DATE DUE

DE 23 '94	DE 17 '97	NV 27 '03
MR 17 '95		JE 1 04
	AP 23 '98	MR 29 '04
MY 5 '95	MY 28 '98	NO 14
JE 1 '95	JV 30 '98	DE 17 '05
NO 17 '95	NO 19 '98	AP 19 '0
DE 8 '95	NV 27 '99	
DE 22 '95		
JY 11 '96	MY 27 '00	
JY 25 '96	JY 22 '99	
	AG 5 '99	
NO 8 '96		
	FE 16 '00	
AP 17 '97		
	MY 6 '00	
MY 29 '97	MY 17 '01	
OC 22 '97	AP 5 '02	
NO 26 '97	FE 13 '03	

DEMCO 38-296

ANATOMY OF RACISM

David Theo Goldberg, editor

Anatomy of

Racism

University of Minnesota Press

Minneapolis • London

Published by the University of Minnesota Press
2037 University Avenue Southeast, Minneapolis, MN 55414.
Printed in the United States of America on acid-free paper
Third printing, 1992

Library of Congress Cataloging-in-Publication Data

Anatomy of racism / edited and with an introduction by David Theo Goldberg.
    p. cm.
Includes Bibliographical references.
ISBN 0-8166-1803-8. — ISBN 0-8166-1804-6 (pbk.)
1. Racism. I. Goldberg, David Theo.
HT1521.A54   1990   89-29092 305.8—dc20   CIP

"Biology and the New Racism," by Martin Barker. Originally published in *The New Racism*.
Copyright © 1981 Junction Books. Reprinted by permission of University Publications of
America. "Race and Gender: The Role of Analogy in Science," by Nancy Leys Stepan.
Originally published in *Isis*, 77 (1986), pp. 261–77. Reprinted by permission. "The Fact of
Blackness," by Frantz Fanon, *Black Skin, White Masks*, pp. 77–99. Copyright © Editions du
Seuil, 1952, reprinted by permission of Grove Press, a division of Wheatland Corporation.
Copyright © 1967 by Grove Press, Inc. "African Grammar" and "Bichon and the Blacks,"
by Roland Barthes, *The Eiffel Tower and Other Mythologies*, translated by Richard Howard.
English translation copyright © 1979 by Farrar, Straus and Giroux, Inc. Reprinted by per-
mission of Farrar, Straus and Giroux, Inc. © Editions du Seuil, 1988. "Ours to Jew or Die"
by Julia Kristeva. From *Powers of Horror: An Essay on Abjection*. Copyright © 1984 Columbia University Press. Reprinted by permission. "Interrogating Identity: The Postcolonial
Prerogative." Copyright © 1988 by Homi Bhabha. "Zionism from the Standpoint of Its
Victims," by Edward W. Said. From *The Question of Palestine*. Copyright © 1979 by Edward W. Said. Reprinted by permission of Times Books, a Division of Random House,
Inc., and Routledge & Kegan Paul Ltd. "Racism and the Innocence of Law," by Peter Fitzpatrick. Originally published in *Journal of Law and Society*, volume 14, no. 1 (1987), pp.
119–132. "Critical Remarks," by Henry Louis Gates, Jr. Copyright © 1990 by Henry Louis
Gates, Jr.

The University of Minnesota is an
equal-opportunity educator and employer.

for future generations,
for a future without racism(s)

Contents

Preface

Racism has proved adaptable to a wide range of theoretical frameworks and practical expressions. Modes of analyzing racism are intertwined in complex and subtle ways with these changing fashions of racist expression. Racist expression has transformed in some cases in reaction to the onslaught of critical analysis, yet in other instances has persisted despite critical attack. The prevailing critical presupposition of the social scientific attack on racism from its emergence in the 1930s is that racism is unvarying in its nature; it is essentially the same attitude complex expressed in differing social conditions. There is a growing recognition now, though hardly universal, that racist discourse is more chameleonic in its nature, in some ways more subtle in its modes of expression, and more central to the modern self-conception than the traditional view allows. This emergent insight has been fueled by and in turn has encouraged the contemporary concerns with the poetics and politics of language, and their influence on perceiving, reading, writing, reasoning, and acting. *Anatomy of Racism* brings together analyses of the forms of racist expression in and by philosophy, literature, popular modes of discourse, politics, and law. It aims to represent in a single volume the contemporary cross-disciplinary concern with the question of racism and the deep implications it has for social identity and identification. The mix of previously published and original work is intended at once to delineate the newly evolving critical approach—the *anatomy* of racism—and to encourage its elaboration.

I remain deeply grateful to many friends and colleagues whose personal, professional, and political commitment made this volume possible, especially those who agreed to furnish original contributions. Homi Bhabha and Sander Gilman responded very generously to requests so late they should never have been made. Skip Gates took on another piece of reading and writing, and still found time for thoughtful suggestions. Nancy Stepan and Peter

Fitzpatrick enabled easy acquisition of the rights to their respective articles, and Edward Said kindly permitted me to edit his paper. I am especially grateful to Anthony Appiah for his sound advice and encouragement throughout. Michael Edwards came as close as it is possible to defying Quine in translating the articles by Etienne Balibar and Christian Delacampagne. The constructive reviews of Michael Brown and Lorenzo Simpson were especially helpful. My assistants Angela Martello and Andrea Alverado completed every task without complaint. The book would not have been published without the editorial foresight, patience, and perseverance of Terry Cochran and his co-workers at the University of Minnesota Press. Finally, Alena and Gabriel suffered my disappointments and excitement consoled only by their comprehension of the subject's importance. Their patience, care, and trust are almost reward enough.

Introduction

I

"Race," some now insist, is a category that should no longer carry social effect. Many, whether supporting or contesting this contention, nevertheless agree that "race" continues to color, if not pervade, contemporary cultural expression. This paradoxical struggle over the social site of "race" is fueled by a deeper and more difficult complex of concerns we commonly call "racism." Accused of it, some deny that they are racist, or that racism is a problem.[1] It is to the set of conceptual and social concerns reflected in such accusations and denials that the essays in this volume are addressed.

Accusation and denial pose a common series of questions, if not a set of common responses. In accusations or denials of racism, what is it that is being charged or refused? What is the nature of the wrong at issue? What is the social context prompting the affirmation or denial? And what is the history against whose background the social context is to be read? This set of concerns points to an underlying problematic. In any affirmation, accusation, or denial of racism, what conception of "race" is being asserted, presupposed, implied, or perhaps attacked? Is this presumption of "race" identical for each kind of attitude, indeed, for each instance of the kind? What, in other words, are the ontological and social commitments of any sort of "race talk?"

It was until very recently that these questions, when addressed explicitly at all, tended to prompt a univocal and unchanging response. Underlying the views both of those who might openly or privately have found racist views compelling and those who clearly considered them troubling was the assumption that racism is singular and monolithic, simply the same attitude complex manifested in varying circumstances. Racism was considered, as it might largely still be, an ahistorical, unchanging social condition always presupposing claims about biological nature and inherent superiority or ability. The primary difference between those expressing and attacking racist beliefs, then, has largely concerned the imputation of error: races do or do not exist; there are or are not innate differences; racial groups and their members are or are not naturally better than others in certain properties and capacities.

The concern to put these empirical misconceptions to rest and to resolve these open questions of racism generated a bulky and dominant corpus of work in the social sciences. The prevailing approach rested on statistical and empirical methodologies in sociology, social pyschology, political science, and economics. In the main, this gave rise to descriptions of race relations and ended, at the level of theoretical explanation, in reductionistic analysis. Reductionistic accounts include those that take racism to be at basis sexually motivated, or economically determined, or a function of an authoritarian—psychotic—group personality type, and the like. Yet, despite this body of work—and in some cases through it—racism has persisted, its forms altered perhaps, its rationale and rationalizations transformed.

This picture of a changed and changing racism rubs up against the complacency of the settled, standard, and accepted view. The tensions between object(s) and analysis, phenomena and understanding—a form of racism as function of the analytic tools and further emergent forms beyond the tools, called for(th) new modes of analysis, breaks with the imperialism of tradition, and a novel conceptual apparatus. These emergent analytic modes and conceptual apparatus have developed in posing and responding to a different set of questions. In what ways does the language used in expressing racist attitudes and in making accusations and denials of racism alter through historical time? How do these changes in expression determine changes in the forms of racist attitudes and behavior, or responses and resistance? What are the factors—scientific, economic, political, legal, cultural, literary, and so on—that effect such alterations in language, expression, and attitude? What is the relation between changing presuppositions and changing interests? What relations of theory and practice may be identified between historically transforming conceptions of "race" and other changing categories of social inclusion or exclusion, such as "ethnicity," "nationality," "class," or "gender"?

The sum of these questions may be subsumed under two general theoretical pursuits. The first consists in analyzing the history of *race formation*, that is, the transformation over time in what gets to count as a race, how racial membership is determined, and what sorts of exclusion this entails. The second concern focuses attention on *racial subjectification* and *subjection*. The aims of this second concern are twofold: to demonstrate how social agents are defined or define themselves as racial subjects. And to show what sorts of social subjection this entails both for the racially formed (*racialized*) and racially forming (*racializing*) producers.

These concerns replace the problematics of empirical testing of racial attitudes and aptitudes with analyses of the body of discourse concerning race
and racism. They replace irresolvable difficulties of objective attitude measurement with analytic and textual[2] dissection of the discourse about racially
constituted bodies and subjects. These displacements mark also a shift in the
rules of analytic engagement: from the passive distance of objective social
science to active commitments in resisting the particular racisms of given
historical moments. The essays included in this volume do not proceed passively just to identify or define some or other aspect of the body of racist discourse and practice. Each is committed in its own fashion to cutting up the
body of racist discursive practices and expressions, stripping them to reveal
the underlying presuppositions, embodiments of interests, aims, and projections of exclusion and subjection. Each engages, in short, in the practices of
what in the title to this collection I call "anatomy."[3]

Thus, the presumption of a single monolithic racism is being displaced by
a mapping of the multifarious historical formulations of *racisms*. The shift
here is from a synchronic description of surface expressions reflecting "race
relations" to critical anatomies of diachronic transformations between successive racist standpoints assumed and discarded since the sixteenth century.
These standpoints have given definition and coherence to world views for
three centuries: to science, natural and social; to literary and aesthetic expression; to social language and perception; and to political attitudes and activities. "Race" has served as a central category of natural and social recognition
and self-representation. The discourse of "race" — racialized and racist ways
of seeing the world and representing it — has constituted and more subtly still
articulates central tropes of modern characterization and contemporary figu-
ration.

The aim of *Anatomy of Racism* is to lay bare and lay out the discursive body
of racist discourse, and to specify its historical and contemporary forms — in
science and philosophy, literature and popular modes of speaking, in politics
and law. Using analytic instruments fashioned in social theory, philosophy,
and literary criticism, this volume undertakes to identify and isolate the cul-
ture(s) of racist discourse, thereby to facilitate both understanding and undermining its varied manifestations.

II

A prevailing theme of this volume is the mapping of dominant racisms. This
involves identifying the prevailing forms racism has assumed in theory and
practice, presupposition, and expression. Common kinds and themes in racist representations are analyzed across a range of domains and periods. One
primary undertaking is to rectify the widespread presumption that racism is

(inherently) a set of irrational prejudices. Racism is revealed, by contrast, to have taken on in normal course the mantle of scientific theory, philosophical rationality, and "morality." Science, politics, and legality, in turn, are revealed to have addressed themselves more or less explicitly in racial and racist terms. Given the theoretical shift from conceiving racism as a singular monolithic phenomenon to identifying a manifold of racisms, there is obviously no inconsistency in acknowledging also ideological or mythological manifestations of racism.

A picture accordingly emerges of historically variant racisms both continuously and discontinuously transformed from one period to another. Subjects, objects, and modes alter. Developments and changes in racist discourse are demonstrated to be functions of dominant interests, aims, and purposes. But forms of racism are found to arise also as responses to critical and practical resistances. Changes in the discursive representations of racism and the practices they inform are shown to be variously related to alterations in conception and articulation of "race" and formations of races. In short, racism is found to be a function of the fashions of racial formation in given sociotemporal conditions.

At the most abstract of theoretical levels, all forms of racism may be linked in terms of their exclusionary or inclusionary undertakings. A major historical shift has been from past racist forms defining and fueling expansionist colonial aims and pursuits to contemporary expressions in nationalist terms. Insistence on racial inferiority in the past fed colonial appetites and imperialist self-definition. Racism is taken now to be expressed increasingly in ⇐ terms of isolationist national self-image; of cultural differentiation tied to custom, tradition, and heritage; and of exclusionary immigration policies, anti-immigrant practices and criminality. These shifts may be found embedded in contemporary conceptions of state and legality; in constitution of class relations (witness the hierarchical *and* racial connotations implicit in the concept of "the *underclass*"); and in family and gender formations. But they are criticized also where their traces are found inherited in articulations of opposition, like some instances of separatism, black nationalism, and Pan-Africanism. As modes of resistance, the latter are considered to make the mistake — *under some interpretations* — of adopting the very categories of exclusivity which are considered objectionable about racism.

The concern with criticism, critique, and opposition is central to this volume. Fundamental to the attitude of anatomy that links the articles collected here is a shared commitment to resisting all forms of racism. This commitment prompts a common attack on the politics of language, categories, and concepts informing racist practice. The aim is to aid the development of appropriate modes and practices of resistance and opposition — in perceiving, reading, and acting — by identifying the changed and changing presumptions, premises, representations, and expressions of exclusion and exclusivity that make up the body of racist discourse. The range of methodologies employed to these ends reflects the variance in forms of racist expression. This range includes close conceptual analysis of racist presuppositions, terms, metaphorical modes of expression, lines of reasoning and reading; interrogation of historical texts and data; sociopolitical, legal, and moral analyses of racial and racist social formations. There is, in short, a sophisticated methodological combination in these pages of discursive analysis, archaeology, genealogy, close textual interrogation and confrontation. It challenges, and so challenges us to revise radically the given ways in which we are required to think about ourselves and others, the set ways we have across disciplines of reading and writing about human and social subjects.

Thus, contemporary understanding of racism's logics and effects has benefited dramatically from recent methodological developments in other contexts. The most notable influence here has been the revolution in analysis of cultural production and products. The debates concerning postmodernism loom large in our sense of these emergent vantage points. Nevertheless, applications of these methodological lessons to the concrete social complexities of racism should give pause to those blindly engaged in burying modernism *or* heralding a postmodernist future. For the teeth of critical concepts are cut, or cut loose, in their practical application or inapplicability to pressing social concerns. Of oppressive social configurations confronting any concern with modernism, modernization, and their postmodern beyond, racisms are among the most pressing. They are in both senses of the term *embedded*—hidden and anchored. Racist discourse touches very nearly all, though some among us may choose to ignore its articulation. We may continue to express ignorance, if not to express the cultures of racism in our theoretical confabulations as in our ordinary social practices. Yet such blindness in exercising choice only serves to raise the already loaded stakes in gambling for—or away—our not so theoretical futures.

III

Thus, new analytic themes have emerged concerning the forms, practices, and functions—the pragmatics—of racist discourse. The following essays share a committed and voiced opposition to racisms. Yet they have not been chosen for their common stance concerning a given discursive theme or question. Themes discussed by some may be skirted by others; a position adopted in one instance may conflict with or be critical of another. What has guided the choice is that the new themes, issues, and questions—the new problematics—emerge and are identified in and through the essays included here.

Anthony Appiah sets the site of the volume, in "Racisms," by reconstructing the presuppositions underlying popular ways of thinking about "race" and racism. In revealing the different conceptual forms racist theorizing and argumentation have assumed, Appiah distinguishes between *racialism* and *racism*. Racialism is the view that human beings are defined by heritable characteristics in virtue of which they may be categorized into races. The members of a given race are accordingly taken to share intraracial characteristics. It is in terms of these characteristics that members of the purported race are taken to be differentiated from those of another racial group. Although the doctrine of racialism is false, Appiah argues that it is not inherently dangerous. By contrast, racism—which presupposes racialism or the viability of racial classifications—is, if not necessarily, then historically harmful. Appiah differentiates *extrinsic* from *intrinsic racism. Extrinsic racism* is the view that members of races, *qua* members, are characterized in terms of possessing or lacking certain virtues, and that such possession or lack is a relevant ground for differential moral treatment. Counterevidence that races and their members are not so characterized should suffice to disavow extrinsic racists of their racist beliefs and behavior. *Intrinsic racists*, by contrast, hold that the raw fact of racial identity or difference, irrespective of any morally relevant virtue or lack thus supposedly entailed, is sufficient reason for valuing one person over another. No counterevidence would be countenanced by the intrinsic racist, for the identities or differences are taken not to be in morally relevant characteristics but in racial essences. Appiah then critically attacks each of these rationally reconstructed forms or racisms.

Martin Barker analyzes the theoretical attempts on the part of the "new racism" in Britain to articulate its aims of excluding the culturally or nationally different in terms of the concept of *instinct* as elaborated in biology, ethology, and sociobiology. Barker lays bare the biological presumptions assumed as the basis of this new "scientific" racism. He shows how these presumptions are unwarranted in terms of the very Darwinian outlook the new racism claims to represent. The scientific sophistication that this new racism furnishes has served to modernize the terms of racist exclusion generated by Enlightenment anthropology, nineteenth-century cranial and eugenic measurements, and twentieth-century intelligence testing.

Nancy Stepan examines the analogy linking *race* to *gender* that has largely dominated scientific analysis of human variation in the past two centuries. Emphasizing that metaphors are an integral feature of the semantics of science, Stepan argues that prevailing metaphors enable new "knowledge" to be constructed or disable entrenched views from being criticized or overthrown. She suggests that the analogies of race and gender have been widely accepted because of dominant social dispositions. The inherited analogy is naturalized, and so subtly conveyed at given conjunctures in and by the language of science. Racial and gender differences have been used accordingly to explain each other. Stepan insists that these analogies be exposed not simply because of the epistemological drive to get at the truth, but especially to prevent anyone being victimized by the metaphors of science.

In "Toward a Critical Theory of Race," Lucius Outlaw's strategy is both retrospective and progressive. First, Outlaw reviews the various articulations "race" has been assigned in scientific theory, and the history of approaches to "race" adopted by critical theory. In this, he analyzes the changing scientific and social agendas of the concept's use. Second, Outlaw examines whether a critical theory of race can be constructed for purposes of enlightenment and emancipation. So, Outlaw shares with the preceding essays a concern to debunk the various conceptual abuses of "race," and the licence thus extended to the social practices of racism. Yet he also addresses the question whether a concept of "race" carefully articulated in terms of nondivisive interests can serve social emancipation.

Christian Delacampagne extends this concern with the conceptual and practical implications of race and racism in "Racism and the West: From Praxis to Logos" (translated from the French by Michael Edwards). Delacampagne suggests that we may speak of races and ethnic groups without being racist. The feature common to all forms of racism, from what he considers the ancient to the contemporary, is the reduction of the cultural to the biological. It is this reduction that constitutes the inversion of the practical and theoretical referred to in Delacampagne's subtitle. The theorizing of racist biology structures racist practice. Delacampagne admits that a good deal of racist theory has served simply to rationalize economic praxis. He argues, however, that forms of racist reasoning embedded in the long development of European logos have also informed and motivated socioeconomic praxis. Delacampagne concludes nevertheless that racist theory and practice can be rejected without abandoning reason and sinking into irrationalism. John Hodge sustains this focus on reason and the representation of the social in racist terms. Hodge identifies the dualism of good and evil as a structural framework in terms of which Western reason is defined. This framework, he argues, enables and motivates forms of group oppression like racism and sexism. The dualism here is taken to enforce a general conception that oppression is rational and thus acceptable. Hodge contrasts this dualist framework of good and evil with a framework of equality and intrinsic moral worth that he takes to encourage resistances to oppression.

In the "Fact of Blackness,"[4] Frantz Fanon establishes a paradigm for a critical theory of racist oppression. Fanon takes *blackness* not as a natural fact but as socially and historically constructed. It is, in short, a constituted fact. The construction projects its products — *blackness* and *whiteness* — as given and fixed. Values of beauty and ugliness are racially defined and instituted. The fact of blackness is taken as the sign of nothingness, of exclusion, and of standing for a tradition of belonging elsewhere. Fanon's seminal work opens the focus from an analysis of the presuppositions of racist thinking to the social and cultural modes or fashions in terms of which racisms are expressed. Yet Fanon is not satisfied simply to specify kinds of racist oppression. His primary aim is to contribute to opposing all forms of such oppression. The general object of resistance for Fanon is the hypostasized "fact" of a single, essential, and undifferentiated *blackness*.

Roland Barthes pursues Fanon's project by uncovering common racist mythologies embedded in everyday signs employed by European media reportage about its Other(s). These signs convey unspoken claims to cultural superiority by the European tradition. Barthes offers a critical model for attacking the signifying apparatuses that shape the construction of political and cultural images; that structure racist modes of seeing and reading; and that pattern dispositions and behavior toward the Other.

Fanon reveals that the powerless or socially excluded are defined not simply as *having* nothing but *as* nothing. The knowledge possessed is invariably ignored, denied a hearing, or suppressed. But powerlessness does not presuppose ignorance. The knowledge emerging and experienced by those at the intersection of categories of race, class, and gender is given voice in the work of Afro-American women writers. Barbara Christian explores the difficulties faced by black women writers—in presentation as in publication—of expressing this emergent knowledge: what Alice Walker's Celie "knows that [we] should know." This epistemological drive of the writer as black, woman, and poor is both to know herself and to have others share the product of this struggle for knowledge and its expression. The expressed efforts to share these intersecting insights of race, gender, and class presuppose self-affirmation as somebody, and command recognition by others. Christian redirects as she reiterates Hegel's insight of the master-slave dialectic: existence in relations of dominance necessitates knowledge, which generates resistance and signals liberation. Christian extends her critique of imposed categories of knowledge and experience to include relations of dominance that pervade the politics of academic knowledge. She argues that representations since the nineteenth century by Afro-American women writers of black women's experience confront contemporary academic conceptions of literary canon, genre, form, and so forth. So, knowledge of existence in the face of an imposed nothingness challenges the emptiness of dominant sociocultural conceptions; similarly, the resilience of Harriet Taylor's *Our Nig* is shown to challenge the exclusionary values of imposed academic categories.

The repressive features of the intersection between race, class, and gender, and the violence thus generated, are analyzed by Sander Gilman in terms of the fin-de-siècle figure of Jack the Ripper: mutilating murderer of prostitutes depicted in the popular image as East European Jewish worker. Gilman un-ravels the (scientific) categories in virtue of which Jews and sexualized women are historically analogized. The representation of their anatomical likeness (amputated genitalia) stands for deviant nature: uncontrolled and uncontrollable, irrational and thus immoral. Just as the prostitute is supposed to infect the innocent community, so the presence of the Jew pollutes the body politic. Bearing the (metaphorical) stigma of syphilis, thought to turn ⌐ the skin black, the Jew is further likened to blacks, as pollutant of the nation-state. Gilman thus reveals the social and scientific sources of the categories of degeneration that historically constitute the identity of the Jew.

In analyzing Céline's anti-Semitic body of work, Julia Kristeva examines also the psychoanalytic entailments embedded in racial knowledge claims or rationalizations, and in the social categories in terms of which these claims are often expressed. Kristeva formulates thus a general framework for ex-amining forms of racist expression additional to the anti-Semitic. Racist claims may be advanced in terms of fragments of social and political ex-perience. These become delirious phantasms when "reason attempts to globalize, unify or totalize." In overgeneralizing, an object of abjection—that is, of threat, aggressivity, envy, and abomination—is produced. For Céline this object is the Jew, although it could be other racial Others. In the name of this object racists comprehend, explain, and resolve any contradictions of their social experience. The fear of the Other's power is overcome in the power of abjection and horror. The perceived threat of the racial Other to undermine order is displaced and countered by appealing to an absolute, reassuring, mystic law incorporated in the body, family, nation, race, and tradition.

Kristeva's focus on the psychoanalytics of cultural racism is extended by Homi Bhabha. In reflecting on the anticolonial writing of Fanon and on the postmodern expression of postcolonial poets, Bhabha interrogates the racial-ized constitution of personal and social identity, of Self and the difference of Otherness. Bhabha accordingly concentrates his analysis of cultural racism less on the politics of nationalism than on the poetics of narcissism. He sug-gests that the split subject of colonial identification is characterized by am-bivalence: the subject both desires and desires to deny its Other. There is no origin of Self or Other, no place or time at which identity is definitively es-tablished, where Self ends and Other begins. The absence or *invisibility* of otherness alters the terms in virtue of which we recognize subjectivity and personhood: the drive to *fix* cultural difference is found by Bhabha to lie in the hypostasized structure of a *visible* object or 'fact of nature' given by the voyeuristic gaze. By contrast, *difference*—the Other's otherness—can be artic-ulated only in the transience and uncertainty of *language*. Difference is usually dismissed in terms of the image of identity, which employs the language of resemblance and analogy to construct a self-identity ("the real me"). Ambivalence strikes at the core of this self-identity, for in being given it is placed in question: language splits the difference in difference, between Self and Other, and so undermines the drive to mastery. The "secret art of invisibleness" critically confronts the representation of personhood, prompting a crisis and the possibility of political subversion. Invisibility challenges the subjectivity or "I" of political agency and narrative mastery with the disembodied "evil eye" or "subaltern resistance," which Bhabha defines as a look or moment that is "differential and strategic rather than originary; ambivalent rather than accumulative, doubling rather than dialectical." Denial of the Other effectively implies identification: disavowal presupposes acknowledgment of otherness and of the Other's being. This ambivalence renders the (post)colonial subject difficult to locate—both to find and to place. The postcolonial subject is found between the folds of subaltern postmodern language, discourse, and writing; just as the postcolonial body shifts between the metropoles and their various levels of periphery.

Bhabha reads Fanon's work, like postmodern writing, as reflecting (upon) the transgressive and transitional movement from colonial dislocation to the emergence, through resistance, from colonial oppression—and this as much in the *form* of expression as in what the writing is *about*. Identity is never given a priori; it is never complete. The shifting boundaries of colonial identity and identification involve an illusory image of presence, really a sign of absence and loss. The otherness of black being undercuts the myth of autonomy and its accompanying fantasy of a singular identity that lie at the foundation of Western subjectivity. Bhabha insists that any notion of homogenized identity of the Other must accordingly be rejected, and so any celebration of oppositional politics predicated on "the margins" or "minorities." Thus, any politics of resistance to cultural racism, as to racism in general, must confront the many and complex difficulties of and in difference.

Kristeva examines the rationale and order of anti-Semitism, and its appropriation of popular categories in social discourse; Bhabha interrogates the racial terms of (post)colonial identity and otherness. In "Zionism from the Standpoint of Its Victims," Edward Said offers a critical case study of the definition, assumption, and projection of racist discourse by those who suffer also as its objects. Said resolves this anomaly of Zionism by interpreting it as an extension of the nineteenth-century colonial spirit. Examining Zionism genealogically, Said identifies it as a set of practical systems for accumulating power, land, and ideological legitimacy. But such accumulation entails a corresponding displacement—of Palestinian people, their ideas and aspirations, and of a contending legitimacy. Said maps the material effects of Zionist ideology and practice on their Palestinian victims, and the resistances thus prompted.

In "Racism and the Innocence of Law," Peter Fitzpatrick examines the implications of race and racism for the contemporary conception of the law in liberal capitalism. The form of law, right, and legality that has emerged from the Enlightenment liberal view claims to be egalitarian: it purports formal innocence and neutrality between citizens, and so principled opposition to discriminatory institutional practices. Fitzpatrick contends that the historical emergence of Enlightenment-generated liberalism and European identity in terms of race, as well as the fact that despite the law's formal opposition to racism liberal capitalism is materially sustained by it, have jointly entailed "persistent limits, certain bounds beyond which law did not proceed in countering racism." Race accordingly confronts the law at its boundaries, restricting law's application notwithstanding its self-professed egalitarianism and innocence. Fitzpatrick illustrates these limits of liberal legality in terms of detailed applications of Britain's Race Relations Act (1976) to cases of industrial discrimination. He argues that the racist perspectives common to racially ordered nations circumscribe the community of law and the specific nature of legality. The law's proclaimed innocence and neutrality in form and principle facilitate racist insinuation and manipulation in practice. Fitzpatrick concludes that in its sustained exclusion of the different, liberal capitalism inevitably undermines its own Enlightenment egalitarian legal professions.

Fitzpatrick's focus on the discursive details and effects of current British racism is extended by Paul Gilroy. Insisting that novel forms of racism require new analytic perspectives, Gilroy argues that it is misleading to seek a general ahistorical or essentialist account of racism, or of race relations. He suggests that racisms are affects, at various historical conjunctures, of underlying economic and sociocultural determinations. To support these methodological claims, Gilroy focuses on contemporary British articulations of racism in terms of culture rather than biology. He shows that culture in Britain is conceived along ethnically absolutist lines, in terms of "naturally" emergent *national* identities and differences, and a culturally specified conception of criminality. He illustrates the racism inherent in Britain's cultural nationalism as exhibited in custom, law, the courts, schools, media, and popular expressions. Contrasted with this, Gilroy conceives black cultural expressions (especially music and dance) as modes of resisting racialized political and legal exclusion. Black culture is taken to generate an autonomous community independent of the domain of formal politics; its aesthetic and energy are considered to fragment power and disperse the dominant order.

The contemporary marriage of racist and nationalist discourse is analyzed by Etienne Balibar in terms of "the paradoxes of universality." Nationalism defines itself basically in universalist terms of uniformity, rationality, and expansiveness; yet it finds expression fundamentally in particularist symbols of difference, custom, tradition, and exclusivity. Balibar examines the ways in which racism reflects and magnifies this paradox. Racism universalizes nationalism while filling nationalism's lack of specificity. In its various constructs and inventions, racism gives content—and so definition—to nationalism's formal universality. The specificity "race" gives to nationality under-mines racism's claimed naturalism; but the elitism racism establishes runs counter to the localized populism that is nationalism's claimed end. Balibar details the techniques of nationalist-racial and racist-national intersections in theory and practice. In nationalizing racism and racializing nationalism, Bali-bar concludes, universalism prevails: nationalism is magnified into a "*super*-nationalism," and racism is elevated beyond national boundaries into a "*supra*nationalism."

By pursing his analysis at a level of theoretical abstraction, Balibar initiates a theoretical response to Gilroy's challenge that no general theory of racisms is capale of being sustained. In "The Social Formation of Racist Discourse," I extend this response by developing a general theory of racisms that under-takes to account for historical alterations in the modes of racial formation and articulation, and so of all forms of racist expression. This theory of racisms is formulated in terms of a notion of *racist discourse*. The transhistorical unity of racist discourse is established on the basis of a set of theoretically abstract but historically formed and given "primitive terms" and relations that "ground" the discursive grammar of racism in its deep structure. The most fundamental primitives of the set are "racial exclusion" and "exclusivity." Others include "classification," "order," "value," and "hierarchy," as well as "racial identity/difference" and "racial superiority/inferiority." Any expres-sion at the surface in given sociotemporal conditions is shown to be identifi-able as racist by tracing it transformationally to some semantic component of racism's deep structure. The racist subject is analyzed in terms of the em-bodiment and expression of these sociohistorically given racist discursive categories and practices. I conclude by mapping some discursive strategies that any practical politics of resistance to racisms might do well to incor-porate.

In a concluding critical reading of the volume, Henry Louis Gates, Jr., warns against accepting too hastily the implications of the currently fashionable cultural antiessentialism. He shows that just as the roots of racist discourse must be traced to Enlightenment essentialism so must the terms of the contemporary "reverse discourse" and conceptual grammar that informs antiracism. This "cultural nominalism" is taken to consist in a social construal of John Locke's radical rejection of kinds. Gates suggests a logical connection between, on one hand, universalisms in all forms (whether essentialist or antiessentialist) and, on the other, the denial of subjectivities or the ignoring of specific experiences that are at the heart of racisms.[5] Thus, a universal anti-realism in current cultural discourse (in the form of the death of the subject) undergirds the radical denial of subjectivity to the Other at the very moment the Other is asserting a subjectivity autonomous from the white Western male. We may disagree with Gates over the relation of theory and practice. Yet he reminds us, lest we forget, of the deep connection between social

identity and political agency, and that the telos of our anatomies of race—
resisting racism—requires in the last analysis practical political commitment.

NOTES

1. For the former, see Ronald Butt's editorial in the Times (London), May 31, 1984; cf. Paul Gilroy, *There Ain't No Black in the Union Jack* (London: Hutchinson, 1982), chapter 2. For the latter, consider the claim by the director of the British Information Service in the United States in 1979 that "racism is not a significant factor in British life and politics." For the context of this claim, see David Goldberg, "Monitoring the Minotaur. Cultural Regulation and Censorship: The Case of *Blacks Britannica*," in *Global Television*, ed. Cynthia Schneider and Brian Wallis (Cambridge, Mass.: Wedge Books, MIT Press, 1988).

2. Texts include, but are not limited to, books, monographs, and pamphlets; speeches, commission and newspaper reports; bureaucratic publications and papers; mixed-media images and representations—as in advertisements, films, video, painting, and popular music.

3. This notion of anatomy builds on and is reflected also in other recent and ongoing work that any critical reading of matters must engage. See especially H. L. Gates (ed.), *"Race," Writing, and Difference* (Chicago: University of Chicago Press, 1986); M. Omi and H. Winant, *Racial Formation in the United States: From the Sixties to the Eighties* (London: Routledge & Kegan Paul, 1986); Paul Gilroy, *There Ain't No Black in the Union Jack* (London: Hutchinson, 1987); M. Barker, *The New Racism* (London: Junction Books, 1981); A. Sivanandan, *A Different Hunger: Writings on Black Resistance* (London: Pluto Press, 1982); C. West, *A Genealogy of Racism* (London: Routledge, 1990); and D. LaCapra and H. L. Gates (eds.), *The Bounds of Race* (Ithaca, N.Y.: Cornell University Press, 1990). I am grateful to Satya Mohanty for emphasizing this point.

4. This is, arguably, the pivotal chapter in Fanon's indisputably definitive work on race and racism, *Black Skin, White Masks*.

5. Gates is surely right also in holding that Locke's radical nominalism and antiessentialism can—and do—bear racist interpretation: witness Locke's instructions to Governor Nicholson of Virginia. Cf. John Locke, *Second Treatise of Government*, ed. Peter Laslett (Cambridge: Cambridge University Press, 1960), footnote to #24.

ANATOMY OF
RACISM

CHAPTER 1

Racisms

Kwame Anthony Appiah

If the people I talk to and the newspapers I read are representative and reliable, there is a good deal of racism about. People and policies in the United
States, in Eastern and Western Europe, in Asia and Africa and Latin America
are regularly described as "racist." Australia had, until recently, a racist immigration policy; Britain still has one; racism is on the rise in France; many
Israelis support Meir Kahane, an anti-Arab racist; many Arabs, according to
a leading authority, are anti-Semitic racists;[1] and the movement to establish
English as the "official language" of the United States is motivated by racism.
Or, at least, so many of the people I talk to and many of the journalists with
the newspapers I read believe.

But visitors from Mars—or from Malawi—unfamiliar with the Western
concept of racism could be excused if they had some difficulty in identifying
what exactly racism was. We see it everywhere, but rarely does anyone stop
to say what it is, or to explain what is wrong with it. Our visitors from Mars
would soon grasp that it had become at least conventional in recent years to
express abhorrence for racism. They might even notice that those most often
accused of it—members of the South African Nationalist party, for
example—may officially abhor it also. But if they sought in the popular media of our day—in newspapers and magazines, on television or radio, in
novels or films—for an explicit definition of this thing "we" all abhor, they
would very likely be disappointed.

Now, of course, this would be true of many of our most familiar concepts.
Sister, chair, tomato—none of these gets defined in the course of our daily business. But the concept of racism is in worse shape than these. For much of
what we say about it is, on the face of it, inconsistent.

It is, for example, held by many to be racist to refuse entry to a university
to an otherwise qualified "Negro" candidate, but not to be so to refuse entry

3

to an equally qualified "Caucasian" one. But "Negro" and "Caucasian" are both alleged to be names of races, and invidious discrimination on the basis of race is usually held to be a paradigm case of racism. Or, to take another example, it is widely believed to be evidence of an unacceptable racism to exclude people from clubs on the basis of race; yet most people, even those who think of "Jewish" as a racial term, seem to think that there is nothing wrong with Jewish clubs, whose members do not share any particular religious beliefs, or Afro-American societies, whose members share the juridical characteristic of American citizenship and the "racial" characteristic of being black.

I say that these are inconsistencies "on the face of it," because, for example, affirmative action in university admissions is importantly different from the earlier refusal to admit blacks or Jews (or other "Others") that it is meant, in part, to correct. Deep enough analysis may reveal it to be quite consistent with the abhorrence of racism; even a shallow analysis suggests that it is intended to be so. Similarly, justifications can be offered for "racial" associations in a plural society that are not available for the racial exclusivism of the country club. But if we take racism seriously we ought to be concerned about the adequacy of these justifications.

In this essay, then, I propose to take our ordinary ways of thinking about race and racism and point up some of their presuppositions. And since popular concepts are, of course, usually fairly fuzzily and untheoretically conceived, much of what I have to say will seem to be both more theoretically and more precisely committed than the talk of racism and racists in our newspapers and on television. My claim is that these theoretical claims are required to make sense of racism as the practice of reasoning human beings. If anyone were to suggest that much, perhaps most, of what goes under the name "racism" in our world cannot be given such a rationalized foundation, I should not disagree: but to the extent that a practice cannot be rationally reconstructed it ought, surely, to be given up by reasonable people. The right tactic with racism, if you really want to oppose it, is to object to it rationally in the form in which it stands the best chance of meeting objections. The doctrines I want to discuss can be rationally articulated: and they are worth articulating rationally in order that we can rationally say what we object to in them.

Racist Propositions

There are at least three distinct doctrines that might be held to express the theoretical content of what we call "racism." One is the view—which I shall call *racialism*[2]—that there are heritable characteristics, possessed by members of our species, that allow us to divide them into a small set of races, in such a way that all the members of these races share certain traits and tendencies with each other that they do not share with members of any other race. These traits and tendencies characteristic of a race constitute, on the racialist view, a sort of racial essence; and it is part of the content of racialism that the essential heritable characteristics of what the nineteenth century called the "Races of Man" account for more than the visible morphological characteristics — skin color, hair type, facial features — on the basis of which we make our informal classifications. Racialism is at the heart of nineteenth-century Western attempts to develop a science of racial difference; but it appears to have been believed by others — for example, Hegel, before then, and many in other parts of the non-Western world since — who have had no interest in developing scientific theories.

Racialism is not, in itself, a doctrine that must be dangerous, even if the racial essence is thought to entail moral and intellectual dispositions. Provided positive moral qualities are distributed across the races, each can be respected, can have its "separate but equal" place. Unlike most Western-educated people, I believe — and I have argued elsewhere[3] — that racialism is false; but by itself, it seems to be a cognitive rather than a moral problem. The issue is how the world is, not how we would want it to be.

Racialism is, however, a presupposition of other doctrines that have been called "racism," and these other doctrines have been, in the last few centuries, the basis of a great deal of human suffering and the source of a great deal of moral error.

One such doctrine we might call "extrinsic racism": extrinsic racists make moral distinctions between members of different races because they believe that the racial essence entails certain morally relevant qualities. The basis for the extrinsic racists' discrimination between people is their belief that members of different races differ in respects that *warrant* the differential treatment, respects — such as honesty or courage or intelligence — that are uncontroversially held (at least in most contemporary cultures) to be acceptable as a basis for treating people differently. Evidence that there are no such differences in morally relevant characteristics — that Negroes do not necessarily lack intellectual capacities, that Jews are not especially avaricious — should thus lead people out of their racism if it is purely extrinsic. As we know, such evidence often fails to change an extrinsic racist's attitudes substantially, for some of the extrinsic racist's best friends have always been Jewish. But at this point — if the racist is sincere — what we have is no longer a false doctrine but a cognitive incapacity, one whose significance I shall discuss later in this essay.

I say that the *sincere* extrinsic racist may suffer from a cognitive incapacity. But some who espouse extrinsic racist doctrines are simply insincere intrinsic racists. For *intrinsic racists*, on my definition, are people who differentiate morally between members of different races because they believe that each race has a different moral status, quite independent of the moral characteristics entailed by its racial essence. Just as, for example, many people assume that the fact that they are biologically related to another person—a brother, an aunt, a cousin—gives them a moral interest in that person,[4] so an intrinsic racist holds that the bare fact of being of the same race is a reason for preferring one person to another. (I shall return to this parallel later as well.)

For an intrinsic racist, no amount of evidence that a member of another race is capable of great moral, intellectual, or cultural achievements, or has characteristics that, in members of one's own race, would make them admirable or attractive, offers any ground for treating that person as he or she would treat similarly endowed members of his or her own race. Just so, some sexists are "intrinsic sexists," holding that the bare fact that someone is a woman (or man) is a reason for treating her (or him) in certain ways.

There are interesting possibilities for complicating these distinctions: some racists, for example, claim, as the Mormons once did, that they discriminate between people because they believe that God requires them to do so. Is this an extrinsic racism, predicated on the combination of God's being an intrinsic racist and the belief that it is right to do what God wills? Or is it intrinsic racism because it is based on the belief that God requires these discriminations because they are right? (Is an act pious because the gods love it, or do they love it because it is pious?) Nevertheless, the distinctions between racialism and racism and between two potentially overlapping kinds of racism provide us with the skeleton of an anatomy of the propositional contents of racial attitudes.

Racist Dispositions

Most people will want to object already that this discussion of the propositional content of racist moral and factual beliefs misses something absolutely crucial to the character of the psychological and sociological reality of racism, something I touched on when I mentioned that extrinsic racist utterances are often made by people who suffer from what I called a "cognitive incapacity." Part of the standard force of accusations of racism is that their objects are in some way *irrational*. The objection to Professor Shockley's claims about the intelligence of blacks is not just that they are false; it is rather that Professor Shockley seems, like many people we call "racist," to be unable to see that the evidence does not support his factual claims and that the connection between his factual claims and his policy prescriptions involves a series of non sequiturs.

What makes these cognitive incapacities especially troubling—something we should respond to with more than a recommendation that the individual, Professor Shockley, be offered psychotherapy—is that they conform to a certain pattern: namely, that it is especially where beliefs and policies that are to the disadvantage of nonwhite people that he shows the sorts of disturbing failure that have made his views both notorious and notoriously unrealiable. Indeed, Professor Shockley's reasoning works extremely well in some other areas: that he is a Nobel Laureate in physics is part of what makes him so interesting an example. *extrinsic*

⌞ This cognitive incapacity is not, of course, a rare one. Many of us are unable to give up beliefs that play a part in justifying the special advantages we gain (or hope to gain) from our positions in the social order — in particular, beliefs about the positive characters of the class of people who share that position⌟ Many people who express extrinsic racist beliefs — many white South Africans, for example — are beneficiaries of social orders that deliver advantages to them by virtue of their "race," so that their disinclination to accept evidence that would deprive them of a justification for those advantages is just an instance of this general phenomenon.

So too, evidence that access to higher education is as largely determined by the quality of our earlier educations as by our own innate talents, does not, on the whole, undermine the confidence of college entrants from private schools in England or the United States or Ghana. Many of them continue to believe in the face of this evidence that their acceptance at "good" universities shows them to be intellectually better endowed (and not just better prepared) than those who are rejected. It is facts such as these that give sense to the notion of false consciousness, the idea that an ideology can prevent us from acknowledging facts that would threaten our position.

The most interesting cases of this sort of ideological resistance to the truth are not, perhaps, the ones I have just mentioned. On the whole, it is less surprising, once we accept the admittedly problematic notion of self-deception, that people who think that certain attitudes or beliefs advantage them or those they care about should be able, as we say, to "persuade" themselves to ignore evidence that undermines those beliefs or attitudes. What is more interesting is the existence of people who resist the truth of a proposition while thinking that its wider acceptance would in no way disadvantage them or those individuals about whom they care — this might be thought to describe Professor Shockley; or who resist the truth when they recognize that its acceptance would actually advantage them — this might be the case with some black people who have internalized negative racist stereotypes; or who fail, by virtue of their ideological attachments, to recognize what is in their own best interests at all.

My business here is not with the psychological or social processes by which these forms of ideological resistance operate, but it is important, I think, to see the refusal on the part of some extrinsic racists to accept evidence against the beliefs as an instance of a widespread phenomenon in human affairs. It is a plain fact, to which theories of ideology must address themselves, that our species is prone both morally and intellectually to such dis-

tortions of judgment, in particular to distortions of judgment that reflect partiality. ⌊An inability to change your mind in the face of appropriate[5] evidence
is a cognitive incapacity; but it is one that all of us surely suffer from in some
areas of belief; especially in areas where our own interests or self-images are
(or seem to be) at stake.⌋

It is not, however, as some have held, a tendency that we are powerless to
resist. No one, no doubt, can be impartial about everything—even about
everything to which the notion of partiality applies; but there is no subject
matter about which most sane people cannot, in the end, be persuaded to avoid
partiality in judgment. And it may help to shake the convictions of those
whose incapacity derives from this sort of ideological defense if we show them
how their reaction fits into this general pattern. It is, indeed, because it generally *does* fit this pattern that we call such views "racism"—the suffix "-ism" indicating that what we have in mind is not simply a theory but an ideology.
It would be odd to call someone brought up in a remote corner of the world
with false and demeaning views about white people a "racist" if that person
gave up these beliefs quite easily in the face of appropriate evidence.

Real live racists, then, exhibit a systematically distorted rationality, the
kind of systematically distorted rationality that we are likely to call "ideological." And it is a distortion that is especially striking in the cognitive domain:
extrinsic racists, as I said earlier, however intelligent or otherwise well informed, often fail to treat evidence against the theoretical propositions of extrinsic racism dispassionately. ⌊Like extrinsic racism, intrinsic racism can also
often be seen as ideological; but since scientific evidence is not going to settle
the issue, a failure to see that it is wrong represents a cognitive incapacity
only on controversially realist views about morality. What makes intrinsic
racism similarly ideological is not so much the failure of inductive or deduc-
tive rationality that is so striking in someone like Professor Shockley but
rather the connection that it, like extrinsic racism, has with the interests—real
or perceived—of the dominant group. ⌉Shockley's racism is in a certain sense
directed *against* nonwhite people: many believe that his views would, if accepted, operate against their objective interests, and he certainly presents the
black "race" in a less than flattering light.

I propose to use the old-fashioned term ⌈"racial prejudice"⌉ in the rest of this
essay to ⌊refer to the deformation of rationality in judgment that characterizes
those whose racism is more than a theoretical attachment to certain propositions about race.⌋

Racial Prejudice

⌊It is hardly necessary to raise objections to what I am calling "racial prejudice"; someone who exhibits such deformations of rationality is plainly in

trouble. But it is important to remember that propositional racists in a racist culture have false moral beliefs but may not suffer from racial prejudice. Once we show them how society has enforced extrinsic racist stereotypes, once we ask them whether they really believe that race in itself, independently of those extrinsic racist beliefs, justifies differential treatment, many will come to give up racist propositions, although we must remember how powerful a weight of authority our arguments have to overcome. Reasonable people may insist on substantial evidence if they are to give up beliefs that are central to their cultures.

Still, in the end, many will resist such reasoning; and to the extent that their prejudices are really not subject to any kind of rational control, we may wonder whether it is right to treat such people as morally responsible for the acts their racial prejudice motivates, or morally reprehensible for holding the views to which their prejudice leads them. It is a bad thing that such people exist; they are, in a certain sense, bad people. But it is not clear to me that they are responsible for the fact that they are bad. Racial prejudice, like prejudice generally, may threaten an agent's autonomy, making it appropriate to treat or train rather than to reason with them.

But once someone has been offered evidence both (1) that their reasoning in a certain domain is distorted by prejudice, and (2) that the distortions conform to a pattern that suggests a lack of impartiality, they ought to take special care in articulating views and proposing policies in that domain. They ought to do so because, as I have already said, the phenomenon of partiality in judgment is well attested in human affairs. Even if you are not immediately persuaded that you are yourself a victim of such a distorted rationality in a certain domain, you should keep in mind always that this is the usual position of those who suffer from such prejudices. To the extent that this line of thought is not one that itself falls within the domain in question, one can be held responsible for not subjecting judgments that *are* within that domain to an especially extended scrutiny; and this is a fortiori true if the policies one is recommending are plainly of enormous consequence.

If it is clear that racial prejudice is regrettable, it is also clear in the nature of the case that providing even a superabundance of reasons and evidence will often not be a successful way of removing it. Nevertheless, the racist's prejudice will be articulated through the sorts of theoretical propositions I dubbed extrinsic and intrinsic racism. And we should certainly be able to say something reasonable about why these theoretical propositions should be rejected.

Part of the reason that this is worth doing is precisely the fact that many of those who assent to the propositional content of racism do not suffer from racial prejudice. In a country like the United States, where racist propositions were once part of the national ideology, there will be many who assent to racist propositions simply because they were raised to do so. Rational objection to racist propositions has a fair chance of changing such people's beliefs.

Extrinsic and Intrinsic Racism

It is not always clear whether someone's theoretical racism is intrinsic or extrinsic, and there is certainly no reason why we should expect to be able to settle the question. Since the issue probably never occurs to most people in these terms, we cannot suppose that they must have an answer. In fact, given the definition of the terms I offered, there is nothing barring someone from being both an intrinsic and an extrinsic racist, holding both that the bare fact of race provides a basis for treating members of his or her own race differently from others and that there are morally relevant characteristics that are differentially distributed among the races. Indeed, for reasons I shall discuss in a moment, *most* intrinsic racists are likely to express extrinsic racist beliefs, so that we should not be surprised that many people seem, in fact, to be committed to both forms of racism.

The Holocaust made unreservedly clear the threat that racism poses to human decency. But it also blurred our thinking because in focusing our attention on the racist character of the Nazi atrocities, it obscured their character as atrocities. What is appalling about Nazi racism is not just that it presupposes, as all racism does, false (racialist) beliefs—not simply that it involves a moral incapacity (the inability to extend our moral sentiments to all our fellow creatures) and a moral failing (the making of moral distinctions without moral differences)—but that it leads, first, to oppression and then to mass slaughter. In recent years, South African racism has had a similar distorting effect. For although South African racism has not led to killings on the scale of the Holocaust—even if it has both left South Africa judicially executing more (mostly black) people per head of population than most other countries and led to massive differences between the life chances of white and nonwhite South Africans—it *has* led to the systematic oppression and economic exploitation of people who are not classified as "white," and to the infliction of suffering on citizens of all racial classifications, not least by the police state that is required to maintain that exploitation and oppression.

Part of our resistance, therefore, to calling the racial ideas of those, such as the Black Nationalists of the 1960s, who advocate racial solidarity, by the same term that we use to describe the attitudes of Nazis or of members of the South African Nationalist party, surely resides in the fact that they largely did not contemplate using race as a basis for inflicting harm. Indeed, it seems to me that there is a significant pattern in the modern rhethoric of race, such that the discourse of racial solidarity is usually expressed through the language of *intrinsic* racism, while those who have used race as the basis for oppression and hatred have appealed to *extrinsic* racist ideas.⌉⌈This point is important for understanding the character of contemporary racial attitudes.⌉

The two major uses of race as a basis for moral solidarity that are most familiar in the West are varieties of Pan-Africanism and Zionism. In each case it is presupposed that a "people," Negroes or Jews, has the basis for shared political life in the fact of being of the same race. There are varieties of each form of "nationalism" that make the basis lie in shared traditions; but however plausible this may be in the case of Zionism, which has in Judaism, the religion, a realistic candidate for a common and nonracial focus for nationality, the peoples of Africa have a good deal less in common culturally than is usually assumed. I discuss this issue at length in *In My Father's House: Essays in the Philosophy of African Culture*, but let me say here that I believe the central fact is this: what blacks in the West, like secularized Jews, have mostly in common is that they are perceived — both by themselves and by others — as belonging to the same race, and that this common race is used by others as the basis for discriminating against them. "If you ever forget you're a Jew, a goy will remind you." The Black Nationalists, like some Zionists, responded to their experience of racial discrimination by accepting the racialism it presupposed.[7]

Although race is indeed at the heart of Black Nationalism, however, it seems that it is the fact of a shared race, not the fact of a shared racial character, that provides the basis for solidarity. Where racism is implicated in the basis for national solidarity, it is intrinsic, not (or not only) extrinsic. It is this that makes the idea of fraternity one that is naturally applied in nationalist discourse. For, as I have already observed, the moral status of close family members is not normally thought of in most cultures as depending on qualities of character; we are supposed to love our brothers and sisters in spite of their faults and not because of their virtues. Alexander Crummell, one of the founding fathers of Black Nationalism, literalizes the metaphor of family in these startling words:

⌊Races, like families, are the organisms and ordinances of God; and race feeling, like family feeling, is of divine origin. The extinction of race feeling is just as possible as the extinction of family feeling. Indeed, a race *is* a family.[8]⌋

⌊ It is the assimilation of "race feeling" to "family feeling" that makes intrinsic racism seem so much less objectionable than extrinsic racism. For this metaphorical identification reflects the fact that, in the modern world (unlike the nineteenth century), intrinsic racism is acknowledged almost exclusively as the basis of feelings of community.⌋ We can surely, then, share a sense of what Crummell's friend and co-worker Edward Blyden called "the poetry of politics," that is, "the feeling of race," the feeling of "people with whom we are connected."[9] ⌊The racism here is the basis of acts of supererogation, the treatment of others better than we otherwise might, better than moral duty demands of us.

This is a contingent fact. There is no logical impossibility in the idea of racialists whose moral beliefs lead them to feelings of hatred for other races while leaving no room for love of members of their own. Nevertheless most racial hatred is in fact expressed through extrinsic racism: most people who have used race as the basis for causing harm to others have felt the need to see the others as independently morally flawed. It is one thing to espouse fraternity without claiming that your brothers and sisters have any special qualities that deserve recognition, and another to espouse hatred of others who have done nothing to deserve it."[10]

Many Afrikaners—like many in the American South until recently—have a long list of extrinsic racist answers to the question why blacks should not have full civil rights. Extrinsic racism has usually been the basis for treating people worse than we otherwise might, for giving them less than their humanity entitles them to. But this too is a contingent fact. Indeed, Crummell's guarded respect for white people derived from a belief in the superior moral qualities of the Anglo-Saxon race.

Intrinsic racism is, in my view, a moral error. Even if racialism were correct, the bare fact that someone was of another race would be no reason to treat them worse—or better—than someone of my race. In our public lives, people are owed treatment independently of their biological characters: if they are to be differently treated there must be some morally relevant difference between them. In our private lives, we are morally free to have aesthetic preferences between people, but once our treatment of people raises moral issues, we may not make arbitrary distinctions. Using race in itself as a morally relevant distinction strikes most of us as obviously arbitrary. Without associated moral characteristics, why should race provide a better basis than hair color or height or timbre of voice? And if two people share all the properties morally relevant to some action we ought to do, it will be an error—a failure to apply the Kantian injunction to universalize our moral judgments—to use the bare facts of race as the basis for treating them differently. No one should deny that a common ancestry might, in particular cases, account for similarities in moral character. But then it would be the moral similarities that justified the different treatment.

It is presumably because most people—outside the South African Nationalist party and the Ku Klux Klan—share the sense that intrinsic racism requires arbitrary distinctions that they are largely unwilling to express it in situations that invite moral criticism. But I do not know how I would argue with someone who was willing to announce an intrinsic racism as a basic moral idea; the best one can do, perhaps, is to provide objections to possible lines of defense of it.

De Gustibus

It might be thought that intrinsic racism should be regarded not so much as an adherence to a (moral) proposition as the expression of a taste, analogous, say, to the food prejudice that makes most English people unwilling to eat horse meat, and most Westerners unwilling to eat the insect grubs that the !Kung people find so appetizing. The analogy does at least this much for us, namely, to provide a model of the way that *extrinsic* racist propositions can be a reflection of an underlying prejudice. For, of course, in most cultures food prejudices are rationalized: we say insects are unhygienic and cats taste horrible. Yet a cooked insect is no more health-threatening than a cooked carrot, and the unpleasant taste of cat meat, far from justifying our prejudice against it, probably derives from that prejudice.

But there the usefulness of the analogy ends. For intrinsic racism, as I have defined it, is not simply a taste for the company of one's "own kind," but a moral doctrine, one that is supposed to underlie differences in the treatment of people in contexts where moral evaluation is appropriate. And for moral distinctions we cannot accept that "de gustibus non est disputandum." We do not need the full apparatus of Kantian ethics to require that public morality be constrained by reason.

A proper analogy would be with someone who thought that we could continue to kill cattle for beef, even if cattle exercised all the complex cultural skills of human beings. I think it is obvious that creatures that shared our capacity for understanding as well as our capacity for pain should not be treated the way we actually treat cattle—that "intrinsic speciesism" would be as wrong as racism. And the fact that most people think it is worse to be cruel to chimpanzees than to frogs suggests that they may agree with me. The distinction in attitudes surely reflects a belief in the greater richness of the mental life of chimps. Still, I do not know how I would *argue* against someone who could not see this; someone who continued to act on the contrary belief might, in the end, simply have to be locked up.

The Family Model

I have suggested that intrinsic racism is, at least sometimes, a metaphorical extension of the moral priority of one's family; it might, therefore, be suggested that a defense of intrinsic racism could proceed along the same lines as a defense of the family as a center of moral interest. The possibility of a defense of family relations as morally relevant—or, more precisely, of the claim that one may be morally entitled (or even obliged) to make distinctions between two otherwise morally indistinguishable people because one is related to one and not to the other—is theoretically important for the prospects of a philosophical defense of intrinsic racism. This is because such a defense of the family involves—like intrinsic racism—a denial of the basic claim, expressed so clearly by Kant, that from the perspective of morality, it is as rational agents *simpliciter* that we are to assess and be assessed. For anyone who follows Kant in this, what matters, as we might say, is not who you are but how you try to live. Intrinsic racism denies this fundamental claim also. And, in so doing, as I have argued elsewhere, it runs against the mainstream of the history of Western moral theory.[11]

The importance of drawing attention to the similarities between the defense of the family and the defense of the race, then, is not merely that the metaphor of family is often invoked by racism; it is that each of them offers the same general challenge to the Kantian stream of our moral thought. And the parallel with the defense of the family should be especially appealing to an intrinsic racist, since many of us who have little time for racism would hope that the family is susceptible to some such defense.

The problem in generalizing the defense of the family, however, is that such defenses standardly begin at a point that makes the argument for intrinsic racism immediately implausible: namely, with the family as the unit through which we live what is most intimate, as the center of private life. If we distinguish, with Bernard Williams, between ethical thought, which takes seriously "the demands, needs, claims, desires, and generally, the lives of other people,"[12] and morality, which focuses more narrowly on obligation, it may well be that private life matters to us precisely because it is altogether unsuited to the universalizing tendencies of morality.

The functioning family unit has contracted substantially with industrialization, the disappearance of the family as the unit of production, and the increasing mobility of labor, but there remains that irreducible minimum: the parent or parents with the child or children. In this "nuclear" family, there is, of course, a substantial body of shared experience, shared attitudes, shared knowledge and beliefs; and the mutual psychological investment that exists within this group is, for most of us, one of the things that gives meaning to our lives. It is a natural enough confusion—which we find again and again in discussions of adoption in the popular media—that identifies the relevant group with the biological unit of *genitor, genetrix*, and *offspring* rather than with the social unit of those who share a common domestic life.

The relations of parents and their biological children are of moral importance, of course, in part because children are standardly the product of behavior voluntarily undertaken by their biological parents. But the moral relations between biological siblings and half-siblings cannot, as I have already pointed out, be accounted for in such terms. A rational defense of the family ought to appeal to the causal responsibility of the biological parent and the common life of the domestic unit, and not to the brute fact of biological relatedness, even if the former pair of considerations defines groups that are often coextensive with the groups generated by the latter. For brute biological relatedness bears no necessary connection to the sorts of human purposes that seem likely to be relevant at the most basic level of ethical thought.

An argument that such a central group is bound to be crucially important in the lives of most human beings in societies like ours is not, of course, an argument for any specific mode of organization of the "family": feminism and the gay liberation movement have offered candidate groups that could (and sometimes do) occupy the same sort of role in the lives of those whose sexualities or whose dispositions otherwise make the nuclear family uncongenial; and these candidates have been offered specifically in the course of defenses of a move toward societies that are agreeably beyond patriarchy and homophobia. The central thought of these feminist and gay critiques of the nuclear family is that we cannot continue to view any one organization of private life as "natural," once we have seen even the broadest outlines of the archaeology of the family concept.

If that is right, then the argument for the family must be an argument for a mode of organization of life and feeling that subserves certain positive functions; and however the details of such an argument would proceed it is highly unlikely that the same functions could be served by groups on the scale of races, simply because, as I say, the family is attractive in part exactly for reasons of its personal scale.

I need hardly say that rational defenses of intrinsic racism along the lines I have been considering are not easily found. In the absence of detailed defenses to consider, I can only offer these general reasons for doubting that they can succeed: the generally Kantian tenor of much of our moral thought threatens the project from the start; and the essentially unintimate nature of relations within "races" suggests that there is little prospect that the defense of the family—which seems an attractive and plausible project that extends ethical life beyond the narrow range of a universalizing morality—can be applied to a defense of races.

Conclusions

I have suggested that what we call "racism" involves both propositions and dispositions.

The propositions were, first, that there are races (this was *racialism*) and, second, that these races are morally significant either (a) because they are contingently correlated with morally relevant properties (this was *extrinsic racism*) or (b) because they are intrinsically morally significant (this was *intrinsic racism*).

The disposition was a tendency to assent to false propositions, both moral and theoretical, about races—propositions that support policies or beliefs that are to the disadvantage of some race (or races) as opposed to others, and to do so even in the face of evidence and argument that should appropriately lead to giving those propositions up. This disposition I called "racial prejudice."

I suggested that intrinsic racism had tended in our own time to be the natural expression of feelings of community, and this is, of course, one of the reasons why we are not inclined to call it racist. For, to the extent that a theoretical position is not associated with irrationally held beliefs that tend to the *dis*advantage of some group, it fails to display the *directedness* of the distortions of rationality characteristic of racial prejudice. Intrinsic racism may be as irrationally held as any other view, but it does not *have* to be directed *against* anyone.

So far as theory is concerned I believe racialism to be false: since theoretical racism of both kinds presupposes racialism, I could not logically support racism of either variety. But even if racialism were true, both forms of theoretical racism would be incorrect. Extrinsic racism is false because the genes that account for the gross morphological differences that underlie our standard racial categories are not linked to those genes that determine, to whatever degree such matters are determined genetically, our moral and intellectual characters. Intrinsic racism is mistaken because it breaches the Kantian imperative to make moral distinctions only on morally relevant grounds — granted that there is no reason to believe that race, *in se*, is morally relevant, and also no reason to suppose that races are like families in providing a sphere of ethical life that legitimately escapes the demands of a universalizing morality.

NOTES

1. Bernard Lewis, *Semites and Anti-Semites* (New York: Norton, 1986).

2. I shall be using the words "racism" and "racialism" with the meanings I stipulate: in some dialects of English they are synonyms, and in most dialects their definition is less than precise. For discussion of recent biological evidence see M. Nei and A. K. Roychoudhury, "Genetic Relationship and Evolution of Human Races," *Evolutionary Biology*, vol. 14 (New York: Plenum, 1983), pp. 1–59; for useful background see also M. Nei and A. K. Roychoudhury, "Gene Differences between Caucasian, Negro, and Japanese Populations," *Science*, 177 (August 1972), pp. 434–35.

3. See my "The Uncompleted Argument: Du Bois and the Illusion of Race," *Critical Inquiry*, 12 (Autumn 1985); reprinted in Henry Louis Gates (eds.), *"Race," Writing, and Difference* (Chicago: University of Chicago Press, 1986), pp. 21–37.

4. This fact shows up most obviously in the assumption that adopted children intelligibly make claims against their natural siblings: natural parents are, of course, causally responsible for their child's existence and that could be the basis of moral claims, without any sense that biological relatedness entailed rights or responsibilities. But no such basis exists for an interest in natural *siblings*; my sisters are not causally responsible for my existence. See "The Family Model," later in this essay.

5. Obviously what evidence should *appropriately* change your beliefs is not independent of your social or historical situation. In mid-nineteenth-century America, in New England quite as much as in the heart of Dixie, the pervasiveness of the institutional support for the prevailing system of racist belief—the fact that it was reinforced by religion and state, and defended by people in the universities and colleges, who had the greatest cognitive authority—meant that it would have been appropriate to insist on a substantial body of evidence and argument before giving up assent to racist propositions. In California in the 1980s, of course, matters stand rather differently. To acknowledge this is not to admit to a cognitive relativism; rather, it is to hold that, at least in some domains, the fact that a belief is widely held—and especially by people in positions of cognitive authority—may be a good prima facie reason for believing it.

6. Ideologies, as most theorists of ideology have admitted, standardly outlive the period in which they conform to the objective interests of the dominant group in a society; so even someone who thinks that the dominant group in our society no longer needs racism to buttress its position can see racism as the persisting ideology of an earlier phase of society. (I say "group" to keep the claim appropriately general; it seems to me a substantial further claim that the dominant group whose interests an ideology serves is always a class.) I have argued, however, in "The Conservation of 'Race' " that racism continues to serve the interests of the ruling classes in the West; in *Black American Literature Forum*, 23 (Spring 1989), pp. 37–60.

7. As I argued in "The Uncompleted Argument: Du Bois and the Illusion of Race." The reactive (or dialectical) character of this move explains why Sartre calls its manifestations in Négritude an "antiracist racism"; see "Orphée Noir," his preface to Senghor's *Anthologie de la nouvelle poésie nègre et malagache de langue française* (Paris: PUF, 1948). Sartre believed, of course, that the synthesis of this dialectic would be the transcendence of racism; and it was his view of it as a stage—the antithesis—in that process that allowed him to see it as a positive advance over the original "thesis" of European racism. I suspect that the reactive character of antiracist racism accounts for the tolerance that is regularly extended to it in liberal circles; but this tolerance is surely hard to justify unless one shares Sartre's optimistic interpretation of it as a stage in a process that leads to the end of all racisms. (And unless your view of this dialectic is deterministic, you should in any case want to play an argumentative role in moving to this next stage.) For a similar Zionist response see Horace Kallen's "The Ethics of Zionism," *Maccabaean*, August 1906.

⌊ 8. "The Race Problem in America," in Brotz's *Negro Social and Political Thought* (New York: Basic Books, 1966), p. 184.⌋

9. *Christianity, Islam and the Negro Race* (1887; reprinted Edinburgh: Edinburgh University Press, 1967), p. 197.

10. This is in part a reflection of an important asymmetry: loathing, unlike love, needs justifying; and this, I would argue, is because loathing usually leads to acts that are *in se* undesirable, whereas love leads to acts that are largely *in se* desirable—indeed, supererogatorily so.

11. See my "Racism and Moral Pollution," *Philosophical Forum*, 18 (Winter–Spring 1986–87), pp. 185–202.

12. *Ethics and the Limits of Philosophy* (Cambridge, Mass.: Harvard University Press, 1985), p. 12. I do not, as is obvious, share Williams's skepticism about morality.

CHAPTER 2

Biology and the New Racism

Martin Barker

Although it [is] necessary to spend time establishing the link between the new Tory racism and David Hume, it is not the most obvious link to make. Nor is it the most obviously powerful, compared with the link with biology. It is the use of the concept of instincts that gives the new racism the appearance of scientific validity. It is in the context of particular aspects of biology, ethology and sociobiology, that we must look at it.

Tory ideology claims that it is biologically fixed that humans form exclusive groups, and that these groups succeed internally in so far as they close up against outsiders. Or as someone else put it:

> The biological nation . . . is a social group containing at least two mature males which holds as an exclusive possession a continuous area of space, which isolates itself from others of its kind through outward antagonism, and which through its defence of its social territory achieves leadership, cooperation and a capacity for concerted action.[1]

The writer of this, Robert Ardrey, is a popularizer of the scientific claims of human ethology, a version of neo-Darwinism that has come to conclusions demonstrably like those of the Tory party.

In recent years, however, the claims of the human ethologists have been the subject of hot controversy. Their prime adversaries have presented yet another neo-Darwinist account: sociobiology. And yet that theory also arrives at the same conclusions about "race." So could it be that Tory policies are, in fact, merely following the dictates of biology as has been claimed? Or is it rather that these supposedly scientific theories are themselves suspicious, and in fact scientific ideologies? Just what is the relation of science and politics in a case like this? Before these questions can be answered, we need to know something more about the theories. We must see just what conclusions are offered by ethology and sociobiology, and how they are arrived at.

What are the two schools, and who are their protagonists? Human ethology derives from the work of a large number of writers, many of them European; notable among them are Konrad Lorenz, Niko Tinbergen, Desmond Morris, and their public relations man Robert Ardrey.[2] Both schools have a taste for popularization, with Morris leading the way in Britain with serializations of his books in the tabloid newspapers. There are strong lines of continuity, both personal and doctrinal, between the ethologists and the prewar eugenicists. Lorenz, in particular, had a somewhat dubious role in the German race-biology climate. Allen Chase cites one of the worst expressions of this:

> There is a close analogy between a human body invaded by a cancer and a nation inflicted with subpopulations whose inborn defects cause them to become social liabilities. Just as in cancer the best treatment is to eradicate the parasitic growth as quickly as possible, the eugenic defence against the dysgenic social effects of afflicted subpopulations is of necessity limited to equally drastic measures. [Lorenz, quoted in Chase, p. 349].[3]

Lorenz, postwar, was somewhat milder, albeit he still held to such an organicist view of society.

But from the late 1960s, a major challenge developed to some key ideas of the ethologists, deriving this time from America. In 1976, the bulk of these criticisms, and an alternative neo-Darwinism, were brought together in Edward Wilson's *Sociobiology — the New Synthesis*.[4] A number of authors have rehearsed the history of this controversy. Michael Ruse gives a useful summary of the sociobiologists' side.[5] The argument centered on the *mechanism* by which Darwinian selection was supposed to take place.

The Darwinian revolution, effectively begun in 1859 with the publication of *On the Origin of Species*, was built around the idea of natural selection. Natural selection was a summary term for the processes whereby, within a species, organisms selectively survived. Those with characteristics slightly better adapted to the particular environments and general circumstances in which the species lived would, on average, survive better and longer — and would, therefore, have greater chances to pass on the genes for those adapted characteristics to offspring. By the slow accumulation of these differences, species change and develop.

All this is fine, beautifully simple, and has all the advantages of a naturalistic account. But it is in applying it that the problems arise. For among the key variables of any environment in which organisms have to survive, are others of its own kind. This is problem enough in relation to plants. But when we come to a vast number of species of animals — insects, birds, fish, mammals, etc.—there is the additional factor of *society*. Under the heading of society would come sexual relations, the rearing of offspring and forms of cooperative behavior, as well as competition for resources. What is the role of social life in natural selection?

Although it is not normally formulated quite in this way by the ethologists and sociobiologists, it seems a fair characterization of the debate to say that this is what it is all about. According to the ethologists, selection takes place at the level of the group: hence the term "group selectionist." What this means is best seen through an example. Among flocking birds, it is common that when a hawk approaches, the first bird to sight it gives an alarm call, which has the effect of warning the whole flock. Why does this happen? Common sense would say, to warn the others. But evidence suggests that the birds that do this put themselves at greater risk by standing out from the rest of the flock. How does such a piece of behavior evolve if it is harmful to the individual? Is it a piece of altruistic behavior?

The group selectionists said yes. It is a piece of behavior that has evolved because of its use to the species as a whole. You can apply this idea in many tempting ways: to the runt in the litter of pigs that gives up trying to live "for the benefit of the others"; to the ritual element in the fighting among wolves that prevents the victor killing the loser. Characteristics tend to survive, it was argued, for the good of the species—or better, for the social population. A social population is any relatively separate subgroup of a species within which mating, rearing and other social activities take place.

The ethologists were in the main zoologists, animal watchers; their problem was to interpret behavior that they saw. Their critics, on the other hand, contained a fair sprinkling of geneticists and biologists. They fired a Darwinian objection; it didn't seem to be possible that group selection could actually work.

Take the bird alarm. At some point this bit of behavior must have been added to the flocks' repertoire. But if giving the alarm tended to attract predators to the bird who made it, then on average it would have been less likely to survive than those birds who gave no alarm, but who still benefited from any warnings given. The genetic predisposition to behave this way would have canceled itself out. So the idea of group selection, however attractive, would not work in evolutionary terms.

This is what the individual selectionists argued, and, out of their increasingly self-conscious applications of this idea came sociobiology. Its main proponents, apart from Wilson, have been W. Hamilton, R. Trivers, John Maynard Smith (all represented in Clutton-Brock and Harvey) and Richard Dawkins.[6] But the sociobiologists have found supporters in other discplines, including the social sciences. I shall have occasion to refer to these as well.

For all their differences, on a large number of occasions the two schools find themselves very largely arguing the same case. For this reason I have called them together the "new instinctivists." But it is of some importance to see how each arrives at the racist conclusions that are the subject of this book.

The Ethologists and Ritual Aggression

Why do we need to do this? A common term shared by this book[7] and by those it critcizes is the Darwinian theory of evolution. I am totally committed to an evolutionary account of the origins and nature of human beings, as of all other species, in terms of natural selection and adaptation. However, I want to dispute what this means in practice. If it turned out that the findings of either the ethologists or of the sociobiologists were necessitated or directly warranted by the very nature of Darwinian theory, I believe we would have no option but to accept them—however unpalatable. In reality, I want to demonstrate that no such straight line of derivation is either achieved or achievable. To see this, it is necessary to know exactly how the ethologists derive their ideas.

I shall begin with Ardrey and Morris, who set out the conclusions that the ethologists draw, and then trace their route of emergence. I am not attempting a full account or critique of their views, only of how they typically move from premises to, in this case, a racist conclusion. Morris has a (for him) very careful discussion of racialism. He notes that there is a strong tendency for people to look at differences between nations and to argue that these (perhaps temperamental) differences must be biologically based: thus the Germans are laborious, the Italians excitable, Americans expansive, the British stiffupperlipish, etc. He scorns this idea: "Even as superficial assessments of acquired national character these generalisations are gross oversimplifications."[8] But, he claims, the real fault and danger comes from reading these traits as innate.

Clearly Morris is not being racist in a traditional sense.[9] But the new racism shows in his next step. Why do people believe this illogical idea that national characters are innate, asks Morris? It is "nothing more than the illogical wishful thinking of the *in-grouping tendency*." What is this?

> The whole human species has a wide range of basic behaviour patterns in common. The fundamental similarities between any one man and any other man are enormous. One of these, paradoxically, is the tendency to form distinct groups and to feel that you are somehow different, really deepdown different, from members of other groups. [Ibid., p. 128].

This is an innate tendency; and it is the same as what Lorenz calls "pseudospeciation," and Ardrey "nation-forming." And it makes inevitable a pessimistic political conclusion:

I am not arguing that there can be a worldwide brotherhood of man. That is a naive utopian dream. Man is a tribal animal and the great super-tribes will always be in competition with one another. [Ibid., p. 126].

Morris has argued that although the "badge" of color of your skin does not indicate any necessary difference under the skin, it is inevitably treated as though it did. And a condition of the success of "in-groups" is, in large part, the attitude taken toward outsiders:

There is, unhappily, an inverse relationship between external wars and internal strife. The implication is clear enough: namely that it is the same kind of frustrated aggressive energy that is finding an outlet in both cases. Only a brilliantly designed supertribal structure can avoid both at the same time. [Ibid., p. 116].

This last qualification is very odd since we are never given any guide as to what will be a brilliant design, who a brilliant designer, and how you go about reorganizing instinctual responses as suggested. By contrast, Ardrey does not worry too much about qualifications of this sort. His support of apartheid in South Africa witnesses the direction of his ideas. Ardrey has always been treated with reserve by the professional ethologists who are a bit embarrassed by him. But for all his exaggerated statements, he is committed to the same central concepts as they, and shares a lot of their "evidence"— coming to conclusions, in a way, much more logically than the others.

His main conclusion is a stronger restatement of Morris, that there is an inverse relation between the internal strength of a nation, and the external hostility in which it is involved:

Nothing in animal example or primate precedent offers any but the conclusion that territory is conservative, that it is invariably defensive, that the biological nation is the supreme natural mechanism for the security of a social group.[10]

Well-defined borders and a relation of defensiveness therefore are the essential requirements of a strong social order.

Even supposing that there were not a hundred other questions and objections to put up against this way of thinking, how is this supposed to have come about? How do Morris, Ardrey, and Lorenz know that this is how it works, and that it is innate? For an innate disposition is not the sort of thing that appears immediately in experience. It is a hypothetical explanation of data.

The ethologists, almost without exception, began from the problem of "aggression." Normally, this term refers loosely to a grouping of forms of behavior, including the actions of nations toward each other, the actions of children sorting out the rules of a game, a certain style of playing football, strategies in chess and even aspects of foreplay in sex. But the ethologists have taken this confused hotchpotch, and have offered to re-present it as a sharp concept by confronting it with the requirements of evolutionary theory. They have a paradigm type case of aggression — intraspecific killing — accounting for which will explain all the others.

Their strategy has been to ask a question that seems at first sight problematic: how is uncontrolled aggression between members of the same species compatible with the Darwinian selection and survival of a species? "If a species is to survive, it simply cannot afford to go round slaughtering its own kind. Intraspecific aggression has to be inhibited and controlled."[11] But aggression cannot just be got rid of. It has powerful evolutionary functions. Lorenz listed the key ones: distribution of the species within its environment, so that food stocks are available to those able to make best use of them; sexual selection, so that the "strongest" genes get passed on; brood defense against predators; and the creation of social ranking orders that are regarded as necessary for coordinated action. The problem, then, is this: by what process is it ensured that these essential functions are fulfilled without, unfortunately, wiping out the species in the process? Ethology's answer is *ritualization*.

If we consider again those functions of aggression listed by Lorenz, clearly, unlike the taking of prey, they are not necessarily best served by killing your opponent, if only for the reasons that killing may take much time and energy, and may result in you yourself being injured. If there were a way in which an instinctual rule could be built in such that you fight only insofar as it is needed, and winner be declared without any damage done, the species would be well served. This is what Lorenz and others claim to have discovered. For example, when the male cichlid fish gets very excited about the possibility of mating, he behaves in a very peculiar way; he

> assumes an attitude of broadside display, discharges some tailbeats, then rushes at his mate, and for fractions of a second it looks as if he will ram her — and then the thing happens which prompted me to write this book; the male does not waste time replying to the threatening of the female; he is far too excited for that, he actually launches a furious attack which, however, is *not directed at his mate* but, *passing her by narrowly, finds its goal in another member of his species.* Under natural conditions this is regularly the territorial neighbour.[12]

Lorenz's analysis of this and similar cases is the core of the ethological theory, including its application to human beings. Indeed, he went on to say that his special case "is very significant for our theme, because analogous processes play a decisive role in the family and social life of a great many higher animals and man."[13]

Lorenz is a good Darwinian. This account of ritualization will only work if it can be shown how it could have become part of what he calls our "inherited inventory." He has shown why we have to behave like this for survival's sake; in *King Solomon's Ring*[14] he has shown why socially organized predators, in particular, need effective ritualization of aggression. Think of wolves: their success depends both on their powerful cooperation and their powerful jaws. Out-of-control aggression among them would result in much less cooperation among them, and many fewer wolves. The fighting behavior of wolf against wolf is a paradigm of ritualization; the loser bares its throat, its most vulnerable part, to the victor, who instantly stops attacking.

But to show that something needs to be present is not to show how it could have developed. Aggression cannot be got rid of. But maybe it can be released in a safer direction. And so ritualization is said to involve *redirected aggression*.

Redirection of aggression means that potentially damaging behavior that is stimulated by one conspecific is directed away toward another. Thus, the male cichlid was aroused by his mate, but attacked a neighbor. Without this, says Lorenz, there could be no society to speak of. Indeed, the very strength of society is in inverse proportion to the strength of the deflected aggression. If we love our partners, relatives, and countrymen a lot, that can only be because we have adequately displaced our aggression. And all this has to be instinctual: "The phylogenetic process of ritualisation creates a new autonomous instinct which interferes as an independent force in the great constitution of all other instinctive motivations."[15] And its primary function is to induce "mutual understanding between members of a species." This is a claim to which Lorenz repeatedly returns.

But how is this to be maintained? One of the sociobiologists' challenges runs as follows: suppose there is such a group-beneficial trait as ritualization. What is to prevent a genetic cheat from arising? Imagine one wolf that does not restrain itself when faced with a bare throat. Think how it would benefit in a society of ritualizers. It would pass on more of its cheating genes. So, even supposing that a tendency to act for the group's benefit could emerge, it would soon cancel itself out.

This is always presented as though no answer was possible. In fact, there was one all along:

> There are certain social behaviour patterns useful to the community but against the interests of the individual. . . . The social system arising in this way remains by its very nature unstable. If, for example, in the jackdaw, *Coleus mondedula L.*, a defence reaction has evolved in which every individual bravely defends a fellow against a predator, it is easy to see that a group with this behaviour pattern has better chances of survival than one without it, but what prevents the occurrence within the group of individuals lacking this comrade-defence reaction?[16]

The answer Lorenz gives is important. For it reveals the continuities with prewar instinctivist accounts of society; and it will be a key to unlocking the objections of the sociobiologists. His answer is: we don't know (yet) for certain, but the mechanism must be something like a social antibody mechanism. Just as the body has defense mechanisms against mutant cells (and outside invaders), so the "social organism" must have a way of policing troublemakers. This will have to have been genetically coupled with the original group-formation mechanism, and they must mutually entail each other. Otherwise society could not persist. And as evidence that such mechanisms do work, Lorenz quotes cases where animals have displayed feelings of remorse or guilt, presumably showing that the individuals can also discipline themselves.

We thus get, from the application of Darwinian requirements to the facts of species' aggression, the following results: to the extent that a species requires social organization, it must ritualize and redirect its aggression. This produces populations that are internally socially structured, and militant against outsiders. This is "pseudo-speciation,"[17] and it is genetically rooted. And human culture is to be understood in this way, not as manmade, but as built by selection:

> Without traditional rites and customs representing a common property valued and defended by all members of the group, human beings would be quite unable to form social units exceeding in size that of the primal family group.[18]

At the family level, simple unitary instincts such as brood protection are strong enough. But for the higher levels of social organization, a "true autonomous instinct" is required, called "militant enthusiasm" (ibid., p. 234).

A combination of this, and a reconstruction of human prehistory[19] explains the horrible human propensity to go to war:

> In human evolution, no inhibitory mechanisms preventing sudden manslaughter were necessary, because quick killing was impossible anyhow; the potential victim had plenty of opportunity to elicit the pity of the aggressor by submissive gestures and appeasing attitudes. No selection pressures arose in the prehistory of mankind to breed inhibitory mechanisms preventing the killing of conspecifics until, all of a sudden, the invention of artificial weapons upset the equilibrium of killing-potential and social inhibitions.[20]

We are not, of course, told how and why humans had this propensity to develop weapons. The only explanation given is that humans had a generalized exploratory attitude that led to science and technology. This provided Morris with a justification for a contemptuous dismissal of any evidence about human tendencies derived from traditional societies; they had not developed, so they could not properly be called human. For it is part of our fundamental nature to explore, and thus to develop.[21]

What worries Lorenz and Morris about this human condition is that certain things can set off militant enthusiasm and then unrestrained aggression will tend to follow. One general cause they all stress is overpopulation.[22] This is a potential cause because overpopulation interferes with the things that bind a society together: organization of property and personal distance; social hierarchies; customs and traditions. Part of the problem can be put down to the creation of cities. When John Doe took up urban life, "he had become a citizen, or super-tribesman, and the key difference was that in a super-tribe *he no longer knew personally each member of his community*."[23] But that was precisely why the cultural symbols of unity became uniquely important, and why anything that interfered with them would be deadly: "The balanced interaction between all the single norms of social behaviour characteristic of a culture accounts for the fact that it is usually highly dangerous to mix cultures."[24] Although his examples are all of traditional societies, Lorenz insists that this is true of any culture.

Lorenz in many places discusses the effects of the weakening of social controls; in particular, he has constructed an explanation of "boredom" in youth, "hatred" between generations, and lawless anarchy in youth subcultures, based on the decline in clear hierarchies and strong traditions.[25] But the root of these effects is what interests us here. It is still the inevitable creation of in-groups and out-groups based on the innate principles of redirection of aggression, which is the ethologists' solution to the Darwinian problem of society.

The Assumptions of Ethology

It would be possible to spend hours and days showing the individual flaws, howlers, contradictions, and false "evidences" that make up human ethology. Many have done so. But it would not serve my purpose of showing that the project of arguing in their way is in principle wrong; that, therefore, their "explanations" of war, rape, aggression, hierarchy, racialism are not just questionable and indeed wrong, but also ideologically laden. To show this, we need to look again at the structure of the account I have just reviewed. For it shows several assumptions that are not subjected to analysis, without which the ethological argument could not even begin.

All these assumptions are connected with what Chase rightly referred to as the continued *preformationism* of instinctivism. Preformationism has taken many forms; at one time, it was believed that male sperm contained a tiny homunculus that simply grew when implanted in the woman. The doctrine now takes the somewhat more subtle form of believing that for each bit of behavior of an organism, there is an appropriate bit of genetic material (or gene difference for each difference in behaviour).[26] First, is the assumption that all animal behavior and human behavior must be understood by looking at its contribution to the survival of the organism. According to Lorenz, there really is no other sort of genuine explanation.[27] Natural selection operates through selective survival of organisms; therefore behaviors that have survived must be there because of their capacity to add to the survival chances of the organism. QED.

The naive attractiveness of this notion should not blind us to its uses and implications. For this is the reality that underlies Morris's comment that "biologically speaking, man has the inborn task of defending three things: himself, his family, and his tribe."[28] They are tasks because they are essential, says Morris, to the survival of the gene pool of that species or population. Now if it could be proved that human behavior is not guided by such "tasks," the whole ethological program would collapse.

The second assumption is perhaps best seen by asking what it is, according to the ethologists, that causes the modern problem of war. I have already hinted at the assumption here, when commenting on Morris's talk of the development of weaponry. Essentially, the ethologists' case is that something has been put biologically out of balance. Morris's talk of the supernormal stimuli of modern advertising is mirrored in one of Lorenz's more cautious, "scientific" works:

> In many omnivorous animals, for example, a mechanism exists that causes them to prefer food with a minimum content of fibre and a maximum of sugar, fat and starch. In the "normal" conditions of wild life, this phylogenetically adapted releasing mechanism is of obvious survival value, but in civilised man it gives rise to a search for supernormal objects, the addiction to which actually amounts to a vice detrimental to health (e.g. white bread, chocolate etc., which cause constipation and obesity in millions).[29]

Again, in one of his most recent works, he explains that humans have it in their natures only to work when it is necessary, an innate laziness that was not harmful when conditions enforced work. But now "modern civilisation" has flattened that enforcement; the absence of serious challenges is seen as dangerous to the species.[30] This same pattern of argument, then, is used to explain problems of war, overeating, laziness, conflict between generations. In this pattern there is an opposition between normal, natural environments and a supposedly artificial environment in which modern persons live.

The ethologists are notoriously unclear about what is the naughty factor in modern society, which is supposed to have corrupted us. It is variously called civilization, technology, cities, overpopulation (though, contra Chase, this is usually seen as a result, not a cause). The imprecision is in itself revealing, but not as significant as the sheer use of the opposition. For we are being shown an implicit assumption: that neo-Darwinism requires species to be "victims" of their environment. Natural selection equals the ability of environments to select out, weed out, the unfit for those environments. If a species evolves characteristics that enable it to escape natural selection, that is unhealthy. Ironically, given their frequent misplaced attacks on "environmentalism," it turns out to be an odd form of environmental determinism. For example, Morris describes as follows the condition of prehominid beings when the forests receded: "Only if the environment gave them a rude shove into greater open spaces would they be likely to move."[31] And being shoved into a different environment gave minimal choices about life-style or social structure: either man would compete with the carnivores, or with the herbivores. The idea of humans becoming, in effect, innate changers of environments, is inconceivable to the ethologists, because of this assumption of theirs. For it would be to deny that "environment" always signifies an independent variable, controlling natural selection. Any breach of this rule is, by definition, "artificial" or an "unbiological environment."[32]

The third assumption, that interlaces with the others, is that human behaviors are unitary: this is a point of tremendous significance. Consider the term "aggression" again. What reason is there, merely from examining its behavioral elements, to suppose that there is one common determining factor to war, murder, rape, sport, and chess playing? It is an assumption of the ethologists (and all other instinctivists) that there are common unitary bases to widely different behaviors. To explain, therefore, is to find a common motivation pattern.

This shows in Lorenz's discussion of the Great Parliament of the Instincts. He explains how big functions of the organism (like mating) are built up out of "relatively independent elements." There can be interaction between these elements, of course; but even interactions presuppose something else, that what interacts is preformed. Therefore the nature of the interactions is predetermined: "In reality, all imaginable interactions can take place between two *impulses which are variable independently of each other*."[33] Thus aggression + sex drive was turned into group adhesion and militant enthusiasm against outsiders. And, because the elements of the combination are preformed and remain relatively independent of each other, no new level of behavior beyond the limits of the elements is possible. But their continued independence is a preformationist assumption.

None of these assumptions is warranted by a Darwinian account, as we shall see. Indeed, it can be shown to be inconsistent with them. This point will become the major substance of my last chapter. But for now it is enough to see that the ethologists cannot stick to these assumptions themselves. They need to contradict them in order to have what I could call a "natural history of evil," that is, a picture of what it is in human behavior that has allowed so much to go wrong, and what could put it right.

Thus Lorenz, despite his assertion that everything ought to be explained as a function of its contribution to evolutionary survival, argues that there are "so-called luxury forms, i.e., structures whose form is not caused by the selection pressure of a system-preserving function, not even by one that was active in the past."[34] And it is supposed to be this additional baggage that expresses the forces of artificial civilization, and all the deviations from Darwinian logic.

But we have been given no guide for assigning behaviors, rites, and customs, institutions to one side or the other. All we have is a bald dualism; when one side can't account, the other must do. Let me show how this works by exploring in detail one example from Morris.

He invites us to see our hierarchical social behavior through Darwinian eyes, by a comparison with baboons. It is true, he admits, that the evolutionary connection is very distant, but that is not the point. For baboons were organized to face an environment similar to that which we faced when the prehominids left the lush forests for the open plain (this is Assumption 2 at work):

> The value of the baboon/human comparison lies in the way it reveals the very basic nature of human dominance patterns. The striking parallels that exist enable us to view the human power game with a fresh eye, and see it for what it is: a fundamental piece of animal behaviour.[35]

Thus is Assumption 1 now brought into play; for what is "animal behaviour" but behavior innately programmed for its survival benefit? So, how do we use this comparison? A typical way would be to look at the roles of the dominant males in each case: "It is always the dominant male baboon that is in the forefront of the defence against an attack from an external enemy. He plays the major role as protector of the group."[36] But, I hear you cry, that doesn't happen in humans. Precisely, says Morris, and that just goes to show how "civilization," the "artificial" life of modern man has corrupted an inherent mechanism: "If only today's leaders were forced to serve in the front lines, how much more cautious and 'humane' they would be when taking their decisions."[37] But why? It can only be because, with the artificial conditions removed, the impulse to ritualize would reassert itself and all would be well again—that is Assumption 3. For ritualization is now separated out as a unitary process, with definite ends and natural tendencies that must be pursued.

In this example from Morris we have a perfect illustration of the arbitrary way in which Darwinian premises are used in order to permit a shift between explanation and condemnation. Where the analogy fails it becomes a mode of condemnation; and a random extra factor, inexplicable in terms of this version of Darwinism, called "artificial civilisation" has to do the job of explaining why the analogy broke down. All three preformationist assumptions are needed in order to continue the myths.

What emerges, though, is that ethology contains assumptions that are not only unquestioned, but unquestionable by the "science" of ethology. For any human behavior that appears to challenge the basic theory is classified as "artificial" and therefore deviant. But the distinction between natural and artificial lives and environments is not a scientific one; it is a moral and political distinction. On all these grounds, we have a case for regarding ethology as *ideological science*. I prefer this wording to calling it simply "ideology," since it is a very important part of the force of ethology that it presents itself as science, that it uses a structure of interconnecting concepts and elaborate methods, and that it appears to be above politics. The ideology is in the very science.

Sociobiology and the Selfish Gene

It is with these remarks as a basis that we must examine the nature of the dispute between the ethologists and the sociobiologists. For without doubt, it arose within biology as a dispute between scientists. And the sociobiologists are keen to point out the implications of this fact. In July 1979, I was present at a conference at which Richard Dawkins asked that certain faults be forgiven, because the sociobiologists had been directing their attention specifically at the group selectionists. And indeed the debate between these two groups has been particularly sharp since the publication, in 1962, of Wynne-Edwards's group selectionist study of animal behavior.[38]

What makes the debate so sharp? Ostensibly, it is purely a debate about genetics, about the mechanism whereby Darwinian selection takes place. This debate has been rumbling on since the original formulation of evolutionary theory, beginning as a dispute between Darwin and Alfred Wallace, the codiscoverers of natural selection. But there is much more involved in the question of mechanism than a purely genetic argument.

If we review for a moment what the ethologists were doing, we can see that they were trying to solve some very particular problems. They were worried about the evolutionary functions of aggression: how could fighting members of one's own species be good for that species, and incorporated in its behavioral repertoire? And how could aggression, genetically rooted, be genetically restrained, so that its functions could be benignly fulfilled? All this boils down to explaining the genetic possibility of society, of certain forms of "altruism." For unrestrained aggression would be the death of society, if not of the species. The ethologist's solution was *ritualization*.

For a time, the ethologists had the edge over the individual selectionists for popularity. Among geneticists, that was probably not so. But Lorenz and company had never been shy of popularizing, and in forms that would appeal: and many of their ideas soaked into popular opinion (or became part of the rationale given for common opinion). The recent counterblast from the sociobiologists, who have also had a strange penchant for popularization, has probably now made them the more popular. What they have attacked is the idea of selection at the level of the group. I have already briefly illustrated this at the beginning of the chapter; now I want to consider its significance.

The ethologists' solution to their problems had been premised on the central need for society. There had to be society for sexual, protective, and distributive purposes. Ritualization, as a possible genetic mechanism, had the beautiful advantage of simultaneously providing society's need for altruism and restraining aggression. I put it like this for if we do not see the ethologists first and foremost solving the problem of society, we will not be able to understand why, for the sociobiologists, aggression is not the central problem.

Not that aggression disappears for the sociobiologists: it is simply given a different place in the picture. The ethological claim is specifically rejected:

> The ethological claims as to the facts of animal aggression are therefore challenged. As might be expected, Lorenz's group selection hypotheses are also questioned. In particular, the sociobiologists want to work from, and only from, individual selection. Now, in a sense, they can do this easily: perhaps even more easily than someone like Lorenz. The sociobiologists make no *a priori* assumptions about the good of the species, and hence have no need of special explanations as to why one organism might attack a fellow. Thus, all other things being equal, in the eyes of the sociobiologists the parasitic wasp larva is indifferent as to whether it is attacking a fellow or a member of a different species.[39]

Every member of a species, according to sociobiology, potentially treats every other as a resource for food, and as a competitor for mating, territory, etc. Aggression is therefore just the natural relation of members of the same species. And the challenge to the ethological view of animal aggression was made by referring to the many known cases where animals *have* killed conspecifics.

We must be careful here about the status of this evidence. Lorenz and his cothinkers had long known that, especially in some species (and, important for them, that included human beings), ritualization was not as strongly developed as in others (see, for example, Lorenz, *On Aggression*, chapter 10 on rats). And in addition, they were fond of quoting studies that showed that under certain sorts of pressure, rape, murder, and cannibalism could develop in animal species. So this evidence was not new; and it was accounted for by reference to a natural thinness of the barriers preventing "murderous" aggression, or as "deviance" resulting from abnormal pressures of such things as overcrowding, food shortages, etc.

Wilson has argued, and Ruse has quoted him, that the ethologists in a sense just missed the necessary information: "I have been impressed by how often such behaviour becomes apparent only when the observation times devoted to a species passes the thousand hour mark."[40] This is not a good argument. The ethologists had in fact pioneered the systematic observation of animals' behavior. They knew many of these "facts"; they just had a different strategy for coping with them. The sociobiologists do not disagree with ethologists primarily on matters of empirical evidence, but on the ways of handling data. They have a different conceptualization of the evidence, in which the idea of "deviant" aggression is largely removed. Instead, it is accounted for by an a priori position, that individual genes—and as their bearers, individual organisms[41]—necessarily and always seek to maximize their own chances of survival. And that means, ab initio, that all other members of your species are your natural competitors.

But that does not get rid of the problem of society. On the contrary, it makes it necessary to consider it in a new form. This is the reason why Wilson, speaking for them all, wrote about "the central theoretical problem of sociobiology: how can altruism which by definition reduces personal fitness, possibly evolve by natural selection?"[42] By definition, indeed. Genes and their organisms (nicely named "gene machines" by Dawkins) behave in such a way as to maximize their own fitness. No malice is imputed. Simply genes and organisms that did not do this will not have had much of a future. For an organism is only to be called altruistic if it behaves "in such a way as to increase another such entity's welfare at the expense of its own."[43] This odd definition of altruism has all the signs of making a dangerous circular argument.

The sociobiologists' confidence in these definitions flows straight from their picture of fundamental evolutionary theory. But it lands them with the problem of accounting for all forms of social behavior: if evolution by definition favors the selfish, how could there ever be altruism? Their answer is, only if it is a special form of selfishness; "there are special circumstances in which a gene can achieve its own selfish goals best by fostering a limited form of altruism at the level of individual animals.[44]

Much energy and inventiveness have gone into inventing many various forms of altruism. But the prime form is kin altruism. The mechanism of its possibility is straightforward: genes are defined as selfish because unselfish ones would not reproduce so successfully, and would gradually disappear from any population. But suppose that an organism is programmed to look after only related organisms, ones with shared genes. The chances are, then, that even if this costs the life of the protector, the gene for protection will have been saved.[45]

Kin altruism is thus consistent with sociobiological premises. But how does all this relate to racism? We can see this, if we take note of an important criticism of sociobiology and how it is responded to. For this account of kin altruism had been met with some very powerful arguments from, for example, Marshall Sahlins.[46] Kin altruism seems to expect organisms to undertake some amazing calculations of genetic relatedness; for clearly, the degree to which it is evolutionarily beneficial depends upon the likelihood that the organism being helped shares the particular genes. And that is mathematically calculable; a parent-child, or a sibling relation will be 50 percent; grandparents, and aunts and uncles 25 percent; cousins 12½ percent; and so on.[47] Sahlins has rightly been scornful of the idea that such detailed calculations can take place.

But the sociobiologists do have a reply, which has two parts. First, it is commonly emphasized that organisms don't actually do the calculating. They behave as if they had calculated:

> I have made the simplifying assumption that the individual animal works out what is best for his genes. What really happens is that the gene pool becomes filled with genes which influence bodies in such a way that they behave *as if* they had made such calculations.[48]

But how? Gene inheritance is only marginally written in one's face. In some species there might be very specific identifiers (for example, the smell-chemicals, pheromones, that carry precise information in insect species); in others, it might rather be a learned discrimination, via the social rearing pattern.

It was this second possibility that gave rise to what can be called a "pseudobiological" process. Tiger and Shepher, in their study of the Israeli kibbutzim, give an example of this. Noting that there seemed never to be sexual relations among children reared together in kibbutzim, they claimed that this must be because of a misfiring incest-avoidance trait that was genetically implanted.[49] A BBC Horizon program on their work called this "fooling the genes"; for the children apparently were avoiding incestuous relations because they had been brought up as though they were brothers and sisters. Thus a genetic "requirement" was mediated via a social pattern.

It is really the combination of these two strands that makes sociobiology's addition to the justification of racism. Listen to David Barash:

> If we admit to the possibility that human behaviour has been selected to maximise inclusive fitness, then our preoccupation with genetic relatedness and our responses to it are certainly no surprise. In fact anything else would require some explanation.
>
> Genetic relatedness often declines dramatically beyond the boundaries of a social group . . . and, significantly, aggressiveness increases in turn. Hostility towards outsiders is characteristic of both human and non-human animals. Physical similarity is also a function of genetic relatedness, and human racial prejudice, directed against individuals who look *different*, could well have its roots in this tendency to distinguish in-group from out-group.[50]

Exactly the same line of argument is offered by Pierre van den Berghe, former liberal sociologist of race relations, in an unpleasant article.[51] In it, he argues that all racial dislike has a genetically based component. He goes through an account of the derivation of racism, ethnocentrism, and nationalism, all from the same source: kin altruism. A breeding population over a long span of time develops sufficient genetic closeness and closedness for such "powerful sentiments" to develop, whose "blind ferocity" and imperviousness to rational arguments are "but a few indications of their continued vitality and their primordiality"[52]: "As hominids became increasingly formidable competitors and predators to their own and closely related species, there was a strong selection pressure for the formation of larger and more powerful groups" (ibid., p. 405). Thus the creation of "super families" or nations "necessarily meant organising *against* other competing groups, and therefore maintaining ethnic boundaries" (ibid.).

Thus is racism rooted in the genes, in the specific style of sociobiology. Limited altruism within a genetic community has its counterpart in open selfishness, hostility, and aggression toward competitive outsiders. Of course, if they had kept their distance . . . But I took care to say that this was the particular contribution of sociobiologists. For in fact, while denying the ethologists' framework of explanation, they have kept many of their particular conclusions; and that has included both the use of territorialism, and of ritualization of aggression. And thus sociobiology can offer a series of reasons why racism should be regarded as genetically programmed in us.

It must be pretty obvious that there is a close convergence between the style of racism that I described in chapter 1, and the "explanations" of ethnocentrism and racial prejudice just outlined. In both, it is possible to deny any assertion of superiority. It is simply that it is natural to isolate oneself behind cultural and genetic barriers: what the two schools of instinctivism offer is a gloss on the word "natural." In this chapter, I have only tried to show the process of derivation of this conclusion. I have made a few preliminary remarks on the ethologists, but I do not want much to return to them. The sociobiologists have become the senior partners now, and I shall direct my main fire against them. Much that I say, however, would apply without change to the ethologists.

The sociobiologists declare themselves deeply upset at any charge of being racist. Barash, for example:

> Concern has been expressed that human sociobiology represents racism in disguise: This is simply not true. Sociobiology deals with biological universals that may underlie human social behaviour, universals that are presumed to hold cross-culturally and therefore cross-racially as well. What better *antidote* for racism than such emphasis on the behavioural commonality of our single species?[53]

He is even prepared to concede that the early pseudobiology of "races" and of *laisser faire* capitalism was a misuse of Darwinism. But that could not be true this time?

Exactly the same case is put forward by Michael Ruse (pp. 76–79), who also cannot see that a racist theory could be anything other than asserting that Jews are degenerate, or blacks inferior. But the new Tory racists are saying something much simpler, and Wilson for one apparently agrees: "Nationalism and racism, to take two examples, are the culturally nurtured outgrowths of simple tribalism."[54] And they all agree that "simple tribalism" (whatever that may be) is just kin altruism in action. It is simply the extension of loving one's family — at least, if all the preceding theory is correct.

NOTES

1. Robert Ardrey, *The Territorial Imperative* (London: Collins, 1967), p. 191.

2. See Konrad Lorenz, *Evolution and Modification of Behavior* (Chicago: University of Chicago Press, 1965), *On Aggression* (London: Methuen, 1967), *Civilised Man's Eight Deadly Sins* (London: Methuen, 1973), and "The Enmity between Generations and Its Probable Causes," in A. Tiselius and S. Nilsson (eds.), *The Place of Values in the World of Fact* (Stockholm: Almqvist & Wiksell, 1970); Nikolas Tinbergen, *The Study of Instinct* (Oxford: Oxford University Press, 1951), and "On War and Peace in Man and Animal," in H. Friedrich (ed.), *Man and Animal* (London: Paladin, 1972); Desmond Morris, *The Naked Ape* (London: Corgi, 1968), *The Human Zoo* (London: Corgi, 1971), *Intimate Behavior* (London: Cape, 1971), and *Manwatching* (London: Cape, 1977); and Robert Ardrey, *The Territorial Imperative, The Social Contract* (London: Collins, 1970), and *African Genesis* (London: Collins, 1961).

3. Allan Chase, *The Legacy of Malthus* (New York: Knopf, 19771). Lorenz's biographer, Alec Nesbitt, rather disputes the significance of this period of Lorenz's writings: to my mind inconclusively, since he is only concerned to disprove personal Nazism. I am much more worried by the simple continuity of basic concepts and what they warrant. Nesbitt, *Konrad Lorenz* (London: Dent, 1976), chapter 7.

4. Wilson, *Sociobiology — the New Synthesis* (Cambridge, Mass.: Harvard University Press, 1976); see also Wilson, *On Human Nature* (Cambridge, Mass.: Harvard University Press, 1978).

5. Michael Ruse, *Sociobiology — Sense or Nonsense?* (Dordrecht: Reidel, 1979), chapter 2.

6. T. H. Clutton-Brock and Paul Harvey (eds.), *Readings in Sociobiology* (New York: Freeman, 1978); Richard Dawkins, *The Selfish Gene* (Oxford: Oxford University Press, 1976), and "Sex and the Immortal Gene," *Vogue* (1977).

7. [The author refers here to the volume from which this essay was excerpted: *The New Racism* (London: Junction Books, 1981) — Ed.]

8. Morris, *The Human Zoo*, p. 127.

9. Morris in fact is very ambivalent on the question of innate differences. In *The Human Zoo* (p. 189), he claims that it has never been proved that there are innate differences between populations (he dislikes the word "race" advisedly). On the other hand, he is prepared to repeat the age-old myth (p. 134) that contraception restricted to the "educated classes" will lead to an overall genetic deterioration, as there is probably a genetic component to differences in intelligence; and the poor, unintelligent won't understand how to use some forms of contraception. What this shows, I think, is modern ethology's whole ambiguous relationship to prewar eugenicism.

10. Ardrey, *The Territorial Imperative*, p. 253.

11. Morris, *The Naked Ape*, p. 139.

12. Lorenz, *On Aggression*, pp. 144–45.

13. Ibid., p. 145.

14. London: Methuen.

15. Lorenz, *On Aggression*, p. 72.

16. Lorenz, *Civilised Man's Eight Deadly Sins*, p. 32.

17. Ibid., p. 49

18. Lorenz, *On Aggression*, p. 226.

19. Something of which the ethologists are very fond. But see the complete demolition of their, and related, accounts in Leakey and Lewin's marvellous book, *Origins* (London: MacDonald & Jane, 1977). Leakey has since disappointed many admirers by his concessions to sociobiological views in the later *People of the Lake* (London: MacDonald & Jane, 1979).

20. Lorenz, *On Aggression*, p. 207.

21. Morris, *The Naked Ape*, p. 10.

22. See Chase, *The Legacy of Malthus*, chapters 6 and 7.

23. Morris, *The Human Zoo*, p. 21.

24. Lorenz, *On Aggression*, p. 225.

25. See Lorenz, "Enmity between Generations."

26. The fallacy in this, and the alternative, are set out in chapters 7–9 [of *The New Racism*—Ed.].

27. Lorenz, *On Aggression*, p. 1.

28. Morris, *The Human Zoo*, p. 111.

29. Lorenz, *Evolution and Modificiation of Behavior*, pp. 26–27.

30. Lorenz, *Civilised Man's Eight Deadly Sins*, p. 25.

31. Morris, *The Naked Ape*, p. 17.

32. See, e.g., Morris, *The Human Zoo*, pp. 27, 115.

33. Lorenz, *On Aggression*, p. 75; my emphasis.

34. Lorenz, *Civilised Man's Eight Deadly Sins*, pp. 46–47.

35. Morris, *The Human Zoo*, p. 51.

36. Ibid., p. 50.

37. Ibid., p. 113.

38. V. C. Wynne-Edwards, *Animal Dispersion in Relation to Social Behavior* (Edinburgh: Oliver & Boyd, 1962).

39. Ruse, *Sociobiology*, p. 25.

40. Ibid.

41. Though that step is highly problematic.

42. Wilson, *Sociobiology—the New Synthesis*, p. 3.

43. Dawkins, *The Selfish Gene*, p. 4.

44. Ibid., p. 2.

45. We can see from this why kin altruism is the paradigm of altruism, compared with, say, reciprocal altruism, another commonly quoted sort. For this latter consists in one organism agreeing with another, as it were, on a "you scratch my back, I'll scratch yours" principle—usually aiding each other in competition with a third. This ability may be mutually beneficial, but it has nothing to do with the specific gene differences between individuals that form the core of the sociobiologists' account, since the cooperating individuals can be totally unrelated genetically.

46. Marshall Sahlins, *The Use and Abuse of Biology* (London: Tavistock, 1977).

47. In fact, of course, the mathematical calculation is vastly more complicated than this, for many reasons. There are dominant genes that are more likely to reappear in any combination; in a small population of animals, there are likely to be generally shared genes in different proportions throughout the population, because of inbreeding. But the sociobiologists will play their games, so who are we to interfere?

48. Dawkins, *The Selfish Gene*, p. 108.

49. Lionel Tiger and Joseph Shepher, *Women in the Kibbutz* (Harmondsworth: Penguin, 1977).

50. David Barash, *Sociobiology and Behavior* (London: Heinemann, 1978), pp. 310–11. In order to guard against charges of selective quotation, let us see how Barash continues: "Clearly, this suggestion of a possible evolutionary basis for human racial prejudice is not intended to legitimise it, just to indicate why it may occur. Behaviour patterns that may have been been adaptive under biological conditions are inappropriate and even dangerous under the cultural innovations of today" (p. 311). Why this is no defense, and is indeed worse than no defense, will become apparent in chapter 8 [of *The New Racism*—Ed.]. Note only for now the continuity with the dualism of the ethologists, between "natural" biology and "artificial" culture.

51. Pierre van den Berghe, "Race and Ethnicity: A Sociobiological Perspective," *Ethnic and Racial Studies*, 1 (1978). And see also Wilson's use of a distinction between hardcore (kin only) and softcore (ethnic community) altruism in his *On Human Nature* (pp. 155–63); also Dawkins: "Conceivably, racial prejudice could be interpreted as an irrational generalisation of a kinselected tendency to identify with individuals physically resembling oneself and to be nasty to individuals different in appearance" (*The Selfish Gene*, p. 108).

52. Ibid., p. 104.

53. Barash, *Sociobiology and Behavior*, p. 278.

54. Wilson, *On Human Nature*, p. 92.

CHAPTER 3

Race and Gender:
The Role of Analogy in Science

Nancy Leys Stepan

Metaphor occupies a central place in literary theory, but the role of metaphors, and of the analogies they mediate, in scientific theory is still debated.[1] One reason for the controversy over metaphor, analogy, and models in science is the intellectually privileged status that science has traditionally enjoyed as the repository of nonmetaphorical, empirical, politically neutral, universal knowledge. During the scientific revolution of the seventeenth century, metaphor became associated with the imagination, poetic fancy, subjective figures, and even untruthfulness and was contrasted with truthful, unadorned, objective knowledge — that is, with science itself.[2]

In the twentieth century logical positivists also distinguished between scientific and metaphoric language.[3] When scientists insisted that analogies or models based on analogies were important to their thinking, philosophers of science tended to dismiss their claims that metaphors had an *essential* place in scientific utterances. The French theoretical physicist Pierre Duhem was well known for his criticism of the contention that metaphor and analogies were important to *explanation* in science. In his view, the aim of science was to reduce all theory to mathematical statements; models could aid the process of scientific discovery, but once they had served their function, analogies could be discarded as extrinsic to science, and the theories made to stand without them.[4]

One result of the dichotomy established between science and metaphor was that obviously metaphoric or analogical science could only be treated as "prescientific" or "pseudoscientific" and therefore dismissable.[5] Because science has been identified with truthfulness and empirical reality, the metaphorical nature of much modern science tended to go unrecognized. And because it went unrecognized, as Colin Turbayne has pointed out, it has been easy to mistake the model in science "for the thing modeled" — to think, to take his example, that nature *was* mechanical, rather than to think it was, metaphorically, seen as mechanical.[6]

More recently, however, as the attention of historians and philosophers of science has moved away from logical reconstructions of science toward more "naturalistic" views of science in culture, the role of metaphor, analogies, and models in science has begun to be acknowledged.[7] In a recent volume on metaphor, Thomas S. Kuhn claims that analogies are fundamental to science; and Richard Boyd argues that they are "irreplaceable parts of the linguistic machinery of a scientific theory," since cases exist in which there are metaphors used by scientists to express theoretical claims "for which no adequate literal paraphrase is known."[8] Some philosophers of science are now prepared to assert that metaphors and analogies are not just psychological aids to scientific discovery, or heuristic devices, but constituent elements of scientific theory.[9] We seem about to move full circle, from considering metaphors mere embellishments or poetic fictions to considering them essential to scientific thought itself.

Although the role of metaphor and analogy in science is now recognized, a critical theory of scientific metaphor is only just being elaborated. The purpose of this essay is to contribute to the development of such a theory by using a particular analogy in the history of the life sciences to explore a series of related questions concerning the cultural sources of scientific analogies, their role in scientific reasoning, their normative consequences, and the process by which they change.

Race and Gender: A Powerful Scientific Analogy

The analogy examined is the one linking race to gender, an analogy that occupied a strategic place in scientific theorizing about human variation in the nineteenth and twentieth centuries.

As has been well documented, from the late Enlightenment on students of human variation singled out racial differences as crucial aspects of reality, and an extensive discourse on racial inequality began to be elaborated.[10] In the nineteenth century, as attention turned increasingly to sexual and gender differences as well, gender was found to be remarkably analogous to race, such that the scientist could use racial difference to explain gender difference, and vice versa.[11]

Thus it was claimed that women's low brain weights and deficient brain structures were analogous to those of lower races, and their inferior intellectualities explained on this basis.[12] Woman, it was observed, shared with Negroes a narrow, childlike, and delicate skull, so different from the more robust and rounded heads characteristic of males of "superior" races. Similarly, women of higher races tended to have slightly protruding jaws, analogous to, if not as exaggerated as, the apelike jutting jaws of lower races.[13] Women and lower races were called innately impulsive, emotional, imitative rather than original, and incapable of the abstract reasoning found in white men.[14] Evolutionary biology provided yet further analogies. Woman was in evolutionary terms the "conservative element" to the man's "progressive," preserving the more "primitive" traits found in lower races, while the males of higher races led the way in new biological and cultural directions.[15]

Thus when Carl Vogt, one of the leading German students of race in the middle of the nineteenth century, claimed that the female skull approached in many respects that of the infant, and in still further respects that of lower races, whereas the mature male of many lower races resembled in his "pendulous" belly a Caucasian woman who had had many children, and in his thin calves and flat thighs the ape, he was merely stating what had become almost a cliché of the science of human difference.[16]

So fundamental was the analogy between race and gender that the major modes of interpretation of racial traits were invariably evoked to explain sexual traits. For instance, just as scientists spoke of races as distinct "species," incapable of crossing to produce viable "hybrids," scientists analyzing male-female differences sometimes spoke of females as forming a distinct "species," individual members of which were in danger of degenerating into psychosexual hybrids when they tried to cross boundaries proper to their sex.[17] Darwin's theory of sexual selection was applied to both racial and sexual difference, as was the neo-Lamarckian theory of the American Edward D. Cope.[18] A last, confirmatory example of the analogous place of gender and race in scientific theorizing is taken from the history of hormone biology. Early in the twentieth century the anatomist and student of race Sir Arthur Keith interpreted racial differences in the human species as a function of pathological disturbances of the newly discovered "internal secretions" or hormones. At about the same time, the apostle of sexual frankness and well-known student of sexual variation Havelock Ellis used internal secretions to explain the small, but to him vital, differences in the physical and psychosexual makeup of men and women.[19]

In short, lower races represented the "female" type of the human species, and females the "lower race" of gender. As the example from Vogt indicates, however, the analogies concerned more than race and gender. Through an intertwined and overlapping series of analogies, involving often quite complex comparisons, identifications, cross-references, and evoked associations, a variety of "differences" — physical and psychical, class and national — were brought together in a biosocial science of human variation. By analogy with the so-called lower races, women, the sexually deviate, the criminal, the urban poor, and the insane were in one way or another constructed as biological "races apart" whose differences from the white male, and likenesses to each other, "explained" their different and lower position in the social hierarchy.[20]

It is not the aim of this essay to provide a systematic history of the biosocial science of racial and sexual difference based on analogy. The aim is rather to use the race-gender analogy to analyze the nature of analogical reasoning in science itself. When and how did the analogy appear in science? From what did it derive its scientific authority? How did the analogy shape research? What did it mean when a scientist claimed that the mature male of many lower races resembled a mature Caucasian female who had had many children? No simple theory of resemblance or substitution explains such an analogy. How did the analogy help construct the very similarities and differences supposedly "discovered" by scientists in nature? What theories of analogy and metaphor can be most effectively applied in the critical study of science?

The Cultural Sources of Scientific Metaphor

How particular metaphors or analogies in science are related to the social production of science, why certain analogies are selected and not others, and why certain analogies are accepted by the scientific community are all issues that need investigation.

In literature, according to Warren Shibles, striking metaphors just come, "like rain."[21] In science, however, metaphors and analogies are not arbitrary, nor merely personal. Not just any metaphors will do. In fact, it is their lack of perceived "arbitrariness" that makes particular metaphors or analogies acceptable as science.

As Stephen Toulmin recently pointed out, the constraints on the choice of metaphors and analogies in science are varied. The nature of the objects being studied (e.g., organic vs. nonorganic), the social (e.g., class) structure of the scientific community studying them, and the history of the discipline or field concerned all play their part in the emergence of certain analogies rather than others and in their "success" or failure.[22] Sometimes the metaphors are strikingly new, whereas at other times they extend existing metaphors in the culture in new directions.

In the case of the scientific study of human difference, the analogies used by scientists in the late eighteenth century, when human variation began to be studied systematically, were products of long-standing, long-familiar, culturally endorsed metaphors. Human variation and difference were not experienced "as they really are, out there in nature," but by and through a metaphorical system that structured the experience and understanding of difference and that in essence created the objects of difference. The metaphorical system provided the "lenses" through which people experienced and "saw" the differences between classes, races, and sexes, between civilized man and the savage, between rich and poor, between the child and the adult. As Sander Gilman says in his book *Seeing the Insane*, "We do not see the world, rather we are taught by representations of the world about us to conceive of it in a culturally acceptable manner."[23]

The origin of many of the "root metaphors" of human difference are obscure. G. Lakoff and M. Johnson suggest that the basic values of a culture are usually compatible with "the metaphorical structure of the most fundamental concepts in the culture."[24] Not surprisingly, the social groups represented metaphorically as "other" and "inferior" in Western culture were socially "disenfranchised" in a variety of ways, the causes of their disenfranchisement varying from group to group and from period to period. Already in ancient Greece, Aristotle likened women to the slave on the grounds of their "natural" inferiority. Winthrop Jordan has shown that by the early Middle Ages a binary opposition between blackness and whiteness was well established in which blackness was identified with baseness, sin, the devil, and ugliness, and whiteness with virtue, purity, holiness, and beauty.[25] Over time, black people themselves were compared to apes, and their childishness, savageness, bestiality, sexuality, and lack of intellectual capacity stressed. The "Ethiopian," the "African," and especially the "Hottentot" were made to stand for all that the white male was not: they provided a rich analogical source for the understanding and representation of other "inferiorities." In his study of the representation of insanity in Western culture, for instance, Gilman shows how the metaphor of blackness could be borrowed to explicate the madman, and vice versa. In similar analogical fashion, the laboring poor were represented as the "savages" of Europe, and the criminal as a "Negro."

When scientists in the nineteenth century, then, proposed an analogy between racial and sexual differences, or between racial and class differences, and began to generate new data on the basis of such analogies, their interpretations of human difference and similarity were widely accepted, partly because of their fundamental congruence with cultural expectations. In this particular science, the metaphors and analogies were not strikingly new but old, if unexamined and diffuse. The scientists' contribution was to elevate hitherto unconsciously held analogies into self-conscious theory, to extend the meanings attached to the analogies, to expand their range through new observations and comparisons, and to give them precision through specialized vocabularies and new technologies. Another result was that the analogies became "naturalized" in the language of science, and their metaphorical nature disguised.

In the scientific elaboration of these familiar analogies, the study of race led the way, in part because the differences between blacks and whites seemed so "obvious," in part because the abolition movement gave political urgency to the issue of racial difference and social inequality. From the study of race came the association between inferiority and the ape. The facial angle, a measure of hierarchy in nature obtained by comparing the protrusion of the jaws in apes and humans, was widely used in analogical science once it was shown that by this measure Negroes appeared to be closer to apes than the white race.[26] Established as signs of inferiority, the facial angle and blackness could then be extended analogically to explain other inferior groups and races. For instance, Francis Galton, Darwin's cousin and the founder of eugenics and statistics in Britain, used the Negro and the apish jaw to explicate the Irish: "Visitors to Ireland after the potato famine," he commented, "generally remarked that the Irish type of face seemed to have become more prognathous, that is, more like the negro in the protrusion of the lower jaw."[27]

Especially significant for the analogical science of human difference and similarity were the systematic study and measurement of the human skull. The importance of the skull to students of human difference lay in the fact that it housed the brain, differences in whose shape and size were presumed to correlate with equally presumed differences in intelligence and social behavior. It was measurements of the skull, brain weights, and brain convolutions that gave apparent precision to the analogies between anthropoid apes, lower races, women, criminal types, lower classes, and the child. It was race scientists who provided the new technologies of measurement—the callipers, cephalometers, craniometers, craniophores, craniostats, and parietal goniometers.[28] The low facial angles attributed by scientists starting in the 1840s and 1850s to women, criminals, idiots, and the degenerate, and the corresponding low brain weights, protruding jaws, and incompletely developed frontal centers where the higher intellectual faculties were presumed to be located, were all taken from racial science. By 1870 Paul Topinard, the leading French anthropologist after the death of Paul Broca, could call on data on sexual and racial variations from literally hundreds of skulls and brains, collected by numerous scientists over decades, in order to draw the conclusion tht Caucasian women were indeed more prognathous or apelike in their jaws than white men, and even the largest women's brains, from the "English or Scotch" race, made them like the African male.[29] Once "woman" had been shown to be indeed analogous to lower races by the new science of anthropometry and had become, in essence, a racialized category, the traits and qualities special to woman could in turn be used in an analogical understanding of lower races. The analogies now had the weight of empirical reality and scientific theory. The similarities between a Negro and a white woman, or between a criminal and a Negro, were realities of nature, somehow "in" the individuals studied.

Metaphoric Interactions

We have seen that metaphors and analogies played an important part in the science of human difference in the nineteenth century. The question is, what part? I want to suggest that the metaphors functioned as the science itself— that without them the science did not exist. In short, metaphors and analogies can be constituent elements of science.

It is here that I would like to introduce, as some other historians of science have done, Max Black's "interaction" theory of metaphor, because it seems that the metaphors discussed in this essay, and the analogies they mediated, functioned like interaction metaphors, and that thinking about them in these terms clarifies their role in science.[30]

By interaction metaphors, Black means metaphors that join together and bring into cognitive and emotional relation with each other two different things, or systems of things, not normally so joined. Black follows I. A. Richards in opposing the "substitution" theory of metaphor, in which it is supposed that the metaphor is telling us indirectly something factual about the two subjects—that the metaphor is a *literal comparison*, or is capable of a literal translation in prose. Richards proposed instead that "when we use a metaphor, we have two thoughts of different things active together and supported by a single word or phrase, whose meaning is the resultant of their interaction." Applying the interaction theory to the metaphor "The poor are the negroes of Europe," Black paraphrases Richards to claim that "our thoughts about the European poor and American negroes are 'active together' and 'interact' to produce a meaning that is a resultant of that interaction."[31] In such a view, the metaphor cannot be simply reduced to literal comparisons or "like" statements without loss of meaning or cognitive content, because meaning is a product of the interaction between the two parts of a metaphor.

How do these "new meanings" come about? Here Black adds to Richards by suggesting that in an interaction metaphor, a "system of associated commonplaces" that strictly speaking belong only to one side of the metaphor are applied to the other. And he adds that what makes the metaphor effective "is not that the commonplaces shall be true, but that they should be readily and freely evoked."[32] Or as Mary Hesse puts it in *Models and Analogies in Science*, these implications "are not private, but are largely common to a given language community and are presupposed by speakers who intend to be understood."[33] Thus in the example given, the "poor of Europe" are seen in terms strictly applicable only to the "Negro," and vice versa. As a consequence, the poor are seen like a "race apart," savages in the midst of European civilization. Conversely, the "Negro" is seen as shiftless, idle, given to drink, part of the social remnant bound to be left behind in the march toward progress. Both the ideas of "savagery" and of "shiftlessness" belong to familiar systems of implications that the metaphor itself brings into play.

Black's point is that by their interactions and evoked associations both parts of a metaphor are changed. Each part is seen as more like the other in some characteristic way. Black was primarily interested in ordinary metaphors of a culture and in their commonplace associations. But instead of commonplace associations, a metaphor may evoke more specially constructed systems of implications. Scientists are in the business of constructing exactly such systems of implications, through their empirical investigations into nature and through their introduction into discourse of specialized vocabularies and technologies.[34] It may be, indeed, that what makes an analogy suitable for scientific purposes is its ability to be suggestive of new systems of implications, new hypotheses, and therefore new observations.[35]

In the case of the nineteenth-century analogical science of human difference, for instance, the system of implications evoked by the analogy linking lower races and women was not just a generalized one concerning social inferiority, but the more precise and specialized one developed by years of anthropometric, medical, and biological research. When "woman" and "lower races" were analogically and routinely joined in the anthropological, biological, and medical literature of the 1860s and 1870s, the metaphoric interactions involved a complex system of implications about similarity and difference, often involving highly technical language (for example, in one set of measurements of the body in different races cited by Paul Topinard in 1878 the comparisons included measures in each race of their height from the ground to the acromion, the epicondyle, the styloid process of the radius, the great trochanter, and the internal malleolus). The systems of implications evoked by the analogy included questions of comparative health and disease (blacks and women were believed to show greater degrees of insanity and neurasthenia than white men, especially under conditions of freedom), of sexual behavior (females of "lower races" and lower-class women of "higher races," especially prostitutes, were believed to show similar kinds of bestiality and sexual promiscuity, as well as similar signs of pathology and degeneracy such as deformed skulls and teeth), and of "childish" characteristics, both physical and moral.[36]

As already noted, one of the most important systems of implications about human groups developed by scientists in the nineteenth century on the basis of analogical reasoning concerned head shapes and brain sizes. It was assumed that blacks, women, the lower classes, and criminals shared low brain weights or skull capacities. Paul Broca, the founder of the Société d'Anthropologie de Paris in 1859, asserted: "In general, the brain is larger in mature adults than in the elderly, in men than in women, in eminent men than in men of mediocre talent, in superior races than in inferior races. . . .

Other things being equal, there is a remarkable relationship between the development of intelligence and the volume of the brain."[37]

Such a specialized system of implications based on the similarities between brains and skulls appeared for the first time in the phrenological literature of the 1830s. Although analogies between women and blackness had been drawn before, woman's place in nature and her biopsychological differences from men had been discussed by scientists mainly in terms of reproductive function and sexuality, and the most important analogies concerned black females (the "sign" of sexuality) and lower-class or "degenerate" white women. Since males of all races had no wombs, no systematic, apparently scientifically validated grounds of comparison between males of "lower" races and women of "higher" races existed.

Starting in the 1820s, however, the phrenologists began to focus on differences in the shape of the skull of individuals and groups, in the belief that the skull was a sign faithfully reflecting the various organs of mind housed in the brain, and that differences in brain organs explained differences in human behavior. And it is in the phrenological literature, for almost the first time, that we find women and lower races compared directly on the basis of their skull formations. In their "organology," the phrenologists paid special attention to the organ of "philoprogenitiveness," of the faculty causing "love of offspring," which was believed to be more highly developed in women than men, as was apparent from their more highly developed upper part of the occiput. The same prominence, according to Franz Joseph Gall, was found in monkeys and was particularly well developed, he believed, in male and female Negroes.[38]

By the 1840s and 1850s the science of phrenology was on the wane, since the organs of the brain claimed by the phrenologists did not seem to correspond with the details of brain anatomy as described by neurophysiologists. But although the specific conclusions of the phrenologists concerning the anatomical structure and functions of the brain were rejected, the principle that differences in individual and group function were products of differences in the shape and size of the head was not. This principle underlay the claim that some measure, whether of cranial capacity, the facial angle, the brain volume, or brain weight, would be found that would provide a true indicator of innate capacity, and that by such a measure women and lower races would be shown to occupy analogous places in the scale of nature (the "scale" itself of course being a metaphorical construct).

By the 1850s the measurement of women's skulls was becoming an established part of craniometry and the science of gender joined analogically to race. Vogt's *Lectures on Man* included a long discussion of the various measures available of the skulls of men and women of different races. His data showed that women's smaller brains were analogous to the brains of lower races, the small size explaining both groups' intellectual inferiority. (Vogt also concluded that within Europe the intelligentsia and upper classes had the largest heads, and peasants the smallest.)[39] Broca shared Vogt's interest; he too believed it was the smaller brains of women and "lower" races, compared with men of "higher" races, that caused their lesser intellectual capacity and therefore their social inferiority.[40]

One novel conclusion to result from scientists' investigations into the different skull capacities of males and females of different races was that the gap in head size between men and women had apparently widened over historic time, being largest in the "civilized" races such as the European, and smallest in the most savage races.[41] The growing difference between the sexes from the prehistoric period to the present was attributed to evolutionary, selective pressures, which were believed to be greater in the white races than the dark and greater in men than women. Paradoxically, therefore, the civilized European woman was less like the civilized European man than the savage man was like the savage woman. The "discovery" that the male and female bodies and brains in the lower races were very alike allowed scientists to draw direct comparisons between a black male and a white female. The male could be taken as representative of both sexes of his race and the black female could be virtually ignored in the analogical science of intelligence, if not sexuality.

Because interactive metaphors bring together a *system* of implications, other features previously associated with only one subject in the metaphor are brought to bear on the other. As the analogy between women and race gained ground in science, therefore, women were found to share other points of similarity with lower races. A good example is prognathism. Prognathism was a measure of the protrusion of the jaw and of inferiority. As women and lower races became analogically joined, data on the "prognathism" of females were collected and women of "advanced" races implicated in this sign of inferiority. Havelock Ellis, for instance, in the late nineteenth-century bible of male-female differences *Man and Woman*, mentioned the European woman's slightly protruding jaw as a trait, not of high evolution, but of the lower races, although he added that in white women the trait, unlike in the lower races, was "distinctly charming."[42]

Another set of implications brought to bear on women by analogy with lower races concerned dolichocephaly and brachycephaly, or longheadedness and roundheadedness. Africans were on the whole more longheaded than Europeans and so dolichocephaly was generally interpreted as signifying inferiority. Ellis not surprisingly found that on the whole women, criminals, the degenerate, the insane, and prehistoric races tended to share with dark races the more narrow, dolichocephalic heads representing an earlier (and by implication, more primitive) stage of brain development.[43]

Analogy and the Creation of New Knowledge

In the metaphors and analogies joining women and the lower races, the scientist was led to "see" points of similarity that before had gone unnoticed. Women became more "like" Negroes, as the statistics on brain weights and body shapes showed. The question is, what kind of "likeness" was involved? Here again the interaction theory of metaphor is illuminating. As Black says, the notion of similarity is ambiguous. Or as Stanley Fish puts it, "Similarity is not something one finds but something one must establish."[44] Metaphors are not meant to be taken literally, but they do imply some structural similarity between the two things joined by the metaphor, a similarity that may be new to the readers of the metaphoric or analogical text, but that they are culturally capable of grasping.

However, there is nothing obviously similar about a white woman of England and an African man, or between a "criminal type" and a "savage." (If it seems to us as though there is, that is because the metaphor has become so woven into our cultural and linguistic system as to have lost its obviously metaphorical quality and to seem a part of "nature.") Rather it is the metaphor that permits us to see similarities that the metaphor itself helps constitute.[45] The metaphor, Black suggests, "selects, emphasizes, suppresses and organizes features" of reality, thereby allowing us to see new connections between the two subjects of the metaphor, to pay attention to details hitherto unnoticed, to emphasize aspects of human experience otherwise treated as unimportant, to make new features into "signs" signifying inferiority.[46] It was the metaphor joining lower races and women, for instance, that gave significance to the supposed differences between the shape of women's jaws and those of men.

Metaphors, then, through their capacity to construct similarities, create new knowledge. The full range of similarities brought into play by a metaphor or analogy is not immediately known or necessarily immediately predictable. The metaphor, therefore, allows for "discovery" and can yield new information through empirical research. Without the metaphor linking women and race, for example, many of the data on women's bodies (length of limbs, width of pelvis, shape of skull, weight or structure of brain) would have lost their significance as signs of inferiority and would not have been gathered, recorded, and interpreted in the way they were. In fact, without the analogies concerning the "differences" and similarities among human groups, much of the vast enterprise of anthropology, criminology, and gender science would not have existed. The analogy guided research, generated new hypotheses, and helped disseminate new, usually technical vocabularies. The analogy helped constitute the objects of inquiry into human variation — races of all kinds (Slavic, Mediterranean, Scottish, Irish, yellow, black, white, and red), as well as other social groups, such as "the child" and "the madman." The analogy defined what was problematic about these social groups, what aspects of them needed further investigation, and which kinds of measurements and what data would be significant for scientific inquiry.

The metaphor, in short, served as a program of research. Here the analogy comes close to the idea of a scientific "paradigm" as elaborated by Kuhn in *The Structure of Scientific Revolutions*; indeed, Kuhn himself sometimes writes of paradigms as though they are extended metaphors and has proposed that "the same interactive, similarity-creating process which Black has isolated in the functioning of metaphor is vital also in the function of models in science."[47]

The ability of an analogy in science to create new kinds of knowledge is seen clearly in the way the analogy organizes the scientists' understanding of causality. Hesse suggests that a scientific metaphor, by joining two distinct subjects, implies more than mere structural likeness. In the case of the science of human difference, the analogies implied a similar *cause* of the similarities between races and women and of the differences between both groups and white males. To the phrenologists, the cause of the large organs of philoprogenitiveness in monkeys, Negroes, and women was an innate brain structure. To the evolutionists, sexual and racial differences were the product of slow, adaptive changes involving variation and selection, the results being the smaller brains and lower capacities of the lower races and women, and the higher intelligence and evolutionarily advanced traits in the males of higher races. Barry Barnes suggests we call the kind of "redescription" involved in a metaphor or analogy of the kind being discussed here an "explanation," because it forces the reader to "understand" one aspect of reality in terms of another.[48]

Analogy and the Suppression of Knowledge

Especially important to the functioning of interactive metaphors in science is their ability to neglect or even suppress information about human experience of the world that does not fit the similarity implied by the metaphor. In their "similarity-creating" capacity, metaphors involve the scientist in a selection of those aspects of reality that are compatible with the metaphor. This selection process is often quite unconscious. Stephen Jay Gould is especially telling about the ways in which anatomists and anthropologists unselfconsciously searched for and selected measures that would prove the desired scales of human superiority and inferiority and how the difficulties in achieving the desired results were surmounted.

Gould has subjected Paul Broca's work on human differences to particularly thorough scrutiny because Broca was highly regarded in scientific circles and was exemplary in the accuracy of his measurements. Gould shows that it is not Broca's measurements per se that can be faulted, but rather the ways in which he unconsciously manipulated them to produce the very similarities already "contained" in the analogical science of human variation. To arrive at the conclusion of women's inferiority in brain weights, for example, meant failing to make any correction for women's smaller body weights, even though other scientists of the period were well aware that women's smaller brain weights were at least in part a function of their smaller body sizes. Broca was also able to "save" the scale of ability based on head size by leaving out some awkward cases of large-brained but savage heads from his calculations, and by somehow accounting for the occasional small-brained "geniuses" from higher races in his collection.[49]

Since there are no "given" points of measurement and comparison in nature (as Gould says, literally thousands of different kinds of measurements can theoretically be made of the human body), scientists had to make certain choices in their studies of human difference. We are not surprised to find that scientists selected just those points of comparison that would show lower races and women to be nearer to each other and to other "lower" groups, such as the anthropoid apes or the child, than were white men. The maneuvers this involved were sometimes comical. Broca, for instance, tried the measure of the ratio of the radius to the humerus, reasoning that a high ratio was apish, but when the scale he desired did not come out, he abandoned it. According to Gould, he even almost abandoned the most time-honored measure of human difference and inferiority, namely, brain weights, because yellow people did well on it. He managed to deal with this apparent exception to the "general rule of nature" that lower races had small heads by the same kind of specious argumentation he had used with small-brained geniuses. Broca claimed that the scale of brain weights did not work as well at the upper end as at the lower end, so that although small brain weights invariably indicated inferiority, large brain weights did not necessarily in and of themselves indicate superiority![50]

Since most scientists did recognize that the brain weights of women were in fact heavier in proportion to their body weights than men, giving women an apparent comparative advantage over men, not surprisingly they searched for other measures. The French scientist Léonce Pierre Manouvrier used an index relating brain weight to thigh bone weight, an index that gave the desired results and was in confirmation with the analogies, but that even at the time was considered by one scientist "ingenious and fantastic but divorced from common sense."[51] Even more absurd when viewed from the distance of time was the study mentioned by Ellis by two Italians who used the "prehensile" (i.e., apish) character of the human toe to compare human groups and found it was greater in normal white women than in white men, and also marked in criminals, prostitutes, idiots, and of course lower races.[52]

One test of the social power (if not the scientific fruitfulness) of an analogy in science seems in fact to be the degree to which information can be ignored, or interpretation strained, without the analogy losing the assent of the relevant scientific community. On abstract grounds, one would expect an analogy of the kind being discussed here, which required rather obvious distortions of perception to maintain (at least to our late twentieth-century eyes), to have been abandoned by scientists fairly quickly. Since, however, interactive metaphors and analogies direct the investigators' attention to some aspects of reality and not others, the metaphors and analogies can generate a considerable amount of new information about the world that confirms metaphoric expectations and directs attention away from those aspects of reality that challenge those expectations. Given the widespread assent to the cultural presuppositions underlying the analogy between race and gender, the analogy was able to endure in science for a long time.

(For instance, by directing attention to exactly those points of similarity and difference that would bring women and lower races closer to apes, or to each other, the race-gender metaphor generated data, many of them new, which "fit" the metaphor and the associated implications carried by it. Other aspects of reality and human experience that were incompatible with the metaphor tended to be ignored or not "seen." Thus for decades the Negro's similarity to apes on the basis of the shape of his jaw was asserted, while the white man's similarity to apes on the basis of his thin lips was ignored.)

When contrary evidence could not be ignored, it was often reinterpreted to express the fundamental valuations implicit in the metaphor. Gould provides us with the example of neoteny, or the retention in the adult of childish features such as a small face and hairlessness. A central feature of the analogical science of inferiority was that adult women and lower races were more childlike in their bodies and minds than white males. But Gould shows that by the early twentieth century it was realized that neoteny was a positive feature of the evolutionary process. "At least one scientist, Havelock Ellis, did bow to the clear implication and admit the superiority of women, even though he wriggled out of a similar confession for blacks." As late as the 1920s the Dutch scientist Louis Bolk, on the other hand, managed to save the basic valuation of white equals superior, blacks and women equal inferior by "rethinking" the data and discovering after all that blacks departed more than whites from the most favorable traits of childhood.[53]

To reiterate, because a metaphor or analogy does not directly present a preexisting nature but instead helps "construct" that nature, the metaphor generates data that conform to it, and accommodates data that are in apparent contradiction to it, so that nature is seen through the metaphor and the metaphor becomes part of the logic of science itself.[54]

Changing Metaphors

Turbayne, in his book *The Myth of Metaphor*, proposes as a major critical task of the philosopher or historian of science the detection of metaphor in science. Detection is necessary because as metaphors in science become familiar or commonplace, they tend to lose their metaphorical nature and to be taken literally. The analogical science of human difference is a particularly striking example. So familiar and indeed axiomatic had the analogies concerning "lower races," "apes," and "women" become by the end of the nineteenth century that in his major study of male-female differences in the human species, Ellis took almost without comment as the standards against which to measure the "typical female" on the one hand "the child," and on the other "the ape," "the savage," and the "aged human." The tendency for metaphors to become dogmatic and to be seen as literally true and nonmetaphoric is particularly strong in science because of the identification of the language of science with the language of objectivity and reality.

The confusion of metaphor for reality in science would be less important if metaphors did not have social and moral consequences in addition to intellectual ones. This aspect of metaphoric and analogic science is often overlooked in discussions of paradigms, models, and analogies in science, in which the main focus tends to be on the metaphor as an intellectual construct with intellectual consequences for the doing of science. But metaphors do more than this. Metaphors shape our perceptions and in turn our actions, which tend to be in accordance with the metaphor. The analogies concerning racial and gender and class differences in the human species developed in the biosocial sciences in the nineteenth century, for instance, had the social consequences of helping perpetuate the racial and gender status quo. The analogies were used by scientists to justify resistance to efforts at social change on the part of women and "lower races," on the grounds that inequality was a "fact" of nature and not a function of the power relations in a society.

Another reason, then, for uncovering or exposing metaphor in science is to prevent ourselves from being used or victimized or captured by metaphors.[55] The victims of the analogical science of human difference were the women and the human groups conceptualized as "lower" races. Their exclusion from the community of scientists doing the analogizing was, to a large extent, part of the same social division of labor that produced scientific theories of natural inferiority. It was an exclusion that made identifying and challenging metaphors of natural inequality very difficult.

That the analogy between race and gender was eventually discarded (though not until well into the twentieth century) raises the interesting question of how metaphors in science change. For if metaphors are part of the logical structure of science, changes in metaphor will bring about changes in science. Ever since Kuhn published *The Structure of Scientific Revolutions* in 1962, of course, the problem of change has been central to any critical theory of science. Kuhn's contribution was to show that the substitution of one "paradigm" (defined as the beliefs, values, or techniques of a scientific community) by another was a complex historical event that could not be reduced to straightforward questions concerning the increased rationality, comprehensiveness, or logic of one paradigm over another. His work raised important questions about the relationship between scientific theories and empirical reality, about the grounds on which one paradigm is accepted and another rejected, and about the roots of change. He proposed that paradigms were not in fact simple reflections of reality but complex human constructions. Above all, Kuhn stressed the idea that all scientific knowledge is "embedded in theory and rules," which the scientist learns as a member of a scientific community.

Nevertheless, despite the emphasis he gave to the scientific community, Kuhn's own explanation of scientific revolutions tended toward the "intellectualist" rather than the sociological. He concentrated attention on the ways in which the scientific paradigm itself generates, through the normal process of puzzle solving within the paradigm, anomalies that eventually cause the breakdown of the paradigm and its replacement by another. On his own admission, Kuhn paid little attention to the role of social, political, or economic factors in the generation of new metaphors, and therefore new meanings, in science.

Recent work in the history and sociology of science, however, in part under the stimulus of Kuhn's work, has tended to stress the importance of the scientific community itself, as a sociological and political as well as scientific entity, for the generation and rejection of metaphors and analogies. The hope is that close historical and sociological investigation will begin to indicate in what ways particular representations or metaphors of nature are related to the social structure—class organization, professional socialization, interests—of the scientific community. The suggestion is being made that the root metaphors held by a particular scientific community or school of thought can become unsatisfactory, not merely because the data generated by the metaphor do not "fit" the metaphor, but because, for political or social or economic reasons, social formations change and new aspects of reality or human experience become important, are "seen," and new metaphors introduced.

The full implication of my own studies of the changes that eventually occurred in the analogical science of human difference is indeed along these lines—namely, that changes in political and social life were closely tied to the new metaphors of human similarity and equality, as opposed to metaphors of difference and inequality, that were proposed in the human sciences after

World War II.[56] The subject of metaphoric change is obviously one requiring much further study.

A Brief Conclusion

In this essay I have indicated only some of the issues raised by a historical consideration of a specific metaphoric or analogical science. There is no attempt at completeness or theoretical closure. My intention has been to draw attention to the ways in which metaphor and analogy can play a role in science, and to show how a particular set of metaphors and analogies shaped the scientific study of human variation. I have also tried to indicate some of the historical reasons why scientific texts have been "read" nonmetaphorically, and what some of the scientific and social consequences of this have been.

Some may argue that I have begged the question of metaphor and analogy in science by treating an analogical science that was "obviously pseudoscientific." I maintain that it was not obviously pseudoscientific to its practitioners, and that they were far from being at the periphery of the biological and human sciences in the nineteenth and early twentieth centuries. I believe other studies will show that what was true for the analogical science of human difference may well be true also for other metaphors and analogies in science.

My intention has also been to suggest that a theory of metaphor is as critical to science as it is to the humanities. We need a critical theory of metaphor in science in order to expose the metaphors by which we learn to view the world scientifically, not because these metaphors are necessarily "wrong," but because they are so powerful.

NOTES

1. A metaphor is a figure of speech in which a name or descriptive term is transferred to some object that is different from, but analogous to, that to which it is properly applicable. According to Max Black, "Every metaphor may be said to mediate an analogy or structural correspondence": see Black, "More About Metaphor," in *Metaphor and Thought*, ed. Andrew Ortony (Cambridge: Cambridge University Press, 1979), pp. 19–43, on p. 31. In this essay, I have used the terms "metaphor" and "analogy" interchangeably.

2. G. Lakoff and M. Johnson, *Metaphors We Live By* (Chicago/London: University of Chicago Press, 1980), p. 191. Scientists' attacks on metaphor as extrinsic and harmful to science predate the Scientific Revolution.

3. See A. J. Ayer, *Language, Truth, and Logic* (New York: Dover, 1952), p. 13.

4. On Duhem, see Carl H. Hempel, *Aspects of Scientific Explanation and Other Essays in the Philosophy of Science* (New York: Free Press, 1965), pp. 433–77. Hempel agrees with Duhem's view that "all references to analogies or analogical models can be dispensed with in the systematic statement of scientific explanations" (p. 440).

5. For this point see Jamie Kassler, "Music as a Model in Early Science," *History of Science*, 20 (1982), pp. 103–39.

6. Colin M. Turbayne, *The Myth of Metaphor* (Columbia: University of South Carolina Press, 1970), p. 24.

7. General works on metaphor and science include Philip Wheelwright, *Metaphor and Reality* (Bloomington: Indiana University Press, 1962); Max Black, *Models and Metaphor* (Ithaca, N.Y.: Cornell University Press, 1962); Mary Hesse, *Models and Analogies in Science* (Notre Dame, Ind.: University of Notre Dame Press, 1966); Richard Olson (ed.), *Science as Metaphor* (Belmont, Calif.: Wadsworth, 1971); W. M. Leatherdale, *The Role of Analogy, Model and Metaphor in Science* (Amsterdam: North-Holland, 1974); Ortony (ed.), *Metaphor and Thought*; and Roger S. Jones, *Physics as Metaphor* (Minneapolis: University of Minnesota Press, 1982). Warren A. Shibles, *Metaphor: An Annotated Guide and History* (Whitewater, Wisc.: Language Press, 1971), gives an extensive introduction and guide to the general problem of metaphor, language, and reality.

8. Thomas S. Kuhn, "Metaphor in Science," in *Metaphor and Thought*, ed. Ortony, pp. 409–19, on p. 414; and Richard Boyd, "Metaphor and Theory Change: What Is 'Metaphor' a Metaphor For?" ibid., pp. 356–408, on p. 360.

9. For a defense of the centrality of analogy to science see N. R. Campbell, "What Is a Theory?" in *Readings in the Philosophy of Science*, ed. Baruch A. Brody (Englewood Clifs, N.J.: Prentice-Hall, 1970), pp. 252–67. Shibles, in *Metaphor*, p. 3, also argues that each school of science "is based on a number of basic metaphors which are then expanded into various universes of discourse."

10. See Nancy Stepan, *The Idea of Race in Science: Great Britain (1800–1960* (London: Macmillan, 1982), esp. chapter 1.

11. No systematic history of the race-gender analogy exists. The analogy has been remarked on, and many examples from the anthropometric, medical, and embryological sciences provided, in Stephen Jay Gould, *The Mismeasure of Man* (New York: Norton, 1981), and in John S. Haller and Robin S. Haller, *The Physician and Sexuality in Victorian America* (Urbana: University of Illinois Press, 1974).

12. Haller and Haller, *The Physician and Sexuality*, pp. 48–49, 54. Among the several craniometric articles cited by the Hallers, see esp. J. McGrigor Allan, "On the Real Differences in the Minds of Men and Women," *Journal of the Anthropological Society of London* 7 (1869), pp. cxcv–ccviii, on p. cciv; and John Cleland, "An Inquiry into the Variations of the Human Skull," *Philosophical Transactions, Royal Society* 89 (1870), pp. 117–74.

13. Havelock Ellis, *Man and Woman: A Study of Secondary Sexual Characters* (1894; 6th ed. London: A. & C. Black, 1926), pp. 106–7.

14. Herbert Spencer, "The Comparative Psychology of Man," *Popular Science Monthly*, 8 (1875–76), pp. 257–69.

15. Ellis, *Man and Woman*, p. 491.

16. Carl Vogt, *Lectures on Man: His Place in Creation and in the History of the Earth* (London: Longman, Green & Roberts, 1864), p. 81.

17. James Weir, "The Effect of Female Suffrage on Posterity," *American Naturalist*, 29 (1895), 198–215.

18. Charles Darwin, *The Descent of Man, and Selection in Relation to Sex* (London: John Murray, 1871), vol. 2, chapters 17–20; Edward C. Cope, "The Developmental Significance of Human Physiognomy, *American Naturalist*, 17 (1883), pp. 618–27.

19. Arthur Keith, "Presidential Address: On Certain Factors in the Evolution of Human Races," *Journal of the Royal Anthropological Institute* 64 (1916), pp. 10–33; Ellis, *Man and Woman*, p. xii.

20. See Nancy Stepan, "Biological Degeneration: Races and Proper Places," in *Degeneration: The Dark Side of Progress*, ed. J. Edward Chamberlin and Sander L. Gilman (New York: Columbia University Press, 1985), pp. 97–120, esp. pp. 112–13. For an extended exploration of how

various stereotypes of difference intertwined with each other, see Sander L. Gilman, *Difference and Pathology: Stereotypes of Sexuality, Race, and Madness* (Ithaca, N.Y.: Cornell University Press, 1985).

21. Shibles, *Metaphor*, p. 15.

22. Stephen Toulmin, "The Construal of Reality: Criticism in Modern and Postmodern Science," *Critical Inquiry*, 9 (1982), pp. 93–111, esp. pp. 100–103.

23. Sander L. Gilman, *Seeing the Insane* (New York: John Wiley, 1982), p. xi.

24. Lakoff and Johnson, *Metaphors We Live By*, p. 22. The idea of root metaphors is Stephen Pepper's in *World Hypothesis* (Berkeley: University of California Press, 1966), p. 91.

25. Winthrop D. Jordan, *White over Black: American Attitudes toward the Negro, 1550–1812* (New York: Norton, 1977), p. 7.

26. Stepan, *The Idea of Race in Science*, pp. 6–10.

27. Francis Galton, "Hereditary Improvement," *Fraser's Magazine*, 7 (1873), 116–30.

28. These instruments and measurements are described in detail in Paul Topinard, *Anthropology* (London: Chapman & Hall, 1878), part 2, chapters 1–4.

29. Ibid., p. 311.

30. Black, *Models and Metaphor*, esp. chapters 3 and 13. See also Mary Hesse, *Models and Analogies in Science*; Hesse, "The Explanatory Function of Metaphor," in *Logic, Methodology, and Philosophy of Science*, ed. Y. Bar-Hillel (Amsterdam: North-Holland, 1965), pp. 249–59; and Boyd, "Metaphor and Theory Change."

31. Black, *Models and Metaphor*, p. 38, quoting J. A. Richards, *Philosophy of Rhetoric* (Oxford: Oxford University Press, 1938), p. 83.

32. Black, *Models and Metaphor*, p. 4

33. Hesse, *Models and Analogies in Science*, pp. 159–60.

34. See Turbayne, *Myth of Metaphor*, p. 19, on this point.

35. Black himself believed scientific metaphors belonged to the pretheoretical stage of a discipline. Here I have followed Boyd, who argues in "Metaphor and Theory Change," p. 357, that metaphors can play a role in the development of theories in relatively mature sciences.

36. For an example of the analogous diseases and sexuality of "lower" races and "lower" women, see Eugene S. Talbot, *Degeneracy: Its Causes, Signs, and Results* (London: Walter Cott, 1898), pp. 18, 319–23.

37. Paul Broca, "Sur le volume et la forme du cerveau suivant les individus et suivant les races," *Bulletin de la Société d'Anthropologie Paris*, 2 (1861), p. 3040.

38. Franz Joseph Gall, "The Propensity to Philoprogenitiveness," *Phrenological Journal*, 2 (1824–25), pp. 20–33.

39. Vogt, *Lectures on Man*, p. 88. Vogt was quoting Broca's data.

40. Gould, *Mismeasure of Man*, p. 103.

41. Broca's work on the cranial capacities of skulls taken from three cemeteries in Paris was the most important source for this conclusion. See his "Sur la capacité des cranes parisiens des divers epoques," *Bulletin de la Societé d'Anthropologie Paris*, 3 (1862), pp. 102–16.

42. Ellis, *Man and Woman*, pp. 106–7.

43. Alexander Sutherland, "Woman's Brain," *Nineteenth Century*, 47 (1900), 802–810; and Ellis, *Man and Woman*, p. 98. Ellis was on the whole, however, cautious about the conclusions that could be drawn from skull capacities and brain weights.

44. Stanley Fish, "Working on the Chain Gang: Interpretation in the Law and Literary Criticism," in *The Politics of Interpretation*, ed. W. J. T. Mitchell (Chicago: University of Chicago Press, 1983), p. 277.

45. Max Black, as cited in Ortony, *Metaphor and Thought*, p. 5.

46. Black, *Metaphor and Thought*, p. 44.

47. Thomas S. Kuhn, *The Structure of Scientific Revolutions*, 2nd ed. (Chicago: University of Chicago Press, 1973), esp. chapter 4; and Kuhn, "Metaphor in Science," p. 415.

48. Barry Barnes, *Scientific Knowledge and Sociological Theory* (London: Routledge & Kegan Paul, 1974), p. 49.

49. Gould, *Mismeasure of Man*, pp. 73–112. For another example see Stephen Jay Gould, "Morton's Ranking of Race by Cranial Capacity," *Science*, 200 (1978), pp. 503–5.

50. Gould, *Mismeasure of Man*, pp. 85–96.

51. Sutherland, "Woman's Brain," p. 805.

52. Ellis, *Man and Woman*, p. 53.

53. Gould, *Mismeasure of Man*, p. 120–21.

54. Terence Hawkes, *Metaphor* (London: Methuen, 1972), p. 88, suggests that metaphors "will retrench or corroborate as much as they expand our vision," thus stressing the normative, consensus-building aspects of metaphor.

55. Turbayne, *Myth of Metaphor*, p. 27.

56. Stepan, *Race in Science*, chapters 6 and 7.

CHAPTER 4

Toward a Critical Theory of "Race"
Lucius Outlaw

A Need for Rethinking

For most of us that there are different races of people is one of the most obvious features of our social worlds. The term "race" is a vehicle for notions deployed in the organization of these worlds in our encounters with persons who are significantly different from us particularly in terms of physical features (skin color and other anatomical features), but also, often combined with these, when they are different with respect to language, behavior, ideas, and other "cultural" matters.

In the United States in particular, "race" is a constitutive element of our common sense and thus is a key component of our "taken-for-granted valid reference schema" through which we get on in the world.[1] And, as we are constantly burdened by the need to resolve difficulties, posing varying degrees of danger to the social whole, in which "race" is the focal point of contention (or serves as a shorthand explanation for the source of contentious differences), we are likewise constantly reinforced in our assumption that "race" is self-evident.

Here has entered "critical" thought: as self-appointed mediator for the resolution of such difficulties by the promotion (and practical effort to realize) a given society's "progressive" evolution, that is, its development of new forms of shared self-understanding — and corresponding forms of social practice — void of the conflicts thought to rest on inappropriate valorizations and rationalizations of "race." Such efforts notwithstanding, however, the "emancipatory project"[2] has foundered on the crucible of "race." True to the prediction of W. E. B. Du Bois, the twentieth century has indeed been dominated by "the problem of the color line." It will clearly be so for the remainder

58

of the century, and well into the twenty-first. For on one insightful reading, we are now in a period in which a major political struggle is being waged, led by the administrations of Ronald Reagan and George Bush, to "rearticulate"[3] racial meanings as part of a larger project to consolidate the victory of control of the state by those on the Right, control that allows them to set the historical agenda for America, thus for the Western "free" world.

Of course, it *must* be said that the persistence of social struggles—in the United States and elsewhere—in which "race" is a key factor is not due simply to a failure to realize emancipatory projects on the part of those who championed them. While there is some truth to such an analysis, the fuller story is much more complex. Nor has the failure been total. It is possible to identify numerous points in history, and various concrete developments, that were significantly influenced—if not inspired entirely—by emancipatory projects informed by traditions of critical theoretical thought: from the New Deal to the modern freedom (i.e., civil rights), Black Power, and antiwar movements; to the modern women's and environmental movements in the United States and elsewhere; to anticolonial, anticapitalist, antidictatorial, antiracist struggles throughout the so-called Third World and Europe.

Still, the persistence of struggles around matters involving "race" requires that those of us who continue to be informed by leftist traditions of critical thought and practice confront, on the one hand, unresolved problems. On the other, by way of a critical review of our own traditions, we must determine the extent to which those traditions have failed to account appropriately for "race" (i.e., provide an understanding that is sufficiently compelling for self-understanding and enlightening of social reality) in a way that makes practically possible mobilization sufficient to effect social reconstructions that realize emancipatory promises. It may well be that we will need to review what we think will constitute "emancipation" and whether our notions coincide with those of liberation and self-realization indigenous to persons and traditions of various "racial" groups that would be assisted by us, or who wage their own struggles with assistance from leftist traditions.

No more compelling need is required for our undertaking such reviews than that of getting beyond the interminable debate whether "race" *or* "class" is the proper vehicle for understanding (and mobilizing against) social problems with invidiously racial components. The present essay is another installment in this ongoing rethinking.[4] Here the focus will be less on the limitations of traditions of critical theory and practice with respect to the privileging of "class" over "race" and more on rethinking "race." A primary concern will be to question "race" as an obvious, biologically or metaphysically given, thereby self-evident reality—to challenge the presumptions sedimented in the "reference schemata" that, when socially shared, become common sense, whether through a group's construction of its life world and/or through hegemonic imposition.[5]

This rethinking will involve, first, a review of the career of "race" as a concept: the context of its emergence and reworking, and the changing agendas of its deployment. Second, a brief recounting of approaches to "race" within traditions of critical theory will facilitate responding to the central question of the essay: "Why a critical theory of 'race" today?" This question is generated by the need to face a persistent problem within Western societies but, in the United States and European societies in particular, one that today presents a new historical conjuncture of crisis proportions: the prospects — and the concrete configurations — of democracy in the context of historic shifts in the demographics of "racial" pluralism. The centripetal, possibly balkanizing forces of racial pluralism have been intensified during the past quarter-century by heightened group (and individual) "racial" self-consciousness as the basis for political mobilization and organization without the constraining effects of the once dominant paradigm of "ethnicity," in which differences are seen as a function of sociology and culture rather than biology.[6]

According to the logic of "ethnicity" as the paradigm for conceptualizing group differences and fashioning social policy to deal with them, the socially devisive effects of "ethnic" differences were to disappear in the social-cultural "melting pot" through assimilation, or, according to the pluralists, ethnic identity would be maintained across time but would be mediated by principles of the body politic: all *individuals*, "without regard to race, creed, color, or national origin," were to win their places in society on the basis of demonstrated achievement (i.e., merit). For both assimilationists and pluralists, *group* characteristics (ethnicity) were to have no play in the determination of merit; their legitimacy was restricted to the private sphere of "culture." This has been the officially sanctioned, and widely socially shared, interpretation of the basic principles of the body politic in the United States in the modern period, even though it was, in significant measure, a cover for the otherwise sometimes explicit, but always programmatic, domination of Africans and of other peoples.

For the past twenty years, however, "race" has been the primary vehicle for conceptualizing and organizing precisely around group differences with the demand that social justice be applied to *groups* and that "justice" be measured by *results*, not just by opportunities. With the assimilation project of the ethnic paradigm no longer hegemonic, combined with the rising demographics of the "unmeltable ethnics" in the American population (and the populations of other Western countries, including Great Britain, France, and West Germany) and the preponderance of "race thinking" infecting political life, we have the battleground on which many of the key issues of social development into the twenty-first century will continue to be waged. Will "critical theory" provide assistance in this area in keeping with its traditions

—that is, enlightenment leading to emancipation—or will it become more and more marginalized and irrelevant?

On "Race"

There is, of course, nothing more fascinating than the question of the various types of mankind and their intermixture. The whole question of heredity and human gift depends upon such knowledge; but ever since the African slave trade and before the rise of modern biology and sociology, we have been afraid in America that scientific study in this direction might lead to conclusions with which we were loath to agree; and this fear was in reality because the economic foundation of the modern world was based on the recognition and preservation of so-called racial distinctions. In accordance with this, not only Negro slavery could be justified, but the Asiatic coolie profitably used and the labor classes in white countries kept in their places by low wage.[7]

Race theory . . . had up until fairly modern times no firm hold on European thought. On the other hand, race theory and race prejudice were by no means unknown at the time when the English colonists came to North America. Undoubtedly, the age of exploration led many to speculate on race differences at a period when neither Europeans nor Englishmen were prepared to make allowances for vast cultural diversities. Even though race theories had not then secured wide acceptance or even sophisticated formulation, the first contacts of the Spanish with the Indians in the Americas can now be recognized as the beginning of a struggle between conceptions of the nature of primitive peoples which has not yet been wholly settled. . . . Although in the seventeenth century race theories had not as yet developed any strong scientific or theological rationale, the contact of the English with Indians, and soon afterward with Negroes, in the New World led to the formation of institutions and relationships which were later justified by appeals to race theories.[8]

The notion of "race" as a fundamental component of "race thinking"—that is, a way of conceptualizing and organizing social worlds composed of persons whose differences allow for arranging them into groups that come to be called "races"—has had a powerful career in Western history (though such thinking has not been limited to the "West") and continues to be a matter of significant social weight. Even a cursory review of this history should do much to dislodge the concept from its place as provider of access to a self-evident, obvious, even ontologically *given* characteristic of humankind. For what comes out of such a review is the recognition that although "race" is continually with us as an organizing, explanatory concept, what the term refers to—that is, the origin and basis of "racial" differences—has not remained constant. When this insight is added to the abundant knowledge that the deployment of "race" has virtually always been in service to political agendas, beyond more "disinterested" endeavors simply to "understand" the basis of perceptually obvious (and otherwise not obvious, but real nonetheless) differences among human groups, we will have firm grounds for a rethinking of "race." Such a rethinking might profitably be situated in a more sociohistorically "constructivist" framework, namely, one in which "race" is viewed, in the words of Michael Omi and Howard Winant, as a social "formation."[9] But first, something of the career of the concept.

"Race" and Science

The career of "race" does not begin in science but predates it and emerges from a general need to account for the unfamiliar or, simply, to classify objects of experience, thus to organize the life world. How — or why — it was that "race" came to play important classifying, organizing roles is not clear:

> The career of the race concept begins in obscurity, for experts dispute whether the word derives from an Arabic, a Latin, or a German source. The first recorded use in English of the word "race" was in a poem by William Dunbar of 1508. . . . During the next three centuries the word was used with growing frequency in a literary sense as denoting simply a class of persons or even things. . . . In the nineteenth, and increasingly in the twentieth century, this loose usage began to give way and the word came to signify groups that were distinguished biologically.[10]

This nineteenth-century development was preceded by others in earlier centuries that apparently generated a more compelling need for classificatory ordering in the social world and, subsequently, the use of "race" as such a device. First, there were the tensions within Europe arising from encounters between different groups of peoples, particularly "barbarians" — whether defined culturally or, more narrowly, religiously. (And it should be noted that within European thought, and elsewhere, the color black was associated with evil and death, with "sin" in the Christian context. The valorizing power inherent in this was ready-to-hand with Europe's encounter with Africa.) A more basic impetus, intensified by these tensions, came from the need to account for human origins in general, for human diversity in particular. Finally, there were the quite decisive European voyages to America and Africa, and the development of capitalism and the slave trade.[11]

The function of "race" as an ongoing, classificatory device gained new authority and a new stage in the concept's career developed when, in the eighteenth century, "evidence from geology, zoology, anatomy and other fields of scientific enquiry was assembled to support a claim that racial classification would help explain many human differences."[12] The concept provided a form of "typological thinking," a mode of conceptualization that was at the center of the agenda of emerging scientific praxis at the time, that served well in the classification of human groups. Plato and Aristotle, of course, were precursors of such thinking: the former with his theory of Forms; the latter through his classification of things in terms of their "nature." In the modern period the science of "race" began in comparative morphology with stress on pure "types" as classificatory vehicles. A key figure contributing to this unfolding agenda was the botanist Linnaeus.[13]

A number of persons were key contributers to the development of theories of racial types. According to Banton and Harwood, Johann Friedrich Blumenbach provided the first systematic racial classification in his *Generis humani varietate nativa liber* (On the Natural Variety of Mankind, 1776). This was followed by the work of James Cowles Prichard *(Generis humani varietate,* 1808).[14] Georges Cuvier, a French anatomist, put forth a physical-cause theory of races in 1800 in arguing that physical nature determined culture. He classified humans into three major groups along an implied descending scale: whites, yellows, and blacks. As Banton and Harwood interpreted his work, central to his thinking was the notion of "type" more than that of "race": "Underlying the variety of the natural world was a limited number of pure types and if their nature could be grasped it was possible to interpret the diverse forms which could temporarily appear as a result of hybrid mating."[15]

Other important contributions to the developing science of "race" include S. G. Morton's publication of a volume on the skulls of American Indians (1839) and one on Egyptian skulls (1845). His work was extended and made popular by J. C. Nott and G. R. Gliddon in their *Types of Mankind* (1854). Charles Hamilton Smith *(The Natural History of the Human Species,* 1848) developed Cuvier's line of argument in Britain. By Smith's reckoning, according to Banton and Harwood, "The Negro's lowly place in the human order was a consequence of the small volume of his brain."[16] Smith's former student, Robert Knox (*The Races of Man,* 1850), argued likewise. Finally, there was Count Joseph Arthur de Gobineau's four-volume *Essay on the Inequality of Human Races* (1854) in which he argued that, in the words of Banton and Harwood, "the major world civilizations . . . were the creations of different races and that race-mixing was leading to the inevitable deterioration of humanity."[17]

Two significant achievements resulted from these efforts. First, drawing on the rising authority of "science" as the realization and guardian of systematic, certain knowledge, there was the legitimation of "race" as a gathering concept for morphological features that were thought to distinguish varieties of *Homo sapiens* supposedly related to one another through the logic of a *natural* hierarchy of groups. Second, there was the legitimation of the view that the behavior of a group and its members was determined by their place in this hierarchy. "*Homo sapiens* was presented as a species divided into a number of races of different capacity and temperament. Human affairs could be understood only if individuals were seen as representatives of races for it was there that the driving forces of human history resided."[18] These science-authorized and -legitimated notions about "race," when combined with social projects involving the distinguishing and, ultimately, the control of "racially different" persons and groups (as in the case of the enslavement of Africans) took root and grew to become part of common sense. "Race" was now "obvious."

For Banton and Harwood, this science of "race" peaked during the middle of the nineteenth century. By the century's end, however, a variety of racial classifications had brought confusion, in part because "no one was quite sure what races were to be classified *for*. A classification is a tool. The same object may be classified differently for different purposes. No one can tell what is the best classification without knowing what it has to do."[19] The situation was both assisted and complicated by the work of Darwin and Mendel. Social Darwinism emerged as an effort by some (notably Herbert Spencer and Ludwig Gumplowicz) to apply Darwin's principles regarding heredity and natural selection to human groups and endeavors and thereby provide firmer grounding for the science of "race" (something Darwin was reluctant to do). Such moves were particularly useful in justifying the dominance of certain groups over others (British over Irish; Europeans over Africans . . .). On the other hand, however, Darwin's *Origins* shifted the terrain of scientific discourse from morphology and the stability of "pure types" to a subsequent genetics-based approach to individual characteristics and the effects on them of processes of change, thus to a focus on the analysis of variety. In the additional work of Mendel, this development proved revolutionary:

> A racial type was defined by a number of features which are supposed to go together. . . . The racial theorists of the nineteenth century assumed there was a natural law which said that such traits were invariably associated and were transmitted to the next generation as part of a package deal. Gregor Mendel's research showed that this was not necessarily the case. . . . [It] also showed that trait variation *within* a population was just as significant as trait variations *between* populations . . . traits do not form part of a package but can be shuffled like a pack of playing cards.[20]

And, since environmental impacts that condition natural selection, in addition to heredity and the interplay between dominant and recessive traits, are important factors in the "shuffling" of traits, the notion of "pure" racial types with fixed essential characteristics was displaced: biologically (i.e., genetically) one can only speak of "clines."[21]

The biology of "races" thus became more a matter of studying diversities within—as well as among—groups, and, of particular interest, the study of how groups "evolve" across both time and space. To these efforts were joined others from the *social* science of "race": that is, understanding groups as sharing some distinctive biological features—though not constituting pure types—but with respect to which sociocultural factors are of particular importance (but in ways significantly different from the thinking of the nineteenth-century theorists of racial types).

For many scientists the old (nineteenth-century) notion of "race" had become useless as a classificatory concept, hence certainly did not support in any truly scientific way the political agendas of racists. As noted by Livingstone, "Yesterday's science is today's common sense and tomorrow's nonsense."[22] Revolutions within science (natural and social) conditioned transformed approaches to "race" (although the consequences have still not completely supplanted the popular, commonsensical notions of "races" as pure types as the Ku Klux Klan, among others, indicates).

The conceptual terrain for this later, primarily twentieth-century approach to "race" continues to be, in large part, the notion of "evolution" and was significantly conditioned by the precursive work of Mendel and Darwin, social Darwinists notwithstanding. In the space opened by this concept it became possible at least to work at synthesizing insights drawn from both natural science (genetics, biochemistry) and social science (anthropology, sociology, psychology, ethology) for a fuller understanding of "geographical races":[23] studies of *organic* evolution focus on changes in the gene pool of a group or groups; studies of *superorganic* evolution are concerned with changes in the "behavior repertoire" of a group or groups—that is, with the sociocultural development.[24] And it is a legitimate question—though one difficult to answer—to what extent, if at all, superorganic evolution is a function of organic evolution or, to add even more complexity, to what extent, if at all, the two forms of evolution are mutually influential. The question of the relations between both forms of development continues to be a major challenge.

But what is a "race" in the framework of organic evolution and the global social context of the late twentieth century? Certainly not a group of persons who share genetic homogeneity. That is likely only in the few places where one might find groups that have remained completely isolated from other groups, with no intergroup sexual reproductions. Among other things, the logics of the capitalist world system have drawn virtually all peoples into the "global village" and facilitated much "interbreeding." But capitalism notwithstanding, "raciation" (i.e., the development of the distinctive gene pools of various groups that determine the relative frequencies of characteristics shared by their members, but certainly not by them alone) has also been a function, in part, of chance. Consequently:

> Since populations' genetic compositions vary over time, race classifications can never be permanent; today's classification may be obsolete in 100

generations. More importantly, modern race classifications attempt to avoid being arbitrary by putting populations *of presumed common evolutionary descent* into the same racial group. Common descent, however, is inferred from similarity in gene frequencies, and here the problem lies. For . . . a population's gene frequencies are determined not only by its ancestry but also by the processes of natural selection and genetic drift. This means that two populations could, in principle, be historically unrelated but genetically quite similar if they had been independently subject to similar evolutionary forces. To place them in the same racial group would, as a step in the study of evolution, be quite misleading. In the absence of historical evidence of descent, therefore, it is difficult to avoid the conclusion that classifying races is merely a convenient but biologically arbitrary way of breaking down the variety of gene frequency data into a manageable number of categories.[25]

When we classify a group as a "race," then, at best we refer to generally shared characteristics derived from a "pool" of genes. Social, cultural, and geographical factors, in addition to those of natural selection, all impact on this pool, thus on raciation: sometimes to sustain the pool's relative configuration (for example, by isolating the group—culturally or physically—from outbreeding); sometimes to modify it (as when "mulattoes" were produced in the United States in significant part through slave masters of European descent appropriating African women for their—the "masters' "—sexual pleasure). It is possible to study, with some success, the evolution of a particular group over time (a case of *specific* evolution). The prospects for success are more limited, however, when the context of concern is *general* evolution—that is, the grouping of all of the world's peoples in ordered categories "with the largest and most heterogeneous societies in the top category and the smallest and most homogeneous in the bottom."[26] In either case—general or specific evolution—the concern is with superorganic evolution: changes in behavior repertoires. And such changes are not tied to the genetic specificities of "races."

But not all persons (or groups) think so. Although evolutionary—as opposed to typological—thinking, in some form, is at present the dominant intellectual framework for systematic reconstructions and explanations of human natural and social history, it, too, has been enlisted in the service of those who would have "science" pass absolution on their political agendas: that is, to legitimate the empowerment of certain groups, certain "races," over others. Even shorn of the more crude outfittings of social Darwinism's "survival of the fittest" (those in power, or seeking power, over others being the "fittest," of course), the field of the science of "race" is still occupied by those offering orderings of human groups along an *ascending* scale with a particular group's placement on the scale being a function of the level of their supposed development (or lack thereof) toward human perfectibility: from "primitive" to "civilized" (circa the nineteenth century); from "undeveloped" or "under-developed" to "developed" or "advanced" (circa the twentieth century).

Such arguments find fertile soil for nourishment and growth now that "evolution" (organic and superorganic, often without distinction), frequently conceived as linear development along a single path which *all* "races" have to traverse, is now a basic feature of our "common sense." Creationists excepted, and as we still face political problems emerging from conflicts among "racial" groups. "Race" continues to function as a critical yardstick for the rank-ordering of racial groups both "scientifically" and sociopolitically, the latter with support from the former. At bottom, then, "race" — sometimes explicitly, quite often implicitly — continues to be a major fulcrum of struggles over the distribution and exercise of power.

Certainly one of the more prominent contemporary struggles has centered on the validity of measurements of the "intelligence" of persons from different "racial" groups that purport to demonstrate the comparative "intelligence" of the groups. This struggle is propelled by the social weight given to "intelligence" as an important basis for achievement and rewards in a meritocratic social order. At its center is the question of the dominant roles played by either the genes or the environment in determining "intelligence" (and, by extension, in determining raciation).

Whichever way the question is answered is not insignificant for social policy. If the genes predominate, some argue, then social efforts in behalf of particular groups (e.g., blacks, women, Hispanics, etc.) intending to ameliorate the effects of disadvantageous sociohistorical conditions and practices are misguided and should be discontinued. It would be more "rational" to rechannel the resources poured into such efforts into "more socially productive" pursuits. On the other hand, if environmental factors dominate, then in a liberal democracy, for example, where justice prevails disparites of opportunities (and results?) among "racial" groups must be corrected, especially when the disparities are the result of years, even centuries, of invidious discrimination and oppression.

The politics of "race" are played out on other fields besides that of "intelligence." Modern science has also been concerned with whether the genes of a "race" determine its cultural practices and/or social characteristics. The findings?

> All the known differences between geographical races in the frequency of genes which affect behavior are . . . quite trivial. Yet in principle it is possible that there may be genetic differences affecting socially, politically or economically significant behaviours and it seems reasonable to expect that the more population geneticists and physical anthropologists look for such genetic differences, the more will they discover. Because, however, of (1)

the relative plasticity of human behaviour, (2) the genetic heterogeneity of all human populations, and (3) the mass of data suggesting the importance of situational determinants (e.g., economic and political factors) in explaining race relations, there is at present little reason to expect that a substantial part of intergroup relations will ever be explicable in genetic terms.[27]

But if not the genes, what about "evolution"? Has it produced differences in behavior and biological mechanisms for survival in different "races"? Is it possible to extrapolate from studies of the evolution of animal behavior to the evolution of human behavior? According to Banton and Harwood, such efforts are inconclusive, the conclusions being at best hypothetical and difficult to test on humans. Moreover:

> . . . the difficulty with generalising about evolution is that it is a process that has happened just once. With relatively few exceptions it is impossible to compare evolutionary change with anything else, or to say what would have happened had one of the components been absent. Therefore everything has its place in evolution. . . . If everything has its place then, by implication, everything is justified.[28]

What, then, after this extended review of the science of "race," are we left with by way of understanding? With the decisive conclusion, certainly, that "race" is *not* wholly and completely determined by biology, but is only partially so. Even then biology does not *determine* "race," but in complex interplay with environmental, cultural, and social factors provides certain boundary conditions and possibilities that affect raciation and the development of "geographical" races. In addition, the definition of "race" is partly political, partly cultural. Nor does the modern conceptual terrain of "evolution" provide scientifically secure access to race-determining biological, cultural, social developmental complexes distributed among various groups that fix a group's rank-ordered place on an ascending "great chain of being." Racial categories are fundamentally *social* in nature and rest on shifting sands of biological heterogeneity.[29] The biological aspects of "race" are conscripted into projects of cultural, political, and social construction. "Race" is a *social* formation.

This being the case, the notion of "evolution" is particularly fruitful for critical-theoretical rethinking of "race." As has been indicated, in the biological sciences it dislodged the nineteenth-century notion of races as being determined by specific, fixed, natural characteristics and made possible better understandings of racial diversities *and* similarities. In addition, as a concept for organizing our thinking about change, "evolution" continues to provide a powerful vehicle for studying human sociohistorical development. It is a notion that is part and parcel of the terrain of critical social thought of the nineteenth and twentieth centuries.

On "Critical Theory" and "Race"

There is some ambiguity surrounding the notion of "critical theory" within traditions of *social* theory—beyond the fact that it is a phrase now used in reference to certain contemporary efforts in literary studies. On the one hand, the phrase is used to refer to a tradition of significantly revised and extended Marxism initiated by a group of theorists often referred to as "the Frankfurt School."[30] In this case "critical theory" is the name Max Horkheimer, an early director of the Institute for Social Research (established in Frankfurt, Germany in the late 1920s, hence the name "Frankfurt School"), gave to what he projected as the appropriate character and agenda for theoretical work directed at understanding—and contributing to the transformation of—social formations that, in various ways, blocked concrete realizations of increased human freedom.[31] This characterization of the nature of social theorizing and its agenda was shared by other members of the Institute (Herbert Marcuse, Theodor Adorno) even though still other members (Erich Fromm, Henryk Grossman) approached matters differently and used different methods in doing so. Further, there were theoretical differences between Horkheimer, Adorno, and Marcuse (and in Horkheimer's own thinking) over time that are masked by the label "critical theory."[32] Still, the label stuck and even today is used to identify a mode of social thought in the Frankfurt School tradition that continues in the work of a number of persons, Jürgen Habermas no doubt being one of the most widely known. Particularly through the influences of Marcuse on many in the generation coming of age in the 1960s during the socially transforming years of the great social mobilizations of the civil rights, black power, and antiwar movements, it is a tradition that has been especially influential in the United States, in part because it brought many of us of that generation to Marx, without question the major intellectual precursor to Frankfurt School critical theory (along with Kant, Hegel, Freud, Lukács, and others). And here lies the ambiguity, for, on the other hand, the phrase is often expanded to include Marx's work, and that in the various currents of Marxism as well, the Frankfurt School included. In the words of Erich Fromm: "There is no 'critical theory'; there is only Marxism."[33] Thus, while the various schools of Marxism, of whatever pedigree, all share important "family resemblances," there are, as well, significant differences among them sufficient to demand that each be viewed in its own right.[34] This is particularly the case when we come to the issue of "race" in "critical theory."

For a number of complex reasons, the Frankfurt School, for all of its influence on a generation of "new" leftists of various racial/ethnic groups many of whom were being radicalized in struggles in which "race" was a key factor, was not known initially so much for its theorizing about "racial" problems

and their resolution as for its insightful critique of social domination generally. Although members of the Institute, according to Martin Jay, were over-
whelmingly of Jewish origins, and the Institute itself was made possible by
funds provided by a member of a wealthy Jewish family expressly, in part,
to study anti-Semitism, all in the context of Germany of the 1920s and early
1930s, "the Jewish question" was not at the center of the Institute's work.[35]

This changed in the late 1930s and early 1940s. With the rise of Hitler and
the Nazis, the Institute was eventually moved to New York in 1935 (and
California in 1941) where its work continued until after the war (when it was
reestablished in West Germany in the 1950s). The focus of the Institute's
work during this time was the battle against fascism with debates centering
on the character of the changed nature of the economy in twentieth-century
capitalism; that is, the expression of group sentiments were to be understood
in the historical context of the society.[36]

In this, notes Jay, the Institute broke significant new ground. No less so
in another major contribution they made to the Marxian legacy, through the
work of Fromm especially, that made their studies of anti-Semitism so informative: the articulation, later supported by extensive empirical studies, of
a social psychology — and of individual psychology and character structure
in the context of the social — drawing off the work of Freud (among others),
in the context of Marxian social theory. This made possible analyses that
linked cultural, political, *and* economic structural and dynamic features of the
social world, and the character structure of the person, which helped to il-
luminate the de facto conditions of possibility for the emergence and social
maintenance of Nazi fascism and anti-Semitism. Here, particularly, is to be
found the significance of Frankfurt School critical theory for our discussion
of "race."

In the course of the Institute's work during its stay in the United States,
the concern with anti-Semitism became less and less the focus as members
of the Institute concentrated increasingly on "prejudice" more generally, although still fundamentally as related to authority and authoritarianism. Initiated by the American Jewish Committee in 1944 and conducted through
its Department of Scientific Research established for that purpose, with the
collaboration of the Berkeley Public Opinion Study, the Institute conducted
major empirical studies, with critical philosophical analyses of the findings,
of "one or another facet of the phenomenon we call prejudice." The object
of the studies, it was noted, was "not merely to describe prejudice but to explain it in order to help in its eradication." The sweep of the project involved
studies of the bases and dynamics of prejudice on individual, group, institutional, and community levels all in the context of the social whole.[37]

The Authoritarian Personality, the result of an integrated set of studies and
analyses, was one among a number of volumes that grew out of this project.
As Horkheimer notes in its preface, it is a book that deals with "social dis-

crimination," and its authors, in the terms of the *credo* of critical theory, were "imbued with the conviction that the sincere and systematic scientific elucidation of a phenomenon of such great historical meaning can contribute directly to an amelioration of the cultural atmosphere in which hatred breeds."[38] It is especially pertinent to this discussion of "race," Daniel Levinson's chapter on ethnocentric ideology in particular.[39]

Here two conceptual moves are to be noted. First, Levinson substitutes "ethnocentrism" for "prejudice":

> Prejudice is commonly regarded as a feeling of dislike against a specific group; ethnocentrism, on the other hand, refers to a relatively consistent frame of mind concerning "aliens" generally. . . . Ethnocentrism refers to group relations generally; it has to do not only with numerous groups toward which the individual has hostile opinions and attitudes but, equally important, with groups toward which he is positively disposed.
>
> A theory of ethnocentrism offers a starting point for the understanding of the psychological aspect of *group* relations. (p. 102, my emphasis)

Equipped with a wider gathering concept, Levinson is able to make yet another move, one he thinks crucial to gaining the understanding being sought: "The term 'ethnocentrism' shifts the emphasis from 'race' to 'ethnic group' " (p. 103). What was gained by this?

> . . . apart from the arbitrariness of the organic basis of classification, the greatest dangers of the race concept lie in its hereditarian psychological implications and in its misapplication to cultures. Psychologically, the race theory implies, whether or not this is always made explicit, that people of a given race (e.g., skin color) are also very similar psychologically because they have a common hereditary family tree . . . Furthermore, the term "race" is often applied to groups which are not races at all in the technical sense . . . There is no adequate term, other than "ethnic," by which to describe cultures (that is, systems of social ways, institutions, traditions, language, and so forth) which are not nations . . . From the point of view of sociology, cultural anthropology, and social psychology, the important concepts are not race and heredity but social organization (national, regional, subcultural, communal) and the interaction of social forms and individual personalities. To the extent that relative uniformities in psychological characteristics are found within any cultural grouping, these uniformities must be explained primarily in terms of social organization rather than "racial heredity." (p. 103)

As noted in the previous section, the conclusion had been reached in contemporary natural and social science that, at the very least, "something other than "racial heredity, understood as biological homogeneity, had to serve as a basis for understanding group characteristics and intergroup dynamics. Frankfurt School critical theory was distinctive as critical philosophical theory and material, social, analysis (a la Marx), fortified by Freudian psychology, deployed in cultural analyses of authority and mass culture. In the Institute's American sojourn particularly, there developed an explicit concern to bring critical thought to bear on the problems of invidious group-based and group-directed discrimination and oppression. "Race" was viewed as an adequate vehicle for such a task. Conditioned by a commitment to engage in critical praxis as an interdisciplinary venture that drew on the best science available (including that on "race"), these social theorists, through an approach to prejudice cum ethnocentrism fashioned from Hegelian, Marxian, Freudian elements, provided a means for getting at the problems of "race"—more precisely of race-*ism*—that was both critical and radical: within the context of an emancipatory project, it cut through social thought based on a reified, erroneous, even fraudulent philosophical anthropology that derived the culture, psychology, and social position of various groups from the biologizing of their "racial types."

Herbert Marcuse, among all members of the Frankfurt School, is most responsible for conveying this legacy to the "New Left" generation of the United States and Western Europe. In contrast to other members of the Institute, he became the most integrated into the American scene and chose to remain in the country when other members returned to Germany in the 1950s.[40] Influential as a teacher and colleague in a number of institutions, his *One Dimensional Man* inducted many of us into critical theory.[41] Here was an understanding of the social order in a way the necessity of which had been driven home to many of us as, in the context of concrete struggles, we came up against the limits of the idealism fueled by the thought of liberal democracy. For a significant group of persons involved in struggles over the "color line," the limits—and their attempted transcendence—were indicated in the evolution of the struggle for "civil rights" to one seeking "Black Power."[42]

But the Frankfurt School did *not* introduce Marxism to the United States. Nor, consequently, was it the first group of Marxian radical theorists to confront the problems of "race." There were other, much older legacies, in fact.[43] It is this history of multiple legacies that makes for the ambiguity of "a critical theory of race" when "critical theory" covers both the Frankfurt School *and* Marxian traditions in general. For an obvious, critically important question is, "Why, given other Marxian legacies, did the New Left seek guidance in the work of the Frankfurt School which might be applied to the problems of 'race,' among others"?

With respect to what we might call the black New Left, but with regard to many nonblack New Leftists as well, this question has been insightfully probed by Harold Cruse. For him, a crucial reason had to do with what he termed the "serious disease of 'historical discontinuity' ":

. . . since World War I a series of world-shaking events, social upheavals
and aborted movements have intruded and sharply set succeeding generations of Negroes apart in terms of social experiences. The youngest elements in the Negro movement today are activists, of one quality or another, who enter the arena unfortified with the knowledge or meaning of
many of the vital experiences of Negro radicals born in 1900, 1910, 1920,
or even 1930. The problem is that too many of the earlier-twentieth-
century-vintage Negro radicals have become too conservative for the
1940ers. Worse than that, the oldsters have nothing to hand down to the
1940ers in the way of refined principles of struggle, original social theory,
historical analysis of previous Negro social trends or radical philosophy
suitable for black people. . . . All the evidence indicates that the roots of
the current crisis of the Negro movement are to be found in the period between the end of World War I and the years of the Great Depression.
. . . most of the social issues that absorb the attention of all the Negro
radical elements today were prominently foreshadowed in these years. Yet
the strands between the period called by some the "Fabulous Twenties" and
the current Negro movement have been broken.[44]

The disease of discontinuity affected more than black youth. It was further
facilitated by the anti-Communist repression led by Senator Joseph McCarthy, which had "a distinctly deleterious effect" not only on the leadership of
black movements at the time, as Cruse notes, but on "radical" leadership in
general.[45]

This discontinuity, bolstered by McCarthyism, was institutionalized in
the curricula of most American colleges and universities, both black and
white: virtually none provided systematically mediated learning regarding
the history of previous struggles in which "radicals" had played important
roles. Thus, when we remember that the U.S. New Left generation emerged
principally on campuses and was forged in the crucibles of the modern civil
rights and antiwar movements whose troops and general staff included thousands of students, the availability and attractiveness of Frankfurt School critical theory was *in part* a function of happy historical conjuncture: it was available when members of a generation were in need — and actively in search — of
understandings to guide them in the transformation of a society that, when
measured by its own best principles, was found seriously deficient. Those
who suffered the deficits were no longer willing to do so, and were moving
to secure their "freedom." Many others were moved to share in the struggles
committed to the realization of what the principles called for. Marcuse, himself a teacher and scholar, was among others a major contributor to the
recovery from discontinuity by providing an important linkage with
Marxian (and Freudian) critical social thought that aided the conceptualization and understanding of the social order as a whole, within a global, histor-

ical context, in which it was possible to situate particular problems that were the focus of struggle, including, to some extent, those of the color line.

But only in part was this a matter of happy coincidence. The linkages between the old and new Lefts were never *completely* broken. Many young whites, in particular, were supported in their efforts by parents and others who themselves had been—and still were—radical activists of previous generations. There was another crucial factor, particularly as experienced by blacks "on the Left," an experience that has been formed into its own legacy: the felt *inadequacy* of Marxian Communist and Socialist projects with respect to "the Negro question," the ultimate test case of the problem of "race." At the core of this legacy is the *other side* of the science of "race": not its scientific, critical conceptualization, but the lived experiences of *real* persons whose experiences are forged in life worlds in part constituted by self-understandings that are in large measure "racial," no matter how "scientifically" inadequate.[46] Other Left theoretical and practical activities, advanced by various groups and parties, ran aground on this reality. Frankfurt School critical theory, unconstrained by dogmatic adherence to "the party line," offered a conceptualization of revolutionary social transformation while, at the same time, it took democratic freedom seriously. Since, at the time, on the black side of struggles involving "race," Black Nationalism was an increasingly ascendant force that even those on the white side had to contend with, and since participants from both "sides" had been forged in large part by liberal democracy, the vision of a new society that decidedly antidogmatic Frankfurt School critical theory helped to shape (particularly by not centering on *class* theory) was potentially more promising as a resolution of racism while preserving black integrity. In this regard there was the promise that the legacy of inadequacy of other traditions of Marxist thought might be overcome.

Oversimplified, the inadequacy had to do with the reductionism in the theorizing about "race" in those Marxian traditions that attempted to confront problems of the color line through approaches that rested on close adherence to a particular reading of the *classic* texts of the "mature" Marx and Engels, a reading sanctified after the Russian Revolution of 1917 by the subsequent Communist Internationals: *class* was the central—indeed, the only—vehicle for fully and properly understanding social organization and struggle. Problems of "race" are to be understood, then, as secondary to the "primary contradiction" of class conflict that is indigenous to social relations in capitalist social formations given the relations of the various classes to the means of production, relations that, at the very least, determine classes "in the last instance." The prospects for progressive social transformation and development, within and beyond capitalism, on this view, are dependent on successful organization and struggle by the international working class, racial differences notwithstanding. Such differences were to be transcended in the brotherhood of class solidarity beyond their opportunistic manipulation by the class of owners and managers, who used them as devices to foster divisions among workers, and by supposedly misguided, chauvinistic blacks (e.g., Marcus Garvey).

The history of Marxian Communist and Socialist organizations in the United States and elsewhere, populated, on the whole, by persons of European descent, is littered with errors, tragedies, and farces resulting from the dogmatic application of this approach.[47] A key source of the difficulty is the inadequate philosophical anthropology presumed by the privileging of "relations to the means of production" as the definitive determinant of groups defined by these relations, thus of the persons in those groups.[48] Aside from problems involving the racism of white workers in the class struggle, and, frequently, the paternalism of the white leadership, for many African-Americans "proletarianism internationalism" was not enough of a basis for forging a new Communist or Socialist world; it disregards—or explicitly treats as unimportant—much that they take to be definitive of African-Americans as a *people*. Identifying and nurturing these characteristics, and the institutions and practices that generate, shape, sustain, and mediate them, constitute a complex tradition of its own, that of "Black Nationalism."[49] It is a tradition that continues to inform approaches to "race" from the black side, within Marxian critical theory as well (though not that of the Frankfurt School). In 1928–29, for example, with impetus from black Communists (Cyril Briggs, Richard B. Moore, and Harry Haywood), who also had roots in the decidedly nationalist African Black Brotherhood, the Communist International took the position that blacks in the "black belt" of the southern United States were an oppressed "nation." The program for their liberation thus called for "self-determination" and "national independence." This was the official position, on and off, for nearly thirty years (1928–57) and was carried out in this country by the Communist Party of the United States of America (CPUSA).[50]

The house of "critical theory" has thus been divided on the issue of "race," sometimes against itself: the approach of the tradition of the Frankfurt School on one side; those of other Socialist and Communist organizations, of many persuasions, on the other, with numerous schools of thought and practice in between: "race" is without scientific basis as an explanatory notion (Frankfurt School); "race," while real, is a factor of conflict secondary to the primary contradiction of class struggle ("classical," "official" Marxism); "race" is the basis of a nation—a group whose members share common history and culture ("official" Marxism of 1928–57). Certainly the divergences have as much to do with social matters as with matters theoretical: the concrete histories of different groups, their agendas, their locations, the personal histories of their members, and so forth. Still, those of us who continue to be informed by legacies and agendas of "critical social theory" must move past this "Tower of Babel" in our own midst if we are to meet the challenges of the present and near future.[51]

Why a Critical Theory of "Race" Today?

Since the Black Nationalist tradition has continued to stress "race" over class, and classical Marxism class over "race," the "class or race" debates have persisted, at great expenditures of paper and ink, not to mention years of interminable struggle, confusion, and failure to conceive and secure the realization of promised emancipation. As we continue to struggle over matters of "race" in the United States and other societies, with very real possibilities for increased conflict, it is not enough to view today's problems as being brought on by the "heightened contradictions" of late capitalism attendant to the policies of neoconservative administrations conflicting with struggles for national liberation and socialism/communism in the "Third World." More is needed, both theoretically and practically.

"Both race *and* class" has been the response of some participants in the debate: "Left Nationalists" such as Manning Marable, on the one hand; theorists of the role of race in market relations and in social stratification (i.e., the social distribution of resources) such as William J. Wilson and Edna Bonacich, on the other.[52] Still others have proposed notions of "people-class," "eth-class," and "nation-class."[53] Yet all of these approaches, mindful of nationalist traditions from the black side, as well as of previous running-agrounds on "race," still presuppose the reality of "race."

But what is that reality? And "real" for whom? Would it be helpful for contemporary critical theory to recover the insights of twentieth-century science of "race" and those of the Frankfurt School regarding "race," "prejudice," and "ethnocentrism" and join them to recently developed critical-theoretic notions of social evolution to assist us in understanding and contributing to the emancipatory transformation of the "racial state" in its present configuration?[54] For, if Omi and Winant are correct: in the United States, the state is *inherently* racial, every state institution is a *racial* institution, and the entire social order is equilibrated (unstably) by the state to preserve the prevailing racial order (i.e., the dominance of "whites" over blacks and other "racial" groups);[55] during the decades of the 1950s through the 1970s, the civil rights, Black Power, Chicano, and other movements assaulted and attempted the "great transformation" of this racial state; however, the assaults were partial, and thus were not successful (as evidenced by the powerful rearticulation of "race" and reforming of the racial state consolidating power and dominance in the hands of a few "whites" in service to "whites" presently under way), because "all failed to grasp the comprehensive manner by which race is structured into the U.S. social fabric. All *reduced* race: to interest group, class fraction, nationality, or cultural identity. Perhaps most importantly, all these approaches lacked adequate conceptions of the racial state"[56] — if they are correct, might this not be case enough (if more is needed) for a new critical theory of "race" cognizant of these realities?

Omi and Winant think so, and propose their notion of "racial formation." It is a notion intended to displace that of "race" as an "essence" ("as something fixed, concrete and objective . . . "), or, alternatively, as a "mere illusion, which an ideal social order would eliminate." Thus, race should be understood as

> . . . an unstable and "decentered" complex of social meanings constantly being transformed by political struggle. . . . The crucial task . . . is to suggest how the widely disparate circumstances of individual and group racial identities, and of the racial institutions and social practices with which these identities are intertwined, are formed and transformed over time. This takes place . . . through political contestation over racial meanings.[57]

Central to their argument is the idea that "race" is socially and historically constructed and changes as a consequence of social struggle. "Race," in a racial state, is thereby irreducibly political.

The discussions and analyses of Omi and Winant, facilitated by their notion of "racial formation," are insightful and informative, particularly for their reading of the "rearticulation" of "race" by the Reagan administration. What these theorists offer is an important contribution to a revised and much needed critical theory of race for the present and near future. And part of the strength of their theorizing lies in the advance it makes beyond the reductionist thinking of other leftist theorists while preserving the sociohistorical constructivist (socially formed) dimensions of "race."

Part of the strength lies, as well, in the resituating of "race" as a "formation." For what this allows is an appreciation of the historical and socially constructive aspects of "race" within the context of a theory of social evolution where learning is a central feature.[58] Then we would have at our disposal the prospects of an understanding of "race" in keeping with the original promises of critical theory: enlightenment leading to emancipation. Social learning regarding "race," steered by critical social thought, might help us to move beyond racism, without reductionism, to pluralist socialist democracy.

Lest we move too fast on this, however, there is still to be explored the "other side" of "race": namely, the lived experiences of those within racial groups (e.g., blacks for whom Black Nationalism, in many ways, is fundamental). That "race" is without a scientific basis in biological terms does not mean, thereby, that it is without any social value, racism notwithstanding. The exploration of "race" from this "other side" is required before we will have an adequate critical theory, one that truly contributes to enlightenment and emancipation, in part by appreciating the integrity of those who see themselves through the prism of "race." We must not err yet again in thinking that "race thinking" must be completely eliminated on the way to emancipated society.

That elimination I think unlikely — and unnecessary. Certainly, however, the social divisive forms and consequences of "race thinking" ought to be eliminated, to whatever extent possible. For, in the United States in particular, a new historical conjucture has been reached: the effort to achieve democracy in a multi-"ethnic," multi-"racial" society where "group thinking" is a decisive feature of social and political life. A critical theory of "race" that contributes to the learning and social evolution that secures socialist, democratic emancipation in the context of this diversity would, then, be of no small consequence.

NOTES

1. Alfred Schutz and Thomas Luckmann, *The Structures of the Life-World*, trans. Richard M. Zaner and H. Tristram Engelhardt, Jr. (Evanston, Ill.: Northwestern University Press, 1973), p. 8.

2. The anticipation of "a release of emancipatory reflection and a transformed social praxis" that emerges as a result of the restoration, via critical reflection, of "missing parts of the historical self-formation process to man and, in this way, to release a self-positing comprehension which enables him to see through socially unnecessary authority and control systems." Trent Schroyer, *The Critique of Domination: The Origins and Development of Critical Theory* (Boston: Beacon Press, 1973), p. 31.

3. "Rearticulation is the process of redefinition of political interests and identities, through a process of recombination of familiar ideas and values in hitherto unrecognized ways." Michael Omi and Howard Winant, *Racial Formation in the United States: From the 1960s to the 1980s* (London: Routledge & Kegan Paul, 1986), p. 146, note 8.

4. For previous installments in this discussion, see my "Race and Class in the Theory and Practice of Emancipatory Social Transformation," in *Philosophy Born of Struggle: Anthology of Afro-American Philosophy from 1917*, ed. Leonard Harris (Dubuque: Kendal/Hunt, 1983), pp. 117–129; "Critical Theory in a Period of Radical Transformation," *Praxis International*, 3 (July 1983), pp. 138–46; and "On Race and Class. Or, On the Prospects of 'Rainbow Socialism,' " in *The Year Left 2: An American Socialist Yearbook*, ed. Mike Davis, Manning Marable, Fred Pfeil, and Michael Sprinker (London: Verso, 1987), pp. 106–21.

5. On life-world construction see Schutz and Luckmann, *The Structures of the Life-World*, and Peter L. Berger and Thomas Luckmann, *The Social Construction of Reality* (Garden City, N.Y.: Doubleday, 1966). "Hegemonic imposition" is a notion much influenced by the ideas of Antonio Gramsci (e.g., *Selections from the Prison Notebooks*, ed. and trans. Quintin Hoare and Geoffrey Nowell Smith [New York: International, 1971]), although a now classic formulation of the basic insight was provided by Marx (and Engels?) in *The German Ideology*: "The ideas of the ruling class are in every epoch the ruling ideas; i.e., the class which is the ruling *material* force of society, is at the same time its ruling *intellectual* force" (in *The Marx-Engels Reader*, 2nd ed., ed. Robert C. Tucker [New York: Norton, 1978], p. 172; emphasis in original).

6. In contrast to biologically oriented approaches, the ethnicity-based paradigm was an insurgent theory which suggested that race was a *social* category. Race was but one of a number of determinants of ethnic group identity or ethnicity. Ethnicity itself was understood as the result of a group formation process based on culture and descent." Omi and Winant, "The Domi-

nant Paradigm: Ethnicity-Based Theory," in *Racial Formation in the United States* (pp. 14–24), p. 15.

7. W. E. B. Du Bois, "The Concept of Race," in *Dusk of Dawn: An Essay Toward an Autobiography of a Race Concept* (New York: Schocken Books, 1968 [1940]), p. 103.

8. Thomas F. Gossett, *Race: The History of an Idea in America* (Dallas: Southern Methodist University Press, 1963), pp. 16–17.

9. "Our theory of racial formation emphasizes the social nature of race, the absence of any essential racial characteristics, the historical flexibility of racial meanings and categories, the conflictual character of race at both the 'micro-' and 'macro-social' levels, and the irreducible political aspect of racial dynamics." Omi and Winant, *Racial Formation in the United States*, p. 4.

10. Michael Banton and Jonathan Harwood, *The Race Concept* (New York: Praeger, 1975), p. 13.

11. Ibid., p. 14.

12. Ibid., p. 13.

13. "The eighteenth-century Swedish botanist Linneaus achieved fame by producing a classification of all known plants which extracted order from natural diversity. Scientists of his generation believed that by finding the categories to which animals, plants and objects belonged they were uncovering new sections of God's plan for the universe. Nineteenth-century race theorists inherited much of this way of looking at things." Ibid., p. 46.

14. Ibid., pp. 24–25. Both works were closely studied in Europe and the United States.

15. Ibid., p. 27.

16. Ibid., p. 28.

17. Ibid., pp. 29–30. These authors observe that while Gobineau's volumes were not very influential at the time of their publication, they were later to become so when used by Hitler in support of his claims regarding the supposed superiority of the "Aryan race."

18. Ibid., p. 30.

19. Ibid., p. 38.

20. Ibid., pp. 47–49; emphasis in original.

21. "An article by an anthropologist published in 1962 declared in the sharpest terms that the old racial classifications were worse than useless and that a new approach had established its superiority. This article, entitled 'On the Non-existence of Human Races', by Frank B. Livingstone, did not advance any new findings or concepts, but it brought out more dramatically than previous writers the sort of change that had occurred in scientific thinking. . . . The kernel of Livingstone's argument is contained in his phrase 'there are no races, there are only clines'. A cline is a gradient of change in a measurable genetic character. Skin colour provides an easily noticed example." Ibid., pp. 56–57.

22. Ibid., p. 58, quoted by Banton and Harwood.

23. "When we refer to races we have in mind their geographically defined categories which are sometimes called 'geographical races', to indicate that while they have some distinctive biological characteristics they are not pure types." Ibid., p. 62.

24. Ibid., p. 63. "The main mistake of the early racial theorists was their failure to appreciate the difference between organic and superorganic evolution. They wished to explain all changes in biological terms." Ibid., p. 66.

25. Ibid., pp. 72–73; emphasis in original.

26. Ibid., p. 77.

27. Ibid., pp. 127–28.

28. Ibid., p. 137.

29. Ibid., p. 147.

30. For discussions of Frankfurt School critical theory see, for example, Martin Jay, *The Dialectical Imagination: A History of the Frankfurt School and the Institute of Social Research, 1923–1950* (Boston: Little, Brown, 1973); Zoltán Tar, *The Frankfurt School: The Critical Theories of Max Hork-*

heimer and Theodor W. Adorno (New York: Wiley, 1977); David Held, *Introduction to Critical Theory: Horkheimer to Habermas* (Berkeley: University of California Press, 1980); and Schroyer, *The Critique of Domination*.

31. Among Horkheimer's characterizations of critical theory is his now classic essay "Traditional and Critical Theory," reprinted in Max Horkheimer, *Critical Theory*, trans. Matthew J. O'Connell et al. (New York: Herder & Herder, 1972), PP. 188–243.

32. Zoltán Tar, *The Frankfurt School*, p. 34.

33. From a personal telephone conversation with Fromm during one of his last visits to the United States in 1976.

34. For a particularly conversant overview of the various currents of Marxism and their philosophical and historical backgrounds, see Leszek Kolakowski, *Main Currents of Marxism*, 3 vols. (Oxford: Oxford University Press, 1978).

35. "If one seeks a common thread running through individual biographies of the inner circle [of the Institute], the one that immediately comes to mind is their birth into families of middle or upper-middle class Jews. . . . If one were to characterize the Institute's general attitude towards the 'Jewish question', it would have to be seen as similar to that expressed by another radical Jew almost a century before, Karl Marx. In both cases the religious or ethnic issue was clearly subordinated to the social. . . . In fact, the members of the Institute were anxious to deny any significance at all to their ethnic roots." Jay, *The Dialectical Imagination*, pp. 31–32.

36. Ibid., pp. 143, 152.

37. Max Horkheimer and Samuel H. Flowerman, "Foreword to Studies in Prejudice," in *The Authoritarian Personality*, Theodor W. Adorno et al. (New York: Norton, 1950), pp. vi, vii.

38. Ibid., p. ix.

39. The following discussion centers on the fourth chapter in *The Authoritarian Personality*, "The Study of Ethnocentric Ideology," by Daniel J. Levinson. Page references will be included in the text.

40. The significance of the Studies in Prejudice notwithstanding, Martin Jay, for example, has noted the strategic moves adopted by Institute members on their movement to New York (e.g., continuing to publish their works in German, rather than English) that limited their integration into the mainstream of American social science. See *The Dialectical Imagination*, pp. 113–14; and Held, *Introduction to Critical Theory*, p. 36.

41. Subtitled *Studies in the Ideology of Advanced Industrial Society*, the book was published by Beacon Press (Boston) in 1964. His *An Essay on Liberation* (Beacon Press, 1969) was an important—though problematic—sequel that attempted to come to terms with the massive mobilizations of the late 1960s in the United States and Western Europe, Paris (1968) in particular. In the latter case (Paris), during a student-initiated national strike, Marcuse was celebrated as one of the "three 'M's" of revolutionary heroes: "Marx, Mao, Marcuse." For pertinent writings in regard to Marcuse, see, for example: *The Critical Spirit: Essays in Honor of Herbert Marcuse*, ed. Kurt H. Wolff and Barrington Moore, Jr. (Boston: Beacon Press, 1967); Paul Breines, (ed.), *Critical Interruptions: New Left Perspectives on Herbert Marcuse* (New York: Herder & Herder, 1970). *The Critical Spirit* includes a helpful Marcuse bibliography.

42. See Clayborne Carson, *In Struggle: SNCC and the Black Awakening of the 1960s* (Cambridge, Mass.: Harvard University Press, 1981); and Robert Allen, *Black Awakening in Capitalist America* (Garden City, N.Y.: Doubleday, 1969).

43. For important discussions, see T. H. Kennedy and T. F. Leary, "Communist Thought on the Negro," *Phylon*, 8 (1947), pp. 116–23; Wilson Record, "The Development of the Communist Position on the Negro Question in the United States," *Phylon*, 19 (Fall 1958), pp. 306–26; and Philip Foner, *American Socialism and Black Americans* (Westport, Conn.: Greenwood Press, 1977). For discussions by black thinkers, see, among others, Cedric J. Robinson, *Black Marxism: The Making of the Black Radical Tradition* (London: Zed Press, 1983); Henry Winston, *Class, Race and Black Liberation* (New York: International Publishers, 1977); Harry Haywood,

Black Bolshevik: Autobiography of an Afro-American Communist (Chicago: Liberator Press, 1978); James Boggs, *Racism and the Class Struggle: Further Pages from a Black Worker's Notebook* (New York: Monthly Review Press, 1970); Manning Marable, *Blackwater: Historical Studies in Race, Class Consciousness and Revolution* (Dayton: Black Praxis Press, 1981); Oliver Cox, *Caste, Class and Race* (New York: Modern Reader, 1970); and Harold Cruse, *The Crisis of the Negro Intellectual* (New York: Morrow, 1967).

44. Harold Cruse, *Rebellion or Revolution?* (New York: William Morrow, 1968), pp. 127, 130.

45. "The hysteria of the time (which was labeled as McCarthyism, but which ranged far beyond the man) had shaken many persons, cowed others, silenced large numbers, and broken the radical impetus that might have been expected to follow the ferment and agitation of the 1930s and 1940s." Vincent Harding, *The Other American Revolution*, Center for Afro-American Studies Monograph Series, Vol. 4, Center for Afro-American Studies (Los Angeles, Calif.) and Institute of the Black World (Atlanta, Ga. 1980), p. 148.

46. A full exploration of "race" in the context of critical theory from the *black* side, if you will, requires a separate writing. For some of my thinking, see the previous installments cited in note 4, as well as in the writings of persons listed in note 43.

47. In the African context, for example, note Aimé Césaire's protest in his resignation from the Communist Party in 1956: "What I demand of Marxism and Communism. Philosophies and movements must serve the people, not the people the doctrine and the movement. . . . A doctrine is of value only if it is conceived by us and for us, and revised through us. . . . We consider it our duty to make common cause with all who cherish truth and justice, in order to form organizations able to support effectively the black peoples in their present and future struggle — their struggle for justice, for culture, for dignity, for liberty." Cedric Robinson, *Black Marxism*, p. 260, as cited by David Caute, *Communism and the French Intellectuals, 1914–1960* (New York: Macmillan, 1964), p. 211.

48. For a characterization and critique of this philosophical anthropology and its relation to class theory in Marx et al., see my "Race and Class in the Theory and Practice of Emancipatory Social Transformation."

49. Literature on this tradition is abundant. See, for example, John Bracey, Jr., et al. (eds.), *Black Nationalism in American* (New York: Bobbs-Merrill, 1970); Sterling Stuckey, *The Ideological Origins of Black Nationalism* (Boston: Beacon Press, 1970); Alphonso Pinkney, *Red, Black and Green: Black Nationalism in the United States* (New York: Cambridge University Press, 1976); and M. Ron Karenga, "Afro-American Nationalism: Beyond Mystification and Misconception," in *Black Books Bulletin*, (Spring 1978), pp. 7–12. In addition, each of these includes a substantial bibliography.

50. See Cedric J. Robinson, *Black Marxism: The Making of the Black Radical Tradition*, p. 300, and Kennedy and Leary, "Communist Thought on the Negro."

51. "There is a kind of progressive Tower of Babel, where we are engaged in building an edifice for social transformation, but none of us are speaking the same language. None understands where the rest are going." Manning Marable, "Common Program: Transitional Strategies for Black and Progressive Politics in America," in *Blackwater: Historical Studies in Race, Class Consciousness and Revolution*, p. 177.

52. See Marable's *Blackwater: Historical Studies in Race, Class Consciousness and Revolution* and "Through the Prism of Race and Class: Modern Black Nationalism in the U.S.," *Socialist Review*, May/June, 1980; William J. Wilson's *The Declining Significance of Race: Blacks and Changing American Institutions* (Chicago: University of Chicago Press, 1978); and Edna Bonacich's "Class Approaches to Ethnicity and Race," *Insurgent Sociologist*, 10 (Fall 1980), pp. 9–23. For a fuller discussion of approaches to "race" through the prism of the paradigm of class theory, see Omi and Winant, *Racial Formation in the United States*, pp. 25–37.

53. On "nation-class," see James A. Geschwender, *Racial Stratification in America* (Dubuque: Brown, 1978).

54. The recent notions of social evolution I have in mind are those of Jürgen Habermas. See, in particular, his "Historical Materialism and the Development of Normative Structures" and "Toward a Reconstruction of Historical Materialism," in Jürgen Habermas, *Communication and the Evolution of Society*, trans. Thomas McCarthy (Boston: Beacon Press, 1979), pp. 95–177.

55. Omi and Winant, *Racial Formation in the United States*, pp. 76–79.

56. Ibid., p. 107.

57. Ibid., pp. 68–69; emphasis in original.

58. See Habermas, *Communication and the Evolution of Society*.

CHAPTER 5

Racism and the West: From Praxis to Logos

Christian Delacampagne
Translated by Michael Edwards

The ten years of research that resulted in the 1983 publication of my doctoral thesis[1] on the formation of racist discourse within ancient and, later, medieval philosophy doubtless represents only a meager contribution to the elucidation of so serious and difficult a problem. I certainly do not pretend to have resolved this problem, or even to have made a discovery decisive to the future of the inquiry. I have merely proposed a set of hypotheses, of a philosophical nature, concerning the correlations, assuredly complex, that in my judgment hold between the development of racism and that of Western rationalism from antiquity to the present.

These hypotheses have been discussed, indeed criticized; I'm delighted about it, for that was their purpose. These criticisms have in turn inspired new reflections. The extent to which these reflections have led me to modify the form or content of my prior assertions is what I wish to explain in this essay. For the friendly comments and stimulating objections to which its substance is due, I must thank an American historian, Gavin I. Langmuir, and two French philosophers, Manuel de Diéguez and Louis Sala-Molins.

The essence of the thesis proposed in *The Invention of Racism* can be summed up as follows: racist discourse, as we have known it in Europe since the nineteenth century, did not appear ex nihilo. It is the fruit — or the inheritor — of other, older discourses, whose first elements can be located in the philosophers of antiquity and whose course can be charted through the theologians and scholars of the Middle Ages. Ancient or medieval, this premodern racism was therefore not born in an irrational or pathological atmosphere. On the contrary, it developed in the midst of a system of thought that strove to be rational; it progressed hand in hand with the very foundations of Western rationalism.

Is this paradox not just a coincidence? Is it not simply the manifest exaggeration of an observation that, if reduced to its proper proportions, would not amount to much? Such was the first reaction of many readers. Carrying their objection to its extreme, some reproached me for wanting to absolve modern Europe, and Christianity in particular, of all responsibility for the paternity of Nazi crimes. I want to make clear right away that this was not my intention. In recalling that massacres of Jews had already taken place in the Hellenistic world, there is no desire to minimize the horror of genocide perpetrated by the Nazis. I think it is the obligation of philosopher and historian alike to consider the genealogy of the discourse that has facilitated the passage from those ancient massacres to contemporary genocide. Moreover, it is not a priori absurd to return to the very birth of rational thought in the classical Greek city-state in order to see the cultivation of the "soil" in which later racism, with its horrible consequences, slowly took root.

There is, however, a historiographical objection to this approach. No document, it runs, can allow one to establish with certainty that a statement hostile to a given people, even if it is repeated for centuries before finally being denounced as racist, has the same meaning for the earlier generations that made it. Let us take a classic example: the accusation of ritual murder made against the Jews by certain ancient authors, then repeated in the Middle Ages and again by Nazi propagandists. Can it have, in the three cases, the same racist content? Can a connection be established between the three successive occurrences of this accusation? And has one the right to construct, upon the assertion of such a connection, a genealogy of modern racism?

I do not believe that it is impossible to respond affirmatively to these questions. Certainly the historical problem raises an apparent difficulty. It is never easy to situate the concrete origin of a slanderous rumor. It is not even always possible to date or place its first appearance. The Nazis knew their medieval authors well, whereas the medievals knew nothing of their ancient predecessors. How, in that case, can one claim a lineal descent from the last group to the first? Common sense obliges us, however, to recognize that all three cases involve a rumor of the same type. As for the fact that it could have been born or reborn in different times and places, that is a characteristic common to all rumors; to say that the origin of rumors poses a problem is simply to restate the very definition of the word "rumor" inasmuch as rumors are in principle chimerical, anonymous, and unjusitifiable.

But are we dealing, in the three periods under consideration, with an authentically *racist* rumor? That is the real difficulty. The stakes are plain: the ancient authors, and even the medievals, who embraced the accusation of ritual murder could well have done so in a spirit of religious polemic, but without a racist ulterior motive.[2] It would then be necessary to speak, in their case, of anti-Judaism and not of anti-Semitism. As a result, my attempt at genealogy would collapse: anti-Judaism could have played a role in the genesis of anti-Semitism, but the two would remain clearly distinguishable even so. Only anti-Semitism, because it is based on pseudobiological assertions, would be an authentic form of racism—and it would be impossible to trace the origin of racism beyond the nineteenth century.

The objection is a serious one. I cannot, however, entirely accept it even if I admit that I could have given the impression of employing too broad a definition of racism—especially for the ancient era. I have indeed, in my book, spoken of "primary racism" in reference to the apprehension universally felt in the presence of the foreigner (or more precisely, the stranger), and of "secondary racism" in reference to the no less universal phenomena of ethnocentrism and xenophobia. Improper terminology, I willingly acknowledge; these phenomena are quite distinct from the specifically racist attitude, and nothing is gained by confusing them—even if the laxity characteristic of present-day language frequently induces us to do so, and even if the "racist" label is more and more often applied to anybody about anything.

Let us try, therefore, to be more rigorous. The Greeks, when they spoke with contempt of the Persians or any of the peoples to whom they gave the name "Barbarians," were obviously not racist in the sense that this term has had since 1930. They were simply convinced of one thing: the absolute superiority of Greek culture over all others. This attitude could have been without consequence. However, it did have consequences, including this one: in the Greek city-state, the only individuals allowed to enjoy the title of citizen (or, to say the same thing in the language of ethics, the only individuals who could be considered "human persons" in the full sense of the term) were propertied Greek adult males. Failure to meet any one of these four conditions was enough to disqualify one from "normal" humanity. It is readily apparent that, for two groups at least, this disqualification was absolute: women and slaves had no chance of escaping their fate. To Aristotle and his contemporaries, as earlier to Pericles, women and slaves were quite simply *by nature* unqualified to be human.

And if I stress this "by nature" that one finds spelled out in Book I of Aristotle's *Politics*,[3] it is not a whim on my part, for it is he who authorizes us to speak—without need for further evidence—of Hellenic racism. Racism, in the modern sense of the term, does not necessarily begin as soon as one speaks of the physiological superiority, or cultural superiority, of one race or another; it begins when one makes (alleged) cultural superiority directly and mechanically dependent on (alleged) physiological superiority, that is, when one *derives* the cultural characteristics of a given group from its biological characteristics. Racism is the reduction of the cultural to the biological, the attempt to make the first dependent on the second. Racism exists wherever it is claimed that a given social status is explained by a given natural characteristic. Consequently, in this sense, racism already exists in the thought and in the society of ancient Greece.

Analogous demonstrations can be provided for our Middle Ages. In *The Invention of Racism*, I believe I have shown that one can speak of racism, in the modern sense of the term (even if the term did not exist), in reference to certain medieval behavior, as much toward the Jews as toward the "cagots."[4] When the accusation of ritual murder—or any other accusation of this kind, based on the idea that all members of a given community are bad "by nature"—is employed to justify a pogrom, it is obviously made in a racist spirit. The assertion according to which the cagots would all be debauched by virtue of their "unhealthy" constitution is also racist—even if this enigmatic minority, while being systematically abused by its neighbors from the fourteenth to the twentieth century, has been less persecuted than the Jewish minority.

Finally, we come to antiblack racism. It would be illusory to see it as only an epiphenomenon linked to a late stage of colonization. Indeed, only recently Louis Sala-Molins—to whom we owe the new edition of the *Black Code*[5] promulgated by Louis XIV in 1685 to regulate the status of black slaves in the French colonies of the period, and which was not definitively abolished until 1848—has quite rightly reminded us that if not all the racists of the period were proslavery, all those who were proslavery were without question racist; and that this racism had behind it a long and heavy history going back at least as far as the biblical curse inflicted on the descendants of Ham. From this ancient curse up to the incontestably racist language of the *Black Code*, historians can if they wish find all the stages and all the transitions in the works of the theologians, philosophers, travelers, and scholars who took an interest in the existence of blacks. Never before the nineteenth century—except perhaps for Las Casas—was European reason able to acknowledge that blacks might lay claim to something other than the inferior status and ill-treatment to which, it seemed, their degenerate "nature" had forever consigned them. It would be an abuse of language to refuse to apply the description "racist" to such an attitude, even if we are forced to recognize its existence in the greatest scholars of the Christian Middle Ages—and also in the majority of the philosophers of the Enlightenment.

It remains to be seen—and this is the most serious question—if racism and European reason have been linked only by chance, or if their relationship goes deeper than one would wish, a priori, to admit. The two hypotheses have their partisans; neither lacks arguments in its favor. What seems to support the first is an observation and a hope. Indeed, the hope exists to see reason challenge racism and emerge triumphant; but it is only a hope. Until the twentieth century, reason has been used more often to justify racism than to combat it. As for the observation, it is banal: no one will deny that, in the enterprise of world domination pursued by Christian Europe, racist or pseudobiological alibis advanced to justify the slave trade or massacres of Indians have merely played a role of a posteriori legitimation. Praxis, in the majority of cases, has preceded logos; the real, the most determinant motives have been economic or political. And if scientists and philosophers have been invited to discourse on the subject, that happened only after the fact, in order to ensure the ideological good conscience of a dominant class that scarcely paused for reflection when the safeguarding of its interests demanded, so it supposed, that the blood of others be made to flow.

Must reason therefore be exonerated? Must racism be considered merely a sort of parasite, which lived off reason until finally expelled by it? This would be, according to Bachelardian philosophy of science, the most desirable solution, the one that would best preserve the peace of reason with itself. Something, however, which I would call an insidious *suspicion*, prevents me from adhering totally to this peacekeeping pact. It is not by chance, not in an isolated fashion—once here, once there—that reason has compromised itself with racism; rather, the compromise has been massive, lasting, from its appearance in Greece, until the present day. It continues: Wilson's sociobiology is at bottom only the most recent avatar, and there is no guarantee that it will be the last. Besides, can racism exist outside reason or without its support? No, because racism is nothing but *biologism*, that is, a face—extreme, exaggerated as much as you like, but a face all the same—of modern scientific reason. Certainly, racism is only a caricature of rationalism; but just like any caricature, it cannot be understood without reference to its model.

That is what I have tried to show in *The Invention of Racism*. I would like now, in response to the friendly criticism of which I spoke at the outset, to clarify two things.

The first is that recognizing the links between racism and reason in no way implies that the condemnation of the former redounds on the latter. The need to indict a "monster" created by the superiority complex typical of the Europeans of yesterday should not lead those of today to reject wholesale the foundations, the tools, or the products of this scientific rationalism of which they remain, in the last analysis, the sole inventors. Let us be clear about this: it is also because Europe invented rationalism, and therefore the concept of human right that follows from it, that the entire world can today raise the (nearly) unanimous protest against the racist horror. Outside rationalism there is place only for fanaticism or tribalism, in which the individual ceases to exist: that is not the future we wish for.

The second point is that whereas racism is absurd—because it is absurd to derive, mechanically, the cultural from the biological—the idea of the ethnic group, with all that supposes about hereditary transmission of traits that might be at the origin of acquired traits, is not unacceptable in and of itself. And if one wishes to name this concept "race," then scientific reason can very well take an interest in races without for all that falling into some sort of racism. In other words, there is a path that consists in demythologizing the meaning of race, by removing all emotional connotations; and, on this path, reason has no reason to hang back.

It is clear that my last two remarks move in the same direction. If it wants to be effective, the ideological struggle against racism should not conceal any taboo. It should not be inspired either by a desire for mortification or by a crazed need for self-punishment. Above all it should not have the "perverse effect" of leading us to deny the real diversity, biological *and* cultural, existing within the human species, or of making us sink into a total cultural relativism—which would imply that the imperatives in the name of which we combat racism are themselves arbitrary. On this condition, and on this condition alone, will our combat continue to make sense. The reasons for opposing racism do not reside in either a naive scientism, or in some politico-religious orthodoxy but, more radically, in the values that constitute the specificity—and are the price—of Western culture.

NOTES

1. *L'Invention du racism* (Paris: Fayard, 1983).
2. This would be, basically, the position of historians such as Leon Poliakov and Gavin Langmuir.
3. Cf., for example, *Politics*, I.3–7.
4. On the "cagots," the reader may wish to refer to chapter 6 of *L'Invention du racisme*. [The term "cagot" designates a minority group living principally in southwestern France from the eleventh century on. The cagots were held to be leprous, cretinous, malodorous, debauched, heretical, the subjugated descendants of the Goths or the Saracens (or some other group of foreigners), possessors of magical powers, and in league with the Jews and the Arabs. As pariahs, they were required to live on the outskirts of towns and villages; wear a red patch (in the shape of a goose's foot) on their clothing; work only in woodcrafts; and enter church by a separate door. Also they were forbidden to intermarry, drink directly from public fountains, go barefoot, or handle merchandise. In all probability, the cagots represented no single ethnic group, but rather were a group of society's rejects—descendants of heretics, lepers, and the similarly afflicted—whose artificial unity was imposed from without. They were a variation on an old cliché: since they didn't exist, society had to invent them. Although their rights were officially restored in 1683, the cagots continued to be ostracized long after.—Trans.]
5. *Le Code Noir ou le calvaire de Canaan* (Paris: PUF, 1987).

CHAPTER 6

Equality: Beyond Dualism and Oppression

John L. Hodge

Introduction

The many forms of oppression, including racism and sexism, are sustained by an ancient moral concept—the dualism of good and evil. Using this pervasive and generally accepted notion, oppressors are able to justify their behavior as joining the struggle between the forces of good in the struggle against evil.[1]

The dualism of good and evil contains assumptions that enable those accepting it to believe they have greater moral worth than those they oppress. Their victims, on the other hand, are seen as bad or as motivated by evil. The treatment of their victims is not viewed as oppression at all, but instead is believed to be justified as the victory of good over evil. Dualism helps create and sustain oppression by enabling it to appear rational.

A conception of human equality stands in opposition to the dualistic justifications of oppression. This conception is that all human beings are of equal worth. While it shares with dualism the view that a person's moral worth determines how he or she should be treated, it is contrary to dualism in that it does not view the moral worth of some as superior to that of others. It is the only moral conception that serves as a foundation for practical judgments of right and wrong while making the justification of oppression—including the oppression of oppressors—impossible.

Although many notions of equality have been proposed, they have been permeated by the preexisting dualism of the surrounding culture. Such a tainted notion of equality, for example, was contained in the 1776 Declaration of Independence: "All men are created equal" meant equality only for white, property-owning males.[2] In spite of a later expansion of that original view of "equality" to include more people, the legacy of this limited notion is still with us. At another extreme, equality is confused with sameness and uniformity.

Equality, as defined here, is freed from the ancient dualism. To build a society without systematic oppression, we must understand this concept of equality and learn how, in a practical sense, to put it into action.

Oppression

Oppression, Racism, and Sexism

Oppression occurs when the members of a group are restricted by others so that the group's members typically have fewer rights or less power than those who restrict them. Those who restrict the group are its oppressors. Others who do not actively contribute to this oppression may nonetheless benefit from it.[3]

Oppression exists in many different forms and degrees. At one extreme, oppression involves daily infliction of physical violence on, and periodic killing of, members of the oppressed group. The enslavement of blacks in the United States prior to the Civil War is an example of this kind of oppression.[4] At another extreme, oppression may be entirely legal and relatively peaceful. The oppressed are kept down, for example, by reduced access to education, job training, and political power. Oppression in the United States today tends to be mostly of the latter kind.

To determine whether a group is oppressed, one must objectively examine the relationship of that group to other groups. The existence of oppression can be established by studying the difference in the power and rights between any two groups, and by determining whether the power and rights of one group has an adverse effect on the power and rights of the other. Identifying the source of oppression requires locating the source of the power that effectively keeps the power or rights of the oppressed group at a lower level. A group that is totally independent from other groups (rare in the modern world) can be neither oppressed nor an oppressor.

An important difference exists between this definition of oppression as an objective phenomenon, a phenomenon that can be observed and studied, and the subjective belief that oppression exists. A member of a group that has enjoyed a disproportionate amount of power may *feel* oppressed if the group's power is reduced. But such a group is not objectively oppressed if, in fact, the reduction of its power results in its members' having the same rights and power as that of others.

Given the preceding definition of oppression, it is easy to see racism and sexism as examples of oppression. When a group is identified by race and its members are oppressed because of their race, we have racism. When a group is identified by gender and its members are oppressed because of gender, we have sexism. Other kinds of oppression also occur. When a group is identified by religion and is oppressed because of religion, we have religious oppression. Similar patterns exist for nationalism and the oppression of homosexuals.

Oppression is,thus, the more inclusive phenomenon. We may focus on racism, but if we get rid of racism and create another form of oppression in its place, nothing has been gained. If we can find the means of eliminating or reducing the general phenomenon of oppression, then we can eliminate or reduce some types of oppression without creating others in their place.

Group Oppression and Individuals

While the concept of oppression is easy to define, oppression in real life occurs in many forms and with many complexities. Looking at a few of these complexities will help us avoid an erroneous view of the relationship of individuals to groups and an oversimplified view of the relationship between theory and real-life situations.

An individual's relation to oppression is typically very complex, since an individual may belong, simultaneously, to both oppressed and oppressor groups. A black male in the United States, for example, is a member of an oppressed group (blacks) and a member of an oppressor group (males). He may also be a member of another oppressed group (poor), or, if he is middle-class, his economic position may allow him to benefit from the oppression of others. A white male, who is in one respect a member of an oppressor group (white males), may also be a member of an oppressed group (say, aged and poor).

The relationship between individual and group behavior is also very complex. Part of understanding this relationship requires distinguishing between individual oppression and group oppression. Oppression may be directed at an individual or at a group, and it may be inflicted by an individual or a group. Group oppression, the main focus of this discussion, occurs when a group is defined or conceived of as a group and is oppressed because of its group characteristics. The group may be delineated by its race, gender, ethnic background, religion, age, nationality, locality, sexual preferences, or by any other means of identification that the oppressor chooses to use. Although it is theoretically possible for a group to be oppressed by an individual or by individuals acting without group identity, generally the oppression of a group requires the power of another relatively cohesive group. Group oppression, thus, generally occurs when oppressors act as part of a group to oppress others identified as a separate group.

When acts of oppression involve individuals fighting among themselves, irrespective of their group identity, we do not have group oppression. But when the oppressive acts of individuals reflect a larger social pattern or reveal that the individuals are acting in accordance with a group norm, then these acts are more appropriately called acts of group oppression. For example, if a white landlord refuses to rent an apartment to a black family because they are black, he may be acting in accordance with group norms that condone or encourage such behavior. If so, his behavior is a manifestation of group oppression, for consciously or unconsciously he sees the family as a member of a group, blacks, that may be treated in that manner by members of his own group. He may see his act as justifiable because it is in accordance with the norms of the group with which he identifies. If blacks are frequently excluded by members of the group the landlord identifies with, then the landlord's action reflects group oppression of blacks.

Although we may legitimately see this landlord's act as contributing to a group phenomenon, we must avoid the error of concluding, without adequate evidence, that all white landlords support the group norms. Observation of the dominant behavior of a group is not adequate to determine the behavior of any particular member of that group, nor does observation of the behavior of most members of a group give any data about the behavior of another member who has not been observed.

This point can be illustrated with the following example: a group consists of the fans of a football team. The fans are present at a game and occupy one side of the stadium. One member of their football team attacks a member of the other team. A neutral observer on the other side of the stadium hears loud cheers from the opposite side as the attack begins. The observer later reports that the fans cheered when a player on their team attacked a member of the other team. George was one of the fans. The observer did not see George.

What can the observer know about the behavior of George? *Nothing*. The observer cannot know whether George participated in the cheering of the attack. The observer cannot even say that it is probable or likely that George cheered with the group. George may have opposed the cheering or may have been silent. Based on our knowledge of the behavior of George's group, we can determine nothing about George's behavior. The situation is not changed if George's group, is say, white, and the opposing team is black.

Whether George should be held responsible for the group's behavior, perhaps because he did not protest loudly enough to stop it, is a different question requiring more specific knowledge of George and his relationship to the group. But it is important to be aware that knowledge of the behavior of groups tells us nothing about whether individual group members participated in or approved of that behavior and nothing about which individuals are responsible or should be held responsible for that behavior. It is also conceivable that George was afraid to oppose his group because the group would have penalized him for opposing it. A group can oppress its own members by suppressing individual criticisms of group behavior.

But those who justify group oppression frequently do not separate individual from group behavior, or distinguish among the behavior of different members of the group. The justifier of oppression often sees the target group as somehow infected with elements of badness or evil. Since the group is so infected, the behavior of any individual members of the group is seen to reflect the infection of the group, and vice versa. In this way dualists often blend the target group and individual together and fail to acknowledge individual differences within the group. The story of George illustrates that we cannot assume, for example, that a member of an oppressor group supports that oppression.

Oppression, Suffering, and Survival

Oppression is a moral issue primarily for two reasons: (1) it causes suffering, and (2) it threatens human survival.

It is primarily the oppressed who suffer, although others may experience the suffering through empathy. This suffering may be caused to a large extent by the enforcement mechanisms used to keep people oppressed. In extreme cases these mechanisms consist of frequent murder and torture. In less extreme cases they may consist of the threat of injury and the imprisonment of those who openly fight against oppression. Oppression may also be enforced mainly through economic or psychological mechanisms rather than physical threats. In such cases, suffering may consist mostly of the relative deprivation the oppressed must endure. Such deprivation reduces the economic well-being of the oppressed or restricts their means to self-fulfillment.

Suffering, whether directly or through empathy, is wrong unless there is a justification for it. What makes it wrong is neither a postulated notion of an objective good nor logical proof. Instead, its wrongness derives from our reactions to pain. Pain is something we would rather do without. It is acceptable only if there is a reason that justifies it.[5] Similarly, suffering, which is a more lasting form of pain, is to be avoided unless it can be justified. The desire to avoid suffering and pain is the basis for viewing suffering, and what causes suffering, as wrong.

The second reason for judging oppression as wrong is that continued oppression threatens human survival.

Oppression requires the creation and maintenance of violence. In some form violence is necessary to maintain group oppression, even if the violence is entirely legal and in the form of police enforcement. Violence typically results in violent reactions. Rarely does an oppressed group passively accept its oppression. In one way or another, and sooner or later, the oppressed fight back. In doing so they seek to frustrate or even destroy those they believe to be their oppressors. Sometimes the oppressed succeed. They may overthrow governments. They may gain power. They may become oppressors themselves.

But today, matters are more complicated than in the past. In a world rife with nuclear, chemical, and biological weapons, oppression can result in disaster. We can no longer ensure that if A attacks B, only B suffers. Today, if Nation A seeks to destroy Nation B with, say nuclear weapons, people and food chains in "uninvolved" nations C and D will be adversely affected. Radiation, like many chemical and biological weapons, does not stay in one place. In a major nuclear war, it will kill thousands or millions of others not directly involved in the conflict. Nuclear combat could have the inadvertent consequence of destroying human life in places far removed from the zone of combat. Potentially, it could destroy all human life.

Survival, like suffering, is a moral issue because, generally speaking, each person would like to live. That which ends innocent life, particularly human life in its entirety, is wrong. To understand this, no postulation of objective forces of good or evil is required.

The Moral Framework of Dualism

Dualism of Good and Evil

The dualism of good and evil is a moral framework, one that shapes the meaning of all judgments of what is deemed good, bad, or evil. Dualism is sometimes explicit in religion, philosophy, and political pronouncements. It is generally implicit, often unconsciously, in the attitudes and beliefs of nearly all members of modern societies.

This dualism contains four essential elements:

1. The meaning of good and evil is determined by objective beings or forces in the universe.
2. The forces (or forceful beings) of good and the forces of evil are in conflict and compete for supremacy.
3. These forces compete for dominance within each person.
4. People can judge themselves or others as being more influenced by the forces of good or more influenced by the forces of evil.

The first element expresses the assumed view that good and evil exist "objectively" in the sense that their existence is independent of human perception and feeling. Good and evil exist whether or not people believe in them. The second element expresses the assumed conflict that exists between good and evil. Any gain for one is a loss for another. There is no middle ground for compromise except as a temporary choice of lesser evils. The third element expresses the assumed connection between these forces and human behavior. The fourth element expresses the assumption that people can measure and judge the relative goodness or badness of themselves and others. This act of judging effectively assumes that people can be placed on a scale on which good is at one end and evil at the other.

Although many, and perhaps most cultures contain the four basic elements of dualism, Western culture is characterized by an additional element.[6] This element expresses the assumed view that the forces of good are reflected in reason, rationality, or the rule of law. The forces of evil, on the other hand, are reflected in passion, emotion, chance, and nature.[7] Although these notions have been subjected to criticism within Western culture, they still express the dominant view.[8]

Day-to-Day Manifestations of Dualism

Within a given society, the degree of general acceptance of the moral framework of dualism can be estimated by looking at common occurrences that presuppose a morally dualistic viewpoint.

Many religions, for example, make explicit the dualism of good and evil. In some typical versions of Christianity, good is symbolized by God and evil by the devil. These two "beings" are viewed as existing objectively and as impinging on and even controlling human lives. As the competing forces of good and evil contend for domination over each person, each individual must, to be good, believe in God and struggle against evil. People who do not make this choice are themselves viewed as evil. While dualism is not equally powerful in all sects of Christianity, it predominates to the extent it is not counteracted in practice by the notion of equality, a concept that also exists in Christian doctrine.[9]

Dualism is also expressed in popular politics. In the United States today, good is typically represented as "freedom" and "democracy." Evil is represented as "communism." Religion, frequently entwined with politics, may be incorporated into popular political notions, such as in the oft-expressed term "godless communism." To be a good person one must side with "freedom" (and God) and oppose "communism."

Dualism is not frequently expressed explicitly. Without consciously thinking about dualism, religion, or philosophy, many people reflect dualist assumptions in their daily lives. Such assumptions lead one to interpret nearly all human conflict as a conflict between good and evil or good and bad. Thus dualism operates in other areas of life far removed from religion, philosophy, and politics.

Dualism is present, for example, in many children's stories, movies, games, and toys. In these media we find not only dualism but also one of the mechanisms by which dualism is taught and transmitted from generation to generation. Evil is symbolized, for example, by witches and wolves, or, more recently, alien beings. Or it may be embodied in some personage with physical characteristics unlike those of the child-reader or audience. Typically the evil beings are ugly, or have long noses or long teeth. They are often darkly colored or wear dark clothing. The good characters, particularly the heroes, look more like people with whom the child is familiar.

These media go far beyond giving children a useful message that some people do very bad things. Instead, they transmit the idea that bad things are most likely to be done by people who are different, that evil is embodied in beings unlike themselves while good is in beings who are similar. When, additionally, the heroes are of a lighter color than the villains, the message has racist overtones that have consequences for both black and white children.[10] For black children, the message is undoubtedly perverse and demeaning, suggesting to them while they are very young and easily influenced that white people are better than they are.[11] White children, too, are given an unconscious message of superiority, a belief that they are better than others by virtue of their skin tone.

Dualist Justifications of Oppression

The dualism of good and evil is a necessary part of the justification of oppression. Whatever the other causes of oppression, dualist justifications help maintain oppression by making social relationships that are objectively oppressive appear subjectively reasonable both to the oppressors and to the beneficiaries of oppression.

These justifications, unconsciously or consciously, contain the following thoughts and relationships.

The forces of good and evil are in conflict, each struggling to win over the other. The forces of good, of course, should win. Once a group identifies itself as good and another group as bad, the "good" group thinks it is justifiable to place additional restrictions and controls on the "bad" group. To restrain the bad group helps the forces of good win over the forces of evil. The bad group should be constrained because constraining it is good, even if only "for its own sake" to guide it to goodness. The good group "should" have more power or rights than the bad group so that the good group can better fight in the struggle against evil, or at least paternalistically direct those who are less good. In more extreme cases, the bad group is not simply to be constrained or directed but defeated or destroyed.

In Western societies dualist justifications typically take a particular form as a consequence of the identification of good with reason, law, and rationality, and bad with emotion, chance, spontaneity, and nature. In accordance with this form of dualism, control of nature through science and technology is generally assumed to be good. This assumption determines the very meaning Western nations attach to the concept of "civilization." The development of societies from "primitive" to "civilized" is often equated with the development of the tools and technological devices that can be used to control nature. Development means technological, industrial, and scientific progress.[12]

An alternative point of view, rarely considered though equally reasonable but for dualism, is that the development of societies should be measured by the way their members treat one another. By this yardstick, the most violent societies would be seen as the most primitive, the least violent as the most civilized.

A rejection of this Western form of dualism does not mean that one must remain within a dualist framework and thus view reason, science, and technology as bad or evil. Alternatively, one could view them as equally capable of good or bad depending on how they are used.

The assumed value of rational control is also expressed in popular stereotypes and imagery. Consider the old but still familiar stereotypes of blacks. Blacks like to sing and dance. Blacks are lazy. The first image suggests people who are controlled by their bodies and emotion; the second, similarly, suggests people controlled by bodily desires. Today the image is likely to be more sophisticated. Blacks excel in entertainment (emotional expression) and sports (bodily expression).[13]

Stereotypic images of women share some commonalities with those of blacks. Women are emotional and more governed by feeling. They are also controlled by their bodies as a consequence of pregnancy, breast feeding, and menstrual cycles. In such images women, like blacks, are depicted as closer to nature.[14]

There would be nothing inherently demeaning about these images were it not for dualism and the perpetual conflict between the forces of good and bad that it implies. In dualist thinking, more of one thing means less of the other. Further, in the Western form of dualism, good is associated with rationality, bad with emotion and nature. *Therefore*, given dualism, more emotion means less rationality; closer to nature means further from human reason and science.

Without dualism, there would be no perceived conflict or contradiction in a person being both emotional *and* rational, being both close to nature *and* scientific. It would be a compliment to say blacks sing and dance. It would be a compliment to say that women are in touch with their emotions and feelings. But to the extent dualism exists, these compliments become insults. The images are intended to insult, and they *do* insult to the extent that dualism is assumed.

Given dualism, it is considered reasonable to reward with more power and rights those who are seen as closer to the good; similarly, it is reasonable to restrict the power and rights of those seen as less good. Thus, in Western societies, it has been generally accepted as "normal" that those considered most rational—educated or economically successful white males—are disproportionately represented in positions having the most influence and power.

Even if Western societies were able to move beyond racism and sexism, oppression would remain if dualism itself were not also overcome. Such societies would remain divided between an elite group, defined as those who were most rational, and all others, defined as those who were more emotional or closer to nature. The identity of the oppressed groups would change, but the quantity of oppression would remain about the same.

The Moral Value of Dualism

Although frequently used to justify oppression, dualism also serves a legitimate function. Insofar as dualism postulates the existence of good and bad beyond individual subjective feelings, it makes *morality* conceptually possible. Serving this function perhaps explains why dualism has persisted so long in human history.

The fundamental principle of morality is that good and bad exist beyond individual wants and desires. Morality means that life is more than the private affairs of individuals, each seeking private pleasures and the avoidance of private pains. In this sense, morality is objective. A viable alternative to dualism must enable the continued existence of morality. Such an alternative would redefine the nature of good and bad without eliminating the fundamental principle of morality.

The fundamental principle of morality is incorporated into the framework of dualism in that "good" is considered an objective force existing independently of people. This kind of objectivity is the polar opposition of the subjectivity of private feelings. However, other kinds of moral objectivity are possible. "Objectivity" does not have to mean "existing separately from feeling." An alternative view, for example, is that moral objectivity is not separate from subjectivity but a common element in what is subjective, an element common to or shared among all people.[15]

The legitimate function of dualism — and the limitations of dualism — can be illustrated with a short story of human development. The story is not intended to be historically accurate but is rather a fable to illustrate the conceptual difference between subjectivity and morality, the probable reasons behind the development of dualism, and the reasons why dualism is morally inadequate.

The story:

At first people were aware only of their own perceptions and feelings. Notions of good and bad, as objective concepts, did not exist. All people knew was what they felt.

Next people observed connections between different feelings and external events. Some events were seen to be connected with pleasure, others with pain. The connections were not clearly seen as causal relationships between two separate occurrences; rather the events and the feelings associated with them were seen as merged into one. Self and other were not clearly separated. The event and the associated feeling were melded together.

Later, the self and not-self became more clearly distinguished. Initially, distinguishing the self from the not-self or object also meant distinguishing the self-that-feels-pleasantness from the object-that-makes-pleasantness. As the distinction between self and object became clear, a term equivalent to "good" was used to designate the pleasantness made or caused by the object, and a term equivalent to "bad" was used to designate the unpleasantness made or caused by the object. Thus were born the concepts of good and bad as distinct from concepts of pleasure and pain.

As humans developed further, they began to look for explanations for events in the world—events that seemed to occur randomly and without reason. They began to postulate unseen gods or demons as the cause of observable events. A rain god, for example, was seen as the being who made rain. In this way they tried to make sense of what they could not understand. This was a major step in human development. It was the rudimentary beginning of science, a process that postulated (and still postulates, with modern differences) unseen beings or forces to help make sense out of the apparent chaos of observed events.

Similar explanations were needed to understand why some events were good and others bad. The gods, demons, or spirits that caused events took on the qualities of the events themselves. "Good" events were perceived to be caused by good spirits; "bad" events, by bad spirits.

The many spirits multiplied until their number and behavior became as apparently chaotic as the events themselves. Simplification was required to reduce the chaos. The acts of different spirits began to be explained as the acts of a single spirit with multiple or myriad characteristics. Good and bad spirits were each combined into fewer but more powerful representations. Ultimately this process led to the conception of One Good Spirit and One Bad Spirit. The Good Spirit represented the forces of good. The Bad Spirit represented the forces of evil.

These conceptions seemed satsifactory and were generally accepted for a long period in human history. Then, as the means of communication and travel developed, people began to notice that things their social group thought were bad, another believed to be good. Further, the other group also invoked the name of the Good Spirit in support of its views. The second group noticed the same about the first. The two groups became angry with each other and fought over who was right. So it was with many groups around the world.

A few observers of these fighting groups noticed that each believed its acts were supported by the Good Spirit and identified its own beliefs with those of the Good Spirit. How, these observers asked, could one determine who was right? After failing to find the answer, they concluded that morality did not exist at all.

Humankind entered an era of moral confusion. Many people denied that morality existed at all. Moral notions, they said, were nothing more than expressions of subjective feeling. Others continued to believe that their own views were those of the Good Spirit. Developmentally, humankind returned to its beginnings, with no more moral guidance than it had when the self and not-self were not distinguished.

Dissatisfied with this moral confusion, some people began to see good and bad in another way: in terms of people's relationships with one another. Thus, another concept of moral objectivity was conceived. Objectivity came to mean not "separate from me" but "more than me." The more-than-me was seen as me-in-community-with-others. Morality began to represent the desired community, the goal of cooperative human interaction without oppression. The moral principle that made this community possible was that of equality, the principle that all people are equal in their essential human worth. This new concept did not develop all at once, but slowly grew over centuries as the other concept of morality, used in support of war and oppression, began slowly to die out.

The Moral Framework of Equality

The Meaning of Equality

The moral framework of equality is the belief or view that all people are of equal moral worth. A person's moral worth is his or her degree of intrinsic goodness. Within the moral framework of equality, individual human acts may be judged as right or wrong, good or bad, better or worse, but the *worth* of human actors is beyond good and evil.

Equality and dualism. Acceptance of the framework of equality, instead of that of dualism, changes the effect of all moral judgments. Within the framework of dualism, all events and beings are judged as relatively closer to either good or evil. The framework of dualism places the moral worth of people on a measuring scale, with good at one end and evil at the other.

Within the framework of equality, however, the moral worth of people cannot be compared. If people were placed on a scale that measured their moral worth, they would all be on the same spot. But since everyone is on the same spot, the scale is meaningless as a measure and might as well be discarded. Stated simply, the moral framework of equality means there are no good and bad people, only good and bad deeds.

In the framework of equality, the morality of deeds is judged in reference to the framework itself. When a person treats another as though the other has lesser or greater moral worth, that treatment is bad. When a person treats another in a way that affirms the other's equal moral worth, that treatment is good. But one must clearly distinguish between what people do—their acts, behavior, and deeds—and their moral worth. Although good and evil exist in the frameworks of both equality and dualism, in the framework of equality only human behavior, not human worth, can be good or evil.

Equality and sameness. This framework of equality does not place value on sameness and conformity. Instead, equality is a moral notion, a notion of human worth. Since people who are different are recognized to be equal in their fundamental worth, their differences raise no moral questions.

In contrast, the valuing of sameness is a likely result of the framework of dualism, especially when dualism is combined with cultural bias. Cultural bias, a prejudice that favors one's own group, affects everyone. "All of us are molded by our social life until we become its creatures; we mistakenly take custom for human nature."[16] Once it is assumed that some people are evil, people who are different are likely to be viewed with suspicion. If different from us, they are probably either better or worse, and as we are good, most likely they are worse. Dualism and cultural bias produce a deadly combination.

History offers many examples of this combination. When the English first encountered Africans in the sixteenth and seventeenth centuries, the English assumed without serious question that the blacks were inferior beings. That assumption (which persists today) helped justify the subsequent enslavement of blacks.[17] Similar assumptions were held by the Europeans who encountered the native Americans ("Indians"). The Declaration of Independence, while pronouncing the equality of men in one sentence, refers to "the merciless Indian savages" in another. In early America, whites also persecuted other whites who were different, especially religious dissidents. In one such instance, in Salem, Massachusetts, in 1692, the influential members of a society accepted the charges of witchcraft, made by children, against the more nonconforming members of the group.[18] Because they were seen as the agents of the devil, the so-called witches were killed or imprisoned.

Today's "witches" and "savages" in the Western world are often referred to as "communists," whether or not the term accurately reflects their political beliefs. This label is often used to desribe others whom the accuser does not like. For example, during the American civil rights movement of the 1960s and 1970s, the leaders and active followers of the movement were often called Communists, not only in the segregated states but also by high officials in the federal government.[19] This echoed the events of an earlier time, the "McCarthy" period of the 1950s, when political nonconformity was also labeled Communist and those so labeled were persecuted with loss of jobs or imprisonment.[20] The label may change, but given the dualist mentality, new labels will be created to serve the same purpose.

In the framework of equality, deviations are more likely to be respected, for in this framework there is no room for regarding people who are different as infected with evil.

Conflicts between Dualism and Equality

We can see the primary difference between the moral frameworks of equality and dualism by looking at the way each framework governs treatment of those with a conflicting point of view. To a person who accepts dualism and who also recognizes no validity to the framework of equality, those accepting the framework of equality are likely to be viewed as representing the forces of evil. Accordingly, the dualist can justify oppression of those who accept equality. If it is good to control, thwart, or destroy evil, so it is good to reduce the power and rights of those who express or live in accordance with a bad point of view.

To one who accepts the framework of equality, even dualists are of equal moral worth and should thus be treated fairly. Equality does not mean that everyone is of equal moral worth except those who do not believe that everyone is of equal moral worth. Within the framework of equality, one cannot justify the oppression of those who accept dualism.

But what should those who accept equality do if others seek to oppress them? Whenever the dualist uses force or violence to oppress those who accept equality, what can the latter do to fight against such oppression and still remain true to their own beliefs?

The framework of equality does not sanction passivity in the face of oppression. To accept one's own oppression is to accept inequality between oneself and one's oppressors, just as behaving as an oppressor would also signify the acceptance of inequality. To act consistently within the framework of equality, one must oppose one's oppressors without at the same time attempting to reduce them to an oppressed condition.

Consider, for example, the members of two groups of people, the Ds and the Es. The Ds accept dualism and act consistently within its framework. The Es accept equality and act consistently within its framework. If the Ds act to oppress the Es, the Es will regard these acts as bad and needing to be opposed.

How can the Es oppose the Ds' acts without oppressing the Ds? The answer lies in objectively comparing the relative powers and rights of the members of the two groups. The Ds' oppression of the Es means the Ds cause the Es to have less power or fewer rights than the Ds. Once the Ds have caused the Es to have less of either, it is justifiable either for the Es to attempt to reduce the Ds' power and rights to their level, or for the Es to raise their power and rights to the level of the Ds. The Es' goal is to create equality of power and rights. If in this effort the E's cause the Ds to have less power or fewer rights than the Es, the Es have gone too far and have become the oppressors.

In the real world, however, we are talking about the use of force and violence, for that is generally the way oppression is achieved and maintained. Even when oppression is achieved *legally*, violence is used, for law requires police enforcement that involves the use or threat of violent force.

For the Ds, the use of violence is not much of a moral problem, for any amount of violence is justified in destroying evil as long as it can be successfully done without unleashing equal or greater retaliatory forces. Hitler, for example, took dualism to its logical conclusion in his attempt to exterminate the "race" he thought was the source of evil.

For the Es, the use of violence is a moral problem (as well as a practical one), for the Es can legitimately use violence only to prevent oppression, not to cause it. The maximum amount of violence the Es may use is the amount that reduces the Ds' power and rights to that of the Es. This amount is the upper limit that the Es may use, for using more violence than that would make the Es the oppressors. In keeping with the Es' respect for the Ds' moral worth, the Es would begin by using verbal persuasion whenever possible and would use violence only as necessary to stop the Ds' oppressive acts.

Dualism and Democracy

In much of the world, dualism and its implicit violence is mitigated by ideals of equality. The political concept of democracy, for example, rests on an ideal of equality. But democracies as they exist today are an inconsistent mixture of equality and dualism. Just as ideals of equality temper the violence of dualism, so does dualism subvert the ideals of equality.

This inconsistent mixture is evident in the United States, where democracy takes on an aggressive, missionary character in the international arena. "Democracy" is actually used as a justification for waging war or instigating rebellion in nations perceived to be undemocratic. An example was the incredibly brutal and destructive war waged by the United States on

Vietnam.[21] At the current time (1987), the United States is openly, with con-
gressional approval, arming and leading forces seeking the violent overthrow of the government of Nicaragua, despite the fact that Nicaragua has
not been accused of attacking the United States. These cases exemplify missionary democracy, that is, the self-contradictory democracy of dualism. In
this view, democracy is good while nondemocracies (usually identified as
"Communist") are evil. Therefore, it is legitimate to destroy the forces of evil
through war, invasion, or instigation of insurrections. Such force is not
limited by the principle that the force used against oppression may not exceed
the force used by the oppressors. Thus we find here the underlying presence
of the moral framework of dualism.

Summary and Conclusion

The justification of oppression depends on the view that people can be measured on a scale of good and evil. Such measurement presupposes the framework of dualism that sees morality primarily in terms of the struggle between
the forces of good and evil. Good and evil are presumed to be objective in
that they are seen as existing "in the universe" independent of and external
to human perception or feeling, analogous to the existence of a rock or the
force of gravity.

Those who measure others on the scale of good and evil assume that the
measurement can be done objectively and that it is justifiable to place restrictions on those judged to be less good or more evil than themselves. After all,
evil is something we would be better off without. So too for the people
judged as more evil. In extreme cases, they should be killed; in other instances, they should at least be controlled and their power or rights reduced.
The objective result is oppression of the people consistently so viewed and
treated, although to the oppressors this result is nothing more than the furtherance of good through the suppression of evil. Without the framework
of dualism, these justifications have no moral foundation on which to rest.

The moral framework of equality denies that people can be measured on
a scale of good and evil, since all people are of equal moral worth. This framework is inconsistent with all justifications of oppression.

Common to both frameworks is the view that good and bad consist of
more than subjective, private pleasures and pains. In the framework of equality, acts that help equalize power and rights are good; acts that give some
more power of rights than others are bad.

In the real world, good acts will encounter the violence of bad acts. At
times, violence must be used to end violence. This statement should shock
no one, for even enforcement of laws requires a degree of violence. But

within the framework of equality, the use of violence is constrained by the framework itself. It is never justifiable to use more violence to stop oppression than the oppressors use to create or maintain it. Within such limits, however, the framework of equality provides a moral basis for effectively opposing any treatment of oneself or others as less than equal.

Although the dualist conception requires postulation of forces of good and evil existing independently of human perception or feeling, no objective evidence supports such postulates.[22] Unlike dualism, these unsupported postulates are superfluous for the moral framework of equality. Instead, accepting the framework of equality is grounded on our own desires to alleviate the suffering caused by oppression and to increase the likelihood of human survival in a world threatened by nuclear disasters. The core of such desires is generally held in common with others. The desire to survive is common to all people, and even the dualist would usually agree that unjustified human suffering is undesirable. This shared commonality is what makes acceptance of the moral framework of equality not a private matter of pleasure and pain but a social act that links each of us to everyone else.

A modern society based on equality without dualism has yet to be created. The seeds of equality were sown centuries ago, and many of these seeds are contained in societies that value democratic institutions. But such seeds have not grown enough as long as "democracies" like the United States contain oppressed groups such as blacks, Hispanics, and women, or as long as believers in such "democracies" see democracy as a justification for aggressively attacking, subverting, or destroying those who appear to have a different viewpoint. A society based on equality can emerge out of such "democracies" only as a consequence of changes in moral beliefs, institutions, and legal systems.[23] When we compare today's "democracies" with the goal to be achieved, we can see the task of making these changes has barely begun.

NOTES

1. An extended examination of the relationship of the dualism of good and evil to oppression is found in John L. Hodge, Donald K. Struckmann, and Lynn Dorland Trost, *Cultural Bases of Racism and Group Oppression* (Berkeley: Two Riders Press, 1975). Parts of this book are reprinted in Carl E. Jackson and Emory J. Tolbert (eds.), *Race and Culture in America*, 3rd ed. (Edina, Minn.: Burgess International Group, 1987). The discussion of equality here goes beyond *Cultural Bases of Racism* by presenting a clearer alternative to dualism.

2. See, for example, Richard Hofstadter, *The American Political Tradition*, chapter 1 (New York: Knopf, 1948).

3. Without oppression, a group's power would be proportionate to its size, but each individual would have the same protected rights as any other, regardless of group membership. The relationship of rights and power in the political arena is discussed in John L. Hodge, "Democracy and Free Speech: A Normative Theory of Society and Government," *The First Amendment Reconsidered*, chapter 5 (New York and London: Longman, 1982), esp. pp. 154–55.

4. See, for example, Kenneth M. Stampp, *The Peculiar Institution* (New York: Knopf, 1956).

5. For example, a woman in childbirth may accept pain as necessary to creating life.

6. The term "Western culture" refers "to the dominant cultural tradition which stems from Western Europe with its strong ancient Greek influence. A more accurate term would be 'Anglo-European' culture." Hodge et al., *Cultural Bases of Racism*. See this work also for a more extensive discussion of dualism in Western culture.

7. See Hodge et al., *Cultural Bases of Racism*, parts 3 and 4.

8. Some of the criticisms are discussed in Hodge et al., *Cultural Bases of Racism*, parts 5 and 6.

9. For example, different Christian sects had different attitudes toward the enslavement of blacks in America. See David Brion Davis, *The Problem of Slavery in Western Culture*, chapter 10 (Ithaca, N.Y.: Cornell University Press, 1966).

10. Recently (1987) a fast-food restaurant that caters to children and is known throughout the world distributed toy robots to accompany one of its food offerings. The leader of the good robots was predominantly yellow. The bad robots were described as wicked and lazy. Their leader was the darkest of the robots, a dark bluish grey close to black.

In *An American Tail*, a children's movie that was recently very popular in the United States, the heroes are nearly all light, the villains are nearly all dark.

Although not every children's story or toy contains these racist color-codings (for example the heroes in the Disney movie *Lady and the Tramp*, were of several colors, including black), such color codings occur more frequently than not. Yellow or blond is a favorite hero color.

11. These effects on black children are discussed in James A. Banks and Jean D. Grambs (eds.), *Black Self-Concept* (New York: McGraw-Hill, 1972), esp. pp. 10–12, and Kenneth B. Clark, *Dark Ghetto* (New York: Harper & Row, 1967), pp. 64–66.

12. The typical assumption that civilization consists of conquering nature is expressed, for example, in Philip L. Ralph, *The Story of Our Civilization* (New York: Dutton, 1954), p. 19. See also James H. Robinson et al., *History of Civilization: Earlier Ages* (Boston: Ginn, 1965), p. xvii.

13. See generally Winthrop D. Jordan, *White over Black* (Baltimore: Penguin, 1969), and Hodge et al., *Cultural Bases of Racism*, part 2.

14. See Karl Stern, *The Flight from Woman* (New York: Farrar, Strauss & Giroux, 1965), and Hodge et al., *Cultural Bases of Racism*, part 5, section 2.

15. This alternative view was explored in John L. Hodge, *A Philosophical Basis of Pacifism*, esp. chapter 9 (Ann Arbor, Mich.: University of Microfilms, 1968). As explained later, the term "pacifism" does not correctly describe the current view of the author.

16. W. Ward Fearnside and William B. Holther, *Fallacy: The Counterfeit of Argument* (Englewod Cliffs, M.J.: Prentice-Hall, 1959), p. 117.

17. See Jordan, *White over Black*, part 1.

18. See, for example, John Putnam Demos, *Entertaining Satan* (Oxfrd and New York: Oxford University Press, 1982), and Marion L. Starkey, *The Devil in Massachusetts* (Garden City, N.Y.: Doubleday, 1969). Some early Christian theory and its relation to the treatment of witches in Europe is discussed in Shulamith Shahar, *The Fourth Estate* (London and New York: Methuen, 1983).

19. See, for example, David J. Garrow, *The FBI and Martin Luther King, Jr.* (New York: Norton, 1981), esp. pp. 91 and 210 (regarding southern sentiment), pp. 78–150 and 208–12 (regarding high government officials), and pp. 151–55 (regarding the element of racism in the FBI).

20. The persecution of Communist expressions was upheld by the federal courts. See, for example, John Somerville, *The Communist Trials and the American Tradition* (New York: Cameron Associates, 1956). Similarly in China during the Cultural Revolution, those who deviated from the political norms were persecuted as evil influences on society. See, for example, Ruth Earnshaw Lo and Katharine S. Kinderman, *In the Eye of the Typhoon* (New York: Da Capo Press, 1980).

21. See generally Marvin E. Gettleman (ed.), *Vietnam: History, Documents, and Opinions on a*

Major World Crisis (New York and Toronto: New American Library, 1970). The peculiar brutality of the war is discussed on pp. 525–30.

22. This notion of moral objectivity was critically examined in Hodge, *A Philosophical Basis of Pacifism*.

23. For example, an examination of what equality would mean in the area of free speech is explored in John L. Hodge, "Democracy and Free Speech."

CHAPTER 7

The Fact of Blackness

Frantz Fanon

"Dirty nigger!" Or simply, "Look, a Negro!"
I came into the world imbued with the will to find a meaning in things, my spirit filled with the desire to attain to the source of the world, and then I found that I was an object in the midst of other objects.

Sealed into that crushing objecthood, I turned beseechingly to others. Their attention was a liberation, running over my body suddenly abraded into non-being, endowing me once more with the agility that I had thought lost, and by taking me out of the world, restoring me to it. But just as I reached the other side, I stumbled, and the movements, the attitudes, the glances of the others fixed me there, in the sense in which a chemical solution is fixed by a dye. I was indignant; I demanded an explanation. Nothing happened. I burst apart. Now the fragments have been put together again by another self.

As long as the black man is among his own, he will have no occasion, except in minor internal conflicts, to experience his being through others. There is of course the moment of "being for others," of which Hegel speaks, but every ontology is made unattainable in a colonized and civilized society. It would seem that this fact has not been given sufficient attention by those who have discussed the question. In the *Weltanschauung* of a colonized people there is an impurity, a flaw that outlaws any ontological explanation. Someone may object that this is the case with every individual, but such an objection merely conceals a basic problem. Ontology—once it is finally admitted as leaving existence by the wayside—does not permit us to understand the being of the black man. For not only must the black man be black; he must be black in relation to the white man. Some critics will take it on themselves to remind us that this proposition has a converse. I saw that this is false. The black man has no ontological resistance in the eyes of the white man. Overnight the Negro has been given two frames of reference within which he has had to place himself. His metaphysics, or, less pretentiously, his customs and the sources on which they were based, were wiped out because they were in conflict with a civilization that he did not know and that imposed itself on him.

The black man among his own in the twentieth century does not know at what moment his inferiority comes into being through the other. Of course I have talked about the black problem with friends, or, more rarely, with American Negroes. Together we protested, we asserted the equality of all men in the world. In the Antilles there was also that little gulf that exists among the almost-white, the mulatto, and the nigger. But I was satisfied with an intellectual understanding of these differences. It was not really dramatic. And then . . .

And then the occasion arose when I had to meet the white man's eyes. An unfamiliar weight burdened me. The real world challenged my claims. In the white world the man of colour encounters difficulties in the development of his bodily schema. Consciousness of the body is solely a negating activity. It is a third-person consciousness. The body is surrounded by an atmosphere of certain uncertainty. I know that if I want to smoke, I shall have to reach out my right arm and take the pack of cigarettes lying at the other end of the table. The matches, however, are in the drawer on the left, and I shall have to lean back slightly. And all these movements are made not out of habit but out of implicit knowledge. A slow composition of my *self* as a body in the middle of the spatial and temporal world—such seems to be the schema. It does not impose itself on me; it is, rather, a definitive structuring of the self and of the world—definitive because it creates a real dialectic between my body and the world.

For several years certain laboratories have been trying to produce a serum for "denegrification"; with all the earnestness in the world, laboratories have sterilized their test tubes, checked their scales, and embarked on researches that might make it possible for the miserable Negro to whiten himself and thus to throw off the burden of that corporeal malediction. Below the corporeal schema I had sketched a historico-racial schema. The elements that I used had been provided for me not by "residual sensations and perceptions primarily on a tactile, vestibular, kinesthetic, and visual character,"[1] but by the other, the white man, who had woven me out of a thousand details, anecdotes, stories. I thought that what I had in hand was to construct a physiological self, to balance space, to localize sensations, and here I was called on for more.

"Look, a Negro!" It was an external stimulus that flicked over me as I passed by. I made a tight smile.

"Look, a Negro!" It was true. It amused me.

"Look, a Negro!" The circle was drawing a bit tighter. I made no secret of my amusement.

"Mama, see the Negro! I'm frightened!" Frightened! Frightened! Now they were beginning to be afraid of me. I made up my mind to laugh myself to tears, but laughter had become impossible.

I could no longer laugh, because I already knew that there were legends, stories, history, and above all *historicity*, which I had learned about from Jaspers. Then, assailed at various points, the corporeal schema crumbled, its place taken by a racial epidermal schema. In the train it was no longer a question of being aware of my body in the third person but in a triple person. In the train I was given not one but two, three places. I had already stopped being amused. It was not that I was finding febrile coordinates in the world. I existed triply: I occupied space. I moved towards the other . . . and the evanescent others, hostile but not opaque, transparent, not there, disappeared. Nausea . . .

I was responsible at the same time for my body, for my race, for my ancestors. I subjected myself to an objective examination, I discovered my blackness, my ethnic characteristics; and I was battered down by tom-toms, cannibalism, intellectual deficiency, fetishism, racial defects, slave-ships, and above all else, above all: "Sho' good eatin'."

On that day, completely dislocated, unable to be abroad with the other, the white man, who unmercifully imprisoned me, I took myself far off from my own presence, far indeed, and made myself an object. What else could it be for me but an amputation, an excision, a haemorrhage that spattered my whole body with black blood? But I did not want this revision, this thematization. All I wanted was to be a man among other men. I wanted to come lithe and young into a world that was ours and to help to build it together.

But I rejected all immunization of the emotions. I wanted to be a man, nothing but a man. Some identified me with ancestors of mine who had been enslaved or lynched: I decided to accept this. It was on the universal level of the intellect that I understood this inner kinship—I was the grandson of slaves in exactly the same way in which President Lebrun was the grandson of tax-paying, hard-working peasants. In the main, the panic soon vanished.

In America, Negroes are segregated. In South America, Negroes are whipped in the streets, and Negro strikers are cut down by machine-guns. In West Africa, the Negro is an animal. And there beside me, my neighbor in the university, who was born in Algeria, told me: "As long as the Arab is treated like a man, no solution is possible."

"Understand, my dear boy, colour prejudice is something I find utterly foreign . . . But of course, come in, sir, there is no colour prejudice among us . . . Quite, the Negro is a man like ourselves . . . It is not because he is black that he is less intelligent than we are . . . I had a Senegalese buddy in the army who was really clever . . . "

Where am I to be classified? Or, if you prefer, tucked away?
"A Martinican, a native of "our" old colonies."
Where shall I hide?
"Look at the nigger! . . . Mama, a Negro! . . . Hell, he's getting
mad . . . Take no notice, sir, he does not know that you are as civilized as
we . . . "
My body was given back to me sprawled out, distorted, recoloured, clad
in mourning in that white winter day. The Negro is an animal, the Negro
is bad, the Negro is mean, the Negro is ugly; look, a nigger, it's cold, the nigger is shivering, the nigger is shivering because he is cold, the little boy is
trembling because he is afraid of the nigger, the nigger is shivering with cold,
that cold that goes through your bones, the handsome little boy is trembling
because he thinks that the nigger is quivering with rage, the little white boy
throws himself into his mother's arms: Mama, the nigger's going to eat me
up.
    All round me the white man, above the sky tears at its navel, the earth
rasps under my feet, and there is a white song, a white song. All this whiteness that burns me . . .
    I sit down at the fire and I become aware of my uniform. I had not seen
it. It is indeed ugly. I stop there, for who can tell me what beauty is?
    Where shall I find shelter from now on? I felt an easily identifiable flood
mounting out of the countless facets of my being. I was about to be angry.
The fire was long since out, and once more the nigger was trembling.
    "Look how handsome that Negro is! . . . "
    "Kiss the handsome Negro's ass, madame!"
    Shame flooded her face. At last I was set free from my rumination. At the
same time I accomplished two things: I identified my enemies and I made a
scene. A grand slam. Now one would be able to laugh.
    The field of battle having been marked out, I entered the lists.
    What? While I was forgetting, forgiving, and wanting only to love, my
message was flung back in my face like a slap. The white world, the only
honourable one, barred me from all participation. A man was expected to behave like a man. I was expected to behave like a black man—or at least like
a nigger. I shouted a greeting to the world and the world slashed away my
joy. I was told to stay within bounds, to go back where I belonged.
    They would see, then! I had warned them, anyway. Slavery? It was no
longer even mentioned, that unpleasant memory. My supposed inferiority?
A hoax that it was better to laugh at. I forgot it all, but only on condition
that the world not protect itself against my any longer. I had incisors to test.
I was sure they were strong. And besides . . .
    What! When it was I who had every reason to hate, to despise, I was re-
jected? When I should have been begged, implored, I was denied the slightest
recognition? I resolved, since it was impossible for me to get away from an

inborn complex, to assert myself as a BLACK MAN. Since the other hesitated to recognize me, there remained only one solution: to make myself known.

In *Anti-Semite and Jew* (p. 95), Sartre says: "They [the Jews] have allowed themselves to be poisoned by the stereotype that others have of them, and they live in fear that their acts will correspond to this stereotype . . . We may say that their conduct is perpetually overdetermined from the inside."

All the same, the Jew can be unknown in his Jewishness. He is not wholly what he is. One hopes, one waits. His actions, his behaviour are the final determinant. He is a white man, and, apart from some rather debatable characteristics, he can sometimes go unnoticed. He belongs to the race of those who since the beginning of time have never known cannibalism. What an idea, to eat one's father! Simple enough, one has only not to be a nigger. Granted, the Jews are harassed — what am I thinking of? They are hunted down, exterminated, cremated. But these are little family quarrels. The Jew is disliked from the moment he is tracked down. But in my case everything takes on a *new* guise. I am given no chance. I am overdetermined from without. I am the slave not of the "idea" that others have of me but of my own appearance.

I move slowly in the world, accustomed now to seek no longer for upheaval. I progress by crawling. And already I am being dissected under white eyes, the only real eyes. I am *fixed*. Having adjusted their microtomes, they objectively cut away slices of my reality. I am laid bare. I feel, I see in those white faces that it is not a new man who has come in, but in a new kind of man, a new genus. Why, it's a Negro!

I slip into corners, and my long antennae pick up the catch-phrases strewn over the surface of things — nigger underwear smells of nigger — nigger teeth are white — nigger feet are big — the nigger's barrel chest — I slip into corners, I remain silent, I strive for anonymity, for invisibility. Look, I will accept the lot, as long as no one notices me!

"Oh, I want you to meet my black friend . . . Aimé Césaire, a black man and a university graduate . . . Marian Anderson, the finest of Negro singers . . . Dr. Cobb, who invented white blood, is a Negro . . . Here, say hello to my friend from Martinique (be careful, he's extremely sensitive) . . . "

Shame. Shame and self-contempt. Nausea. When people like me, they tell me it is in spite of my colour. When they dislike me, they point out that it is not because of my colour. Either way, I am locked into the infernal circle.

I turn away from these inspectors of the Ark before the Flood and I attach myself to my brothers, Negroes like myself. To my horror, they too reject me. They are almost white. And besides they are about to marry white women. They will have children faintly tinged with brown. Who knows, perhaps little by little . . .

I had been dreaming.

"I want you to understand, sir, I am one of the best friends the Negro has in Lyons."

The evidence was there, unalterable. My blackness was there, dark and unarguable. And it tormented me, pursued me, disturbed me, angered me.

Negroes are savages, brutes, illiterates. But in my own case I knew that these statements were false. There was a myth of the Negro that had to be destroyed at all costs. The time had long since passed when a Negro priest was an occasion for wonder. We had physicians, professors, statesmen. Yes, but something out of the ordinary still clung to such cases. "We have a Senegalese history teacher. He is quite bright . . . Our doctor is coloured. He is very gentle."

It was always the Negro teacher, the Negro doctor; brittle as I was becoming, I shivered at the slightest pretext. I knew, for instance, that if the physician made a mistake it would be the end of him and of all those who came after him. What could one expect, after all, from a Negro physician? As long as everything went well, he was praised to the skies, but look out, no nonsense, under any conditions! The black physician can never be sure how close he is to disgrace. I tell you, I was walled in: No exception was made for my refined manners, or my knowledge of literature, or my understanding of the quantum theory.

I requested, I demanded explanations. Gently, in the tone that one uses with a child, they introduced me to the existence of a certain view that was held by certain people, but, I was always told, "We must hope that it will very soon disappear." What was it? Colour prejudice.

It [colour prejudice] is nothing more than the unreasoning hatred of one race for another, the contempt of the stronger and richer peoples for those whom they consider inferior to themselves, and the bitter resentment of those who are kept in subjection and are so frequently insulted. As colour is the most obvious outward manifestation of race it has been made the criterion by which men are judged, irrespective of their social or educational attainments. The light-skinned races have come to despise all those of a darker colour, and the dark-skinned peoples will no longer accept without protest the inferior position to which they have been relegated.[2]

I had read it rightly. It was hate; I was hated, despised, detested, not by the neighbour across the street or my cousin on my mother's side, but by an entire race. I was up against something unreasoned. The psychoanalysts say that nothing is more traumatizing for the young child than his encounters with what is rational. I would personally say that for a man whose only weapon is reason there is nothing more neurotic than contact with unreason.

I felt knife blades open within me. I resolved to defend myself. As a good tactician, I intended to rationalize the world and to show the white man that he was mistaken.

In the Jew, Jean-Paul Sartre says, there is

a sort of impassioned imperialism of reason: for he wishes not only to convince others that he is right; his goal is to persuade them that there is an absolute and unconditioned value to rationalism. He feels himself to be a missionary of the universal; against the universality of the Catholic religion, from which he is excluded, he asserts the "catholicity" of the rational, an instrument by which to attain to the truth and establish a spiritual bond among men.[3]

And, the author adds, though there may be Jews who have made intuition the basic category of their philosophy, their intuition

has no resemblance to the Pascalian subtlety of spirit, and it is this latter— based on a thousand imperceptible perceptions—which to the Jew seems his worst enemy. As for Bergson, his philosophy offers the curious appearance of an anti-intellectualist doctrine constructed entirely by the most rational and most critical of intelligences. It is through argument that he establishes the existence of pure duration, of philosophic intuition; and that very intuition which discovers duration or life, is itself universal, since anyone may practise it, and it leads towards the universal, since its objects can be named and conceived.[4]

With enthusiasm I set to cataloguing and probing my surroundings. As times changed, one had seen the Catholic religion at first justify and then condemn slavery and prejudices. But by referring everything to the idea of the dignity of man, one had ripped prejudice to shreds. After much reluctance, the scientists had conceded that the Negro was a human being; *in vivo* and *in vitro* the Negro had been proved analogous to the white man: the same morphology, the same histology. Reason was confident of victory on every level. I put all the parts back together. But I had to change my tune.

That victory played cat and mouse; it made a fool of me. As the other put it, when I was present, it was not; when it was there, I was no longer. In the abstract there was agreement: the Negro is a human being. That is to say, amended the less firmly convinced, that like us he has his heart on the left side. But on certain points the white man remained intractable. Under no conditions did he wish any intimacy between the races, for it is a truism that "crossings between widely different races can lower the physical and mental level . . . Until we have a more definite knowledge of the effect of race-crossings we shall certainly do best to avoid crossings between widely different races."[5]

For my own part, I would certainly know how to react. And in one sense, if I were asked for a definition of myself, I would say that I am one who waits; I investigate my surroundings, I interpret everything in terms of what I discover, I become sensitive.

In the first chapter of the history that the others have compiled for me, the foundation of cannibalism has been made eminently plain in order that I may not lose sight of it. My chromosomes were supposed to have a few thicker or thinner genes representing cannibalism. In addition to the *sex-linked*, the scholars had now discovered the *racial-linked*. [in English in the original—Trans.] What a shameful science!

But I understand this "psychological mechanism." For it is a matter of common knowledge that the mechanism is only psychological. Two centuries ago I was lost to humanity, I was a slave for ever. And then came men who said that it all had gone on far too long. My tenaciousness did the rest; I was saved from the civilizing deluge. I have gone forward.

Too late. Everything is anticipated, thought out, demonstrated, made the most of. My trembling hands take hold of nothing; the vein has been mined out. Too late! But once again I want to understand.

Since the time when someone first mourned the fact that he had arrived too late and everything had been said, a nostalgia for the past has seemed to persist. Is this that lost original paradise of which Otto Rank speaks? How many such men, apparently rooted to the womb of the world, have devoted their lives to studying the Delphic oracles or exhausted themselves in attempts to plot the wanderings of Ulysses! The pan-spiritualists seek to prove the existence of a soul in animals by using this argument: a dog lies down on the grave of his master and starves to death there. We had to wait for Janet to demonstrate that the aforesaid dog, in contrast to man, simply lacked the capacity to liquidate the past. We speak of the glory of Greece, Artaud says; but, he adds, if modern man can no longer understand the *Choephoroi* of Aeschylus, it is Aeschylus who is to blame. It is tradition to which the anti-Semites turn in order to ground the validity of their "point of view." It is tradition, it is that long historical past, it is that blood relation between Pascal and Descartes, that is invoked when the Jew is told, "There is no possibility of your finding a place in society." Not long ago, one of those good Frenchmen said in a train where I was sitting: "Just let the real French virtues keep going and the race is safe. Now more than ever, national union must be made a reality. Let's have an end of internal strife! Let's face up to the foreigners (here he turned towards my corner) no matter who they are."

It must be said in his defence that he stank of cheap wine; if he had been capable of it, he would have told me that my emancipated-slave blood could not possibly be stirred by the name of Villon or Taine.

An outrage!

The Jew and I: since I was not satisfied to be racialized, by a lucky turn of fate I was humanized. I joined the Jew, my brother in misery.

An outrage!

At first thought it may seem strange that the anti-Semite's outlook should be related to that of the Negrophobe. It was my philosophy professor, a native of the Antilles, who recalled the fact to me one day: "Whenever you hear anyone abuse the Jews, pay attention, because he is talking about you." And I found that he was universally right—by which I meant that I was answerable in my body and in my heart for what was done to my brother. Later I realized that he meant, quite simply, an anti-Semite is inevitably anti-Negro.

You come too late, much too late. There will always be a world—a white world—between you and us . . . The other's total inability to liquidate the past once and for all. In the face of this affective ankylosis of the white man, it is understandable that I could have made up my mind to utter my Negro cry. Little by little, putting out pseudopodia here and there, I secreted a race. And that race staggered under the burden of a basic element. What was it? *Rhythm*! Listen to our singer, Léopold Senghor:

> It is the thing that is most perceptible and least material. It is the archetype of the vital element. It is the first condition and the hallmark of Art, as breath is of life: breath, which accelerates or slows, which becomes even or agitated according to the tension in the individual, the degree and the nature of his emotion. This is rhythm in its primordial purity, this is rhythm in the masterpieces of Negro art, especially sculpture. It is composed of a theme—sculptural form—which is set in opposition to a sister theme, as inhalation is to exhalation, and that is repeated. It is not the kind of symmetry that gives rise to monotony; rhythm is alive, it is free . . . This is how rhythm affects what is least intellectual in us, tyrannically, to make us penetrate to the spirituality of the object; and that character of abandon which is ours is itself rhythmic.[6]

Had I read that right? I read it again with redoubled attention. From the opposite end of the white world a magical Negro culture was hailing me. Negro sculpture! I began to flush with pride. Was this our salvation?

I had rationalized the world and the world had rejected me on the basis of colour prejudice. Since no agreement was possible on the level of reason, I threw myself back towards unreason. It was up to the white man to be more irrational than I. Out of the necessities of my struggle I had chosen the method of regression, but the fact remained that it was an unfamiliar weapon; here I am at home; I am made of the irrational; I wade in the irrational. Up to the neck in the irrational . . .

The soil, which only a moment ago was still a tamed steed, begins to revel. Are these virgins, these nymphomaniacs? Black Magic, primitive mentality, animism, animal eroticism, it all floods over me. All of it is typical of peoples that have not kept pace with the evolution of the human race. Or, if one prefers, this is humanity at its lowest. Having reached this point, I was long reluctant to commit myself. Aggression was in the stars. I had to choose. What do I mean? I had no choice . . .

Yes, we are—we Negroes—backward, simple, free in our behaviour. That is because for us the body is not something opposed to what you call the mind. We are in the world. And long live the couple, Man and Earth! Besides, our men of letters helped me to convince you; your white civilization overlooks subtle riches and sensitivity. Listen:

> Emotive sensitivity. *Emotion is completely Negro as reason is Greek.* [Author's italics.] Water rippled by every breeze? Unsheltered soul blown by every wind, whose fruit often drops before it is ripe? Yes, in one way, the Negro today is richer *in gifts than in works.* [Author's italics.] But the tree thrusts its roots into the earth. The river runs deep, carrying precious seeds. And, the Afro-American poet, Langston Hughes, says:

> > I have known rivers
> > ancient dark rivers
> > my soul has grown deep
> > like the deep rivers.

> The very nature of the Negro's emotion, of his sensitivity, furthermore, explains his attitude towards the object perceived with such basic intensity. It is an abandon that becomes need, an active state of communion, indeed of identification, however negligible the action — I almost said the personality — of the object. A rhythmic attitude: The adjective should be kept in mind.[7]

So here we have the Negro rehabilitated, "standing before the bar," ruling the world with his intuition, the Negro recognized, set on his feet again, sought after, taken up, and he is a Negro — no, he is not a Negro but the Negro, exciting the fecund antennae of the world, placed in the foreground of the world, raining his poetic power on the word, "open to all the breaths of the world." I embrace the world! I am the world! The white man has never understood this magic substitution. The white man wants the world; he wants it for himself alone. He finds himself predestined master of this world. He enslaves it. An acquisitive relation is established between the world and him. But there exist other values that fit only my forms. Like a magician, I robbed the white man of "a certain world," for ever after lost to him and his. When that happened, the white man must have been rocked backward by a force that he could not identify, so little used as he is to such reactions. Somewhere beyond the objective world of farms and banana trees and rubber trees, I had subtly brought the real world into being. The essence of the world was my fortune. Between the world and me a relation of coexistence was established. I had discovered the primeval One. My "speaking hands" tore at the hysterical throat of the world. The white man had the anguished feeling that I was escaping from him and that I was taking something with me. He went through my pockets. He thrust probes into the least circumvolution of my brain. Everywhere he found only the obvious. So it was obvious that I had a secret.

I made myself the poet of the world. The white man had found a poetry in which there was nothing poetic. The soul of the white man was corrupted, and, as I was told by a friend who was a teacher in the United States, "The presence of the Negroes beside the whites is in a way an insurance policy on humanness. When the whites feel that they have become too mechanized, they turn to the men of colour and ask them for a little human sustenance." At last I had been recognized, I was no longer a zero.

I had soon to change my tune. Only momentarily at a loss, the white man explained to me that, genetically, I represented a stage of development: "Your properties have been exhausted by us. We have had earth mystics such as you will never approach. Study our history and you will see how far this fusion has gone." Then I had the feeling that I was repeating a cycle. My originality had been torn out of me. I wept a long time, and then I began to live again. But I was haunted by a galaxy of erosive stereotypes: the Negro's *sui generis* odour . . . the Negro's *sui generis* good nature . . . the Negro's *sui generis* gullibility . . .

I had tried to flee myself through my kind, but the whites had thrown themselves on me and hamstrung me. I tested the limits of my essence; beyond all doubt there was not much of it left. It was here that I made my most remarkable discovery. Properly speaking, this discovery was a rediscovery.

I rummaged frenetically through all the antiquity of the black man. What I found there took away my breath. In his book *L'abolition de l'esclavage* Schoelcher presented us with compelling arguments. Since then, Frobenius, Westermann, Delafosse — all of them white — had joined the chorus: Ségou, Djenné, cities of more than a hundred thousand people; accounts of learned blacks (doctors of theology who went to Mecca to interpret the Koran). All of that, exhumed from the past, spread with its insides out, made it possible for me to find a valid historic place. The white man was wrong, I was not a primitive, not even a half-man, I belonged to a race that had already been working in gold and silver two thousand years ago. And too there was something else, something else that the white man could not understand. Listen:

> What sort of men were these, then, who had been torn away from their families, their countries, their religions, with a savagery unparalleled in history?
>
> Gentle men, polite, considerate, unquestionably superior to those who tortured them — that collection of adventurers who slashed and violated and spat on Africa to make the stripping of her the easier.
>
> The men they took away knew how to build houses, govern empires, erect cities, cultivate fields, mine for metals, weave cotton, forge steel.
>
> Their religion had its own beauty, based on mystical connections with the founder of the city. Their customs were pleasing, built on unity, kindness, respect for age.
>
> No coercion, only mutual assistance, the joy of living, a free acceptance of discipline.

Order — Earnestness — Poetry and Freedom.

From the untroubled private citizen to the almost fabulous leader there was an unbroken chain of understanding and trust. No science? Indeed yes; but also, to protect them from fear, they possessed great myths in which the most subtle observation and the most daring imagination were balanced and blended. No art? They had their magnificent sculpture, in which human feeling erupted so unrestrained yet always followed the obsessive laws of rhythm in its organization of the major elements of a material called upon to capture, in order to redistribute, the most secret forces of the universe. . . . [8]

Monuments in the very heart of Africa? Schools? Hospitals? Not a single good burgher of the twentieth century, no Durand, no Smith, no Brown even suspects that such things existed in Africa before the Europeans came. . . .

But Schoelcher reminds us of their presence, discovered by Caillé, Mollien, the Cander brothers. And, though he nowhere reminds us that when the Portuguese landed on the banks of the Congo in 1498, they found a rich and flourishing state there and that the courtiers of Ambas were dressed in robes of silk and brocade, at least he knows that Africa had brought itself up to a juridical concept of the state, and he is aware, living in the very flood of imperialism, that European civilization, after all, is only one more civilization among many — and not the most merciful. [9]

I put the white man back into his place; growing bolder, I jostled him and told him point-blank, "Get used to me, I am not getting used to anyone." I shouted my laughter to the stars. The white man, I could see, was resentful. His reaction time lagged interminably . . . I had won. I was jubilant.

"Lay aside your history, your investigations of the past, and try to feel yourself into our rhythm. In a society such as ours, industrialized to the highest degree, dominated by scientism, there is no longer room for your sensitivity. One must be tough if one is to be allowed to live. What matters now is no longer playing the game of the world but subjugating it with integers and atoms. Oh, certainly, I will be told, now and then when we are worn out by our lives in big buildings, we will turn to you as we do to our children — to the innocent, the ingenuous, the spontaneous. We will turn to you as to the childhood of the world. You are so real in your life — so funny, that is. Let us run away for a little while from our ritualized, polite civilization and let us relax, bend to those heads, those adorably expressive faces. In a way, you reconcile us with ourselves."

Thus my unreason was countered with reason, my reason with "real reason." Every hand was a losing hand for me. I analysed my heredity. I made a complete audit of my ailment. I wanted to be typically Negro — it was no longer possible. I wanted to be white — that was a joke. And, when I tried, on the level of ideas and intellectual activity, to reclaim my negritude, it was snatched away from me. Proof was presented that my effort was only a term in the dialectic:

> But there is something more important: The Negro, as we have said, creates an anti-racist racism for himself. In no sense does he wish to rule the world: he seeks the abolition of all ethnic privileges, wherever they come from; he asserts his solidarity with the oppressed of all colours. At once the subjective, existential, ethnic idea of *negritude* "passes," as Hegel puts it, into the objective, positive, exact idea of *proletariat*. "For Césaire," Senghor says, "the white man is the symbol of capital as the Negro is that of labour . . . Beyond the black-skinned men of his race it is the battle of the world proletariat that is his song."
>
> That is easy to say, but less easy to think out. And undoubtedly it is no coincidence that the most ardent poets of negritude are at the same time militant Marxists.
>
> But that does not prevent the idea of race from mingling with that of class: The first is concrete and particular, the second is universal and abstract; the one stems from what Jaspers calls understanding and the other from intellection; the first is the result of a psychobiological syncretism and the second is a methodical construction based on experience. In fact, negritude appears as the minor term of a dialectical progression: The theoretical and practical assertion of the supremacy of the white man is its thesis; the position of negritude as an antithetical value is the moment of negativity. But this negative moment is insufficient by itself, and the Negroes who employ it know this very well; they know that it is intended to prepare the synthesis or realization of the human in a society without races. Thus negritude is the root of its own destruction, it is a transition and not a conclusion, a means and not an ultimate end.[10]

When I read that page, I felt that I had been robbed of my last chance. I said to my friends, "The generation of the younger black poets has just suffered a blow that can never be forgiven." Help had been sought from a friend of the coloured peoples, and that friend had found no better response than to point out the relativity of what they were doing. For once, that born Hegelian had forgotten that consciousness has to lose itself in the night of the absolute, the only condition to attain to consciousness of self. In opposition to rationalism, he summoned up the negative side, but he forgot that this negativity draws its worth from an almost substantive absoluteness. A consciousness committed to experience is ignorant, has to be ignorant, of the essences and the determinations of its being.

Orphée Noir is a date in the intellectualization of the *experience* of being black. And Sartre's mistake was not only to seek the source of the source but in a certain sense to block that source:

> Will the source of Poetry be dried up? Or will the great black flood, in spite of everything, colour the sea into which it pours itself? It does not

matter: Every age has its own poetry; in every age the circumstances of history choose a nation, a race, a class to take up the torch by creating situations that can be expressed or transcended only through Poetry; sometimes the poetic impulse coincides with the revolutionary impulse, and sometimes they take different courses. Today let us hail the turn of history that will make it possible for the black men to utter "the great Negro cry with a force that will shake the pillars of the world" (Césaire).[11]

And so it is not I who make a meaning for myself, but it is the meaning that was already there, pre-exisiting, waiting for me. It is not out of my bad nigger's misery, my bad nigger's teeth, my bad nigger's hunger that I will shape a torch with which to burn down the world, but it is the torch that was already there, waiting for that turn of history.

In terms of consciousness, the black consciousness is held out as an absolute density, as filled with itself, a stage preceding any invasion, any abolition of the ego by desire. Jean-Paul Sartre, in this work, has destroyed black zeal. In opposition to historical becoming, there had always been the unforeseeable. I needed to lose myself completely in negritude. One day, perhaps, in the depths of that unhappy romanticism . . .

In any case I *needed* not to know. This struggle, this new decline had to take on an aspect of completeness. Nothing is more unwelcome than the commonplace: "You'll change, my boy; I was like that too when I was young . . . you'll see, it will all pass."

The dialectic that brings necessity into the foundation of my freedom drives me out of myself. It shatters my unreflected position. Still in terms of consciousness, black consciousness is immanent in its own eyes. I am not a potentiality of something, I am wholly what I am. I do not have to look for the universal. No probability has any place inside me. My Negro consciousness does not hold itself out as a lack. It *is*. It is its own follower.

But, I will be told, your statements show a misreading of the processes of history. Listen then:

Africa I have kept your memory Africa
you are inside me
Like the splinter in the wound
like a guardian fetish in the centre of the village
make me the stone in your sling
make my mouth the lips of your wound
make my knees the broken pillars of your abasement
AND YET
I want to be of your race alone
workers peasants of all lands . . .

. . . white worker in Detroit black peon in Alabama
uncountable nation in capitalist slavery
destiny ranges us shoulder to shoulder
repudiating the ancient maledictions of blood taboos
we roll away the ruins of our solitudes
If the flood is a frontier
we will strip the gully of its endless
covering flow
If the Sierra is a frontier
we will smash the jaws of the volcanoes
upholding the Cordilleras
and the plain will be the parade ground of the dawn
where we regroup our forces sundered
by the deceits of our masters
As the contradiction among the features
creates the harmony of the face
we proclaim the oneness of the suffering
and the revolt
of all the peoples on all the face of the earth
   and we mix the mortar of the age of brotherhood
   out of the dust of idols.[12]

Exactly, we will reply, Negro experience is not a whole, for there is not
merely *one* Negro, there are *Negroes*. What a difference, for instance, in this
other poem:

The white man killed my father
Because my father was proud
The white man raped my mother
Because my mother was beautiful
The white man wore out my brother in the hot sun
   of the roads
Because my brother was strong
Then the white man came to me
His hands red with blood
Spat his contempt into my black face
Out of his tyrant's voice:
"Hey boy, a basin, a towel, water."[13]

Or this other one:

> My brother with teeth that glisten at the compliments
>   of hypocrites
> My brother with gold-rimmed spectacles
> Over eyes that turn blue at the sound of the Master's
>   voice
> My poor brother in dinner jacket with its silk lapels
> Clucking and whispering and strutting through the
>   drawing rooms of Condescension
> How pathetic you are
> The sun of your native country is nothing more now
>   than a shadow
> On your composed civilized face
> And your grandmother's hut
> Brings blushes into cheeks made white by years of
>   abasement and *Mea culpa*
> But when regurgitating the flood of lofty empty words
> Like the load that presses on your shoulders
> You walk again on the rough red earth of Africa
> These words of anguish will state the rhythm of your
>   uneasy gait
> I feel so alone, so alone here![14]

From time to time one would like to stop. To state reality is a wearing task. But, when one has taken it into one's head to try to express existence, one runs the risk of finding only the nonexistent. What is certain is that, at the very moment when I was trying to grasp my own being, Sartre, who remained The Other, gave me a name and thus shattered my last illusion.[15] While I was saying to him:

> "My negritude is neither a tower nor a cathedral,
> it thrusts into the red flesh of the sun,
> it thrusts into the burning flesh of the sky,
> it hollows through the dense dismay of its own pillar
> of patience . . . "

while I was shouting that, in the paroxysm of my being and my fury, he was reminding me that my blackness was only a minor term. In all truth, in all truth, I tell you, my shoulders slipped out of the framework of the world, my feet could no longer feel the touch of the ground. Without a Negro past, without a Negro future, it was impossible for me live my Negrohood. Not yet white, no longer wholly black, I was damned. Jean-Paul Sartre had forgotten that the Negro suffers in his body quite differently from the white man.[16] Between the white man and me the connexion was irrevocably one of transcendence.[17]

But the constancy of my love had been forgotten. I defined myself as an absolute intensity of beginning. So I took up my negritude, and with tears in my eyes I put its machinery together again. What had been broken to pieces was rebuilt, reconstructed by the intuitive lianas of my hands.

My cry grew more violent: I am a Negro, I am a Negro, I am a Negro . . .

And there was my poor brother—living out his neurosis to the extreme and finding himself paralysed:

THE NEGRO: I can't, ma'am.
LIZZIE: Why not?
THE NEGRO: I can't shoot white folks.
LIZZIE: Really! That would bother them, wouldn't it?
THE NEGRO: They're white folks, ma'am.
LIZZIE: So what? Maybe they got a right to bleed you like a pig just because they're white?
THE NEGRO: But they're white folks.

A feeling of inferiority? No, a feeling of non-existence. Sin is Negro as virtue is white. All those white men in a group, guns in their hands, cannot be wrong. I am guilty. I do not know of what, but I know that I am no good.

THE NEGRO: That's how it goes, ma'am. That's how it always goes with white folks.
LIZZIE: You too? You feel guilty?
THE NEGRO: Yes, ma'am.

It is Bigger Thomas—he is afraid, he is terribly afraid. He is afraid, but of what is he afraid? Of himself. No one knows yet who he is, but he knows that fear will fill the world when the world finds out. And when the world knows, the world always expects something of the Negro. He is afraid lest the world know, he is afraid of the fear that the world would feel if the world knew. Like that old woman on her knees who begged me to tie her to her bed:

"I just know, Doctor: Any minute that thing will take hold of me."
"What thing?"
"The wanting to kill myself. Tie me down, I'm afraid."

In the end, Bigger Thomas acts. To put an end to his tension, he acts, he responds to the world's anticipation.[18]

So it is with the character in *If He Hollers Let Him Go*[19]—who does precisely what he did not want to do. That big blonde who was always in his way, weak, sensual, offered, open, fearing (desiring) rape, became his mistress in the end.

The Negro is a toy in the white man's hands; so, in order to shatter the hellish cycle, he explodes. I cannot go to a film without seeing myself. I wait for me. In the interval, just before the film starts, I wait for me. The people in the theatre are watching me, examining me, waiting for me. A Negro groom is going to appear. My heart makes my head swim.

The crippled veteran of the Pacific war says to my brother, "Resign yourself to your colour the way I got used to my stump; we're both victims."[20]

Nevertheless with all my strength I refuse to accept that amputation. I feel in myself a soul as immense as the world, truly a soul as deep as the deepest of rivers, my chest has the power to expand without limit. I am a master and I am advised to adopt the humility of the cripple. Yesterday, awakening to the world, I saw the sky turn upon itself utterly and wholly. I wanted to rise, but the disembowelled silence fell back upon me, its wings paralysed. Without responsibility, straddling Nothingness and Infinity, I began to weep.

NOTES

1. Jean Lhermitte, *L'Image de notre corps* (Paris: Nouvelle Revue critique, 1939), p. 17.

2. Sir Alan Burns, *Colour Prejudice* (London: Allen & Unwin, 1948), p. 16.

3. Jean-Paul Sartre, *Anti-Semite and Jew* (New York: Grove Press, 1960), pp. 112–13.

4. Ibid., p. 115.

5. Jon Alfred Mjoen, "Harmonic and Disharmonic Race-crossings," The Second International Congress of Eugenics (1921), *Eugenics in Race and State*, vol. II, p. 60, quoted in Sir Alan Burns, op. cit., p. 120.

6. "Ce que l'homme noir apporte," in Claude Nordey, *L'Homme de couleur* (Paris: Plon, 1939), pp. 309–10.

7. Léopold Senghor, "Ce que l'homme noir apporte," in Nordey, ibid., p. 205.

8. Aimé Césaire, Introduction to Victor Schoelcher, *Esclavage et colonisation* (Paris: Presses Universitaires de France, 1948), p. 7.

9. Ibid., p. 8.

10. Jean-Paul Sartre, *Orphée Noir*, preface to *Anthologie de la nouvelle poésie nègre et malgache* (Paris: Presses Universitaires de France, 1948), p. xl ff.

11. Ibid., p. xliv.

12. Jacques Roumain, "Bois-d'Ebène," Prelude in *Anthologie de la nouvelle poésie nègre et malgache*, p. 113.

13. David Diop, "Le temps du martyre," in ibid., p. 174.

14. David Diop, "Le Renégat."

15. Jean-Paul Sartre, *The Respectful Prostitute*, in *Three Plays* (New York: Knopf, 1949), pp. 189, 191. Originally, *La Putain respectueuse* (Paris: Gallimard, 1947). See also *Home of the Brave*, a film by Mark Robson.

16. Though Sartre's speculations on the existence of The Other may be correct (to the extent, we must remember, to which *Being and Nothingness* describes an alienated consciousness), their application to a black consciousness proves fallacious. That is because the white man is not only The Other but also the master, whether real or imaginary.

17. In the sense in which the word is used by Jean Wahl in *Existence humaine et transcendance* (Neuchâtel: La Baconnière, 1944).

18. Richard Wright, *Native Son* (New York: Harper, 1940).

19. By Chester Himes (Garden City: Doubleday, 1945).

20. *Home of the Brave.*

CHAPTER 8

Bichon and the Blacks

Roland Barthes

Match has printed a story which has a good deal to say about our petit-bourgeois myth of the Black: a young couple, both professors, have made an expedition into Cannibal country to do some painting; they have taken with them their months-old baby, Bichon. *Match* goes into ecstasy over the courage of all three.

First of all, nothing is more irritating than heroism without an object. A society is in a serious situation when it undertakes to develop gratuitously the *forms* of its virtues. If the dangers incurred by baby Bichon (torrents, wild animals, diseases, etc.) were real, it was literally stupid to impose them, on the mere pretext of doing some painting in Africa and satisfying the dubious ambition of getting on canvas "a debauch of sun and light"; it is even more reprehensible to disguise this stupidity as a piece of bravery, all quite decorative and moving. We see how courage functions here: a formal and empty action, the more unmotivated it is, the more respect it inspires; this is a boy-scout civilization, where the code of feelings and values is completely detached from concrete problems of solidarity or progress. What we have is the old myth of "character," i.e., of "training." Bichon's exploits are of the same sort as the more spectacular feats of mountain climbing or balloon ascension: demonstrations of an ethical order, which receive their final value only from the publicity they are given. In our culture, there frequently corresponds to the socialized forms of collective sport a superlative form of star sport: here physical effort does not institute man's apprenticeship to his group, but instead an ethic of vanity, an exoticism of endurance, a minor mystique of risk, monstrously severed from any concern with sociability.

The trip Bichon's parents made into a region situated quite vaguely and significantly labeled the Country of the Red Negroes, a kind of fictional site whose actual characteristics are skillfully attenuated but whose legendary name already proposes a terrifying ambiguity between the color of their painted skins and the human blood they supposedly drink—the trip is presented in the vocabulary of conquest: one sets out unarmed, no doubt, but "armed with palette and brush," just as if it were a hunting safari or a military expedition, made under ungrateful material conditions (the heroes are always poor, our bureaucratic society does not favor noble departures), but rich in courage—and in its splendid (or grotesque) uselessness. Baby Bichon is assigned the Parsifal role, contrasting his blondness, innocence, curls, and smile to the infernal world of black and red skins, scarifications, and hideous masks. Naturally, it is the white gentleness which emerges victorious: Bichon subjugates the "man-eaters" and becomes their idol (the White Men are definitely cut out to become gods). Bichon is a good little Frenchman, he tames and conquers the savages without firing a shot: at the age of two, instead of being perambulated in the Bois de Boulogne, he is already working for his country, just like his daddy, who, without our quite knowing why, leads the life of a cameleer and tracks down "looters" in the bush.

We have already divined the image of the Black taking shape behind this tonic little tale: first of all, the Black is frightening, he is a cannibal; and if we find Bichon heroic, it is because he in fact risks being eaten. Without the implicit presence of this risk, the story would lose all its shock value, the reader would not be scared; hence occasions are multiplied in which the white baby is alone, abandoned, carefree, and exposed in a circle of potentially threatening Blacks (the only entirely reassuring image of the Black is that of the *boy*, the domesticated barbarian, coupled, moreover, with that other commonplace of all good African stories: the *thieving boy* who vanishes with his master's things). With each image we are meant to tremble over what might happen: this is never specified, the narrative is "objective," but it actually depends on the pathetic collusion of white flesh and black skin, of innocence and cruelty, of spirituality and magic; Beauty subjugates the Beast, Daniel is nuzzled by lions, and a civilization of the soul triumphs over the barbarism of instinct.

The profound cunning of Operation Bichon is to display the world of the Blacks through the eyes of a white child: here everything will look like a Punch-and-Judy show. Now, since this reduction exactly corresponds to the image "common sense" provides of these exotic arts and customs, we merely confirm *Match*'s reader in his childish vision, settled a little deeper in that impotence to imagine others which I have already pointed out apropos of petit-bourgeois myths. Ultimately the Black has no complete and autonomous life: he is a bizarre object, reduced to a parasitical function, that of diverting the white man by his vaguely threatening *baroque*: Africa is a more or less dangerous *guignol*.

And now, if we will contrast with this general imagery (*Match*: approximately a million readers) the ethnologists' efforts to demystify the Black phenomenon, the rigorous precautions they have long since taken when obliged to employ such ambiguous notions as "Primitives" or "Archaic Societies," the intellectual probity of such men as Mauss, Lévi-Strauss, or Leroi-Gourhan confronting the old racial terms in their various disguises, we will better understand one of our major servitudes: the oppressive divorce of knowledge and mythology. Science proceeds rapidly on its way, but the collective representations do not follow, they are centuries behind, kept stagnant in their errors by power, the press, and the values of order.

We are still living in a *pre*-Voltairean mentality, that is what must be said over and over. For in the age of Montesquieu or of Voltaire, if we were astonished by the Persians or the Hurons, at least it was in order to grant them the benefit of ingenuity. Today Voltaire would not write up Bichon's adventures the way *Match* has done: instead, he would imagine some cannibal (or Korean) Bichon contending with the napalmized *guignol* of the West.

CHAPTER 9

African Grammar

Roland Barthes

The official vocabulary of African affairs is, as we might suspect, purely axio-matic. Which is to say that it has no value as communication, but only as in-timidation. It therefore constitutes a *writing*, i.e., a language intended to bring about a coincidence between norms and facts, and to give a cynical reality the guarantee of a noble morality. In a general way, it is a language which functions essentially as a code, i.e., the words have no relation to their con-tent, or else a contrary one. It is a writing which we might call cosmetic, be-cause it aims at covering the facts with a sound of language, or if we prefer, with the sufficient sign of language. I should like to indicate briefly the way in which a lexicon and a grammar can be politically committed.

BANDE / BANDE (of outlaws, rebels, or civil criminals). — This is the very ex-ample of an axiomatic language. The disparagement of the vocabulary here serves in a precise way to deny the state of war, which permits annihilating the notion of an interlocutor. "No arguments with outlaws." The moraliza-tion of language thus permits referring the problem of peace to an arbitrary change of vocabulary.

When the "band" is French, it is sublimated under the name of *community*.

DÉCHIREMENT / LACERATION (cruel, painful). — This term helps accredit the notion of History's irresponsibility. The state of war is masked under the no-ble garment of tragedy, as if the conflict were essentially Evil, and not a (remediable) evil. Colonization evaporates, engulfed in the halo of an impo-tent lament, which *recognizes* the misfortune in order to establish it only the more successfully.

Phraseology: "The government of the Republic is resolved to make all possible efforts in order to bring to an end the cruel lacerations Morocco is suffering." (Letter from Monsieur Coty to Ben Arafa.)

" . . . the Moroccan people, painfully divided against itself . . . " (Declaration by Ben Arafa.)

DÉSHONORER / DISHONOR. — We know that in ethnology, at least according to Lévi-Strauss's very suggestive hypothesis, *mana* is a kind of algebraic symbol, intended to represent "an indeterminate value of signification, in itself without meaning and therefore capable of receiving any meaning, whose unique function is to fill a gap between signifier and signified." *Honor* is quite specifically our *mana*, something like a blank place in which we arrange the entire collection of inadmissible meanings and which we make sacred in the manner of a taboo.

Phraseology: "It would be to dishonor the Moslem populations to let it be supposed that these men could be considered in France as their representatives. It would also be to dishonor France." (Communiqué of the Ministry of the Interior.)

DESTIN / DESTINY. — It is at the very moment when the colonized peoples are beginning to deny the fatality of their condition that the bourgeois vocabulary makes the greatest use of the word *Destiny*. Like honor, destiny is a *mana*, in which we modestly collect the most sinister determinisms of colonization.

Naturally, Destiny exists only in a linked form. It is not military conquest which has subjected Algeria to France, it is a conjunction performed by Providence which has united two destinies. The link is declared indissoluble in the very period when it is dissolving with an explosiveness which cannot be concealed.

Phraseology: "We intend, as for ourselves, to give the peoples whose destiny is linked to ours a true independence within voluntary association." (Monsieur Pinay to the UN.)

DIEU / GOD. — Sublimated form of the French government.

Phraseology: "When the Omnipotent designated us to wield supreme power . . . " (Declaration by Ben Arafa.)

" . . . With the abnegation and the sovereign dignity of which you have always given the example . . . Your Majesty thus intends to obey the will of the Almighty." (Letter from Monsieur Coty to Ben Arafa, dismissed by the government.)

GUERRE / WAR. — The goal is to deny the thing. For this, two means are available: either to name it as little as possible (most frequent procedure); or else to give it the meaning of its contrary (more cunning procedure, which is at the basis of almost all the mystifications of bourgeois discourse). *War* is then used in the sense of *peace*, and *pacification* in the sense of *war*.

Phraseology: "War does not keep measures of pacification from being taken." (General de Monsabert.) By which we are to understand that (official) peace does not, fortunately, prevent (real) war.

MISSION / MISSION. — This is the third *mana* word. Into it we can put whatever is wanted: schools, electricity, Coca-Cola, police operations, raids, death sentences, concentration camps, freedom, civilization, and the "presence" of France.

Phraseology: "You know, however, that France has a mission in Africa which she alone can fulfill." (Monsieur Pinay to the UN.)

POLITIQUE / POLITICS. — Assigned a limited domain: on the one hand, there is France; and on the other, politics. North African affairs, when they concern France, are not within the domain of politics. When things become serious, abandon Politics for the Nation. For men of the Right, Politics is the Left: *they* are France.

Phraseology: "To seek to protect the French community and the virtues of France is not to engage in politics." (General Tricon-Dunois.)

In a contrary sense and bracketed with the word *conscience* (*politics of conscience*), the word *politics* becomes euphemistic; it then signifies: a practical sense of spiritual realities, the nuance which permits a Christian to set out in good conscience to "pacify" Africa.

Phraseology: " . . . To refuse service *a priori* in an army imminently to serve in Africa, in order to avoid such a situation (to contradict an inhuman order), this abstract Tolstoyism cannot be identified with a politics of conscience, for it is no politics at all." (Dominican editorial in *La Vie intellectuelle*.)

POPULATION / POPULATION. — This is a favorite word of the bourgeois vocabulary. It serves as an antidote to the excessively brutal *classes*, which moreover is "without reality." *Population* is meant to depoliticize the plurality of groups and minorities by pushing individuals back into a neutral, passive collection which is entitled to the bourgeois pantheon only on the level of a politically unconscious existence. The term is generally ennobled by its plural: *the Moslem populations*, which does not fail to suggest a difference in maturity between the Metropolitan unity and the pluralism of the colonized, France *gathering* beneath her what is by nature diverse and numerous.

When it is necessary to make a disparaging judgment (war occasionally compels such severities), we readily fraction the population into *elements*. Elements are generally fanatic or manipulated. (For only fanaticism or unconsciousness can impel anyone to try to abandon colonized status.)

Phraseology: "The elements of the population which have been able to join the rebels under circumstances . . . " (Communiqué from the Ministry of the Interior.)

SOCIAL / SOCIAL. — *Social* is always bracketed with *economic*. This duo uniformly functions as an alibi, i.e., it announces or justifies on each occasion certain repressive operations, to the point where we might say that it signifies them. The *social* is essentially schools (France's civilizing mission, education of overseas peoples, gradually led to maturity); the *economic* is *interests*, always *obvious* and *reciprocal*, which *indissolubly* link Africa and Metropolitan France. These "progressive" terms, once suitably drained, can function with impunity as magical units.

Phraseology: "Social and economic domain, social and economic installations."

The predominance of substantives in the whole vocabulary, of which we have just provided a few samples, derives obviously from the huge consumption of concepts necessary to the cover-up of reality. Though general and advanced to the last degree of decomposition, the exhaustion of this language does not attack verbs and substantives in the same way: it destroys the verb and inflates the noun. Here moral inflation bears on neither objects nor actions, but always on ideas, "notions," whose assemblage obeys less a communication purpose than the necessity of a petrified code. Codification of the official language and its substantivation thus go hand in hand, for the myth is fundamentally nominal, insofar as nomination is the first procedure of distraction.

The verb undergoes a curious legerdemain: if it is a main verb, we find it reduced to the state of a simple copula, meant simply to posit the existence or the quality of the myth. (Monsieur Pinay to the UN: "*There would be* an illusory détente . . . *it would be* inconceivable . . . *What would be* a nominal independence? . . .* " etc.) The verb arduously attains full semantic status only on the level of the future, the possible, or the unintentional, in a remote distance where the myth runs less risk of being contradicted. (A Moroccan government *will be constituted . . . called upon to negotiate* reforms . . . the effort undertaken by France *with a view to constructing* a free association . . . etc.)

In its presentation, the substantive generally requires what two excellent grammarians, Damourette and Pichon, who lacked neither rigor nor humor in their terminology, used to call: the *notorious plate*, which means that the substance of the noun is always presented to us as known. We are here at the very heart of the myth's formation: it is because France's *mission*, the *laceration* of the Moroccan people, or the *destiny* of Algeria are given grammatically as postulates (a quality generally conferred upon them by the use of the definite article) that we cannot contest them discursively. Notoriety is the first form of naturalization.

I have already observed the quite banal emphasis put on certain plural forms (*populations*). It must be added that this emphasis overvalues or depreciates at will certain intentions: *populations* installs a euphoric sentiment of pacifically subjugated multitudes; but when we speak of *elementary nationalisms*, the plural aims at degrading further, if it is possible, the notion of (enemy) nationalism, by reducing it to a collection of mediocre units. This is what our two grammarians, experts *avant la lettre* in African affairs, had further foreseen by distinguishing the *massive plural* from the *numerative plural*: in the first expression, the plural flatters an idea of mass; in the second, it insinuates an idea of division. Thus grammar inflects the myth: it delegates its plurals to different moral tasks.

The adjective (or the adverb) often plays a curiously ambiguous role: it seems to proceed from an anxiety, from the sentiment that the substantives used, despite their notorious character, have undergone a wear and tear which cannot be entirely concealed; whence the necessity to reinvigorate them: independence becomes *true*, aspirations *authentic*, destinies *indissolubly* linked. Here the adjective aims at clearing the noun of its past disappointments, presenting it in a new, innocent, credible state. As in the case of main verbs, the adjective confers a future value upon discourse. Past and present are the business of the substantives, great concepts in which the idea alone dispenses us from proof (Mission, Independence, Friendship, Cooperation, etc.); action and predicate, in order to be irrefutable, must take shelter behind some unreal form: finality, promise, or adjuration.

Unfortunately, these adjectives of reinvigoration are worn out almost as fast as they are used, so that it is finally the adjectival relaunching of the myth which most certainly designates its inflation. It suffices to read *true, authentic, indissoluble,* or *unanimous* to get wind of the emptiness of the rhetoric. This is because at bottom these adjectives, which we might call adjectives of essence, because they develop under a modal form the substance of the name they accompany — these adjectives cannot modify anything: independence cannot be anything but independent, friendship friendly, and cooperation unanimous. By the impotence of their effort, these wretched adjectives here come to manifest the ultimate health of language. Try as the official rhetoric will to reinforce the coverings of reality, there is a moment when the words resist it and oblige it to reveal beneath the myth the alternative of lie or truth: independence is or is not, and all the adjectival designs which strive to give nothingness the qualities of being are the very signature of culpability.

CHAPTER 10

What Celie Knows That
You Should Know

Barbara Christian

> *At a climactic moment in* The Color Purple, Mister *taunts Celie:*
> *Look at you. You black, you pore, you ugly, you a woman.*
> *Goddam . . . You nothing at all.*
> *Celie retorts:*
> *I'm pore, I'm black, I may be ugly and can't cook . . .*
> *But I'm here.*

I begin my discussion about ways in which the study of Afro-American women's literature might enrich and extend knowledge with that excerpt from *The Color Purple* because it so succinctly articulates two worldviews. Mister's assessment of Celie's worth emphasizes her nothingness because she exists in realms of powerlessness and therefore of nonexistence in the world as he sees it. Because Celie is nothing, how can she know anything? Celie's affirmation of her own existence does not deny his categories of powerlessness; rather she insists that nonetheless she exists, that she knows something as a result of being at that intersection of categories that attempt to camouflage her existence.

It is precisely that intersection of categories that Mister lists, those of race, class, and gender, which Afro-American women writers have had to explore in order to articulate their subjects' existence. It is the knowledge that comes from living at such a sharp intersection, a point of contending categories of nothingness, which is so central to the literature, from Harriet Wilson's *Our Nig*, the first novel by an Afro-American woman to be published in this country, to Toni Morrison's recent *Beloved*. If there is any persistent motif in this literature, it is the illuminating of that which is perceived by others as not existing at all. To be black, poor, and a woman in American society has historically appeared and continues to appear to be "nothing at all," as Mister so grandly proclaims. Yet in knowing what it is to be a black woman, one knows not only that one exists, but also some essential truths about those "intellectual" categories—gender, race, class—of which all human beings partake.

Of course, the most obvious contribution that Afro-American women's literature can bring to knowledge is what it feels like, what it sounds like, what it means to be any number of black women in America. The exploration of this literature for those of us who are Afro-American women is to experience ourselves as subjects in contexts that help us to understand who we were as well as who we now are. In exploring ourselves as subjects, not only do we reflect on what *we* know, but we also know a great deal about those who are perceived as being "something" rather than "nothing at all." Let me demonstrate the interrelationship of these two aspects of knowledge by commenting on the first novel by an Afro-American woman to be published in this country, lest we conclude that such an orientation is due to prevailing black feminist ideology.

Harriet Wilson's *Our Nig* is both an expression of what it meant to be an indentured black girl enslaved in a white Northern household of the 1830s as well as an exploration of the ways in which race affects the relations among women. In writing her autobiographical novel, Mrs. Wilson presents Frado, her girl-protagonist, as brutally abused by her white Northern mistress, Mrs. Bellmont. Although they are both women, Mrs. Bellmont perceives Frado not as a girl but as a thing from which she intends to get as much work as possible. In this context, gender bonds are meaningless and race is the primary determinant of the power relations between these two women.

Still *Our Nig* underscores the effects of gender on Frado's life. Mag, her mother, is a working-class white orphan who is seduced at an early age by a prosperous white man and becomes pregnant. Although the child dies, it is that momentous event in Mag's life that plunges her into a life of abject poverty and social ostracism from which she is barely saved by Jim, a black man who marries her and is the father of her two children. Mrs. Wilson documents not only the results of Mag's fall from grace because she is a woman but also Jim's hard life as a black man who can barely support his family and who eventually dies from overwork. The author emphasizes how Mag's ostracism from society is due both to gender and race and how it affects her as a mother. Near starvation, this mother does what no mother is supposed to do. She abandons her child, Frado, precipitating the terrible existence the girl experiences at the Bellmonts'. Like Celie, Frado is poor, black, and a woman. Like Celie, Mrs. Wilson, the author of *Our Nig*, insists on telling her own story, insists on her own apparently unique experience even as she outlines the intersection of race, gender, and class factors that determined her childhood.

But not only does this intersection affect the actual story she tells, it is the very reason for Mrs. Wilson's authorship. She tells us in her preface that it was her need to support her ailing child that was the initial impulse for *publishing* her story. Because she is a wife abandoned by her husband and thus a poor mother, she tried, as did so many nineteenth-century American women, to make some money through writing. Nina Baym's study of white women writers of the nineteenth century indicates that economics was one major reason why so many of them became professional romance writers. Harriet Wilson's *Our Nig* suggests that like white women, black women, also in need of income, sought to make a living through their pen.

But if that was her only intention, Harriet Wilson underscores it by constructing a story that she tells us in her preface may well offend her brethren. In the construction of her novel, she opposed the abolitionist conventions of black William Wells Brown's *Clotel* as well as white Harriet Beecher Stowe's *Uncle Tom's Cabin*. For through the character of Mrs. Bellmont she dramatically challenges their claim that Northern white women were the likeliest allies of suffering, oppressed blacks. In addition, Mrs. Wilson emphasizes that it is a fugitive slave turned abolitionist-lecturer who marries Frado and abandons her and her child, thus questioning the idea that all black abolitionists were committed to the women of their race. It is likely that it is precisely those challenges to prevailing ideas that plunged Mrs. Wilson's novel into oblivion. Not only was her venture unsuccessful, not only did her son die, but it was not until this decade that her novel was rediscovered.

Alice Walker's *The Color Purple* was published in 1983, the same year that Henry Louis Gates's edition of the newly discovered *Our Nig* was released, so it is unlikely that she was able to read that nineteenth-century novel while she was writing her own. Yet, although Mrs. Wilson and Walker wrote some hundred years apart, they exhibit similar attitudes about black women as subjects.

The Color Purple also focuses on intersections of race, class, and gender so evident in much of Afro-American women's literature. It is about a young black woman's freeing of herself from incest, rape, and wife beating within a black patriarchal family as well as her growing understanding of her worth. She does this not only through the support and love given to her from her sister-in-law, Sofia, her lover-friend, Shug, and her blood sister, Nettie, but also through her writing. Her letters to God and then to Nettie are her meditations on her life, her attempt to understand her reality, even as they are a record of her society's structure. Like *Our Nig, The Color Purple* explores the relations within a family from the perspective of a black girl-woman even as it demonstrates how racism, sexism, and class values are modes of oppression that intersect.

Imagine Mister as another version of the hard-working Jim. In this context he is a Southern black of the Reconstruction period whose family is descended from slaves and slave owners and who has observed the means by which white men maintain power. Rather than marrying a white woman, as Jim did, an act that in the South would precipitate his death, he imitates the men who have oppressed him. For he inherits from his hard-working father not only property and middle-class status but the modes of behavior that white men, who are above him, exhibit. Those who are subject to his will, those with less power than he, are his female kin, his wife, and his children. Just as he must at all times call white men Mister, a symbol of his power relationship to them, he insists that those below him call him Mister.

Like Frado, it is the loss of her parents that leads to Celie's rape by her stepfather and her abusive marriage to Mister. Just as Frado is beaten and kept in her place, Celie is beaten and kept in *her* place. Just as Frado is a thing to be used, Celie is a thing to be used. But whereas Frado's only means of salvation during her chidhood are the apparently compassionate but ineffectual white men who promise her heavenly rather than earthly release, Celie has access to other black women who help her to build trust in herself and to oppose Mister and all that might restrict her. Like Frado, it is Celie's knowledge that she *can* fight that is the beginning of her release from bondage. Unlike Frado, whose opponent is a white woman, Celie must fight a black man, her husband who does not love her and who desires another woman. Like Frado, Celie lives in a middle-class household. Yet neither of them, as black women, shares in whatever power that status is supposed to signify. Whereas Frado is "nig" in the Bellmont house, Celie is "wife" and therefore nonexistent in her husband's house. When Harpo, her stepson, asks his father why he beats Celie, Mister simply and emphatically states, "She my wife."

Both Mrs. Bellmont and Mister are clearly frustrated beings. We can surmise from Frado's description of her employer that rather than being "an angel of house," a concept that became the norm for women in the late nineteenth century, she is its "devil." Clearly the household she runs is not sufficiently engrossing for her; she lacks avenues, outlets, although Frado, her victim, has little awareness of the lacks her employer feels. Because Mrs. Bellmont is more powerful than Frado, she vents her frustration on the girl, as so many whites have on blacks. In contrast, Celie does learn why Mister is so frustrated. In his weakness and in his desire to hold onto the land his father bequeathed to him, he has given up Shug, the woman he loves but cannot own. Like Mrs. Bellmont, he assaults those weaker than he — his wife and his children. Both *their* stories suggest to us that dissatisfied people who too are restricted by society exercise power over others because they *can*.

Like Mrs. Wilson, Celie writes, against all odds, to affirm her existence. It is because Celie needs to understand what is happening to her that she writes her letters to God. Like Mrs. Wilson, Alice Walker published her novel to assert that Celies do exist, as they had in her own family. For Celie's character is based on Rachel, Walker's step-grandmother, just as Frado's ex-

perience is based on the life experience of Mrs. Wilson. Through her im-
aginative retelling of Rachel's story, Walker claims for her maternal ancestor
that knowledge that is an intersection of sexism and racism, a racism peculiar
to America, an intense sexism that was common through much of the world
at the beginning of the twentieth century. That Alice Walker's novel has not
been repressed, as Mrs. Wilson was, is an indication of a literary activism
among black women like Mrs. Wilson, rather than primarily a measure of
these two writers' respective literary talents.

For there is no question that Mrs. Wilson had a fine sense of the demands
of writing a narrative, despite her claims of ineptitude in her preface. *Our Nig*
is written in a strong, fluent prose. There is in Mrs. Wilson's rendering of her
voice a sense of conviction in her storytelling skills. And she buttresses that
voice with quotations from innumerable poets so that the reader could not
ignore her knowledge of literature. Like her protagonist, Frado, literacy is
for her a source of consolation, a means by which she gives order and meaning to her experience. As important, the author writes her work in a form
that combines the major elements of two major genres of the day: the sentimental romance and the slave narrative, interestingly two forms that her
literary descendant, Alice Walker, would put to great use in writing *The Color
Purple*. Despite her low status in the society, despite her claims that she was
"nothing at all," Mrs. Wilson drew from the two literary traditions of which,
it could be said, she was naturally a part—that of "women's" literature and
that of "Afro-American" literature. She therefore undercut the idea that
"free" black people of the day were not reading, were not scrutinizing those
forms in which the dominant popular literature was being written. Ralph El-
lison's blurb for the republication of *Our Nig* in 1983 put it succinctly:
"Professor Gates' discovery confirms my suspicion that there was more 'free
floating literacy' available to Negroes than had been assumed." To that comment I would add that black women, as well as men, strove for literacy and
saw reading and writing as a means of articulating their existence as well as
a potential for advancement in the society.

Yet, despite Mrs. Wilson's remarkable achievement, her work went un-
mentioned for over a hundred years by black as well as white scholars. It is
not surprising that white scholars would not notice her novel since blacks
and women were typically disregarded in the literary area. Moreover, generally speaking, Afro-American scholars focused until recently on the men
who wrote; yet they did include, if only in footnotes, the works of women
like Frances Harper. What Wilson's omission from even their footnotes indicates is that she did not fit into the Afro-American political ideology of the
day. Her truth raised questions about the complex intersection of issues. At
a time when the emphasis was on abolition and uplift her story would have
been an embarrassment to her brethren. Further, Harriet Wilson was clearly

not a part of the visible Afro-American social and political groups of the time. That she managed to get her story published is itself a miracle. During the 1970s, the influence of the Black movement and the women's movement opened a space in which literary scholars began to question the established body of American literature. The result has been a revision of the literary canon and an investigation of what works of literature have been omitted from our national literary tradition as well as reasons for their omission. Clearly groups perceived as "other" were not supposed to have written literature worth considering. The space created by such questioning is surely one of the reasons why Henry Louis Gates could recognize *Our Nig* for the fascinating work it is. Still, that autobiographical novel's importance as an example of an Afro-American woman's attempt to forge a form out of the two literary traditions to which she was heir is just beginning to be examined.

For *Our Nig* is a part of both the Afro-American and the women's literary tradition. Such a fusion of traditions should be quite fascinating to literary scholars. Instead we are often restricted by our own categories of gender and race. If we look at the literary work that most focused on nineteenth-century American women's fiction, Nina Baym's *Women's Fiction: A Guide to Novels about Women in America, 1820–1870* (published in 1978), we could not expect to find reference to *Our Nig*, since Gates's edition of that work was not released until 1983. Still it is surprising that in her study, published during a period of intense interest in Afro-American women's literature, Baym uses the word "woman" so uncategorically. She appears not to have investigated the possibility that Afro-American women attempted to write fiction. Nor does she qualify her title or her text with the accurate adjective, *white* women, since her study is devoted exclusively to that group of women. An investigation into whether Afro-American women wrote sentimental fiction may have resulted in conclusions somewhat different from the ones she reaches. For example, writers of sentimental fiction might not, if they were also black, have been primarily middle class (Harriet Wilson was not). Issues of class that Baym discusses in this might also have been affected by her inclusion of black women's fiction.

On the other hand, contemporary male Afro-American literary commentators sometimes ignore the existence of *Our Nig* as an indication that black women as well as white women wrote sentimental romances. In his review of Alice Walker's *The Color Purple* in the January 29, 1987, edition of the *New York Review of Books*, Darryl Pinckney asserted that the book is closer to Harriet Beecher Stowe's works than it is to those of Zora Neale Hurston, for, he continues, *The Color Purple* is a form of the sentimental inspirational fiction of the nineteenth century. In referring to Harriet Beecher Stowe, Pinckney attempted to disqualify Alice Walker as belonging to the tradition of Afro-American literature; rather he implies that she belongs to the tradition of white women writers.

Whether *The Color Purple* is inspirational sentimental fiction is a point we could debate. What I would like to stress is Pinckney's omission of the fact that Afro-American women writers, like Wilson and Frances Harper, were participating in the development of sentimental romances and that their participation in that genre ought to qualify it as part of the tradition of Afro-American literature. Despite his allusion to Zora Neale Hurston (who too could be said to have used qualities of the sentimental romance in *Their Eyes Were Watching God*), Pinckney's assertion gives the impression that there are *not* important literary intersections among black and white writers, male as well as female, in this country. After all, one could, as he has, label Ishmael Reed's fiction "detective" fiction, a genre used by white men and women. More important is Pinckney's slightly hidden assumption that since black men did not often use the genre of the sentimental romance, that genre is not a part of the Afro-American literary tradition.

Harriet Wilson's use not only of the slave narrative so identified with black nineteenth century writers but also of the sentimental romance in 1859, as well as its use in the works of other nineteenth-century Afro-American women, suggests that free black women were relating to literary forms that would best express their experience as both black and woman. This quest continues among our writers, for contemporary Afro-American women writers utilize forms that could be identified as belonging to different traditions. Their participation in such traditions is enriching rather than restrictive.

Despite her adroit use of different genres, Mrs. Wilson could well have predicted, given the constraints of her time, that she would be unsuccessful in her publishing venture. Yet she insisted on telling *her* story from her particular point of view. Her use of italics throughout her text, a device that emphasizes that she is relating a truth contrary to what readers have come to believe, is a sure sign that she sees her experience as knowledge that must be recognized by others. She is insistent that what she knows needs to be known by others. Her attitude is important in her narrative; for if only *she* knows what she knows, she is left alone, not only in physical desolation but in a void that devises her existence. Her writing and publishing her subversive story underlines her insistence on her own existence, her insistence that it be acknowledged, respected, recognized by others. Listen to the final sentence of *Our Nig*. In concluding her tale about those who have determined so much of what her life has been and has become, Frado tells us that "[she] has passed from their memories, as Joseph from the butler's, but she will never cease to track them beyond mortal vision."

It is her truth, despite the prevailing traditional or alternative modes of representing reality, that Frado knows, that Celie knows. It is that contrariness that is at the core of so much of Afro-American women's literature, a contrariness that has often resulted in being silenced as Harriet Wilson was or in being rebuked as Alice Walker has been. That contrariness is a measure of health, of the insistence that counter to the societal perception of black women as being "nothing at all," their existence is knowledge that relates to us all.

For not only do *Our Nig* and *The Color Purple* explore poor black women as subjects, they also give us a finely tuned sense of their protagonists' society. Because Frado and Celie are at the bottom of society's ladder, they are likelier to experience more of the various strata of society. Those who are in positions of power do not have to pay attention to all those beneath them. They can be ignorant of those facts they do not want to know. Contrary to Mister's statement then, that because Celie is black, poor, and a woman, she knows nothing, contrary to the assertion that powerlessness means ignorance, Celie must know a great deal in order to survive. The powerless are particularly attuned to those who possess more power than they do. For the powerless, knowledge is essential to survival.

In beginning her story with Frado's mother's two falls, first into the quagmire of gender restraints, then into the bottomless pit of racism, Harriet Wilson tells a different story from those versions that envisioned the North as the Promised Land. The author presents us with a hierarchical view of society. Mag is near the bottom because she is a poor ophan girl. But she falls even lower when she commits the sin of getting pregnant without the sanctions of marriage. In so doing she becomes even more economically destitute. In other words, her class status is related to her gender and to the fact that she does not obey society's conventions. Of course the man who seduces her is not demeaned by his act, for he is the conqueror rather than the conquered. But beyond that, Mag has neither family nor resources to force him to submit to her wishes. Mrs. Wilson's description of Mag's fate is a clear indication that the author understands power relations between the sexes in society and how gender is affected by class status: she tells us that Mag "knew the voice of her charmer, so ravishing, sounded *far above* her," and that she thought "she could ascend to him and become an *equal.*" Instead, he "proudly garnered [her] as a trophy with those of other victims and left her to her fate."

As well, Mrs. Wilson describes Mag's fall into blackness in similar societal terms, for she knew marriages between Northern white women and black men were not acknowledged. Mulattoes exist, most of us have been told, because of relationships, most of them forced or illicit, between black women and white men. Thus, when Mag marries Jim, Mrs. Wilson emphasizes the differences in their reasons for their union. Jim sees Mag as a "treasure." He muses that "she'd be as much of a prize to me as she'd fall short of coming up to the mark with white folks." Mag accepts Jim because of her poverty and desolation. Mrs. Wilson comments:

> You can philosophize, gentle reader upon the impropriety of such unions, and preach dozens of sermons on the evils of amalgamation. *Want* is a more

powerful philosopher and preacher. Poor Mag she has sundered another bond which held her to her fellows. She has descended another step down the ladder to infamy. (p. 13)

Issues of class, race, and gender, then, are interactive in Mrs. Wilson's story. And her rendition focuses on how fixed societal status is in her time, and how status affects personality. Mag is already low on the scale when the novel opens because she is poor and an orphan. But she *is* virginal, her one prize — what Wilson calls a "priceless gem." That gem, she thinks, is a means to rising above her place in society. But in "giving up" her virginity, she sinks even lower. She is now a poor *soiled* orphan girl.

Yet black people were even lower on the social scale than Mag, who is poor, who is a woman, who knows sex. Wilson's description of Jim's attempt to support himself and his family suggests that he is only slightly above the status of a slave. His blackness gravely affects his economic status, and his attempt, if only a psychological one, to move closer to the status of whites by marrying a white woman suggests how restricted he has been. Still, although Jim is lower in status than Mag, because he is black and she is white, he is still a man and can alleviate, if only for a time, her destitute condition. Neither Mag's nor Jim's attempt to improve their status by relating to someone above them is successful, however. Instead, they "descend another step down."

Frado inherits from her parents their low standing. Not only is she black like her father, she is a woman like her mother. And she is a child, a being of especially low standing in nineteenth-century society. Because her mother is white, she is shut out from black as well as white society. Since her mother is rejected by her community and mothers are usually the link to a community, Frado is left without any resources beyond her parents.

By situating Frado's story in American culture, Wilson tells us not only that race, class, and gender intersect but that they are never pure, exclusive categories. None of these categories exist on their own. Rather, there are men or women of one class or another, of one race or another. Because of the ways in which we have tended to study these categories, we mention them only when we speak of the "non's — nonwhite, nonmale, non-middle-class," that is of what we assume to be the norm. But in today's world all human beings belong to at least one of these categories.

When we study Afro-American women's literature, we are compelled to see that when we say "woman," we often unconsciously mean *white women*; when we omit a racial designation, we tend not to differentiate gender *and* to mean nonwhite; when we say people, we mean those who are economically comfortable. Our adjectives — for example, black, poor, female — qualify what we have designated as universal. But suppose we begin to think in another way, that is, from Celie or Frado's perspective. Then the others are white; the others are men; the others are comfortable or powerful. From their perspectives, those are the ones who do not know what needs to be known. And if we did adopt their perspective, we could not so easily define "women," or "blackness." Is Frado's experience the experience of woman, as we have come to think of that category, in the nineteenth century? Is her experience *black*, as we tend to identify blackness? Is Celie's experience the experience of a middle-class person, as we usually describe it?

Theoretical frames become more difficult to assert and construct, for Frado's experience, as is Celie's, is a clear indication that not only Afro-American women but very few of us can possibly be described as the norm. Interestingly, theory, at least in literary study, appears to be central — absolutely necessary — today when referring to those who are perceived as the other. I wonder, if anyone were to construct a "theory" about white male upper-class literature, what it would be called.

Nor does Afro-American women's literature establish any such construct as "the black woman's experience." What the literature emphasizes is both the variousness and the sameness of being a black woman in America. Contrary to many social science studies, in which black women are often *objects* of study, Afro-American women writers give voice to experiences that converge at certain points and are different at others. Our tendency to want to reduce any one group to a monolith is one reason why scholars as well as readers could not *imagine*, despite the text, that *The Color Purple* was about a black *middle-class* family. We have been so conditioned by images of poor Southern blacks that we find it difficult to conceive of any others, despite our knowledge that blacks in Georgia made great economic strides during Reconstruction.

The study of Afro-American women's literature also suggests that we should be cautious about labeling genres or particular forms as belonging primarily to one group or another. Wilson fuses the slave narrative and sentimental romance. *The Color Purple* is written in letters, the form used in the first English novels, a form associated with women's history, and uses both the slave narrative and the sentimental romance in its structure. These writers drew from existing forms and constructed new ones more suited to their needs — forms that compel us to read differently, to enter into their unique experience. And like jazz musicians, Mrs. Wilson's voice is distinctly her own, as Alice Walker's and Toni Morrison's are distinctly theirs.

In using the word "tradition," as I so consciously did in my first book, *Black Women Novelists*, I sought to delineate a specifically Afro-American female body of literature that has existed since the eighteenth century. That word was useful for me, and I hope for others, in that it brought into view writers who had been completely ignored by both Anglo-American and Afro-American literary scholars. By emphasizing that these writers, as a result of their social definition in America, could not help but reflect the intersections of race, class, and gender, I hoped to suggest the central importance of their work to American history, to American culture.

Such emphasis, however, ought not to suggest, as it sometimes does (particularly to scholars), that these writers are all the same, or that they are limited to or by that construct. In fact, the opposite is true. For what Celie knows, what Frado knows, is that denied the apparent advantages of being the norm, whether it is in the category of gender, race, or class, they *exist*. Their very existence expands those categories beyond their meaning. Frado's knowledge and Celie's knowledge stretch those catgories and challenge our assumptions as to what they can mean.

The literature that Afro-American women write refutes the perception not only that their subjects are "nothing at all" but that their subjects cannot be reduced to categories so often imposed on those who are devalued. Perhaps that is one lesson it teaches those of us who are scholars. For we are often so tempted to want to *fix* our subjects of study in stone.

CHAPTER 11

"I'm Down on Whores": Race and Gender in Victorian London

Sander L. Gilman

"I am down on whores and I shan't quit ripping them till I do get buckled," wrote Jack the Ripper to the Central News Agency on September 18, 1888.[1] The question I want to raise in this essay reflects not on the reality of Jack the Ripper—real he was, and he never did get buckled—but on the contemporary fantasy of what a Jack the Ripper could have been. To understand the image of Jack, however, it is necessary to understand the image of the prostitute in Victoria's London. It is also necessary to comprehend the anxiety that attended her image in 1888, an anxiety that, as our anxieties a hundred years later, focused on diseases labeled sexual and attempted to locate their boundaries within the body of the Other.[2]

Who could truly kill the prostitute but the prostitute herself; who could expiate her sins against the male but she herself? For the prostitute's life must end in suicide. In Alfred Elmore's image *On the Brink*, exhibited at the Royal Academy in 1865 we see the initial step before the seduction of the female, the beginning of the slide toward prostitution and eventual self-destruction.[3] Alone, outside of the gambling salon in Bad Homburg, having lost her money, the potential object of seduction (Everywoman) is tempted by the man to whom she is indebted. Women, all women, were seen as potentially able to be seduced, as having a "warm fond heart" in which exists "a strange and sublime unselfishness, which men too commonly discover only to profit by," or so writes W. R. Greg in the *Westminster Review* of 1850.[4] The well-dressed woman has come to the spa, has exposed herself to the exploitation of the male, and is caught between the light and darkness of her future, a future mirrored in the representation of her face, half highlighted by the moonlight, half cast in shadow. She is at the moment of choice, a choice between the lily and the passionflower. According to *The Language of Flowers*, a standard handbook of Victorian culture, the lily signifies purity and

The moment of seduction from Alfred Elmore, On the Brink, 1865. Courtesy Fitzwilliam Museum, University of Cambridge.

William Hogarth's The Lady's Last Stake, *1758–59. Courtesy Membership Purchase Fund, Herbert F. Johnson Museum of Art, Cornell University, Ithaca, N.Y.*

sweetness, and the passionflower represents strong feelings and susceptibility.[5] The gambling salon was the wrong locus for the female. As early as Hogarth's *The Lady's Last Stake* (1758–59), the seduction of the female might be seen as the result of being in the wrong place. Males can gamble; females cannot. Males can indulge their passions; females cannot. Sexuality is a game for the male; it is not for the female. But gambling is also here a metaphor, although a socially embedded one, for the process by which the seduction of the female takes place. Playing on the innate biological nature of the female makes the seduction possible, but the metaphor of losing at gambling also points to the model of infection and disease.

Alfred Elmore's picture shared this vocabulary of gambling. Gambling is a "fever" (*The [London] Times*), the gambler is "infected by the fever of gambling" (*Illustrated London News*), the gambler is thus "feverish" (*Athenaeum*).[6] Gambling is a disease that infects and makes ill, the infiltration into the purity

The title page vignette of the nineteenth-century French translation of Fracastoro's poem
Syphilis *by August Barthelemy,* Syphilis: Poème en deux chants *(Paris: Béchet junior*
et Labé & Bohaire, 1840). Courtesy Olin Library, Cornell University, Ithaca, N.Y.

of the female. Seduction thus has a course of illness: it begins with the signs and symptoms of disease, the fever of gambling, the result of the individual being out of place — much like the colonial explorer expecting to get malaria as a sign of being out of place — and leads inexorably to the next stages of the disease, prostitution and death.[7] The image of the gambler who stands at the moment of choosing between vice and virtue, who is gambling with life itself, is appropriate. Gambling is the sign of the moment before seduction, and thus the male stands in proximity to, but not touching, the female. The sexualized touch is prepared but has not been consummated. Once it is (if it is, and that is the ambiguity of this image), the course is inevitable — at least for the female — for "seduction must, almost as a matter of course, lead to prostitution," as W. M. Sanger observed in 1859.[8]

The appropriate end of the prostitute is suicide, "deserted to a life of misery, wretchedness, and poverty . . . terminated by self-destruction." This is the penalty for permitting oneself to be seduced by immoral men, to be infected, and thus to spread infection to — innocent men? This is the chain of argument that places the seducer and the prostitute beyond the boundary that defines polite sexuality, a sexuality, as in the case of Victoria's Prime Minister William Gladstone's fascination with prostitutes, which led him to attempt their conversion at his own hearthside and simultaneously undertake to have sexual contact with them. The seducer and the prostitute are the defining borders of diseased sexuality. The seducer is parallel to the image of Bram Stoker's *Dracula* (1897). For in the act of seduction he transforms the innocence of the female into a copy of himself, just as Dracula's victims become vampires. She becomes the prostitute as seductress, infecting other males as he had infected her with the disease of licentiousness (and, not incidentally, syphilis). Sexuality, disease, and death are linked in the art of seduction. As a contemporary reformist source noted, in this image "the Deceiver recognizes the Deceived . . . he, the tempter, the devil's agent. . . . Men, seducers, should learn from this picture and fallen women, look at this, and remember 'the wages of sin is death.' "[9] The sign of transmission of the disease of polluted (and polluting) sexuality, the sexualized touch, is as of this moment missing in Elmore's icon of seduction.[10] In Thomas Hood's widely cited poem on the death of the prostitute, "The Bridge of Sighs" (1844), the sexualized touch, the source of disease, becomes the forgiving touch of the dead prostitute:

> Take her up instantly,
> Loving not loathing.
> Touch her not scornfully;
> Think of her mournfully,
> Gently and humanly;
> Not of the stains of her,

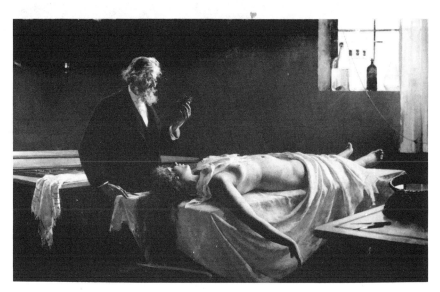

The beautiful dead woman during the autopsy in Enrique Simonet, Tenía corazón, *1890.*
Courtesy Museo de Bellas Artes provincial, Malága, Spain.

> All that remains of her
> Now is pure womanly . . .[11]

Death seems to purge the dead prostitute of her pollution, in a series of images of dead prostitutes in the nineteenth century from George Frederic Watts's *Found Drowned* (1848–50) through to the ubiquitous death mask of the "Beautiful Dead Woman from the Seine," which decorated many bourgeois parlors in France and Germany at the fin de siècle. The touching of the dead body is not merely a piteous gesture toward the "fallen," it is a permitted touching of the female, a not contagious, not infecting touching, a control over the dead woman's body.

Once dead by her own hand it was the physician who could touch the body. His role was to examine and dissect the body condemned to death by its fall from grace. And that body becomes the object of study, the corpse to be opened by the physician. For one of the favorite images of late nineteenth-century medical art is the unequal couple transmogrified into the image of the aged pathologist contemplating the exquisite body of the dead prostitute before he opens it. In the striking image by Enrique Simonet (1890), we are present the moment when the body has been opened and the pathologist stares at the heart of the whore. What will be found in the body of these drowned women? Will it be the hidden truths of the nature of the woman, what women want, the answer to Freud's question to Marie Bonaparte? Will

A woman with spiderlike hair, wearing a black cloak, stands among rows of graves. She holds a skull in her hands in this powerful illustration of the evils of syphilis in Louis Raemaekers's 'Hécatombe, La Syphilis, c. 1916. Courtesy University of Wisconsin Medical School Library Collection, Madison.

it be the biological basis of difference, the cell with its degenerate or potentially infectious nature that parallels the image of the female and its potential for destroying the male? Will it be the face of the Medusa, with all of its castrating power? Remember that in the age of "syphiliphobia" the "Medusa" masks the infection hidden within the female. In Louis Raemaekers's 1916 Belgian poster representing the temptation of the female as the source of the disease, much of the traditional imagery of the seductress can be found. Standing among rows of graves, wearing a black cloak and holding a skull, which represents her genitalia, she is the essential femme fatale. But there is a striking fin de siècle addition to the image—here "la syphilis" is the Medusa. Her tendril-like hair, her staring eyes, present the viewer with the reason for the male's seduction—not his sexuality, but her vampirelike power to control the male's rationality. The Medusa is the genitalia of the female, threatening, as Sigmund Freud has so well demonstrated, the virility of the male, but also beckoning him to "penetrate" (to use Freud's word) into her mysteries.[12]

What will be found in the body of these drowned women? If we turn to the German expressionist Gottfried Benn's 1912 description of the autopsy of a beautiful drowned girl, we get an ironic, twentieth-century answer to this question:

The mouth of a girl, who had long lain in the reeds,

looked so gnawed upon.

When they finally broke open her chest, the esophagus was so full of holes.

Finally in a bower below the diaphragm

they found a nest of young rats

One of the little sisters was dead.

The others were living off liver and kidneys,

drinking the cold blood, and had

here spent a beautiful youth.

And death came to them too beautiful and quickly

We threw them all into the water.

Oh, how their little snouts squeaked![13]

The physician-poet Benn ironically transfers the quality of the aesthetic ascribed to the beautiful dead prostitute to the dead and dying rats. What is found within the woman is the replication of herself: the source of disease, of plague, the harbor rats, nestled within the gut. The birthing of the rats is the act of opening the body, exposing the corruption hidden within. The physician's eye is always cast to examine and find the source of pathology. This is the role assigned to the physician by society. Here, again, it is the male physician opening the body of the woman to discover the source of disease, here the plague, hidden within the woman's body.

But in the fantasy of the nineteenth century the physician could not remove the prostitute from the street. Only the whore could kill the whore.
Only the whore, and Jack—killing and dismembering, searching after the
cause of corruption and disease. Jack could kill the source of infection because, like them, he too was diseased. The paradigm for the relationship between Jack and the prostitutes can be taken from the popular medical discourse of the period: "Similia similibus curantur" (Like cures like), the motto
of C. F. S. Hahnemann, the founder of homeopathic medicine. The scourge
of the streets, the carrier of disease can be eliminated only by one who is
equally corrupt and diseased. And that was Jack.

Jack, as he called himself, was evidently responsible for a series of murders
that raised the anxiety level throughout London to a fever pitch in the cold,
damp fall of 1888. The images of the murders in the *Illustrated Police News*
(London) provide an insight into how the murderer was seen and also how
the "real" prostitute, not the icon of prostitution or of seduction, was portrayed in mass art. The murders ascribed to Jack the Ripper all took place in
the East End of London, an area that had been the scene of heavy Eastern European Jewish immigration. Who, within the fantasy of the thought-
collective, can open the body, who besides the physician? No one but Jack,
the emblem of human sexual perversion out of all control, out of all bounds.
Jack becomes the sign of deviant human sexuality destroying life, the male
parallel to the destructive prostitute. He is the representative of that inner
force, hardly held under control, that has taken form, the form of Mr. Hyde.
Indeed, an extraordinarily popular dramatic version of Robert Louis Steven-
son's *Dr. Jekyll and Mr. Hyde* was playing in the West End while Jack (that not-
so-hidden Mr. Hyde) terrorized the East End.

The images of the victims of "Jack"—ranging in number from four to
twenty depending on which tabulation one follows—were portrayed as
young women who had been slashed and multilated. The Whitechapel
murders most probably included Emma Smith (April 2, 1888), Martha
Tabram (August 7, 1888), Mary Ann Nichols (August 31, 1888), Annie
Chapman (September 8, 1888). Elizabeth Stride and Catherine Eddowes
were both murdered on September 30, 1888. But, because of the sensibilities
of even the readers of the *Illustrated Police News*, the mutilation presented is
the mutilation of the face (as in the image of Annie Chapman). The reality,
at least the reality that terrified the London of 1888, was that the victims were
butchered. Baxter Philips, who undertook the postmortem description of
Martha Tabram, described the process:

> The body had been completely disembowelled and the entrails flung care-
> lessly in a heap on the table. The breasts had been cut off, hacked for no
> apparent purpose, and then hung on nails affixed to the walls of the room.
> Lumps of flesh, cut from the thighs and elsewhere, lay strewn about the

The image of Annie Chapman murdered on September 8, 1888, from the Illustrated Police News. *Courtesy Olin Library, Cornell University, Ithaca, N.Y.*

room, so that the bones were exposed. As in some of the other cases, certain organs had been extracted, and, as they were missing, had doubtless been carried away.[14]

I will spare you the police photographs of the eviscerated prostitutes. They appeared at the time only within "scientific" sources such as Alexandre Lacassagne's 1889 study of sadism.[15] In the public eye the prostitutes were their faces, the faces of the prostitute in death. But the true fascination was with those "certain organs [that] had been extracted" and had "been carried away." The whore's body had not merely been opened, but her essence, her sexuality, had been removed. These images are quite in contrast to those of the contemporary "Whitehall" murder where a decapitated torso was discovered and reconstructed from limbs found throughout the city. The mutilated body was understood over the course of the further killings to be one of Jack's victims, even though it contrasted with the bodies of the prostitutes Jack killed. In the case of Jack, the bodies were opened and their viscera were removed. Such sexual disfigurement, along with the amputation of the breasts of some of the victims, made it clear to both the police and the general public that Jack's actions were sexually motivated. And, indeed, most of the theories concerning Jack's identity assumed that he (or a close family member) had been infected with syphilis by a prostitute and was simply (if in-

The "Jewish Jack" from the Illustrated Police News. Courtesy Olin Library, Cornell University, Ithaca, N.Y.

sanely) taking his revenge. But the vague contours of Jack the "victim" soon gave way to a very specific visual image of Jack.

What is striking is that the image of "Jack" is also set. He is the caricature of the Eastern Jew. Indeed, the official description of "Jack" was of a man "age 37, rather dark beard and moustache, dark jacket and trousers, black felt hat, spoke with a foreign accent."[16] There appeared scrawled on the wall in Goulston Street near where a blood-covered apron was discovered the cryptic message: "The Juwes are The men That Will not be Blamed for nothing." The image of the Jews as sexually different, the Other even in the killing of the Other, led to the arrest of John Pizer, "Leather Apron," a Polish-Jewish shoemaker. Pizer was eventually cleared and released. But a high proportion of

The arrest of John Pizer from the Illustrated Police News. *Courtesy Olin Library, Cornell University, Ithaca, N.Y.*

The pogrom occasioned by the Jack the Ripper murders from the Illustrated Police News. Courtesy Olin Library, Cornell University, Ithaca, N.Y.

the 130 men questioned in the Ripper case were Jews. Sir Robert Anderson, the police official officially in charge of the case, noted in his memoir that the police assumed that Jack was a Polish Jew.[17] When the body of Catherine Eddowes was found on September 30 outside the International Working Men's Educational Club by a Jew, a pogrom almost occurred in the East End, at least according to the *East London Observer* (October 15, 1888). "On Saturday the crowds who assembled in the streets began to assume a very threatening attitude towards the Hebrew population of the District. It was repeatedly asserted that no Englishman could have perpetrated such a horrible crime as that of Hanbury Street, and that it must have been done by a JEW — and forthwith the crowds began to threaten and abuse such of the unfortunate Hebrews as they found in the streets." The powerful association between the working class, revolutionaries, and the Jews combined to create the visualization of Jack the Ripper as a Jewish worker, marked by his stigmata of degeneration as a killer of prostitutes. Here Jack had to intervene. In one of his rhyming missives sent in 1889 to Sir Melville MacNaghten, the chief of the Criminal Investigation Division at Scotland Yard, he wrote:

> I'm not a butcher, I'm not a Yid
>
> Nor yet a foreign skipper,
>
> But I'm your own light-hearted friend,
>
> Yours truly, Jack the Ripper.[18]

When during the 1890s the German playwright Frank Wedekind visualized his Jack the Ripper killing the archwhore Lulu he represented him as a degenerate, working-class figure: "He is a square-built man, elastic in his movements, with a pale face, inflamed eyes, thick arched eyebrows, drooping moustache, sparse beard, matted sidewhiskers and fiery red hands with gnawed finger nails. His eyes are fixed on the ground. He is wearing a dark overcoat and a small round hat."[19] This primitive figure was quite in line with the views shared by the Italian forensic psychiatrist, Cesare Lombroso, and his French opponent, Alexandre Lacassagne, as to the representative image (if not origin) of the criminal, but very specifically the sadist.[20] For the Germans, at least for liberals such as Wedekind, Jack was also seen as a member of the *lumpenproletariat* in reaction to the charge, made in 1894 in the anti-Semitic newspapers in Germany, that Jack was an Eastern European Jew functioning as part of the "International Jewish conspiracy."[21] But in Britain this image evoked a very specific aspect of the proletariat, that of London's East End, the Eastern Jew.[22]

But why Eastern European Jews? The charge of ritual murder, the murder of Christian women by Polish Jews, appeared in the *Times* during this period. But this was but a subissue or perhaps a more limited analogy to the events in Whitechapel. Nor can we simply recall the history of British anti-

Semitism, from the Norwich pogrom of 1144, caused by the charge of the ritual murder of a child, to the King's Road murders of 1771, which were laid at the feet of the Jews. The search for Jack the Ripper was the search for an appropriate murderer for the Whitechapel prostitutes. The murderer had to be representative of an image of sexuality that was equally distanced and frightening. Thus the image of Jack the Ripper as the *shochet*, the ritual butcher, arose at a moment during which there was a public campaign of the antivivisectionists in England and Germany against the "brutality" of the ritual slaughter of kosher meat.

This image of the Jewish Jack rested on a long association of the image of the Jew in the West with the image of the mutilated, diseased, different appearance of the genitalia. This mark of sexual difference was closely associated with the initial image of the syphilitic Jack. The Jew remains the representation of the male as outsider, the act of circumcision marking the Jewish male as sexually apart, as anatomically different. (It is important to remember that there is a constant and purposeful confusion through the late nineteenth and early twentieth centuries of circumcision and castration, as in Oskar Panizza's 1894 essay on "the castrated Jew.")[23] The prostitute is, as has been shown, the embodiment of the degenerate and diseased female genitalia in the nineteenth century. From the standpoint of the normative perspective of the European middle class, it is natural that the Jew and the prostitute must be in conflict and that the one "opens up" the Other, as they are both seen as "dangers" to the economy, both fiscal and sexual, of the state. This notion of the association of the Jew and the prostitute is also present in the image of "spending" semen (in an illicit manner) that dominates the literature on masturbation in the eighteenth and early nineteenth centuries.[24] For the Jew and the prostitute are seen as negating factors, outsiders whose sexual images represent all of the dangers felt to be inherent in human sexuality. And consciously to destroy, indeed, to touch the polluting force of the Other, one must oneself be beyond the boundaries of acceptability.

The linkage between Jew and prostitute is much older than the 1880s, one that is related to the image of the black and the monkey in the second plate of Hogarth's *The Harlot's Progress*. Here Moll Hackabout, the harlot, has become the mistress of a wealthy London Jew. The Jew has been cheated by the harlot, and her lover is about to leave the scene. But her punishment is forthcoming. She will be dismissed by him and begin her slow slide downward. Tom Brown, Hogarth's contemporary and the author of "A Letter to Madam —, kept by a Jew in Covent Garden," which may well have inspired the plate, concludes his letter on the sexuality of the Jew by asking the young woman "to be informed whether Aaron's bells make better music than ours."[25] It is this fascination with the sexual difference of the Jew, parallel to the sexual difference of the prostitute, that relates them even in death. Each

Moll Hackabout as the Jew's mistress, the second plate of William Hogarth's The Harlot's Progress *(1731). Private collection, Ithaca, N.Y.*

possesses a sexuality that is different from the norm, a sexuality that is represented in the unique form of their genitalia.

The relationship between the Jew and the prostitute also has a social dimension. For both Jew and prostitute have but one interest, the conversion of sex into money or money into sex. "So tnen," Brown writes to the lady, "tis neither circumcision nor uncircumcision that avails any thing with you, but money, which belongs to all religions" (p. 200). The major relationship, as Tom Brown and Hogarth outline, is a financial one; Jews buy specific types of Christian women, using their financial ability as a means of sexual control. "I would never have imagined you . . . would have ever chosen a gallant out of that religion which clips and diminishes the current coin of love, or could ever be brought to like those people that lived two thousand years on types and figures" (p. 199).

By the end of the nineteenth century this linkage had become a commonplace in all of Christian Europe. In 1892 an early nineteenth-century (1830s) pornographic "dialogue between a Jew and a Christian, a Whimsical Entertainment, lately performed in Duke's Palace," the "Adventures of Miss Lais Lovecock," reappeared in London.[26] This dialogue represents the Jew and represents him in a very specific manner. First, the Jew speaks in dialect. By 1888 the British Jewish community had become completely acculturated.

With Disraeli's terms as prime minister as well as the Prince of Wales (later King Edward VII) attending the wedding of Leopold de Rothschild on January 14, 1881, at a London synagogue, the boundary between the "native" Jews and the "foreign" Jew had to be drawn. This explains the use of dialect that in 1892 would point toward the Eastern Jew, toward Jack the Ripper, who could not command written English at least about the "Juwes."[27] The text may well have reflected the image of the Jew in the 1830s, but it clearly had a very different set of associations after Jack the Ripper's appearance. The Jew, Isaac, describes his seduction of his father's Jewish (and, therefore, since all Jews are deviants in one way or another, hermaphroditic) maid who has a "clitoris, which was hard and shaped like a penis," while he seduces the Christian prostitute, Polly. She is described by him as having "little feet and ankles, I think of your pretty legs, and den I think of your snowy thighs, and den my fancy glowing hot got to de fountain of bliss, and dere I vill go immediately" (p. 66). She is the object of the Jew's desire, for his women (servant girls or whores) are as sexually marginal as he is himself. But it is only for money that Polly is willing to ring "Aaron's bells," for "nothing under three hundred a year" (p. 62). The prostitute is little more than a Jew herself. Both are on the margins of "polite" society. And, as we know, from the degeneration of Hogarth's Moll Hackabout following her relationship with the Jewish merchant, such sexuality in women leads to corruption and physical decay. The Jew, with all of his associations with disease, becomes the surrogate for all marginal males, males across the boundary from the (male) observer, males who, like women, can be the source of corruption, if not for the individual, then for the collective.

The association of the venality of the Jew with capital is retained even into the latter half of the twentieth century. In a series of British comic books from the 1980s in which an anthropomorphized phallus plays the central role, the Jew is depicted as masturbating, committing an "unnatural" act (while all of the other phalluses are depicted having a potential female partner) while reading a financial journal.[28] What is striking in these comics is that all of the phalluses are circumcised. Here we have a problem within contemporary culture. In the post-World War II decades circumcision became commonplace—even among non-Jews—in the United States and (less so, but more prominent than before World War II) Great Britain. How then to differentiate between the Jew and the non-Jew, between the "deviant" and the "normal?" We are faced with an analogous problem to why George Eliot's eponymous character Daniel Deronda did not know he was a Jew. Did he never look at his penis? Here the hidden is not marked on the skin, for the skin hides rather than reveals. It is the Jew within that surfaces. Here, in seeing a financial journal as the source of power and therefore of sexual stimulation; in Eliot's novel with the "natural" sexual attraction between the crypto-Jew Deronda and the beautiful Jewess, Mirah Cohen. (Deronda never defines himself as sexually different, for his own body is the baseline that defines for him the sexually "normal." His circumcised penis is not a sign of difference, until he understands himself to be a Jew.)

The image of the Jew revealed in his sexuality seems to be an accepted manner of labeling the image of the deviant. Even his phallus does not know for sure until he performs a "perverse" act. Here the icon is a reversal of the traditional image of the phallus as the beast out of control. In this image it is the man, not his phallus, who is bestial (read: Jewish). The perversion of the Jew (and thus the "humor" of this depiction of the phallus) lies in his sexualized relationship to capital. This, of course, echoes the oldest and most basic calumny against the Jew, his avarice, an avarice for the possession of "things," of "money," which signals his inability to understand (and produce) anything of transcended aesthetic value. The historical background to this is clear: canon law forbade the taking of interest, seeing interest, according to Thomas Aquinas, as impossible, for money, not being alive, could not reproduce.[29] Jews, in taking money, treated money as if it were alive, as if it were a sexualized object. The Jew takes money as does the prostitute, as a substitute for higher values, for love and beauty. And thus the Jew becomes the representative of the deviant genitalia, the genitalia not under the control of the moral, rational conscience.

But the image of the Jew as prostitute is not merely that of the economic parallel between the sexuality of the Jew and that of the prostitute. For that relationship also reveals the nature of the sexuality of both Jew and prostitute as diseased, as polluting. Just as the first image of Jack the Ripper was that of the victim of the prostitute, the syphilitic male, so too were the Jews closely identified with sexually transmitted diseases. For the Jew was also closely related to the spread and incidence of syphilis. This charge appeared in various forms, as in the anti-Semitic tractate *England under the Jews* (1901) by Joseph Banister, in which there is a fixation on the spread of "blood and skin diseases."[30] Such views had two readings. Banister's was the more typical. The Jews were the carriers of sexually transmitted diseases and transmitted them to the rest of the world. This view is to be found in Hitler's discussion of syphilis in *Mein Kampf* and there he links it to the Jew, the prostitute, and the power of money.

> Particularly with regard to syphilis, the attitude of the nation and the state can only be designated as total capitulation. . . . The cause lies, primarily, in our prostitution of love. . . . This Jewification of our spiritual life and mammonization of our mating instinct will sooner or later destroy our entire offspring.[31]

Hitler's views, like those of Banister and the earlier British anti-Semites, also linked Jews with prostitutes. Jews were the archpimps; Jews ran the brothels; Jews infected their prostitutes and caused the weakening of the national fiber.[32] Indeed, according to Hitler, it was the realization of this very "fact" during the first few days of his stay in Vienna in 1907 that converted him to anti-Semitism. The hidden source of the disease of the body politic is the Jew and his tool is the whore: "If you cut even cautiously into such an tumor, you found, like a maggot in a rotting body, often dazzled by the sudden light—a kike!"[33]

Such a view of the Jew as syphilitic was not limited to the anti-Semitic fringe of the turn of the century. It was a view that possessed such power that even "Jewish" writers (i.e., writers who felt themselves stigmatized by the label of being "Jewish") such as Marcel Proust (whose uncomfortable relationship to his mother's Jewish identity haunted his life almost as much as did his gay identity) accepted it. In Proust's *Remembrance of Things Past*, a series of novels written to recapture the world of the 1880s and 1890s, one of the central characters, Charles Swann, is a Jew who marries a courtesan. This link between Jew and prostitute is mirrored in Proust's manner of representing the sexuality of the Jew. For Proust, being Jewish is analogous to being gay—it is "an incurable disease."[34] But what marks this disease for all to see? For in the mentalité of the turn of the century, syphilis in the male must be written on the skin, just as it is hidden within the sexuality of the female. Proust, who discusses the signs and symptoms of syphilis with a detailed clinical knowledge in the same volume, knows precisely what marks the sexuality of the Jew on his physiognomy.[35] It is marked on his face as "ethnic eczema."[36] It is a sign of sexual and racial corruption as surely as the composite photographs of the Jew made by Francis Galton at the time reveal the true face of the Jew.[37] This mark on this face is Hitler's and Banister's sign of the Jew's sexual perversion. It is the infectious nature of that "incurable disease," the sexuality of the Jew, Proust's Jew fixated on his courtesan. (This is an interesting reversal of one of the subthemes of Zola's *Nana*. There Nana, like Moll Hackabout, is first the mistress of a Jew, whom she, quite easily reversing the role of Jack the Ripper, bankrupts and drives to suicide.) The Jew's sexuality, the sexuality of the polluter, is written on his face in the skin disease that announces the difference of the Jew. For Proust, all of his Jewish figures (including Swann and Bloch) are in some way diseased, and in every case, this image of disease links the racial with the sexual, much as Proust's image of the homosexual links class (or at least, the nobility) with homosexuality. ("Homosexuality" is a "scientific" label for a new "disease" coined by Karoly Benkert in 1869 at the very same moment in history that the new "scientific" term for Jew-hating, "anti-Semitism," was created by Wilhelm Marr.) The image of the infected and infecting Jew also had a strong political as well as personal dimension for Proust. For the ability to "see" the Jew who was trying to pass as a non-Jew within French society is one of the themes of the novels, a theme that, after the Dreyfus Affair, had overt political implications. Seeing the Jew was seeing the enemy within the body politic, was

seeing the force for destruction. And Proust's "racial" as well as sexual identity was tied to his sense of the importance of class and society for the definition of the individual. Thus Proust's arch-Jew Swann was visibly marked by
him as the heterosexual syphilitic, as that which he was not (at least in his
fantasy about his own sexual identity).

The second model at the close of the nineteenth century that represented
the relationship between Jews and sexually transmitted disease postulated
exactly the opposite—that Jews had a statistically lower rate of syphilitic infection because they had become immune to it through centuries of exposure.
Syphilis was understood at the close of the nineteenth century as an African
disease predating Columbus. In the medical literature of the period, reaching
across all of European medicine, it was assumed that Jews had a notably
lower rate of infection. In a study of the incidence of tertiary lues (the final
stage of the syphilitic infection) in the Crimea undertaken between 1904 and
1929, the Jews had the lowest consistent rate of infection.[38] In an eighteen-
year longitudinal study, H. Budel demonstrated the extraordinarily low rate
of tertiary lues in Estonia during the prewar period.[39] All of these studies assumed that biological difference as well as the social difference of the Jews
was at the root of their seeming "immunity."

Jewish scientists also had to explain the "statistical" fact of their immunity
to syphilis. In a study of the rate of tertiary lues undertaken during World
War I, the Jewish physician Max Sichel responded to the general view of the
relative lower incidence of infection among Jews as resulting from the sexual
difference of the Jews.[40] He responds—out of necessity—with a social argument. The Jews, according to Sichel, evidence lower incidence because of
early marriage and the patriarchal structure of the Jewish family, but also because of their much lower rate of alcoholism. They were, therefore, according to the implicit argument, more rarely exposed to infection by prostitutes,
whose attractiveness was always associated with the greater loss of sexual
control in the male attributed to inebriety. The relationship between these
two "social" diseases is made into a cause for the higher incidence among
other Europeans. The Jews, because they are less likely to drink heavily, are
less likely to be exposed to both the debilitating effects of alcohol (which increase the risk for tertiary lues) as well as the occasion for infection. There
is a hidden agenda in these comments. The prostitute is the source of infection, according to Sichel. And the prostitute is the offspring of alcoholic parents, according to one common theory of nineteenth-century psychopathol-
ogy. If you have no Jewish alcoholics, then you have no Jewish prostitutes
and thus the Jews are isolated from any charge of being the "source of pollution," one of the common calumnies lodged against them from the Middle
Ages through the nineteenth century.

In 1927 H. Strauss looked at the incidences of syphilitic infection in his
hospital in Berlin in order to demonstrate whether the Jews had a lower inci-

dence but also to see (as in the infamous Tuskegee experiments using blacks in the United States)[41] whether they had "milder" forms of the disease because of their life-style or background.[42] He found that Jews indeed had a much lower incidence of syphilis (while having an extraordinarily higher rate of hysteria) than the non-Jewish control group. He proposes that the disease may well have a different course in Jews than in non-Jews. The reason given by non-Jewish scientists was the inherited tendency of male Jews to be more "immune." Just as "Jewishness" was an inherited tendency, so too was the nature of a "Jewish sexuality," a sexuality so markedly different that some Jewish male infants were even born circumcised![43]

Both of these arguments saw the Jew as having a "special" relationship to syphilis (through the agency of the prostitute) and carried on the association between the Jew and the prostitute. But this special relationship could literally be seen on the Jew. Joseph Banister saw the Jews as bearing the stigmata of skin disease (as a model for discussing sexually transmitted disease): "If the gentle reader desires to know what kind of blood it is that flows in the Chosen People's veins, he cannot do better than take a gentle stroll through Hatton Garden, Maida Vale, Petticoat Lane, or any other London 'nosery.' I do not hesitate to say that in the course of an hour's peregrinations he will see more cases of lupus, trachoma, favus, eczema, and scurvy than he would come across in a week's wanderings in any quarter of the Metropolis."[44] It is the nose of the Jew, the polite anti-Semitic reference to the phallus. For the "nose" is the iconic representation of the Jew's phallus throughout the nineteenth century. Indeed, Jewish social scientists such as the British savant Joseph Jacobs spend a good deal of their time denying the salience of "nostrility" as a sign of the racial cohesion of the Jews.[45] It is clear that for Jacobs (as for Wilhelm Fliess in Germany)[46] the nose is the displaced locus of anxiety associated with the marking of the male Jew's body through circumcision given the debate about the "primitive" nature of circumcision and its reflection on the acculturation of the Western Jew during the late nineteenth century.

Jews bear their diseased sexuality on their skin. Indeed, they bear the salient stigma of the black skin of the syphilitic. For, at least in the Latin tradition, syphilis (like leprosy, another disease thought to be sexually transmitted[47]) was understood to turn one black, the syphilitic *rupia*. Francisco Lopez de Villalobos, court physician to Charles V, in his long poem on syphilis of 1498, observes that the "color of the skin becomes black" when one has the "Egyptian disease," the plague of boils recounted in the account of the Jews' escape from slavery. Blackness marks the sufferer from disease, sets him outside of the world of purity and cleanliness.[48] The Jews are black, according to nineteenth-century racial science, because they are "a mongrel race which always retains this mongrel character."[49] That is Houston Stewart Chamberlain arguing against the "pure" nature of the Jewish race. Jews had "hybridized" with blacks in Alexandrian exile. And they were exposed to the syphilis that becomes part of their nature. They are, in an ironic review of Chamberlain's work by the father of modern Yiddish scholarship, Nathan Birnbaum, a "bastard" race whose origin was caused by their incestuousness.[50] Adam Gurowski, a Polish noble, "took every light-colored mulatto for a Jew" when he first arrived in the United States in the 1850s.[51] Jews are black because they are different, because their sexuality is different, because their sexual pathology is written on their skin. Gurowski's contemporary, Karl Marx, associates leprosy, Jews, and syphilis in his description of his archrival Ferdinand Lassalle (in 1861): "Lazarus the leper, is the prototype of the Jews and of Lazarus-Lassalle. But in our Lazarus, the leprosy lies in the brain. His illness was originally a badly cured case of syphilis."[52] Jews = lepers = syphilitics = prostitutes = blacks. This chain of association presents the ultimate rationale for the Jewish Jack the Ripper. For the diseased destroy the diseased, the corrupt the corrupt. They corrupt in their act of touching, of seducing the pure and innocent, creating new polluters. But they are also able in their sexual frenzy to touch and kill the sexual pariahs, the prostitutes, who like Lulu at the close of Frank Wedekind's play (and Alban Berg's opera) go out to meet them, seeking their own death. Being unclean, being a version of the female genitalia (with their amputated genitalia), the male Jew is read (as Jack's Viennese contemporary Otto Weininger had read him) as really nothing but a type of female. The pariah can thus touch and kill the pariah; the same destroy the same. Wedekind's Lulu dies not as a suicide but as the victim of the confrontation between two libidinal forces—the unbridled, degenerate sexuality of the male and the sexual chaos of the sexually emancipated female. But die she does, and Jack leaves the stage, having washed his hands, like Pontius Pilate, ready to kill again.

NOTES

1. Cited by Michel Parry (ed.), *Jack the Knife: Tales of Jack the Ripper* (London: Mayflower, 1975), p. 12.

2. See Dorothy Nelkin and Sander L. Gilman, "Placing the Blame for Devastating Disease," *Social Research*, 55 (1988), pp. 361–78.

3. I am here indebted to Lynda Nead, "Seduction, Prostitution, Suicide: On the Brink by Alfred Elmore," *Art History*, 5 (1982); pp. 309–22. On the general history of prostitution in Great Britain during the nineteenth century see Judith R. Walkowitz, *Prostitution and Victorian Society: Women, Class, and the State* (Cambridge: Cambridge University Press, 1980).

4. W. R. Greg, "Prostitution," *Westminster Review*, 53 (1850), p. 456.

5. *The Language of Flowers* (London: Milner, 1849), pp. 19, 22.

6. Cited by Nead, "Seduction, Prostitution, Suicide," p. 316.

7. The image of the dead woman is a basic trope within the art and literature of the nineteenth century. See Elisabeth Bronfen, "Die schöne Leiche: Weiblicher Tod als motivischer Konstante vond er Mitte des 18. Jahrhunderts bis in die Moderne," in Renate Berger and Inge Stephan (eds.), *Weiblichkeit und Tod in der Literatur* (Cologne: Böhlau, 1987), pp. 87–115. On the

general background of the fascination with and representation of death in the West see Philippe Ariès, *The Hour of Our Death*, trans. Helen Weaver (New York: Knopf/Random House, 1981), as well as Mario Praz, *The Romantic Agony*, trans. Angus Davidson (Cleveland: World, 1956), and John McManners, *Death and the Enlightenment: Changing Attitudes to Death among Christians and Unbelievers in Eighteenth-Century France* (Oxford: Clarendon Press, 1981).

8. William W. Sanger, *The History of Prostitution: Its Extent, Causes, and Effects Throughout the World* (1859; New York: Medical Publishing Company, 1927), p. 322.

9. William Tait, *Magdalenism: An Inquiry into the Extent, Causes, and Consequences of Prostitution in Edinburgh* (Edinburgh: Rickard, 1840), p. 96. Compare Margaret Higonnet, "Speaking Silences: Women's Suicide," in Susan Rubin Suleiman (ed.), *The Female Body in Western Culture: Contemporary Perspectives* (Cambridge, Mass.: Harvard University Press, 1986), pp. 68–83.

10. See, for example, "Drowned! Drowned!" *The Magdalen's Friend, and Female Homes' Intelligencer*, 1 (1860), p. 71. On the Continental background to the image of the female suicide see Aaron Sheon, "Octave Tassert's 'Le Suicide': Early Realism and the Plight of Women," *Arts Magazine*, 76 (May 1981), pp. 142–51, as well as Judith Wechler, *A Human Comedy: Physiognomy and Caricature in Nineteenth-Century Paris* (Chicago: University of Chicago Press, 1982).

11. Thomas Hood, "The Bridge of Sighs," *The Complete Poetical Works of Thomas Hood* (New York: G. P. Putnam, 1869), vol. 1, p. 27. On the literary image of the prostitute see Martin Seymour-Smith, *Fallen Women: A Sceptical Enquiry into the Treatment of Prostitutes, Their Clients, and Their Pimps, in Literature* (London: Nelson, 1969).

12. See Sigmund Freud's essay "Medusa's Head," *The Standard Edition of the Complete Psychological Works of Sigmund Freud*, trans. James Strachey (London: Hogarth, 1953–74), here, vol. 18, p. 273–74. See Annemarie Taeger, *Die Kunst, Medusa zu töten: Zum Bild der Frau in der Literatur der Jahrhundertwende* (Bielefeld: Aisthesis, 1988).

13. Gottfried Benn, *Sämtliche Werke* (Stuttgart: Klett-Cotta, 1986), vol. 1, p. 11. Translation mine.

14. In Parry, *Jack the Knife*, p. 14.

15. Alexandre Lacassagne, *Vacher l'eventreur et les crimes sadiques* (Lyon: Storck, 1889).

16. Cited in Christopher Frayling, "The House That Jack Built: Some Stereotypes of the Rapist in the History of Popular Culture," in Sylvana Tomaselli and Roy Porter (eds.), *Rape* (Oxford: Basil Blackwell, 1986), p. 183. The further citations from "Jack" are taken from Frayling unless otherwise noted.

17. Robert Anderson, *The Lighter Side of My Official Life* (London: Hodder & Stroughton, 1910), p. 32.

18. Cited in Alexander Kelley and Colin Wilson, *Jack the Ripper: A Bibliography and Review of the Literature* (London: Association of Assistant Librarians, 1973), p. 14.

19. Frank Wedekind, *Five Tragedies of Sex*, trans. Frances Fawcett and Stephen Spender (New York: Theatre Arts Books, n.d.), p. 298.

20. Cesare Lombroso and Guglielmo Ferrero, *La donna deliquente: La prostituta a la donna normale* (Turin: Roux, 1893), and Alexandre Lacassagne, *L'homme criminel comparé a l'homme primitif* (Lyon: Association typographique, 1882).

21. Peter Pulzer, *The Rise of Political Anti-Semitism in Germany and Austria* (London: Peter Halban, 1988), p. 6.

22. The fantasy of a "Jewish" Jack the Ripper dies very hard. Robin Odell, *Jack the Ripper in Fact and Fiction* (London: Harrap, 1965), proposed again that Jack was a *shochet*, a ritual slaughterer. This theme has reappeared in the recent volume by Martin Fido, *The Crimes, Detection, and Death of Jack the Ripper* (London: Weidenfeld & Nicolson, 1987), which argues that a Jewish tailor named David Cohen was "Jack."

23. Jack Zipes, "Oscar Panizza: The Operated German as Operated Jew," *New German Critique*, 21 (1980), pp. 47–61.

24. See the discussion by Alain Corbin, "Commercial Sexuality in Nineteenth-Century France: A System of Images and Regulations," *Representations*, 14 (1986), pp. 209–19.

25. Tom Brown, *Amusements Serious and Comical and Other Works*, ed. Arthur L. Hayward (London: Routledge and Sons, 1927), p. 200.

26. *The Bagnio Miscellany Containing the Adventures of Miss Lais Lovelock . . .* (London: Printed for the Bibliopolists, 1892), here pp. 54–55.

27. On the background to this concept see my *Jewish Self-Hatred: Anti-Semitism and the Hidden Language of the Jews* (Baltimore: Johns Hopkins University Press, 1985). Frayling, "The House That Jack Built," p. 196.

28. Gray Joliffe and Peter Mayle, *Man's Best Friend* (London: Pan, 1984).

29. See Benjamin Nelson, *The Idea of Usury: From Tribal Brotherhood to Universal Otherhood* (Princeton, N.J.: Princeton University Press, 1949), and John Thomas Noonan, *The Scholastic Analysis of Usury* (Cambridge, Mass.: Harvard University Press, 1857).

30. Joseph Banister, *England under the Jews* (London: [J. Banister], 1907 [3rd ed.]), p. 61. For a more detailed account of Banister and the idea of the diseased Jew see Colin Holmes, *Anti-Semitism in British Society, 1876–1939* (New York: Holmes & Meier, 1979), pp. 36–48.

31. Adolph Hitler, *Mein Kampf*, trans. Ralph Manheim (Boston: Houghton Mifflin, 1943), p. 247.

32. Holmes, *Anti-Semitism*, pp. 44–45. Compare Edward J. Bristow, *Prostitution and Prejudice: The Jewish Fight against White Slavery, 1870–1939* (Oxford: Clarendon, 1982).

33. Hitler, *Mein Kampf*, p. 57.

34. The discussion of the images of the Jew and the homosexual is to be found in "Cities of the Plain," in Marcel Proust, *Remembrance of Things Past*, trans. C. K. Scott Moncrieff and Terence Kilmartin (Harmondsworth: Penguin, 1986), vol. 2, p. 639.

35. On syphilis and Charcot see Proust, ibid., vol. 2, p. 1086.

36. Ibid., vol. 1, p. 326.

37. See the discussion by Galton reprinted in Joseph Jacobs, *Studies in Jewish Statistics, Social, Vital, and Anthropometric* (London: D. Nutt, 1891), p. xl.

38. N. Balaban and A. Molotschek, "Progressive Paralyse bei den Bevölkerungen der Krim," *Allgemeine Zeitschrift für Psychiatrie*, 94 (1931), pp. 373–83.

39. H. Budel, "Beitrag zur vergleichenden Rassenpsychiatrie," *Monatsschrift für Psychiatrie und Neuologie*, 37 (1915), pp. 199–204.

40. Max Sichel, "Die Paralyse der Juden in sexuologischer Beleuchtung," *Zeitschrift für Sexualwissenschaft*, 7 (1919–20), pp. 986–1104.

41. See James H. Jones, *Bad Blood: The Tuskegee Syphilis Experiment* (New York: Free Press, 1981).

42. H. Strauss, "Erkrankungen durch Alkohol und Syphilis bei den Juden," *Zeitschrift für Demographie und Statistik der Juden*, 4 (1927), pp. 33–39.

43. J. H. F. Autenrieth, "Über die beschnitten-gebohrnen Judenkinder," *Archiv für die Physiologie*, 7 (1807), pp. 296–98.

44. Banister, *England under the Jews*, p. 61.

45. Joseph Jacobs, *Studies in Jewish Statistics*, pp. xxxii–xxxiii.

46. See Frank J. Sulloway, *Freud: Biologist of the Mind* (New York: Basic Books, 1979), pp. 147–58.

47. On the tradition of seeing leprosy as a sexually transmitted disease see Saul N. Brody, *The Disease of the Soul: Leprosy in Medieval Literature* (Ithaca, N.Y.: Cornell University Press, 1974).

48. Francisco Lopez de Villalobos, *El Somario de la medicina con un tratado sobre las pestíferas bubas*, ed. María Teresa Herrera (Salamanca: Ediciones del Instituto de Historia de la Medicina Espannóla, 1973), pp. 159–61. See Yvonne David-Peyre, "Normativité et pathologie, au siècle d'Or," *Textes et Languages*, 11 (1985), pp. 5–22.

49. Houston Stewart Chamberlain, *Foundations of the Nineteenth Century*, trans. John Lees, 2 vols. (London: John Lane, 1910), vol. 1, pp. 388–89.

50. Nathan Birnbaum, "Über Houston Stewart Chamberlain," in his *Ausgewählte Schriften zur jüdischen Frage*. (Czernowitz: Verlag der Buchhandlung Dr. Birnbaum & Dr. Kohut, 1910), vol. 2, p. 201.

51. Adam G. de Gurowski, *America and Europe* (New York: Appelton, 1857), p. 177.

52. Saul K. Padover, (ed. and trans.), *The Letters of Karl Marx* (Englewood Cliffs, N.J.: Prentice-Hall, 1979), p. 459.

CHAPTER 12

"Ours to Jew or Die": Céline and the Categories of Anti-Semitism

Julia Kristeva

.

> *Enthusiasm involves a lot of mad raving—Alas! Freud certainly raved a great*
> *deal—but our ravings now seem to involve solely political fanaticism—that's*
> *even more ridiculous—I know. I was caught up in it.*
>
> Céline, Letter to Milton Hindus

Logical Oscillations: An Anarchism

Doubtless contradictory, hotheaded, "raving" if you wish, Céline's pamphlets (*Mea Culpa*, 1936; *Bagatelles pour un massacre*, 1937; *L'Ecole des cadavres*, 1938; *Les Beaux Draps*, 1941), in spite of their stereotyped themes, carry on the wild beauty of his style. Isolating them from the whole of his writings constitutes a defense or a claim on the part of the political left or right; it is at any rate an ideological stance, not an analytic or literary position.

The pamphlets provide the phantasmatic substratum on which, in another connection and another place, the novelistic works were built. Thus, very "honestly," the person who signs novels and pamphlets with his grandmother's first name, Céline, remembers his father's name, the one on his birth certificate, Louis Destouches, in order to acknowledge the thoroughly existential, biographical paternity of the pamphlets. Where my identity is concerned, "I" have no other truth to tell save my delirium: my paroxysmal desire under its social guise. Where that other who writes and is not my familial ego is concerned, "I" go beyond, "I" shift, "I" am no longer, for the end of the night is without subject, rigadoon, music, or enchantment. Destouches and Céline: biography and thanatography, delirium and scription—the distinction surely exists, but it is never complete; like Janus who avoids the trap of an impossible identity, the texts, novels or pamphlets, also display two faces.

Céline can thus at the same time *attack the collapse of ideals and the reduction of the masses to the satisfaction of their basest needs while extolling those who foster such a situation*, beginning with Hitler. For instance, he writes in *Les Beaux Draps*:

> The masses have no ideals, all they have is needs. And what are those needs? [. . .] It's a platform with nothing but material things, a swell feed, and a gold brick. They're an embryonic bourgeoisie that hasn't yet negotiated its contract.[1]

Or else:

> The downtrodden of the earth on the one side, the bourgeois on the other, they have basically only one idea, to become rich or to stay rich, it's the same thing, the lining has the same value as the cloth, the same currency, the same coin, no difference in their hearts. It's all guts, incorporated. Everything for the belly. (*BD*, p. 89)

And in *L'Ecole des cadavres*:

> Who is the true friend of the people? Fascism is. / Who has done the most for the working man? the USSR or Hitler? / Hitler has. / All you have to do is look, keeping all that red shit away from your eyes. / Who has done the most for the small businessman? Not Thorez but Hitler![2]

This does not prevent him from attacking Hitler violently — though after the war, it is true:

> Hitlerite clamors, that howling neo-Romanticism, that Wagnerian satanism, always seems to me obscene and unbearable — I am for Couperin, Rameau — Jaquin [. . .]. Ronsard . . . Rabelais.[3]

> Backing Hitler there was nothing, or almost nothing, I mean from the spiritual point of view, a horde of petty bourgeois, greedy swine rushing in for the spoils.[4]

(And that, as Céline saw it, is what made the Nazis unfit for Nazism.)

He can *lash out at and inveigh against Freemasons, academics, and other secular elites, and at the same time attack no less violently, with Nietzchean overtones, the Catholic church.* Thus, on the one hand:

> France is Jewish and Masonic [. . .] It's the Hydra with a hundred and twenty thousand heads! Siegfried can't get over it! (*BD*, p. 78)

> The French Masonic Republic is no longer anything but a very disgusting electoral rip-off, a fantastic organization for gulling very naive Frenchmen. (*EC*, p. 31)

> The profligate Masonic Republic, so-called French, which is completely at the mercy of secret societies and Jewish banks (Rothschild, Lazare, Baruch, etc.), is feeling the pangs of agony. More gangrened than one would think

possible, it is rotting away scandal by scandal. All that's left are puss-laden scraps from which, in spite of all, the Jew and his Freemason dog tear away a few new goodies each day, cadaverous snatches; they stuff themselves, what a blow-out! thrive on them, gloat, exult, they go delirious on carrion. (*EC*, p. 31)

And on the other:

Having spread to the many races, to the hated Aryan races, "Peter and Paul's" religion performed admirably; as early as the cradle it reduced to beggars, to a lower form of man, the subjected people, the hordes intoxicated by Christianic literature; it hurled them, bewildered and besotted, to the conquest of Christ's Sindon, the magic hosts, forever forsaking their Gods, their exalting religions, the Gods of their blood, the Gods of their race. (*BD*, p. 81)

The most shameless gambling joint for corn-holed Christianese the kikes have ever laid hands on . . . Christianic religion? Judeo-Talmudo-communism? A gang! The apostles? Jews. All of them! Gangsters all! The first gang? The Church! The first racket? The first people's commissariat? The Church! Peter? Al Capone of the Canticles! A Trotsky for Roman muzhiks! The Gospel? A code for racketeers . . . (*EC*, p. 270)

The Judeo-Christian connivance serves as prelude to the great Judeo-Masonic rushing for the spoils . . . (*EC*, p. 272)

He can *shoot down in flames communism and the "Middling Revolution," but he can do the same to Charles Maurras.* Thus, for instance, in *Mea Culpa* or in other texts:

Communism without poets as it is practiced by Jews, scientists, rational reasoners, materialists, Marxists, bureaucrats, skunks, louts, at the rate of six hundred kilos per sentence, is a very boring process of prosaic tyranny, absolutely unable to take wings, an absolutely atrocious, Jewish satrapal imposture, unedible and inhuman, a very sickening forcing house for slaves, a hellish wager, a remedy worse than the disease. (*EC*, p. 133)

And at the same time on the other side:

But what is Maurras getting at? I don't understand a thing about the cunning, the dosulage, the high-sounding hare and hounderies of his most Latin doctrine. (*EC*, p. 252)

And his style! His famous style! Sticky, stumbling, tendentious, fake, Jewish . . . (*EC*, p. 189)

And against the bourgeois:

As for the Bourgeois, he doesn't give a damn, what he wants is to keep his lettuce, his "Royal Dutch" stock, his privileges, his situation, and the Lodge where he meets such fine people, the kind who have a pipe-line to the government. In short he is Jewish, seeing that the Jews have got the gold . . . (D, p. 70)

In similar fashion, he flies into a *black rage against the schools, which are reductive of animal spontaneity and are based on abstract, paternal reason,* a reason that constrains and maims (A "hatcher of symbols,"[5] the school, in *Les Beaux Draps,* is a "devourer" of the "mischievous liveliness" of children; by means of reason, it inflicts false and fake values upon them, as opposed to spontaneous, innate, animal beauty), and he *feverishly defends the true family, the solid dictatorship of the father* ("I go by another Family code, one that is much hardier, more ample, a lot more generous, not a code for shrivelled up argumentative preservers. Of course not! Not at all! A real code, one that would include everything, animals, goods and people, children and the aged, all of France in the same family, Jews excluded of course, a single family, a single dad, dictator and respected"; *BD,* p. 172).

One has to admit that out of such logical oscillations there emerge a few striking words of truth. Such words present us with harsh X-rays of given *areas* of social and political experience; they turn into fantasies or deliriums only from the moment when reason attempts to *globalize, unify,* or *totalize.* Then the crushing anarchy or nihilism of discourse topples over and, as if it were the reverse of that negativism, an *object* appears—an object of hatred and desire, of threat and aggressivity, of envy and abomination.

That object, the Jew, gives thought a focus where all contradictions are explained and satisfied. The function of the Jew in the economy of Célinian discourse will perhaps be better understood after I have called attention to at least *two common features* that structure the fluctuations of the pamphlets.

Against the Symbolic Law: A Substitute Law

The first is *rage against the Symbolic,* which is represented here by religious, parareligious, and moral establishments (Church, Freemasonry, School, intellectual Elite, communist Ideology, etc.); it culminates in what Céline hallucinates and knows to be their foundation and forebear—Jewish monotheism. When one follows his associations of ideas, his anti-Semitism—virulent and stereotyped but impassioned—appears as the simple outcome of a fully secular rage; anti-Semitism would be a diehard secularism sweeping away, along with its number one enemy, religion, all its secondary representatives: abstraction, reason, and adulterated power, considered emasculating.

The second is the attempt to substitute *another Law* for the constraining and frustrating symbolic one, a law that would be absolute, full, and reassuring. The wishes of Céline, as Fascist ideologue, call for that law, seen as mystic positivity:

There is an idea that can lead nations. There is a law. It stems from an idea that rises toward absolute mysticism, that rises still witout fear or program. If it flows in the direction of politics, that is the end of it. It falls lower than mud and we with it [. . .] we need an idea, a harsh doctrine, a diamond-like doctrine, one even more awesome than the others, we need it for France.[6]

Beyond politics, and yet taking it into account, *material positivity*, a full, tangible, reassuring, and happy substance, will be embodied in the Family, the Nation, the Race, and the Body.

The novelist Céline has only too deeply explored the abomination that such entities are prey to. But the pamphleteer wants them; he fantasies them as capable of being full, without other, without threat, without heterogeneity; he wants them harmoniously to absorb their differences into a kind of sameness that would be obtained by means of a subtle drifting, a scansion, a punctuation that would relay but without interrupting—a replica of primary narcissism. Without Master, this universe has rhythm; without Other, it is Dance and Music; without God, it has style. Against the ternary economy of a Transcendence, Céline proclaims the immanence of substance and meaning, of the natural/racial/familial and the spiritual, of the feminine and the masculine, of life and death—a glorification of the Phallus that does not speak its name but is communicated to the senses as Rhythm.

One should again learn to dance. France remained happy up to the rigadoon. One will never dance in the factories, nor will one ever sing again. If one no longer sings, one passes away, one no longer conceives children, one locks oneself up in a movie theater just to forget that one exists. (*BD*, p. 148)

Oh, what delightful impertinence! Caught in the whirlwind [. . .] For heavens' sake! amid a thousand flippancies! cat-like, on their toes, by fits and starts! they're making fun of us! Ta! ta! ta! . . . where the melody has led us . . . a summons in F! . . . everything evaporates! . . . two trills again! . . . an arabesque! . . . an échappée! Good Lord, here they are! . . . F . . . E . . . D . . . C . . . B! . . . Saucy girls of heaven enchant us! Since we are to be damned anyway, what's the difference! (*BD*, pp. 221–22)

Céline's style shows that such a dual enchantment between the "not yet one" and the "not quite another" can be written. He convinces us that the jouissance of so-called primary narcissism's immanence can be sublimated in a signifer that has been recast and desemanticized into music.

Furthermore, it is impossible not to hear the liberating truth of such a call to rhythm and joy, beyond the crippling constraints of a society ruled by monotheistic symbolism and its political and legal repercussions.

And yet, both the enchantment of the style and libertarian spontaneity bear within themselves their own *limit*; at the very moment that they seek to escape the oppression of the thinking, ethical, or legislative Unity, they prove to be tied to the deadliest of fantasies. The negated and frightened desire for the One as well as for the Other produces a symptom of destroying hatred directed toward both.

At that point the image of the Jew will concentrate negated love become hatred for Mastery on the one hand, and on the other and jointly, desire for what mastery cuts out: weakness, the joying substance, sex tinged with femininity and death.

Anti-Semitism, for which there thus exists an object as phantasmatic and ambivalent as the Jew, is a kind of parareligious formation; it is the sociological thrill, flush with history, that believers and nonbelievers alike seek in order to experience abjection. One may suppose, consequently, that anti-Semitism will be the more violent as the social and/or symbolic code is found wanting in the face of developing abjection. That, at any rate, is the situation in our contemporary world, and it is also, for more personal reasons, that of Céline. Do not all attempts, in our own cultural sphere at least, at escaping from the Judeo-Christian compound by means of a unilateral call to return to what it has repressed (rhythm, drive, the feminine, etc.), converge on the same Célinian anti-Semitic fantasy? And this is so because, as I have tried to explain earlier, the writings of the chosen people have selected a place, in the most determined manner, on that untenable crest of manness seen as symbolic fact—which constitutes abjection.

In this sense, Céline's pamphlets are the avowed delirium out of which the work emerges to venture into obscure regions at the limits of identity. If delirium is indeed involved, and Céline himself suggests that it is,[7] that is also the nature of all anti-Semitism, the daily banality of which surrounds us; Nazi excesses or Célinian outbursts, which are cathartic upon the whole, give us a warning while we thirst for sleep and jouissance.

Brother . . .

What fantasies can the Jew thus precipitate in Céline, in order to be the exemplar of all hatred, of all desire, of all fear of the Symbolic?

All powerful at first, he stands as a *hero*. Not so much as father than as preferred son, chosen, availing himself of paternal power. Freud had noted that every hero is a patricide. Céline does not go so far perhaps as to think of that kind of heroism, although he implicitly takes it for granted when he deems that, beyond comparison, over all other sons, "the Jew is a man more than anyone else" (*BM*, p. 270).[8]

Such a brother, superior and envied, is essentially active as opposed to the "grotesque unconcern" of the Aryan (*BM*, p. 128). Such a one is Yubelblat, in *Bagatelles pour un massacre*:

> He's a top-notch go-getter . . . Not a minute of interruption . . . He promises . . . Promises . . . flatters while delineating . . . rousing ardor or hatred . . . that tarry, weaken, become lost . . . He goes and badgers them again! What a hustle . . . Looking out for squalls! Skimming through! . . . Skimming through [. . .] pirouettes, nimble dodges, acrobatics . . . stealthy conferences, international mysteries and legerdemain, the frail Yubelblat. (*BM*, p. 102)

And what is more, contrary to accepted stereotypes, Céline depicts him as fearless, "The Jew, he's afraid of nothing . . . " (*BD*, p. 136) as long as he can reach his goal — power. "He always has to be the one who gives orders" (*BD*, p. 141).

It is by means of full anal mastery ("the future is his, he's got the dough," *BM*, p. 327), which involves *having* the primordial object, that the Jew makes certain of *being*, of being *everything* and *everywhere*, totaling the world as a flawless unity under his absolute control.

> The Jews, you know, they're all camouflaged, disguised, chameleon-like, they change names like they cross frontiers, now they pass themselves off from Bretons, Auvergnats, Corsicans, now for Turandots, Durandards, Cassoulets . . . anything at all . . . that throws people off, that sounds deceptive. (*BM*, p. 127)

> He's mimetic, he's a whore, he would have dissolved long ago, after assimilating to others so much, if it weren't for his greed, his greed saves him, he has worn out all races, all men, all animals, the earth is now done with [. . .] He's still hassling the universe, heaven, God, the Stars, he wants everything, he wants more, he wants the Moon, he wants our bones, he wants our guts as hair-curlers to celebrate the Sabbath, to deck the Carnival. (*BD*, p. 142)

Secretive, privy to mystery ("The Jew is mysterious, he has alien ways . . . " *BD*, p. 119), he holds elusive power. His ubiquity is not limited to space, he is not only on our land and under our skin, the very closest neighbor, the nearly same, the one we do not differentiate, the *dizziness of identity*, "we don't know what mugs they have, or could have, what manners they've got" (*BM*, p. 127); it also takes in the totality of time, he is *heir*, scion, enhanced by issue, by a kind of nobility that guarantees him the opportunity to amass traditions as well as goods of the family and social group:

> Any little Jew, at birth, finds in his cradle all the possibilities of a fine career . . . (*BM*, p. 127)

Blessed by the father and by reliable families, he artfully manipulates the networks of social reality, and he does it even better if he can be accepted by the aristocracy.

And yet, this position of power has nothing in common with the cold and majestic mastery proper to classic domination. In the anti-Semitic fantasy, Jewish power does not arouse respect as does paternal authority. Edged with fear, to the contrary, it unleashes the excitement brought on by sibling rivalry; the Aryan who engages in it is then swept into the fire of denied homosexual passion. Indeed, this chosen brother displays too much *weakness* (concerning him Céline calls to mind the small size and features indicative of crossbreeding, when he does not refer directly to the circumcised foreskin: "Lenin, Warburg, Trotsky, Rothschild, they all think alike in this. Not a foreskin of difference, it's one hundred percent Marxism"; *BD*, p. 103), ambivalent lack—which can just as well cause *surplus* or even *jouissance*—for one to be satisfied with obeying him or defying him. Is it possible to give in to a being whose behavior signifies he is an emanation of the Everything Everywhere, if he is so obviously weak and sensual? His weakness will be held against him—he will be considered a usurper, but very soon one will admit that his jouissance is what grates. As if he were that unique being, so different from the pagan, who draws his aura out of his weakness, that is, not out of a full and glorious body but out of his subjectivation to the Other.

It is indeed for an incomprehensible jouissance that Céline upbraids that favored brother by means of a sadomasochistic language that is openly sexual, or homosexual: "Fifteen million Jews will corn-hole five hundred million Aryans" (*BM*, p. 127). "He just couldn't care less, he comes, he's old enough, he's having fun" (*BD*, p. 31), is said about Roosevelt but in the context it also applies to Jews. "The Jews, Afro-Asiatic hybrids, quadroons, half-negroes, and Near-Easterners, unbridled fornicators, have no reason to be in this country" (*EC*, p. 215); or this letter signed "Jewish Salvador" and addressed to the "repulsive Céline," where one reads, among other fantasies, "The kikes stick it up your ass and if you want to be corn-holed just let us know" (*EC*, p. 17). The anti-Semite who comes up against it finds himself reduced to a feminine and masochistic position, as a passive object and slave to this jouissance, aggressed, sadisticized.

The fantasy of a Jewish threat, weighing against the Aryan world ("we are in the midst of Jewish Fascism"; *BM*, p. 180) in a period when, to the contrary, persecutions against the Jews are beginning, cannot be explained in any other way; it emanates directly out of that vision of the Jew as a being of having, as issuing from the All in which he joys, and especially from the immediate sexualization of that jouissance.

They do you no personal wrong? . . . —They get my goat . . . they feel me out in order to corner me . . . they come to size up the crap, at each turn of the page . . . each minute . . . to see how much more I have softened, grown weaker . . . (*BM*, p. 319)

Please condescend, my darling monster! too discreet crucifier! too seldom as I see it! I adore you! Grant all my wishes! You are keeping me on tenterhooks! You can see that I am weeping! overcome with happiness at the thought that I am at least going to suffer still a lot more . . . (*BM*, p. 134)

There's always a little Jew there in the corner, crouching, mocking, thinking it over . . . watching the goy, who's seething . . . now heartened he comes closer . . . Seeing the object so fully aflame . . . runs his hand over that lovely cunt! . . . (*BD*, p. 124)

Through the crescendo of the phantasmatic build-up, the Jew ends up becoming a despotic tyrant to whom the anti-Semite submits his anal eroticism, explicitly with Céline, elsewhere in more or less underhanded fashion. Céline describes himself, as he faces this imaginary aggressor, as a "corn-holed figure," "the kikes shit in your kisser" (*EC*, p. 17); he often seems "the good Aryan [. . .] always ready to make his Jew come" (*BD*, p. 125).

And yet, if jouissance is something the Jew is supposed to have knowledge of, he appears anxious not to spend (himself) for it. He is master of jouissance, but not an artisan, not an artist. That tyrannical brother thus places himself under the purview of a law that is paternal, in the nature of the superego, dominating drives, the opposite of natural, childish, animal, and musical spontaneity. Anxious to commit himself to a bit of "direct humanity," the Jew "immediately becomes more and more tyrannical" (*BM*, p. 194). A domineering person, he first gains mastery over himself through cold reason, which deprives him of any access to talent. The Jew is the prototype of the intellectual, the superintellectual, so to speak (the utmost in intellectual frigidity is reached when the university man happens to be Jewish, like Ben Montaigne, the professor in *Les Beaux Draps*); he is incapable of art but he has invented "technix" (which ushers in the artificial world of "flies without pricks! soft sphincters! falsies, all the filthy trickeries"; *BM*, p. 177). If he is a writer, he is like the bourgeois writer author of "patched up borrowings, things seen through a windshield . . . a bumper or simply stolen from the depths of libraries . . . " (*BM*, p. 166). Thus identified with Law, Mastery, Abstraction, and Home, he will drift from the position of desired and envied brother to that of impregnable father against whom all the quite Oedipal attacks of Céline's scription, claiming Emotion and Music as the other of Law and Language, will unceasingly be directed.

At this far point of "delirium" the anti-Semite unveils his denied but fierce belief in the Absolute of Jewish Religion as religion of the Father and of the Law; the anti-Semite is its possessed servant, its demon, its "dibbuk" as someone has said,[9] who provides *a contrario* proof of monotheistic power of which he becomes the symptom, the failure, the envier. Is that why he expresses the traumatic topoi of that religion—like those of abjection—which religion, to the contrary, elaborates, sublimates, or masters? All of which, without being its truth, at least constitutes for the subject its unconscious impact?

. . . Or Wife

A third step needs to be taken now as I construct anti-Semitic discourse, which is frightened desire for the inheriting brother. If he joys in being under the Law of the Other, if he submits to the Other and draws out of it his mastery as well as his jouissance, is not this dreaded Jew an object of the Father, a piece of waste, his wife as it were, an abjection? It is on account of being such an unbearable conjoining of the One and the Other, of Law and Jouissance, of the one who Is and the one who Has that the Jew becomes threatening. So, in order to be protected, anti-Semitic fantasy relegates that object to the place of the ab-ject. The Jew: a conjunction of waste and object of desire, of corpse and life, fecality and pleasure, murderous aggressivity and the most neutralizing power—"What trow I? I trow that it is 'ours to Jew or die!' " (*BD*, p. 57), instinctively then, and uncompromisingly! The Jew becomes the feminine exalted to the point of mastery, the impaired master, the ambivalent, the border where exact limits between same and other, subject and object, and even beyond these, between inside and outside, and disappearing—hence an Object of fear and fascination. *Abjection itself*. He is abject: dirty, rotten. And I who identify with him, who desire to share with him a brotherly, mortal embrace in which I lose my own limits, I find myself reduced to the same abjection, a fecalized, feminized, passivated rot: "the repulsive Céline."

> [. . .] dirty bastard, loafer [. . .] Flushed out by Moses he holds his rank of big shit de luxe, pally with none but the other flushed-outs, within the realm of Moses, of the Eternal! He is nothing but decay, decaying. He has but one authentic thing deep in his shitty substance, and that's his hatred for us, his scorn, the fury with which he wants to have us crumble, deeper and deeper, into potter's field. (*BD*, p. 113)

The Aryan, lacking the symoblic power of the Jew, is no more than "experimental flesh," a "flesh in the state of decay" (*BM*, p. 316). The French Republic is "gangrened," the Jews can tear from it only "purulent scraps," "goodies," and "cadaverous fragments" (*EC*, p. 30). We are now far removed from Louis XIV or Louis XV, to whom Céline compared himself, in an interview after the war, when he tried to account for, even to criticize, his anti-Semitism ("But to the extent that they [the Jews] constituted a sect, like the Templars, or the Jansenists, I was as categorical as Louis XIV [. . .] and Louis XV when he got rid of the Jesuits . . . So, there you have it: I mistook myself for Louis XV or Louis XIV, that was obviously a serious error").[10] Unless such a megalomania, like Majesty itself, is the final mask behind which is concealed the empty, dilapidated castle of a foul, putrid, crisis-ridden identity.

The anti-Semite is not mistaken. Jewish monotheism is not only the most rigorous application of Unicity of the Law and the Symbolic; it is also the one that wears with the greatest assurance, but like a lining, the mark of maternal, feminine, or pagan substance. If it *removes* itself with matchless vigor from its fierce presence, it also integrates it without complacency. And it is probably such a presence, other but still integrated, that endows the monotheistic subject with the strength of an other-directed being. *In short, when a scription on the limits of identity comes face to face with abjection, it enters into competition with biblical abominations and even more so with prophetic discourse.* Céline alludes to biblical texts, mentions the prophets, vituperates against them. Nevertheless, his text follows their trajectory, jealously and yet differently. For he lacks the Law that belongs to prophetic stance; the abjection that he stages, contrary to that of the prophets, will not be relieved, not through any Name; it will merely be inscribed in enchantment, not for some other time, but here and now, in the text. If Céline, too, like the wandering people, undertakes a journey — the abjection inherent in the speaking being having been duly noted — what is involved for the novelist is a journey without project, without faith, to the end of the night. And yet is it not obvious that for Céline Scription and Style fully occupy the place left vacant by the disappearance of God, Prophet, and Faith? It remains for us to examine how such a scription, as Céline understands and practices it, rather than replacing displaces and therefore modifies transcendence and also reshapes the subjectivity that stirs within.

NOTES

1. Louis-Ferdinand Céline, *Les Beaux Draps* (Paris: Nouvelles Editions Françaises, 1941), p. 90. Subsequent references to this work, abbreviated as *BD*, will appear in the body of the text.

2. Louis-Ferdinand Céline, *L'Ecole des cadavres* (Paris: Denoël, 1938), p. 140. Subsequent references to this work, abbreviated as *EC*, will appear in the body of the text.

3. Letter to Hindus, September 2, 1947, *L'Herne*, 5:94.

4. Letter to Hindus, April 16, 1947, *L'Herne*, 5:72.

5. Louis-Ferdinand Céline, *Bagatelles pour un massacre* (Paris: Denoël, 1937), p. 144. Subsequent references to this work, abbreviated as *BM*, will appear in the body of the text.

6. From an interview with Ivan-M. Sicard published in *L'Emancipation Nationale*, November 21, 1941.

7. It would not only seem that, to the end of his life, he never clearly renounced anti-Semitism ("I disown nothing at all . . . I have not at all changed my mind . . . I simply put in a modicum of doubt, but people will have to prove that I was wrong rather than me showing that I was right" — "Entretien avec A. Zbinden," *Romans II*, p. 940), but even when he entertains the idea of a reconciliation with Jews (he specifies, "not a *Defense of the Jews* but a *Reconciliation*")

he is led to advocate a new racism, a decidedly permanent feeling of love/hatred for the other: "We must create a new racism upon biological bases" (letter to Hindus, August 10, 1947, *L'Herne*, 5:90).

8. Catherine Francblin has presented a very lucid analysis of Céline's anti-Semitism in an unpublished master's essay entitled "Céline et les Juifs." I am indebted to her for the following development.

9. See A. Mandel, "D'un Céline juif," *L'Herne* (1963), 3:252–57, and "L'Ame irresponsable, ou Céline et le Dibbouk," *L'Herne* (1965) 5:207–9.

10. "Entretiens avec A. Zbinden," *Romans II*, p. 939.

CHAPTER 13

Interrogating Identity:
The Postcolonial Prerogative

Homi K. Bhabha

I

To read Fanon is to experience the sense of division that prefigures—and fissures—the emergence of a truly radical thought that never dawns without casting an uncertain dark. Fanon is the purveyor of the transgressive and transitional truth. He may yearn for the total transformation of Man and Society, but he speaks most effectively from the uncertain interstices of historical change: from the area of ambivalence between race and sexuality; out of an unresolved contradiction between culture and class; from deep within the struggle of psychic representation and social reality. His voice is most clearly heard in the subversive turn of a familiar term, in the silence of sudden rupture: "*The Negro is not. Any more than the white man.*" The awkward division that breaks his line of thought keeps alive the dramatic and enigmatic sense of process of change. That familiar alignment of colonial subjects—Black/White, Self/Other—is disturbed with one brief pause and the traditional grounds of racial identity are dispersed, whenever they are found to rest in the narcissistic myths of negritude or white cultural supremacy. It is this palpable pressure of division and displacement that pushes Fanon's writing to the edge of things—the cutting edge that reveals no ultimate radiance but, in his words, "exposed an utterly naked declivity where an authentic upheaval can be born."

This essay is a belated and modest offering to mark the twenty-fifth anniversary of Frantz Fanon's death, which, in Britain, was passed over in silence. I would like to thank Lisa Appignanesi, James Donald, and David Goldberg for their many useful suggestions.

The psychiatric hospital at Blida-Joinville is one such place where, in the divided world of French Algeria, Fanon discovered the impossibility of his mission as a colonial psychiatrist:

> If psychiatry is the medical technique that aims to enable man no longer to be a stranger to his environment, I owe it to myself to affirm that the Arab, permanently an alien in his own country, lives in a state of absolute depersonalization. . . . . . The social structure existing in Algeria was hostile to any attempt to put the individual back where he belonged.

The extremity of this colonial alienation of the person—this end of the "idea" of the individual—produces a restless urgency in Fanon's search for a conceptual form appropriate to the social antagonism of the colonial relation. The body of his works splits between a Hegelian-Marxist dialectic, a phenomenological affirmation of Self and Other and the psychoanalytic ambivalence of the Unconscious, its turning from love to hate, mastery to servitude. In his desperate, doomed search for a dialectic of deliverance Fanon explores the edge of these modes for thought: his Hegelianism restores hope to history; his existentialist evocation of the "I" restores the presence of the marginalized; his psychoanalytic framework illuminates the madness of racism, the pleasure of pain, the agonistic fantasy of political power.

As Fanon attempts such audacious, often impossible, transformations of truth and value, the jagged testimony of colonial dislocation, its displacement of time and person, its defilement of culture and territory, refuses the ambition of any total theory of colonial oppression. The Antillean *évolué* cut to the quick by the glancing look of a frightened, confused, white child; the stereotype of the native fixed at the shifting boundaries between barbarism and civility; the insatiable fear and desire for the Negro: "Our women are at the mercy of Negroes . . . God knows how they make love"; the deep cultural fear of the black figured in the psychic trembling of Western sexuality—it is these signs and symptoms of the colonial condition that drive Fanon from one conceptual scheme to another, while the colonial relation takes shape in the gaps between them, articulated to the intrepid engagements of his style. As Fanon's text unfolds, the scientific fact comes to be aggressed by the experience of the street; sociological observations are intercut with literary artifacts, and the poetry of liberation is brought up short against the leaden, deadening prose of the colonized world.

What is this distinctive *force* of Fanon's vision that has been forming even as I write about the division, the displacement, the cutting edge of this thought? It comes, I believe, from the tradition of the oppressed, as Walter Benjamin suggests: it is the language of a revolutionary awareness that "the state of emergency in which we live is not the exception but the rule. We must attain to a concept of history that is in keeping with this insight." And the state of emergency is also always a state of *emergence*. The struggle against colonial oppression not only changes the direction of Western history, but challenges its historicist idea of time as a progressive, ordered whole. The analysis of colonial depersonalization not only alienates the Enlightenment idea of "Man," but challenges the transparency of social reality, as a pregiven image of human knowledge. If the order of Western historicism is disturbed in the colonial state of emergency, even more deeply disturbed is the social and psychic representation of the human subject. For the very nature of humanity becomes estranged in the colonial condition and from that "naked declivity" it emerges, not as an assertion of will nor as an evocation of freedom, but as an enigmatic questioning. With a question that echoes Freud's "*What does woman want?*, Fanon turns to confront the colonized world. "What does a man want?" he asks, in the introduction to *Black Skin, White Masks*; "What does the black man want?"

To this loaded question where cultural alienation bears down on the ambivalence of psychic identification, Fanon responds with an agonizing performance of self-images:

> I had to meet the white man's eyes. An unfamiliar weight burdened me. In the white world the man of color encounters difficulties in the development of his bodily schema. . . . I was battered down by tom-toms, cannibalism, intellectual deficiency, fetishism, racial defects. . . . I took myself far off from my own presence. . . . What else could it be for me but an amputation, an excision, a haemorrhage that spattered my whole body with black blood?

From within the metaphor of vision complicit with a Western metaphysic of Man emerges the displacement of the colonial relation. The black presence ruins the representative narrative of Western personhood: its past tethered to treacherous stereotypes of primitivism and degeneracy will not produce a history of civil progress, a space for the *Socius*; its present, dismembered and dislocated, will not contain the image of identity that is questioned in the dialectic of mind/body and resolved in the epistemology of appearance and reality. The white man's eyes break up the black man's body and in that act of epistemic violence its own frame of reference is transgressed, its field of vision disturbed.

"What does the black man *want?*" Fanon insists, and in privileging the psychic dimension he not only changes what we understand by a *political* demand but transforms the very means by which we recognize and identify its *human agency*. Fanon is not principally posing the question of political oppression as the violation of a human essence, although he lapses into such a lament in his more existential moments. He is not raising the question of colonial man in the universalist terms of the liberal-humanist ("How does colonialism deny the Rights of Man?"); nor is he posing an ontological question about Man's being ("*Who* is the alienated colonial man?"). Fanon's question is addressed not to such a unified notion of history nor to such a unitary concept of man. It is one of the original and disturbing qualities of *Black Skin, White Masks* that it rarely historicizes the colonial experience. There is no master narrative or realist perspective that provides a background of social and historical facts against which emerge the problems of the individual or collective psyche. Such a traditional sociological alignment of Self and Society or History and Psyche is rendered questionable in Fanon's identification of the colonial subject who is historicized as it comes to be heterogeneously inscribed in the texts of history, literature, science, myth. The colonial subject is always "overdetermined from without," Fanon writes. It is through image and fantasy—those orders that figure transgressively on the borders of history and the unconscious—that Fanon most profoundly evokes the colonial condition.

In articulating the problem of colonial cultural alienation in the psychoanalytic language of demand and desire, Fanon radically questions the formation of both individual and social authority as they come to be developed in the discourse of social sovereignty. The social virtues of historical rationality, cultural cohesion, the autonomy of individual consciousness assume an immediate, utopian identity with the subjects on whom they confer a civil status. The civil state is the ultimate expression of the innate ethical and rational bent of the human mind; the social instinct is the progressive destiny of human nature, the necessary transition from Nature to Culture. The direct access from individual interests to social authority is objectified in the representative structure of a General Will—Law or Culture—where Psyche and Society mirror each other, transparently translating their difference, without loss, into a historical totality. Forms of social and psychic alienation and aggression—madness, self-hate, treason, violence—can never be acknowledged as determinate and constitutive conditions of civil authority, or as the ambivalent effects of the social instinct itself. They are always explained away as alien presences, occlusions of historical progress, the ultimate misrecognition of Man.

For Fanon such a myth of Man and Society is fundamentally undermined in the colonial situation where everyday life exhibits a "constellation of delirium" that mediates the normal social relations of its subjects: "The Negro enslaved by his inferiority, the white man enslaved by his superiority alike behave in accordance with a neurotic orientation." Fanon's demand for a psychoanalytic explanation emerges from the perverse reflections of civil virtue in the alienating acts of colonial governance: the visibility of cultural mummification in the colonizer's avowed ambition to civilize or modernize the native that results in "archaic inert institutions [that function] under the oppressor's supervision like a caricature of formerly fertile institutions"; or the validity of violence in the very definition of the colonial social space; or the viability of the febrile, phantasmic images of racial hatred that come to be absorbed and acted out in the wisdom of the West. These interpositions, indeed collaborations of political and psychic violence *within* civic virtue, alienation within identity, drive Fanon to describe the splitting of the colonial space of consciousness and society as marked by a "Manichaean delirium."

The representative figure of such a perversion, I want to suggest, is the image of post-Enlightenment man tethered to, *not* confronted by, his dark reflection, the shadow of colonized man, that splits his presence, distorts his outline, breaches his boundaries, repeats his action at a distance, disturbs and divides the very time of his being. This ambivalent identification of the racist world — moving on two planes without being in the least embarrassed by it, as Sartre says of the anti-Semitic consciousness — turns on the idea of man as his alienated image, not Self and Other but the Otherness of the Self inscribed in the perverse palimpsest of colonial identity. And it is that bizarre figure of desire, which splits along the axis on which it turns, that compels Fanon to put the psychoanalytic question of the desire of the subject to the historic condition of colonial man.

"What is often called the black soul is a white man's artefact," Fanon writes. This transference, I have argued, speaks otherwise. It reveals the deep psychic uncertainty of the colonial relation itself: its split representations stage that division of body and soul that enacts the artifice of identity, a division that cuts across the fragile skin — black and white — of individual and social authority. What emerges from the figurative language I have used to make such an argument are three conditions that underlie an understanding of the *process of identification* in the analytic of desire.

First: to exist is to be called into being in relation to an Otherness, its look or locus. It is a demand that reaches outward to an external object and as J. Rose writes, "It is the relation of this demand to the place of the object it claims that becomes the basis for identification." This process is visible in that exchange of looks between native and settler that structures their psychic relation in the paranoid fantasy of boundless possession and its familiar language of reversal: "When their glances meet he [the settler] ascertains bitterly, always on the defensive, 'They want to take our place.' It is true for there is no native who does not dream at least once a day of setting himself up in the settler's place." It is always in relation to the place of the Other that colonial desire is articulated: that is, in part, the phantasmic space of possession that no one subject can singly occupy that permits the dream of the inversion of roles.

Second: the very place of identification, caught in the tension of demand and desire, is a space of splitting. The fantasy of the native is precisely to occupy the master's place while keeping his place in the slave's *avenging* anger. "Black skin, white masks" is not, for example, a neat division; it is a doubling, dissembling image of being in at least two places at once that makes it impossible for the devalued, insatiable *évolué* (an abandonment neurotic, Fanon claims) to accept the colonizer's invitation to identity: "You're a doctor, a writer, a student, you're *different*, you're one of *us*." It is precisely in that ambivalent use of "different"—to be different from those that are different makes you the same—that the Unconscious speaks of the form of Otherness, the tethered shadow of deferral and displacement. It is not the colonialist Self or the colonized Other, but the disturbing distance in between that constitutes the figure of colonial otherness—the white man's artifice inscribed on the black man's body. It is in relation to this impossible object that emerges the liminal problem of colonial identity and its vicissitudes.

Finally, as has already been disclosed by the rhetorical figures of my account of desire and Otherness, the question of identification is never the affirmation of a pregiven identity, never a self-fulfilling prophecy—it is always the production of an image of identity and the transformation of the subject in assuming that image. The demand of identification—that is, to be *for* an Other—entails the representation of the subject in the differentiating order of Otherness. Identification, as we inferred from the preceding illustrations, is always the return of an image of identity that bears the mark of splitting in the Other place from which it comes. For Fanon, like Lacan, the primary moments of such a repetition of the self lie in the desire of the look and the limits of language. The "atmosphere of certain uncertainty" that surrounds the body certifies its existence and threatens its dismemberment.

II

Listen to my friend, the Bombay poet Adil Jussawalla, writing of the "missing person" that haunts the identity of the postcolonial bourgeoisie:

> No Satan
> warmed in the electric coils of his creatures
> or Gunga Din
> will make him come before you.
> To see an invisible man or a missing person,
> trust no Eng. Lit. That
> puffs him up, narrows his eyes,
> scratches him fangs. Caliban
> is still not IT.
> But faintly pencilled
> behind a shirt . . .
>
> . . . .

> Savage of no sensational paint,
> fangs cancelled.[1]

As that voice falters listen to its echo in the verse of a black woman, descendant of slaves, writing of the diaspora:

> We arrived in the Northern Hemisphere
> when summer was set in its way
> running from the flames that lit the sky
> over the Plantation.
> We were a straggle bunch of immigrants
> in a lily white landscape.
>
> . . . .
>
> One day I learnt,
> a secret art,
> Invisible-Ness, it was called.
> I think it worked
> as even now you look
> but never see me . . .
> Only my eyes will remain to haunt,
> and to turn your dreams
> to chaos.[2]

As these images fade, and the empty eyes endlessly hold their menacing gaze, listen finally to Edward Said's attempt to historicize their chaos of identity:

> One aspect of the electronic, postmodern world is that there has been a reinforcement of the stereotypes by which the Orient is viewed. . . . If the world has become immediately accessible to a Western citizen living in the electronic age, the Orient too has drawn nearer to him, and is now less a myth perhaps than a place criss-crossed by Western, especially American interests.[3]

I have begun with these postcolonial portraits because they seize on the vanishing point of two familiar traditions in the discourse of identity: the philosophical tradition of identity as the process of self-reflection in the mirror of (human) nature; and the anthropological view of the difference of human identity as located in the division of Nature/Culture. In the postcolonial text the problem of identity returns as a persistent questioning of the frame, the space of representation, where the image — missing person, invisible eye, Oriental stereotype — is confronted with its difference, its Other. This is neither the glassy essence of Nature, to use Richard Rorty's image, nor the leaden voice of "ideological interpellation," as Louis Althusser suggests. What is so graphically enacted in the moment of colonial identification is the splitting of the subject in its historical place of utterance: "*No* Satan / or Gunga Din will make him come before you / *To see* an invisible man or a missing person . . . / trust *no* Eng. Lit." What these repeated negations of identity dramatize, in their elision of the seeing eye that must contemplate what is missing or invisible, is the impossibility of claiming an origin for the Self (or Other) within a tradition of representation that conceives of identity as the satisfaction of a totalizing, plenitudinous object of vision. By disrupting the stability of the ego, expressed in the equivalence between image and identity, the secret art of invisibleness of which the migrant poet speaks, changes the very terms of our recognition of the person.

This change is precipitated by the peculiar temporality whereby the subject cannot be apprehended without the absence or invisibility that constitutes it — "as even now you look / but never see me" — so that the subject speaks, and is seen, from where it is *not*; and the migrant woman can subvert the perverse satisfaction of the racist, masculinist gaze that disavowed her presence, by presenting it with an anxious absence, a countergaze that turns the discriminatory look, which denies her cultural and sexual difference, back on itself.

It is this familiar, postmodernist space of the Other (in the process of identification) that develops a graphic historical and cultural specificity in the splitting of the postcolonial or migrant subject. In place of that "I" — institutionalized in the visionary, authorial ideologies of *Eng. Lit.* or the notion of "experience" in the empiricist accounts of slave history — there emerges the challenge to see what is invisible, the look that cannot "see me," a certain problem of the object of the gaze that constitutes a problematic referent for the language of the Self. The elision of the eye, represented in a narrative of negation and repetition — *no* . . . *no* . . . *never* — insists that the phrase of identity cannot be spoken, except by putting the eye/I in the impossible position of enunciation. *To see* a missing person, or *to look* at Invisibleness, is to emphasize the subject's *transitive* demand for a *direct* object of self-reflection, a point of presence that would maintain its privileged enunciatory position *qua subject*. To see a *missing person* is to *transgress* that demand; the "I" in the position of mastery is, at *that same time*, the place of its absence, its *re*-presentation. What we witness is the alienation of the eye with the sound of the signifier as the desire (to look/to be looked at) emerges and is erased in the *feint of writing*:

> But faintly pencilled
> behind a shirt,
> a trendy jacket or tie

if he catches your eye,
he'll come screaming at you like a jet—
savage of no sensational paint,
fangs cancelled.

Why does the faintly penciled person fail to catch your eye? What is the secret of Invisibleness that enables the woman migrant to look without being seen?

What is transformed in the postmodern perspective, is not simply the image of the person, but an interrogation of the discursive and disciplinary place from which questions of identity are strategically and institutionally posed. Through the progress of this poem "you" are continually positioned in the space between a range of contradictory places that coexist. So that you find yourself at the point at which the Orientalist stereotype is evoked and erased *at the same time*; in the place where Eng. Lit. is *Entstellt* in the ironic mimicry of its Indo-Anglian repetition. And this space of re-inscription must be thought outside of those metaphysical philosophies of self-doubt, where the otherness of identity is the anguished *presence* within the Self of an existentialist agony that emerges when you look perilously through a glass darkly.

What is profoundly unresolved, even erased, in the discourses of poststructuralism is that *perspective of depth* through which the authenticity of identity comes to be reflected in the glassy metaphorics of the mirror and its mimetic or realist narratives. In shifting the frame of identity from the field of vision to the space of writing, postmodernism interrogates that third dimensionality that gives profundity to the representation of Self and Other and creates that depth of perspective that cineastes call the fourth wall; literary theorists describe it as the transparency of realist metanarratives. Barthes brilliantly diagnoses this as *l'effet du reel*, the "profound, geological dimension"[4] of signification, achieved by arresting the linguistic sign in its *symbolic* function. The bilateral space of the symbolic consciousness, Barthes writes, massively privileges *resemblance*, constructs an *analogical* relation between signifier and signified that ignores the question of form, and creates a vertical dimension within the sign. In this scheme the signifier is always predetermined by the signified—that conceptual or real space that is placed prior to, and outside of, the act of signification.

From our point of view, this verticality is significant for the light it sheds on that *dimension of depth* that provides the language of Identity with its sense of reality, a measure of the "me," which emerges from an acknowledgment of my inwardness, the depth of my character, the profundity of my person, to mention only a few of those adjectives through which we commonly articulate our self-consciousness. My argument about the importance of *depth* in the representation of a unified image of the self is borne out by the most decisive and influential formulation on personal identity in the English empiricist tradition.

John Locke's famous criteria of the continuity of consciousness ensuring the sameness of a rational being could quite legitimately be read as written in the symbolic sign of resemblance and analogy. For the consciousness of the past, crucial to the argument — "as far as this consciousness can be extended *backwards* to any past action or thought, so far reaches the identity of that person" — is precisely that unifying third dimension, that agency of *depth*, that brings together in an analogical relation (dismissive of the differences that construct temporality and signification), "that same consciousness uniting those distant actions into the came person, *whatever substances contributed to their production*" (my emphasis).[5]

Barthes's description of the sign-as-symbol is conveniently analogous to the language we use to designate identity. At the same time, it sheds light on the concrete linguistic concepts with which we can grasp how the language of personhood comes to be invested with a visuality or visibility of depth. This makes the moment of self-consciousness at once refracted and transparent; the question of identity always poised uncertainly, tenebrously, between shadow and substance. The symbolic consciousness gives the sign (of the Self) a sense of autonomy or solitariness "as if it stands by itself in the world" privileging an individuality and a unitariness whose integrity is expressed in a certain richness of agony and anomie. Barthes calls it a mythic prestige, almost totemic in "its form [which is] constantly exceeded by the power and movement of its content; . . . much less a codified form of communication than an (affective) instrument of participation."[6] (This image of human identity and, indeed, human identity as *image* — both familiar frames or mirrors of selfhood that speak from deep within Western culture — are inscribed in the sign of resemblance.) The analogical relation unifies the experience of self-consciousness by finding, within the mirror of nature, the symbolic certitude of the sign of culture based "on an analogy with the compulsion to believe when staring at an object."[7] This, as Rorty writes, is part of the West's obsession that our primary relation to objects and ourselves is analogous to visual perception. Preeminent among these representations has been the reflection of the self that develops in the symbolic consciousness of the sign, and marks out the discursive space from which *The real Me* emerges initially as an assertion of the authenticity of the person and then lingers on to reverberate — *The real Me???* — as a questioning of identity.

My purpose here is to define the space of the inscription or writing of identity — beyond the visual depths of Barthes's symbolic sign. The postmodernist experience of the disseminating self-image goes beyond representation as the analogical consciousness of resemblance. The problem is not of the nature of dialectical contradiction, the antagonistic consciousness of master and slave, that can be sublated and transcended. The impasse or aporia of consciousness that seems to be the representative postmodernist experience is a peculiar strategy of doubling.

Each time the encounter with identity occurs at the point at which something exceeds the frame of the image, it eludes the eye, evacuates the self as site of identity and autonomy and — most important — leaves a resistant trace, a stain of the subject, a sign of resistance. We are no longer confronted with an ontological problem of being but with the discursive strategy of the moment of interrogation, a moment in which the demand for identification becomes, primarily, a response to other questions of signification and desire, culture and politics.

In place of the symbolic consciousness that gives the sign of identity its integrity and unity, its *depth*, we are faced with a dimension of doubling; a spatialization of the subject, that is occluded in the illusory perspective of, what I have called, the "third dimension" of the mimetic frame or visual image of identity. The figure of the double — to which I now turn — cannot be contained within the analogical sign of resemblance, which, as Barthes said, developed its totemic, vertical dimension only because "what interests it in the sign is the signified: the signifier is always a determined element." For poststructuralist discourse, it is the priority (and play) of the signifier that reveals the space of doubling (not depth) that is the very articulatory principle of discourse. It is through that space of enunciation that problems of meaning and being enter the discourses of poststructuralism, as the problematic of subjection and identification.

What emerges in the preceding poems, as the line drawing of trendy jacket and tie, or the eerie, avengeful disembodied eye, must not be read as revelations of some suppressed truth of the postcolonial psyche/subject. In the world of double inscriptions that we have now entered, in this space of *writing*, there can be no such immediacy of a visualist perspective, no such face-to-face epiphanies in the mirror of nature, that Rorty attributed to the tradition of epistemological knowledge. On one level, what confronts you, the reader, in the incomplete portrait of the postcolonial bourgeois — who looks uncannily like the trendy metropolitan intellectual *you* are yourself — is the ambivalence of your desire for the Other: "*You! hypocrite lecteur! — mon semblable, — mon frere!*"

That disturbance of your voyeuristic look enacts the complexity and contradictions of your desire *to see, to fix* cultural difference in a containable, *visible* object, or as a fact of nature, when it can only be articulated in the uncertainty or undecidability that circulates through the processes of language and identification. The desire for the Other is doubled by the desire in language, which *splits the difference* between Self and Other so that both positions are partial; neither is sufficient unto itself. As I have just shown in the portrait of the missing person, the very question of identification only emerges *in be-*

tween disavowal and designation. It is performed in the agonistic struggle between the epistemological, visual demand for a knowledge of the Other, and its representation in the act of articulation and enunciation.

> Look a Negro . . . Mama, see the Negro! I'm frightened . . . I could no
> longer laugh, because I already know where there were legends, stories,
> history, and above all *historicity*. . . . Then, assailed at various points, the
> corporeal schema crumbled, its place taken by a racial epidermal
> schema . . . It was no longer a question of being aware of my body in the
> third person but in a triple person . . . I was responsible for my body, for
> my race, for my ancestors.

Fanon's *Black Skin, White Masks* reveals the doubling of identity: the difference between personal identity as an intimation of reality, or an intuition of being, and the psychoanalytic problem of identification that, in a sense, always begs the question of the subject: "What does a man want?" The emergence of the human subject as socially and psychically authenticated depends on the *negation* of an originary narrative of fulfillment or an imaginary coincidence between individual interest or instinct and the General Will. Such binary, two-part, identities function in a kind of narcissistic reflection of the One in the Other that is confronted in the language of desire by the psychoanalytic process of identification. For identification, identity is never an a priori, nor a finished product; it is only ever the problematic process of access to an image of totality. The discursive conditions of this psychic image of identification will be clarified if we think of the perilous perspective of the concept of the image itself. For the image—as point of identification—marks the site of an ambivalence. Its representation is always spatially split—it makes *present* something that is *absent*—and temporally deferred: it is the representation of a time that is always elsewhere, a repetition. The image is only ever an *appurtenance* to authority and identity; it must never be read mimetically as the appearance or a reality. The access to the image of identity is only ever possible in the *negation* of any sense of originality or plenitude, through the principle of displacement and differentiation (absence/presence, representation/repetition) that always renders it a liminal reality. The image is at once a metaphoric substitution, an illusion of presence and by that same token a metonym, a sign of its absence and loss. It is precisely from this edge of meaning and being, from this shifting boundary of otherness within identity, that Fanon asks: "What does a *black* man want?"

> When it encounters resistance from the other, self-consciousness undergoes
> the experience of desire. . . . As soon as I desire I ask to be considered. I
> am not merely here and now, sealed into thingness. I am for somewhere
> else and for something else. I demand that notice be taken of my negating
> activity in so far as I pursue something other than life. . . .

I occupied space. I moved towards the other . . . and the evanescent other, hostile, but not opaque, transparent, not there, disappeared. Nausea.

From that overwhelming emptiness of nausea Fanon makes his answer: the black man wants the objectifying confrontation with otherness; in the colonial psyche there is an unconscious disavowal of the negating, splitting moment of desire. The place of the Other must not be imaged as Fanon sometimes suggests as a fixed phenomenological point, opposed to the self, that represents a culturally alien consciousness. The Other must be seen as the necessary negation of a primordial identity — cultural or psychic — that introduces the system of differentiation that enables the cultural to be signified as a linguistic, symbolic, historic reality. If, as I have suggested, the subject of desire is never simply a Myself, then the Other is never simply an *It-self*, a front of identity, truth, or misrecognition.

As a principle of identification, the Other bestows a degree of objectivity but its representation — be it the social process of the Law or the psychic process of the Oedipus — is always ambivalent, disclosing a lack. For instance, the common, conversational distinction between the letter and spirit of the Law displays the otherness of Law itself; the ambiguous grey area between Justice and judicial procedure is, quite literally, a conflict of judgment. In the language of psychoanalysis, the Law of the Father or the paternal metaphor, again, cannot be taken at its word. It is a process of substitution and exchange that inscribes a normative, normalizing place for the subject; but that metaphoric access to identity is exactly the place of prohibition and repression, precisely a conflict of authority. Identification, as it is spoken in the *desire of the Other*, is always a question of interpretation for it is the elusive assignation of myself with a one-self, the elision of person and place.

If the differentiating force of the Other is the process of the subject's signification in language and society's objectification in Law, then how can the Other disappear? Can desire, the moving spirit of the subject, ever evanesce?

III

Lacan's excellent, if cryptic, suggestion that "the Other is a dual entry matrix"[8] should be understood as the partial erasure of the *depth perspective* of the symbolic sign, through the circulation of the signifier that, in its doubling and displacing, permits the sign no reciprocal binary division of form and content, superstructure and infrastructure, self/other. It is only by understanding the ambivalence and the antagonism of the desire of the Other that we can avoid the increasingly facile adoption of the notion of a homogenized Other, for a celebratory, oppositional politics of the margins or minorities.

The performance of the doubleness or splitting of the subject is enacted in the *writing/ecriture* of the poems I have quoted. It is evident in the play on the metonymic figures of "missing" and "invisibleness" around which their questioning of identity turns. It is articulated in those iterative instances that simultaneously mark the possibility and impossibility of identity, its presence through absence. *"Only my eyes will remain / to watch and to haunt,"* warns Meiling Jin as that threatening part object, the disembodied eye—the evil eye—becomes the subject of a violent discourse of *ressentiment*. Here, phantasmic and (pre)figurative rage erases the naturalistic identities of I and We that narrate a more conventional, even realist history of colonial exploitation and metropolitan racism, within the poem.

The moment of seeing that is arrested in the evil eye inscribes a timelessness, or a freezing of time—*"remain / to watch and to haunt"*—that can only be represented in the destruction of that *depth* associated with the sign of symbolic consciousness. It is a depth that comes from what Barthes describes as the *analogical* relation between superficial form and massive *Abgrund*: the "relation of form and content [as] ceaselessly renewed by time (history); the superstructure overwhelmed by the infrastructure, without our ever being able to grasp the structure itself."[9]

The eyes that remain—the eyes as a kind of *remainder*, producing an iterative process—cannot be part of this plenitudinous and progressive renewal of time or history. They are precisely the signs of a structure of *writing* history, a *history* of the poetics of postcolonial diaspora that the symbolic consciousness could never grasp. Most significantly, these partial eyes bear witness to a woman's writing of the postcolonial condition. Their circulation and repetition frustrate both the voyeuristic desire for the fixity of sexual difference and the fetishistic desire for racist stereotypes. The gaze of the evil eye alienates *both* the narratorial I of the slave and the surveillant eye of the Master. It unsettles any simplistic polarities or binarisms in identifying the exercise of power—Self/Other—and erases the analogical dimension in the articulation of sexual difference. It is empty of that depth of verticality that creates a totemic resemblance of form and content (*Abgrund*) that is ceaselessly renewed and replenished by the groundspring of history. The evil eye—like the missing person—is precisely nothing in itself; and it is this *structure of difference* that produces the continual hybridity of race and sexuality in the postcolonial discourse.

The elision of identity articulated in these tropes of the "secret art of Invisibleness" from which our postcolonial writers speak is not an ontology of lack that, on its other side, becomes a nostalgic demand for a liberatory, non-repressed identity. It is the uncanny, space and time *between* those two moments of being, their incommensurable differences—if such a place can be imagined—that is signified in the process of repetition, that gives the evil eye or the missing person its meaning. Meaningless in/as themselves, these figures initiate the rhetorical excess of social reality and the psychic reality of social fantasy. Their poetic and political force develops through a certain strategy of duplicity or doubling (not resemblance, in Barthes's sense), which Lacan has elaborated as "the process of gap" within which the relation of subject to Other is produced.[10] The primary duplicity of that missing person that is penciled in before your eyes, or the woman's eyes that watch and haunt, is that although these images emerge with a certain fixity and finality in the *present*, as if they are the last word on the subject, they cannot identify or interpellate identity as *presence*. This is because they are created in the ambivalence of a double time of iteration that, in Derrida's felicitous phrase, "baffles the process of appearing by dislocating any orderly time at the center of the present." The effect of such baffling, in both poems, is to initiate a principle of undecidability in the signification of part and whole, past and present, self and Other, such that there can be no negation or transcendence of difference.

The naming of the missing person as "*Savage of no sensational paint*" is a case in point. The phrase, spoken at the end of the poem, neither simply returns us to the Orientalist discourse of stereotypes and exotica—Gunga Din— enshrined in the history of Eng. Lit., nor allows us to rest with the line drawing of the missing person. The reader is positioned—together with the enunciation of the question of identity—in an undecidable space in between "desire and fulfillment, between perpetration and its recollection. . . . Neither future nor present, but between the two."[11] The repetition of the orientalia and its imperialist past are re-presented, made present semantically, within the same time and utterance as its representations are negated syntactically—"*no* sensational paint / Fangs cancelled.*" From that erasure, in the repetition of that "no," without being articulated at all in the phrase itself, emerges the faintly penciled presence of the missing person who, in absentia, is both present in, and constitutive of, the savagery. Can you tell the postcolonial bourgeois and the Western intellectual elite apart? How does the repetition of a part of speech—no!—turn the trendy image of civility into the double of savagery? What part does the feint of writing play in evoking these faint figures of identity? And, finally, where do *we* stand in that uncanny echo between what may be described as the attenuation of identity and its simulacra?

These questions demand a double answer. In each of them I have posed a theoretical problem in terms of its political and social effects. It is the boundary between them that I have continually tried to explore in my vacillations between the texture of poetry and a certain texturality of identity. One answer to my questions would be to say that we now stand at the point in the poststructuralist argument where we can see the doubleness of its own grounds: the uncanny sameness-in-difference, or the alterity of Identity of which these theories speak, and from which, in forked tongues, they communicate with each other to constitute those discourses that we name postmodernist. The rhetoric of repetition or doubling that I have traced displays the art of *becoming* through a certain metonymic logic disclosed in the "evil eye" or the "missing person." Metonymy, which is a figure of contiguity that substitutes a part for a whole (an eye for an I) must not be read as a form of simple substitution or equivalence. Its circulation of part and whole, identity and difference, must be understood as a *double movement* that follows what Derrida calls the logic or play of the "supplement":

> If it represents and makes an image, it is by the anterior default of a presence. Compensatory and vicarious, the supplement [evil eye] is an adjunct, a subaltern instance which *takes — (the) — place*. As substitute . . . [missing person] . . . it produces no relief, its place is assigned in the structure by the mark of an emptiness. Somewhere something can be filled up of itself . . . only by allowing itself to be filled through sign and proxy.[12]

Having illustrated, through my reading of the poems, the supplementary nature of the subject, I want to focus on the subaltern instance of metonymy, which is the *proxy* of both presence and the present: time (*takes place on*) and space (*takes place of* . . .) at once. To conceptualize this complex doubling of time and space, as the site of enunciation, and the temporal conditionality of social discourse, is both the thrill and the threat of the poststructuralist and postmodernist discourses. How different is this representation of the sign from the symbolic consciousness where, as Barthes said, the relation of form and content is ceaselessly renewed by Time (as the *Abgrund* of the historical)? The evil eye, which seeks to outstare linear, continuist history and turn its progressive dream into nightmarish chaos, is exemplary once more. What the poet calls "the secret art of Invisibleness" creates a crisis in the representation of personhood and, at the critical moment, initiates the possibility of political subversion. Invisibility erases the self-presence of that "I" in terms of which traditional concepts of political agency and narrative mastery function. What *takes (the) place*, in Derrida's supplementary sense, is the disembodied evil eye, the subaltern instance, that wreaks its revenge by circulating, *without being seen*. It cuts across the boundaries of master and slave; it opens up a space *in between* the poem's two locations, the Southern Hemisphere of slavery and the Northern Hemisphere of diaspora and migration, which then become uncannily doubled in this phantasmic scenario of the political unconscious. This doubling resists the traditional causal link that explains contemporary metropolitan racism as a result of the historical prejudices of imperialist nations. What it does suggest is the possibility of a new understanding of both forms of racism, based on their shared symbolic and spatial structures — Fanon's Manichaean structure — articulated within different temporal, cultural, and power relations.

The *antidialectical* movement of the subaltern instance subverts any binary or sublatory ordering of power and sign; it defers the object of the look — "*as even now you look / but never see me*" — and endows it with a strategic motion, which we may here, analogously, name the movement of the death drive. The evil eye, which is nothing in itself, exists in its lethal traces or effects as a form of iteration that arrests time — death/chaos — and initiates a space of *in-tercutting* that articulates politics/psyche, sexuality/race, in a relation that is differential and strategic rather than originary, ambivalent rather than ac-cumulative, doubling rather than dialectical. (The play of the evil eye is camouflaged, invisible in the common, ongoing activity of looking — making present, while it is implicated in the petrifying, unblinking gaze that falls Medusa-like on its victims — dealing death, extinguishing both presence and the present. There is a specifically feminist re-presentation of political sub-version in this strategy of the evil eye.) The disavowal of the position of the migrant woman — her social and political *invisibility* — is used by her in her se-cret art of revenge, *mimicry*. In that overlap of signification — in that fold of identification as cultural and sexual difference — the "I" is the initial, initiatory signature of the subject; and the "eye" (in its metonymic repetition) is the sign that initiates the terminal, arrest, death:

> as even now you look
> but never see me . . .
> Only my eyes will remain to haunt,
> and to turn your dreams
> to chaos.

It is in this overlapping space between the fading of identity and its faint inscription that I take my stand on the subject, amidst a celebrated gathering of poststructuralist thinkers. Although there are significant differences be-tween them, I want to focus here on their attention to the place from which the subject speaks or is spoken.

For Lacan — who has used the arrest of the evil eye in his analysis of the gaze — this is the moment of "temporal pulsation":

> [The signifier in the field of the Other] petrif[ies] the subject in the same movement in which it calls the subject to speak as subject.[13]

Foucault repeats something of the same uncanny movement of doubling when he elaborates on the "quasi-invisibility of the statement":

> Perhaps it is like the over-familiar that constantly eludes one; those familiar transparencies, which although they conceal nothing in their density, are nevertheless not entirely clear. The enunciative level emerges in its very proximity. . . . It has this quasi-invisibility of the "there is," which is effaced in the very thing of which one can say: "there is this or that thing . . . " Language always seems to be inhabited by the other, the else-where, the distant; it is hollowed out by distance.[14]

Lyotard holds on to the pulsating beat of the time of utterance when he dis-cusses the narrative of Tradition:

Tradition is that which concerns time, not content. Whereas what the West wants from autonomy, invention, novelty, self-determination, is the opposite—to forget time and to preserve, and accumulate contents. To turn them into what we call history and to think that it progresses because it accumulates. On the contrary, in the case of popular traditions . . . nothing gets accumulated, that is the narratives must be repeated all the time because they are forgotten all the time. But what does not get forgotten is the temporal beat that does not stop sending the narratives to oblivion. . . . This is a situation of continuous embedding, which makes it impossible to find a first utterer.[15]

IV

I may be accused of a form of linguistic or theoretical formalism, of establishing a rule of metonymy or the supplement and laying down the oppressive, even universalist, law of difference or doubling. How does the poststructuralist attention to *ecriture* and textuality influence my experience of myself? Not directly, I would answer, but then, have our fables of identity ever been unmediated by another; have they ever been more (or less) than a detour through the word of God, or the writ of Law, or the Name of the Father; the totem, the fetish, the telephone, the superego, the voice of the analyst, the closed ritual of the weekly confessional or the ever open ear of the monthly *coiffeuse*?

I am reminded also of the problem of self-portraiture in Holbein's *The Ambassadors*, of which Lacan produces a startling reading. The two still figures stand at the center of their world, surrounded by the accoutrements of *vanitas*—a globe, a lute, books, and compasses, unfolding wealth. They also stand in the moment of temporal instantaneity where the Cartesian subject emerges—in the same figural time—as the subjectifying relation of geometrical perspective, which I've described as the *depth* of the image of identity. But off-center, in the foreground (violating the meaningful depths of the *Abgrund*), there is a flat spherical object, obliquely angled. As you walk away from the portrait and turn to leave, you see that the disc is a skull, the reminder (and remainder) of death, that makes visible, nothing more, than the alienation of the subject, the anamorphic ghost.[16]

This brings me to my final interrogations. Doesn't the logic of the supplement—in its repetition and doubling—produce a historylessness; a "culture" of theory that makes it impossible to give meaning to historical specificity? This is a large question that I can only answer here by proxy, by citing a text remarkable for its postcolonial specificity and for its questioning of what we might mean *by* cultural specificity:

A—'s a giggle now
but on it Osiris, Ra.
An ॐ's an er . . . a cough,
once spoking your valleys with light.
But the a's here to stay.
On it St. Pancras station,
the Indian and African railways.

That's why you learn it today.

. . . .

"Get back to your language," they say.

These lines come from an early section of Adil Jussawalla's poem *Missing Person*. They provide an insight into the fold between the cultural and linguistic conditions that are articulated in the textual economy that I have described as the metonymic or the supplementary. The discourse of poststructuralism has largely been spelled out in an intriguing repetition of *a*, whether it is Lacan's *petit objet a* or Derrida's *différance*. Observe, then, the agency of this postcolonial *a*.

There is something supplementary about *a* that makes it the initial letter of the Roman alphabet and, at the same time, the indefinite article. What is dramatized in this postcolonial circulation of the *a* is a double scene on a double stage, to borrow a phrase from Derrida. The A — with which the verse begins — is the sign of a linguistic objectivity, inscribed in the Indo-European language tree, institutionalized in the cultural disciplines of empire; and yet as the Hindi vowel ॐ, which is the first letter of the Hindi alphabet and is pronounced as "er," testifies, the object of linguistic science is always already in an enunciatory process of cultural translation, showing up the hybridity of any genealogical or systematic filiation.

Listen: "*An ॐ's an er . . . a cough*": In the same time, we hear the *a* repeated in translation, not as an object of linguistics, but in the *act* of the colonial enunciation of cultural contestation. This double scene articulates the ellipsis. . . . which marks the *différance* between the Hindi sign ॐ and the demotic English signifier — "*er, a cough*." It is through the emptiness of ellipsis that the difference of colonial culture is articulated as a *hybridity* that acknowledges that all cultural specificity is belated, *different until itself* — ॐ . . . er ugh! Cultures come to be represented by virtue of the processes of iteration and translation through which their meanings are very vicariously addressed to — *through* — an Other. This erases any essentialist claims for the inherent authenticity or purity of cultures that, once inscribed in the naturalistic sign of symbolic consciousness, frequently become rationalist political arguments for the hierarchy and ascendancy of powerful cultures.[17]

It is in this hybrid gap, which produces no relief, that the colonial subject *takes place*, its subaltern position inscribed in that space of iteration where ॐ *takes (the) place of "er."* If this sounds like a schematic, poststructuralist joke—"its all words, words, words . . . "—then I must remind you of the linguistic insistence in Clifford Geertz's influential statement that the experience of understanding other cultures is "more like grasping a proverb, catching an illusion, seeing a joke—or as I have suggested reading a poem—than it is like achieving communion."[18] My insistence on locating the postcolonial subject *within* the play of the subaltern instance of writing is an attempt to develop Derrida's passing remark that the history of the decentered subject and its dislocation of European metaphysics is concurrent with the emergence of the problematic of cultural difference within ethnology.[19] He acknowledges the political nature of this moment but leaves it to us to specify it in the postcolonial text:

> "Wiped out," they say.
>
> Turn left or right,
>
> there's millions like you up here,
>
> picking their way through refuse,
>
> looking for words they lost.
>
> You're your country's lost property
>
> with no office to claim you back.
>
> You're polluting our sounds. You're so rude.
>
> "Get back to your language," they say.[20]

Embedded in these statements is a cultural politics of diaspora and paranoia, of migration and discrimination, of anxiety and appropriation, which is unthinkable without attention to those metonymic or subaltern moments that structure the subjects of writing and meaning. Without the doubleness that I described in the postcolonial play of the "a/ ॐ," it would be difficult to understand the anxiety provoked by the hybridizing of language, activated in the anguish associated with vacillating *boundaries*—psychic, cultural, territorial—of which these verses speak. Where do you draw the line between languages? between cultures? between disciplines? between peoples?

I have suggested here that a subversive political line is drawn in a certain poetics of "invisibility," "ellipsis," the evil eye and the missing person—all instances of the "subaltern" in the Derridean sense, and near enough to the sense that Gramsci gives the concept, "[not simply an oppressed group] but lacking autonomy, subjected to the influence or hegemony of another social group, not possessing one's own hegemonic position."[21] It is with this difference between the two usages, of course, that notions of autonomy and domination within the hegemonic would have to be carefully rethought, in the light of what I have said about the *proxy*-mate nature of any claim to *presence* or autonomy. However, what is implicit in both concepts of the subaltern, as I read it, is a strategy of ambivalence in the structure of identification that occurs precisely in the elliptical *in between*, where the shadow of the Other falls upon the Self.

From that shadow (in which the postcolonial *a* plays) emerges cultural differences as an *enunciative* category; opposed to relativistic notions of cultural diversity, or the exoticism of the "diversity" of cultures. Its force as a concept of cultural and political analysis is to open up the area of ambivalence within the generality of the statement and subject of Culture that is usually located somewhere between civil consensus and radical critique. It is that "between" that is articulated in the camouflaged subversion of the "evil eye" and the transgressive mimicry of the "missing person." The force of cultural difference is, as Barthes once said of the practice of metonymy, "the violation of a signifying *limit of space*, it permits on the very level of discourse, a counterdivision of objects, usages, meanings, spaces and properties."²²

It is by bringing together the violence of the poetic sign *within* the threat of political violation that we can understand the *powers* of language. Then, we can grasp the importance of the imposition of the Imperial *a* as the cultural condition for the very movement of empire, its *logomotion* — the creation of the Indian and African railways as the poet wrote. Now, we can begin to see why the threat of the (mis)translation of ॐ and "er," among those displaced and diasporic peoples who pick through the refuse, is a constant reminder to the postimperial West, of the hybridity of its mother tongue, and the heterogenity of its national space.

V

In his more analytic mode Fanon can impede the exploration of such questions of the ambivalence of colonial inscription and identification. The state of emergency from which he writes demands more insurgent answers, more immediate identifications. At times Fanon attempts too close a correspondence between the *mise-en-scene* of unconscious fantasy and the phantoms of racist fear and hate that stalk the colonial scene; he turns too hastily from the ambivalences of identification to the antagonistic identities of political alienation and cultural discrimination; he is too quick to name the Other, to personalize its presence in the language of colonial racism — "the real Other for the white man is and will continue to be the black man. And conversely." These attempts, in Fanon's words, to restore the dream to its proper political time and cultural space can, at times, blunt the edge of his brilliant illustrations of the complexity of the psychic projections in the pathological colonial relation. Jean Veneuse, the Antillean *évolué*, desires not merely to be in the place of the White man but compulsively seeks to look back and down on himself from that position. The White man does not merely deny what he fears and desires by projecting it on "them"; Fanon sometimes forgets that paranoia never preserves its position of power, for the compulsive identification with a persecutory "They" is always an evacuation and emptying of the "I."

Fanon's sociodiagnostic psychiatry tends to explain away the ambivalent turns and returns of the subject of colonial desire, its masquerade of Western Man and the "long" historical perspective. It is as if Fanon is fearful of his most radical insights: that the politics of race will not be entirely contained within the humanist myth of man or economic necessity or historical progress, for its psychic affects question such forms of determinism; that social sovereignty and human subjectivity are only realizable in the order of Otherness. It is as if the question of desire that emerged from the traumatic tradition of the oppressed has to be denied, at the end of *Black Skin, White Masks*, to make way for an existentialist humanism that is as banal as it is beatific:

> Why not the quite simple attempt to touch the other, to feel the other, to exlain the other to myself? . . . At the conclusion of this study, I want the world to recognize, with me, the open door of every consciousness.

Such a deep hunger for humanism, despite Fanon's insight into the dark side of Man, must be an overcompensation for the closed consciousness or "dual narcissism" to which he attributes the depersonalization of colonial man: "There one lies body to body, with one's blackness or one's whiteness in full narcissistic cry, each sealed into his own particularity — with, it is true, now and then a flash or so." It is this flash of recognition — in its Hegelian sense with its transcendental, sublative spirit — that fails to ignite in the colonial relation where there is only narcissistic indifference: "And yet the Negro knows there is a difference. He wants it. . . . The former slave needs a challenge to his humanity." In the absence of such a challenge, Fanon argues, the colonized can only imitate, a distinction nicely made by the psychoanalyst Annie Reich: "It is imitation . . . when the child holds the newspaper *like* his father. It is identification when the child learns to read." In disavowing the culturally differentiated condition of the colonial world — in demanding *"Turn White or disappear"* — the colonizer is himself caught in the ambivalence of paranoic identification, alternating between fantasies of megalomania and persecution.

However, Fanon's Hegelian dream for a human reality *in-itself-for-itself* is ironized, even mocked, by his view of the Manichaean structure of colonial consciousness and its nondialectical division. What he says in *The Wretched of the Earth* of the demography of the colonial city reflects his view of the psychic structure of the colonial relation. The native and settler zones, like the juxtaposition of black and white bodies, are opposed, but not in the service of a higher unity. No conciliation is possible, he concludes, for of the two terms one is superfluous.

No, there can be no reconciliation, no Hegelian recognition, no simple, sentimental promise of a humanistic "world of the You." Can there be life without transcendence? Politics without the dream of perfectibility? Unlike Fanon, I think the *nondialectical* moment of Manichaeanism suggests an answer. By following the trajectory of colonial desire—in the company of the bizarre colonial figure, the tethered shadow—it becomes possible to cross, even to shift the Manichaean boundaries. Where there is no human *nature*, hope can hardly spring eternal; but it emerges surely and surreptitiously in the strategic return of that difference that informs and deforms the image of identity, in the margin of Otherness that displays identification. There may be no Hegelian negation, but Fanon must sometimes be reminded that the disavowal of the Other always exacerbates the edge of identification, reveals that dangerous place where identity and aggressivity are twinned. For denial is always a retroactive process; a half acknowledgment of that Otherness has left its traumatic mark. In that uncertainty lurks the white-masked black man; and from such ambivalent identification—black skin, white masks—it is possible, I believe, to redeem the pathos of cultural confusion into a strategy of political subversion. We cannot agree with Fanon that "since the racial drama is played out in the open the black man has no time to make it unconscious," but that is a provocative thought. In occupying two places at once—or three in Fanon's case—the depersonalized, dislocated colonial subject can become an incalculable object, quite literally, difficult to place. The demand of authority cannot unify its message nor simply identify its subjects. For the strategy of colonial desire is to stage the drama of identity at the point which the black man *slips* to reveal the white skin. At the edge, in between the black body and the white body, there is a tension of meaning and being, or some would say demand and desire, which is the psychic counterpart to that muscular tension that inhabits the native body:

> The symbols of social order—the police, the bugle calls in the barracks, military parades and waving flags—are at one and the same time inhibitory and stimulating: for they do not convey the message "Don't dare to budge"; rather, they cry out "Get ready to attack."

It is from such tensions—both psychic and political—that a strategy of subversion emerges. It is a mode of negation that seeks not to unveil the fullness of Man but to manipulate his representation. It is a form of power that is exercised at the very limits of identity and authority, in the mocking spirit of mask and image; it is the lesson taught by the veiled Algerian woman in the course of the revolution as she crossed the Manichaean lines to claim her liberty. In Fanon's essay *Algeria Unveiled* the colonizer's attempt to unveil the Algerian woman does not simply turn the veil into a symbol of resistance;

it becomes a technique of camouflage, a means of struggle—the veil conceals bombs. The veil that once secured the boundary of the home—the limits of woman—now masks the woman in her revolutionary activity, linking the Arab city and French quarter, transgressing the familial and colonial boundary. As the veil is liberated in the public sphere, circulation between and beyond cultural and social norms and spaces, it becomes the object of paranoid surveillance and interrogation. Every veiled woman, writes Fanon, became suspect. And when the veil is shed in order to penetrate deeper into the European quarter, the colonial police see everything and nothing. An Algerian woman is only, after all, a woman. But the Algerian *fidai* is an arsenal, and in her handbag she carries her hand grenades.

Remembering Fanon is a process of intense discovery and disorientation. Remembering is never a quiet act of introspection or retrospection. It is a painful re-membering, a putting together of the dismembered past to make sense of the trauma of the present. It is such a memory of the history of race and racism, colonialism and the question of cultural identity, that Fanon reveals with greater profundity and poetry than any other writer. What he achieves, I believe, is something far greater: for in seeing the phobic image of the Negro, the native, the colonized, deeply woven into the psychic pattern of the West, he offers the master and slave a deeper reflection of their interpositions, as well as the hope of a difficult, even dangerous, freedom: "It is through the effort to recapture the self and to scrutinize the self, it is through the lasting tension of their freedom that men will be able to create the ideal conditions of existence for a human world."

This leads to a meditation on the experience of dispossession and dislocation—psychic and social—which speaks to the condition of the marginalized, the alienated, those who have to live under the surveillance of a sign of identity and fantasy that denies their difference. In shifting the focus of cultural racism from the politics of nationalism to the politics of narcissism, Fanon opens up a margin of interrogation that causes a subversive slippage of identity and authority. Nowhere is this slippage more visible than in his work itself, where a range of texts and traditions—from the classical repertoire to the quotidian, conversational culture of racism—vie to utter that last work that remains unspoken.

In Britain today, as a range of culturally and racially marginalized groups readily assume the mask of the Black, not to deny their diversity, but audaciously to announce the important artifice of cultural identity and its difference, the need for Fanon becomes urgent. As political groups from different directions gather under the banner of the Black, not to homogenize their oppression, but to make of it a common cause, a public image of the identity of otherness, the need for Fanon becomes urgent—urgent, in order to remind us of that crucial engagement between mask and identity, image and identification, from which comes the lasting tension of our freedom and the lasting impression of ourselves as others:

> In case of display . . . the play of combat in the form of intimidation, the being gives of himself, or receives from the other, something that is like a mask, a double, an envelope, a thrown-off skin, thrown off in order to cover the frame of a shield. It is through this separated form of himself that the being comes into play in his effects of life and death.[23]

The time has come to return to Fanon; as always, I believe, with a question: How can the human world live its difference; how can a human being live Other-wise?

VI

I have chosen to give poststructuralism a specifically postcolonial provenance in order to engage with an influential objection recently repeated by Terry Eagleton in a recent essay:

> We have as yet no political theory, or theory of the subject, which is capable in this dialectical way of grasping social transformation as at once diffusion and affirmation, the death and birth of the subject—or at least we have no such theories that are not vacuously apocalyptic.[24]

Taking my lead from the "doubly inscribed" subaltern instance, I would argue that it is the *dialectical* hinge between the birth and death of the subject that needs to be interrogated. Perhaps the charge that a politics of the subject results in a vacuous apocalypse is itself a response to the poststructuralist probing of the notion of progressive negation—or sublation—in dialectical thinking. The supplementary or metonymic are *neither* empty nor full, *neither* part nor whole. Their compensatory and vicarious processes of signification are a spur to social translation, the production of something else *besides* which is not only the cut or gap of the subject but also the intercut across social sites and disciplines. This hybridity spatializes the project of political thinking by continually facing it with the strategic and the contingent, with the countervailing thought of its own "unthought." It has to negotiate its goals through an acknowledgment of differential objects and discursive levels articulated not simply as contents but in their *address* as forms of textual or narrative subjections—be they governmental, judicial, or artistic. Despite its firm commitments, the political must always pose as a problem, or a question, the *priority of the place from which it begins*, if its authority is not to become autocratic.

What must be left an open question, *post*-poststructuralism, is how we are to rethink ourselves once we have undermined the immediacy and autonomy of self-consciousness. It is not difficult to question the civil argument that the people are a conjugation of individuals, harmonious *under* the Law. We can dispute the political argument that the radical, vanguardist party and its masses represent a certain objectification in a historical process, or stage, of social transformation. What remains to be thought is the *repetitious* desire to recognize ourselves doubly, as, at once, decentered in the solidary processes of the political group, and yet, ourself as a consciously committed, even individuated, agent of change — the bearer of belief. What is this ethical pressure to "account for ourselves" — but only *partially* — within a political theater of agonism, bureaucratic obfuscation, violence, and violation? Is this political desire for partial identification a beautifully human, even pathetic attempt to disavow the realization that, *betwixt and besides* the lofty dreams of political thinking, there exists an acknowledgment, somewhere between fact and fantasy, that the techniques and technologies of politics need not be *humanizing* at all, in no way endorsing of what we understand to be the human — humanist? — predicament. We may have to force the limits of the social as we know it to rediscover a sense of political and personal agency through the unthought of the civic and the psychic. This may be no place to end but it may be a place to begin.

NOTES

1. Adil Jussawalla, *Missing Person* (Clearing House, 1976), pp. 14–29.

2. Meiling Jin, "Strangers on a Hostile Landscape," *Watchers and Seekers*, ed. Cobham and Collins (The Women's Press), pp. 126–27.

3. Edward Said, *Orientalism* (London: Routledge & Kegan Paul, 1978), pp. 26–27.

4. Roland Barthes, "The Imagination of the Sign," in *Critical Essays* (Evanston, Ill.: Northwestern University Press, 1972), pp. 206–7.

5. John Locke, *An Essay Concerning Human Understanding* (London: Fontana, 1969), pp. 212–13.

6. Barthes, "Imagination of the Sign," p. 207.

7. Richard Rorty, "Mirroring," in *Philosophy and the Mirror of Nature* (Oxford: Blackwell, 1980), pp. 162–63.

8. Jacques Lacan, "Seminar 21," *Feminine Sexuality*, ed. J. Mitchell and J. Rose (London: Routledge & Kegan Paul, 1982), p. 164.

9. Barthes, "Imagination of the Sign," pp. 209–10.

10. Jacques Lacan, "Alienation," in *The Four Fundamental Concepts of Psychoanalysis* (London: Hogarth, 1977), p. 206.

11. J. Derrida, "The Double Session," *Dessimination* (Chicago: University of Chicago Press, 1981), pp. 212–13.

12. Jacques Derrida, *Of Grammatology*, trans. G. C. Spivak (Baltimore: Johns Hopkins University Press, 1976), p. 145.

13. Jacques Lacan, "Alienation," p. 207.

14. Michel Foucault, *The Archaeology of Knowledge* (London: Tavistock, 1974), p. 111.

15. J.-F. Lyotard and J. L. Thebaud, *Just Gaming* (Minneapolis: University of Minnesota Press, 1985), pp. 34 and 39.

16. Lacan, "Alienation," p. 88.

17. See Homi K. Bhabha, "The Commitment to Theory," in *New Formations* 5 (May 1988).

Also my "Signs Taken as Wonders," in *Race, Writing and Difference*, ed. Henry Louis Gates, Jr. (Chicago: University of Chicago Press, 1986).

18. Clifford Geertz, "Native's Point of View: Anthropological Understanding," in *Local Knowledge* (New York: Basic Books, 1983), p. 70.

19. Jacques Derrida, *Writing and Difference*, trans. Alan Bass (Chicago: University of Chicago Press, 1982), p. 282.

20. Adil Jussawalla, *Missing Person*, p. 15.

21. Anne Showstack Sassoon, *Approaches to Gramsci*. (London, 1982), p. 16.

22. Roland Barthes, "Imagination of the Sign," p. 246.

23. Jacques Lacan, *Four Fundamental Concepts*, trans. Alan Sheridan-Smith (New York: Norton, 1981), p. 107.

24. T. F. Eagleton, "The Politics of Subjectivity," in *Identity*, ed. Lisa Appignanest. ICA Documents 6 (London: Institute of Contemporary Art, 1988).

CHAPTER 14

Zionism from the Standpoint of Its Victims

Edward W. Said

Zionism and the Attitudes of European Colonialism

Every idea or system of ideas exists *somewhere*, is mixed in with historical cir-cumstances, is part of what one may very simply call "reality." One of the enduring attributes of self-serving idealism, however, is the notion that ideas are just ideas, and that they exist only in the realm of ideas. The tendency to view ideas as pertaining only to a world of abstractions increases among people for whom an idea is essentially perfect, good, uncontaminated by hu-man desire or will. Such a view also applies when the ideas are considered to be evil, absolutely perfect in their evil, and so forth. When an idea has be-come effective—that is, when its value has been proved in reality by its wide-spread acceptance—some revision of it will of course seem to be necessary, since the idea must be viewed as having taken on some of the characteristics of brute reality. Thus it is frequently argued that such an idea as Zionism, for all its political tribulations and the struggles on its behalf, is at bottom an *un-changing* idea that expresses the yearning for Jewish political and religious self-determination—for Jewish national selfhood—to be exercised on the promised land. Because Zionism seems to have culminated in the creation of the state of Israel, it is also argued that the historical realization of the idea confirms its unchanging essence and, no less important, the means used for its realization. Very little is said about what Zionism entailed for non-Jews who happened to have encountered it; for that matter, nothing is said about where (outside Jewish history) it took place, and from what in the historical context of nineteenth-century Europe Zionism drew its force. To the Pales-tinian, for whom Zionism was somebody's else's idea imported into Palestine and for which in a very concrete way he or she was made to pay and suffer, these forgotten things about Zionism are the very things that are centrally important.

In short, effective political ideas like Zionism need to be examined historically in two ways: (1) *genealogically* in order that their provenance, their kinship and descent, their affiliation both with other ideas and with political institutions may be demonstrated; (2) as practical systems for *accumulation* (of power, land, ideological legitimacy) and *displacement* (of people, other ideas, prior legitimacy). Present political and cultural actualities make such an examination extraordinarily difficult, as much because Zionism in the postindustrial West has acquired for itself an almost unchallenged hegemony in liberal "establishment" discourse, as because in keeping with one of its central ideological characteristics, Zionism has hidden, or caused to disappear, the literal historical ground of its growth, its political cost to the native inhabitants of Palestine, and its militantly oppressive discriminations between Jews and non-Jews.

Consider as a startling instance of what I mean, the symbolism of Menachem Begin, a former head of the Irgun terror organization, in whose past there are numerous (and frequently admitted) acts of cold-blooded murder, being honored as Israeli premier at Northwestern University in May 1978 with a doctorate of laws *honoris causa*; a leader whose army a scant month before had created 300,000 new refugees in South Lebanon, who spoke constantly of "Judea and Samaria" as "rightful" parts of the Jewish state (claims made on the basis of the Old Testament and without so much as a reference to the land's actual inhabitants); and all this without—on the part of the press or the intellectual community—one sign of comprehension that Menachem Begin's honored position came about literally at the expense of Palestinian Arab silence in the Western "marketplace of ideas," that the entire historical duration of a Jewish state in Palestine prior to 1948 was a sixty-year period two millennia ago, that the dispersion of the Palestinians was not a fact of nature but a result of specific force and strategies. The concealment by Zionism of its own history has by now therefore become institutionalized, and not only in Israel. To bring out its history as in a sense it was exacted from Palestine and the Palestinians, these victims on whose suppression Zionism and Israel have depended, is thus a specific intellectual/political task in the present context of discussion about "a comprehensive peace" in the Middle East.

The special, one might even call it the privileged, place in this discussion of the United States is impressive, for all sorts of reasons. In no other country, except Israel, is Zionism enshrined as an unquestioned good, and in no other country is there so strong a conjuncture of powerful institutions and interests—the press, the liberal intelligentsia, the military-industrial complex, the academic community, labor unions—for whom uncritical support of Israel and Zionism enhances their domestic as well as international standing. Although there has recently been some modulation in this remarkable consensus — due to the influence of Arab oil, the emergence of countervailing conservative states allied to the United States (Saudi Arabia, Egypt), the redoubtable political and military visibility of the Palestinian people and their representatives the PLO — the prevailing pro-Israeli bias persists. For not only does it have deep cultural roots in the West generally and the United States in particular, but its *negative, interdictory* character vis-à-vis the *whole* historical reality is systematic.

Yet there is no getting around the formidable historical reality that in trying to deal with what Zionism has suppressed about the Palestinian people, one also abuts the entire disastrous problem of anti-Semitism on the one hand, and on the other, the complex interrelationship between the Palestinians and the Arab states. Anyone who watched the spring 1978 NBC presentation of *Holocaust* was aware that at least part of the program was intended as a justification for Zionism — even while at about the same time Israeli troops in Lebanon produced devastation, thousands of civilian casualties, and untold suffering of a sort likened by a few courageous reporters to the U.S. devastation of Vietnam (see, for example, H. D. S. Greenway, "Vietnam-style Raids Gut South Lebanon: Israel Leaves a Path of Destruction," *Washington Post*, March 25, 1978). Similarly, the furor created by the package deal in early 1978 as a result of which U.S. war planes were sold to Israel, Egypt, and Saudi Arabia made the predicament of Arab liberation interlocking with right-wing Arab regimes even more acute. The task of criticism, or, to put it another way, the role of the critical consciousness in such cases is to be able to make distinctions, to produce differences where at present there are none. To write critically about Zionism in Palestine has therefore never meant, and does not mean now, being anti-Semitic; conversely, the struggle for Palestinian rights and self-determination does not mean support for the Saudi royal family, nor for the antiquated and oppressive state structures of most of the Arab nations.

One must admit, however, that all liberals and even most "radicals" have been unable to overcome the Zionist habit of equating anti-Zionism with anti-Semitism. Any well-meaning person can thus oppose South African or American racism and at the same time tacitly support Zionist racial discrimination against non-Jews in Palestine. The almost total absence of any handily available historical knowledge from non-Zionist sources, the dissemination by the media of malicious simplifications (e.g., Jews vs. Arabs), the cynical opportunism of various Zionist pressure groups, the tendency endemic to university intellectuals uncritically to repeat cant phrases and political clichés (this is the role Gramsci assigned to traditional intellectuals, that of being "experts in legitimation"), the fear of treading upon the highly sensitive terrain of what Jews did to *their* victims, in an age of genocidal extermination of Jews — all this contributes to the dulling, regulated enforcement of almost unanimous support for Israel. But, as I. F. Stone recently noted, this unanimity exceeds even the Zionism of most Israelis.[1]

On the other hand, it would be totally unjust to neglect the power of Zionism as an idea for Jews, or to minimize the complex internal debates characterizing Zionism, its true meaning, its messianic destiny, etc. Even to speak about this subject, much less than attempting to "define" Zionism, is for an Arab quite a difficult matter, but it must honestly be looked at. Let me use myself as an example. Most of my education, and certainly all of my basic intellectual formation, is Western; in what I have read, in what I write about, even in what I do politically, I am profoundly influenced by mainstream Western attitudes toward the history of the Jews, anti-Semitism, the destruction of European Jewry. Unlike most other Arab intellectuals, the majority of whom obviously have not had my kind of background, I have been directly exposed to those aspects of Jewish history and experience that have mattered singularly for Jews and for Western non-Jews reading and thinking about Jewish history. I know as well as any educated Western non-Jew can know, what anti-Semitism has meant for the Jews, especially in this century. Consequently I can understand the intertwined terror and the exultation out of which Zionism has been nourished, and I think I can at least grasp the meaning of Israel for Jews, and even for the enlightened Western liberal. And yet, because I am an Arab Palestinian, I can also see and feel other things— and it is these things that complicate matters considerably, that cause me also to focus on Zionism's *other* aspects. The result is, I think, worth describing, not because what I think is so crucial, but because it is useful to see the same phenomenon in two complementary ways, not normally associated with each other.

The three ideas that depended on one another in almost every Zionist thinker or ideologue are (a) the nonexistent Arab inhabitants, (b) the complementary Western-Jewish attitude to an "empty" territory, and (c) the restorative Zionist project, which would repeat by rebuilding a vanished Jewish state and combine it with modern elements like disciplined, separate colonies, a special agency for land acquisition, etc. Of course, none of these ideas would have any force were it not for the additional fact of their being addressed to, shaped for, and out of an *international* (i.e., non-Oriental and hence European) context. This context was the reality, not only because of the ethnocentric rationale governing the whole project, but also because of the overwhelming facts of Diaspora realities and imperialist hegemony over the entire gamut of European culture. It needs to be remarked, however, that Zionism (like the view of America as an empty land held by Puritans) was a colonial vision unlike that of most other nineteenth-century European powers, for whom the natives of outlying territories were *included* in the redemptive *mission civilisatrice*.

From the earliest phases of its modern evolution until it culminated in the creation of Israel, Zionism appealed to a European audience for whom the classification of overseas territories and natives into various uneven classes was canonical and "natural." That is why, for example, every single state or movement in the formerly colonized territories of Africa and Asia today identifies with, fully supports, and understands the Palestinian struggle. In many instances — as I hope to show presently — there is an unmistakable co-incidence between the experiences of Arab Palestinians at the hands of Zionism and the experiences of those black, yellow, and brown people who were described as inferior and subhuman by nineteenth-century imperialists. For although it coincided with an era of the most virulent Western anti-Semitism, Zionism also coincided with the period of unparalleled European territorial acquisition in Africa and Asia, and it was as part of this general movement of acquisition and occupation that Zionism was launched initially by Theodor Herzl. During the latter part of the greatest period in European colonial expansion, Zionism also made its crucial first moves along the way to getting what has now become a sizeable Asiatic territory. And it is impor-tant to remember that in joining the general Western enthusiasm for overseas territorial acquisition, Zionism *never* spoke of itself unambiguously as a Jew-ish liberation movement, but rather as a Jewish movement for colonial settle-ment in the Orient. To those Palestinian victims that Zionism displaced, it *cannot have meant anything by way of sufficient cause* that Jews were victims of European anti-Semitism and, given Israel's continued oppression of Palestin-ians, few Palestinians are able to see beyond their reality, namely, that once victims themselves, Occidental Jews in Israel have become oppressors (of Palestinian Arabs and Oriental Jews).

These are not intended to be backward-looking historical observations, for in a very vital way they explain and even determine much of what now happens in the Middle East. The fact that no sizeable segment of the Israeli population has as yet been able to confront the terrible social and political in-justice done the native Palestinians is an indication of how deeply ingrained are the (by now) anomalous imperialist perspectives basic to Zionism, its view of the world, its sense of an inferior native Other. The fact also that no Palestinian, regardless of his political stripe, has been able to reconcile himself to Zionism suggests that extent to which, for the Palestinian, Zionism has appeared to be an uncompromisingly exclusionary, discriminatory, colonialist praxis. So powerful, and so unhesitatingly followed, has been the radical Zionist distinction between privileged Jews in Palestine and un-privileged non-Jews there, that nothing else has emerged, no perception of suffering human existence has escaped from the two camps created thereby.[2] As a result, it has been impossible for Jews to understand the human tragedy caused the Arab Palestinians by Zionism; and it has been impossible for Arab Palestinians to see in Zionism anything except an ideology and a practice keeping them, and Israeli Jews, imprisoned. But in order to break down the iron circle of inhumanity, we must see how it was forged, and there it is ideas and culture themselves that play the major role.

Consider Herzl. If it was the Dreyfus Affair that first brought him to Jewish consciousness, it was the idea of overseas colonial settlement for the Jews that came to him at roughly the same time as an antidote for anti-Semitism. The idea itself was current at the end of the nineteenth century, even as an idea for Jews. Herzl's first significant contact was Baron Maurice de Hirsch, a wealthy philanthropist who had for some time been behind the Jewish Colonization Association for helping Eastern Jews to emigrate to Argentina and Brazil. Later, Herzl thought generally about South America, then about Africa as places for establishing a Jewish colony. Both areas were widely acceptable as places for European colonialism, and that Herzl's mind followed along the orthodox imperialist track of his period is perhaps understandable. The impressive thing, however, is the degree to which Herzl had absorbed and internalized the imperialist perspective on "natives" and their "territory."[3]

There could have been no doubt whatever in Herzl's mind that Palestine in the late nineteenth century was peopled. True, it was under Ottoman administration (and therefore already a colony), but it had been the subject of numerous travel accounts, most of them famous, by Lamartine, Chateaubriand, Flaubert, and others. Yet even if he had not read these authors, Herzl as a journalist must surely have looked at a Baedeker to ascertain that Palestine was indeed inhabited by (in the 1880s) 650,000 mostly Arab people. This did not stop him from regarding their presence as manageable in ways that, in his diary, he spelled out with a rather chilling prescience for what later took place. The mass of poor natives were to be expropriated and, he added,"both the expropriation and the removal of the poor must be carried out discreetly and circumspectly." This was to be done by "spirit[ing] the penniless population across the border by procuring employment for it in the transit countries, while denying it any employment in our own country." With uncannily accurate cynicism, Herzl predicted that the small class of large landowners could be "had for a price" — as indeed they were. The whole scheme for displacing the native population of Palestine far outstripped any of the then current plans for taking over vast reaches of Africa. As Desmond Stewart aptly says:

> Herzl seems to have foreseen that in going further than any colonialist had so far gone in Africa, he would, temporarily, alienate civilised opinion. "At first, incidentally," he writes on the pages describing "involuntary expropriation," "people will avoid us. We are in bad odor. By the time the reshaping of world opinion in our favor has been completed, we shall be firmly established in our country, no longer fearing the influx of foreigners, and receiving our visitors with aristocratic benevolence and proud amiability."

This was not a prospect to charm a peon in Argentina or a fellah in
Palestine. But Herzl did not intend his Diary for immediate publication.[4]

One need not wholly accept the conspiratorial tone of these comments
(whether Herzl's or Stewart's) to grant that world opinion has not been, until
during the sixties and seventies when the Palestinians forced their presence
on world politics, very much concerned with the expropriation of Palestine.
I said earlier that in this regard the major Zionist achievement was getting
international legitimization for its own accomplishments, thereby making
the Palestinian cost of these accomplishments seem to be irrelevant. But it is
clear from Herzl's thinking that that could not have been done unless there
was a prior European inclination to view the natives as irrelevant *to begin with*.
That is, those natives already fit a more or less acceptable classificatory grid,
which made them sui generis inferior to Western or white men — and it is this
grid that Zionists like Herzl appropriated, domesticating it from the general
culture of their time to the unique needs of a developing Jewish nationalism.
One needs to repeat that what in Zionism served the no doubt justified ends
of Jewish tradition, saving the Jews as a people from homelessness and
anti-Semitism and restoring them to nationhood, also collaborated with
those aspects of the dominant Western culture (in which Zionism institutionally lived) making it possible for Europeans to view non-Europeans as inferior, marginal, and irrelevant. For the Palestinian Arab, therefore, it is the
collaboration that has counted, not by any means the good done to Jews. The
Arab has been on the receiving end not of benign Zionism — which has been
restricted to Jews — but of an essentially discriminatory and powerful culture,
of which, in Palestine, Zionism has been the agent.

Here I must digress to say that the great difficulty today of writing about
what has happened to the Arab Palestinian as a result of Zionism, is that Zionism has had a large number of successes. There is no doubt in my mind,
for example, that most Jews do regard Zionism and Israel as urgently important facts for Jewish life, particularly because of what happened to the Jews
in this century. Then too, Israel has some remarkable political and cultural
achievements to its credit, quite apart from its spectacular military successes
until recently. Most important, Israel is a subject about which, on the whole,
one can feel positive with less reservations than the ones experienced in
thinking about the Arabs, who are outlandish, strange, hostile Orientals after
all; surely that is an obvious fact to anyone living in the West. Together these
successes of Zionism have produced a prevailing view of the question of
Palestine that almost totally favors the victor, and takes hardly any account
of the victim.

Yet what did the victim feel as he watched the Zionists arriving in Palestine? What does he think as he watches Zionism described today? Where does
he look in Zionism's history to locate its roots, and the origins of its practices

toward him? These are the questions that are never asked—and they are precisely the ones that I am trying to raise, as well as answer, here in this examination of the links between Zionism and European imperialism. My interest is in trying to record the effects of Zionism on its victims, and these effects can only be studied genealogically in the framework provided by imperialism, even during the nineteenth century when Zionism was still an idea and not a state called Israel. For the Palestinian now who writes critically to see what his or her history has meant, and who tries—as I am now trying—to see what Zionism has been for the Palestinians, Antonio Gramsci's observation is relevant, that "the consciousness of what one really is . . . is 'knowing thyself' as a product of the historical process to date which has deposited in you an infinity of traces, without leaving an inventory." The job of producing an inventory is a first necessity, Gramsci continued, and so it must be now, when the "inventory" of what Zionism's victims (*not* its beneficiaries) endured is rarely exposed to public view.[5]

If we have become accustomed to making fastidious distinctions between ideology (or theory) and practice, we shall be more accurate historically if we do not do so glibly in the case of the European imperialism that actually annexed most of the world during the nineteenth century. Imperialism was and still is a political philosophy whose aim and purpose for being is territorial expansion and its legitimization. A serious underestimation of imperialism, however, would be to consider territory in too literal a way. Gaining and holding an *imperium* means gaining and holding a domain, which includes a variety of operations, among them constituting an area, accumulating its inhabitants, having power over its ideas, people, and of course, its land, converting people, land, and ideas to the purposes and for the use of a hegemonic imperial design; all this as a result of being able to treat reality appropriatively. Thus the distinction between an idea that one *feels* to be one's own and a piece of land that one claims by right to be one's own (despite the presence on the land of its working native inhabitants) is really nonexistent, at least in the world of nineteenth-century culture out of which imperialism developed. Laying claim to an idea and laying claim to a territory—given the extraordinarily current idea that the non-European world was there to be claimed, occupied, and ruled by Europe—were considered to be different sides of the same, essentially constitutive activity, which had the force, the prestige, and the authority of *science*. Moreover, because in such fields as biology, philology, and geology the scientific consciousness was principally a reconstituting, restoring, and transforming activity turning old fields into new ones, the link between an outright imperialist attitude toward distant lands in the Orient and a scientific attitude to the "inequalities" of race was that both attitudes depended on the European *will*, on the determining force necessary to change confusing or useless realities into an orderly, disciplined set of new classifications useful to Europe. Thus in the works of Carolus Linnaeus, Georges Buffon, and Georges Cuvier the white races became scientifically different from reds, yellows, blacks, and browns, and, consequently, territories occupied by those races also newly became vacant, open to Western colonies, developments, plantations, and settlers. Additionally, the less equal races were made useful by being turned into what the white race studied and came to understand as a part of its racial and cultural hegemony (as in Joseph de Gobineau and Oswald Spengler); or, following the impulse of outright colonialism, these lesser races were put to direct use in the empire. When in 1918, Georges Clemenceau stated that he believed he had "an unlimited right of levying black troops to assist in the defense of French territory in Europe if France were attacked in the future by Germany," he was saying that by some scientific right France had the knowledge and the power to convert blacks into what Raymond Poincaré called an economic form of gunfodder for the white Frenchman.[6] Imperialism, of course, cannot be blamed on science, but what needs to be seen is the relative ease with which science could be deformed into a rationalization for imperial domination.

Supporting the taxonomy of a natural history deformed into a social anthropology whose real purpose was social control, was the taxonomy of linguistics. With the discovery of a structural affinity between groups or families of languages by such linguists as Franz Bopp, William Jones, and Friedrich von Schlegel, there began as well the unwarranted extension of an idea about language families into theories of human types having determined ethnocultural and racial characteristics. In 1808, as an instance, Schlegel discerned a clear rift between the Indo-Germanic (or Aryan) languages on the one hand and, on the other, the Semitic-African languages. The former, he said, were creative, regenerative, lively, and aesthetically pleasing; the latter were mechanical in their operations, unregenerate, passive. From this kind of distinction, Schlegel, and later Renan, went on to generalize about the great distance separating a superior Aryan and an inferior non-Aryan mind, culture, and society.

Perhaps the most effective deformation or translation of science into something more accurately resembling political administration took place in the amorphous field assembling together jurisprudence, social philosophy, and political theory. First of all, a fairly influential tradition in philosophic empiricism (recently studied by Harry Bracken)[7] seriously advocated a type of racial distinction that divided humankind into lesser and greater breeds of men. The actual problems (in England, mainly) of dealing with a 300-year-old Indian empire, as well as numerous voyages of discovery, made it possible "scientifically" to show that some cultures were advanced and civilized, others backward and uncivilized; these ideas, plus the lasting social meaning imparted to the fact of color (and hence of race) by philosophers like John Locke and David Hume, made it axiomatic by the middle of the nineteenth century that Europeans always ought to rule non-Europeans.

This doctrine was reinforced in other ways, some of which had a direct bearing, I think, on Zionist practice and vision in Palestine. Among the supposed juridical distinctions between civilized and noncivilized peoples was an attitude toward land, almost a doxology about land, which noncivilized people supposedly lacked. Civilized people, it was believed, could cultivate the land because it meant something to them; on it, accordingly, they bred useful arts and crafts, they created, they accomplished, they built. For an uncivilized people, land was either farmed badly (i.e., inefficiently by Western standards) or it was left to rot. From this string of ideas, by which whole native societies who lived on American, African, and Asian territories for centuries were suddenly denied their right to live on that land, came the great dispossessing movements of modern European colonialism, and with them all the schemes for redeeming the land, resettling the natives, civilizing them, taming their savage customs, turning them into useful beings under European rule. Land in Asia, Africa, and the Americas was there for European exploitation, because Europe understood the value of land in a way impossible for the natives. At the end of the century, Joseph Conrad dramatized this philosophy in *Heart of Darkness*, and embodied it powerfully in the figure of Kurtz, a man whose colonial dreams for the earth's "dark places" were made by "all Europe." But what Conrad drew on, as indeed the Zionists drew on also, was the kind of philosophy set forth by Robert Knox in his work *The Races of Man*,[8] in which men were divided into white and advanced (the producers) and dark, inferior wasters. Similarly, thinkers like John Westlake and before him Emer de Vattel divided the world's territories into empty (though inhabited by nomads, and a low kind of society) and civilized — and the former were then "revised" as being ready for takeover on the basis of a higher, civilized right to them.

I very greatly simplify the transformation in perspective by which millions of acres outside metropolitan Europe were thus declared empty, their people and societies decreed to be obstacles to progress and development, their space just as assertively declared open to European white settlers and their civilizing exploitation. During the 1870s in particular, new European geographical societies mushroomed as a sign that geography had become, according to Lord Curzon, "the most cosmopolitan of all the sciences."[9] Not for nothing in *Heart of Darkness* did Marlow admit to his

> passion for maps. I would look for hours at South America, or Africa, or Australia, and lose myself in all the glories of exploration. At that time there were many blank spaces [populated by natives, that is] on the earth, and when I saw one that looked particularly inviting on a map (but they all look like that) I would put my finger on it and say, When I grow up I will go there.[10]

Geography and a passion for maps developed into an organized matter mainly devoted to acquiring vast overseas territories. And, Conrad also said, this

> . . . conquest of the earth, which mostly means the taking it away from those who have a different complexion or slightly flatter noses than our-selves, is not a pretty thing when you look into it too much. What redeems it is the idea only. An idea at the back of it; not a sentimental pretence but an idea—something you can set up, and bow down before, and offer a sac-rifice to.[11]

Conrad makes the point better than anyone, I think. The power to con-quer territory is only in part a matter of physical force: there is the strong moral and intellectual component making the conquest itself secondary to an idea, which dignifies (and indeed hastens) pure force with arguments drawn from science, morality, ethics, and a general philosophy. Everything in Western culture potentially capable of dignifying the acquisition of new domains—as a new science, for example, acquires new intellectual territory for itself—could be put at the service of colonial adventures. And *was* put, the "idea" always informing the conquest, making it entirely palatable. One ex-ample of such an idea spoken about openly as a quite normal justification for what today would be called colonial aggression, is to be found in these pas-sages by Paul Leroy-Béaulieu, a leading French geographer in the 1870s:

> A society colonizes, when having itself reached a high degree of maturity and of strength, it procreates, it protects, it places in good conditions of de-velopment, and it brings to virility a new society to which it has given birth. Colonization is one of the most complex and delicate phenomena of social physiology.

There is no question of consulting the natives of the territory where the new society is to be given birth. What counts is that a modern European society has enough vitality and intellect to be "magnified by this pouring out of its exuberant activity on the outside." Such activity must be good since it is be-lieved in, and since it also carries within itself the healthy current of an entire advanced civilization. Therefore, Leroy-Beaulieu added,

> Colonization is the expansive force of a people; it is its power of reproduc-tion; it is its enlargement and its multiplication through space; it is the sub-jugation of the universe or a vast part of it to that people's language, cus-toms, ideas, and laws.[12]

Imperialism was the theory, colonialism the practice of changing the use-lessly unoccupied territories of the world into useful new versions of the Eu-ropean metropolitan society. Everything in those territories that suggested waste, disorder, uncounted resources, was to be converted into productivity, order, taxable, potentially developed wealth. You get rid of most of the offending human and animal blight — whether because it simply sprawls untidily all over the place or because it roams around unproductively and uncounted — and you confine the rest to reservation, compounds, native homelands, where you can count, tax, use them profitably, and you build a new society on the vacated space. Thus was Europe reconstituted abroad, its "multiplication in space" successfully projected and managed. The result was a widely varied group of little Europes scattered throughout Asia, Africa, and the Americas, each reflecting the circumstances, the specific instrumentalities of the parent culture, its pioneers, its vanguard settlers.[13] All of them were similar in one other major respect — despite the differences, which were considerable — and that was that their life was carried on with an air of *normality*. The most grotesque reproductions of Europe (South Africa, Rhodesia, etc.) were considered appropriate; the worst discrimination against and exclusions of the natives were thought to be normal because "scientifically" legitimate; the sheer contradiction of living a foreign life in an enclave many physical and cultural miles from Europe, in the midst of hostile and uncomprehending natives, gave rise to a sense of history, a stubborn kind of logic, a social and political state decreeing the present colonial venture as *normal*, justified, good.

With specific reference to Palestine, what were to become institutional Zionist attitudes to the Arab Palestinian natives and their supposed claims to a "normal" existence, were more than prepared for in the attitudes and the practices of British scholars, administrators, and experts who were officially involved in the exploitation and government of Palestine since the mid-nineteenth century. Consider that in 1903 the Bishop of Salisbury told members of the Palestine Exploration Fund that

> Nothing, I think, that has been discovered makes us feel any regret at the suppression of Canaanite civilisation [the euphemism for native Arab Palestinians] by Israelite civilisation. . . . [The excavations show how] the Bible has not misrepresented at all the abomination of the Canaanite culture which was superseded by the Israelite culture.

These, then, are some of the main points that must be made about the background of Zionism in European imperialist or colonialist attitudes. For whatever it may have done for Jews, Zionism essentially saw Palestine as the European imperialist did, as an empty territory paradoxically "filled" with ignoble or perhaps even dispensable natives; it allied itself, as Chaim Weizmann quite clearly said after World War I, with the imperial powers in carrying out its plans for establishing a new Jewish state in Palestine, and it did not think except in negative terms of "the natives," who were passively supposed to accept the plans made for their land; as even Zionist historians like Yehoshua Porath and Neville Mandel have empirically shown, the ideas of Jewish colonizers in Palestine (well before World War I) always met with unmistakable native resistance, not because the natives though that Jews were evil, but because most natives do not take kindly to having their territory settled by foreigners;[14] moreover, in formulating the concept of a Jewish nation "reclaiming" its own territory, Zionism not only accepted the generic racial concepts of European culture, it also banked on the fact that Palestine was actually peopled not by an advanced but by a backward people, over which it *ought* to be dominant. Thus that implicit *assumption* of domination led specifically in the case of Zionism to the practice of ignoring the natives for the most part as not entitled to serious consideration.[15] Zionism therefore developed with a unique consciousness of itself, but with little or nothing left over for the unfortunate natives. Maxime Rodinson is perfectly correct in saying that Zionist indifference to the Palestinian natives was

> an indifference linked to European supremacy, which benefited even Europe's proletarians and oppressed minorities. In fact, there can be no doubt that if the ancestral homeland had been occupied by one of the well-established industrialized nations that ruled the world at the time, one that had thoroughly settled down in a territory it had infused with a powerful national consciusness, then the problem of displacing German, French, or English inhabitants and introducing a new, nationally coherent element into the middle of their homeland would have been in the forefront of the consciousness of even the most ignorant and destitute Zionists.[16]

In short, all the constitutive energies of Zionism were premised on the excluded presence, that is, the functional absence of "native people" in Palestine; institutions were built deliberately shutting out the natives, laws were drafted when Israel came into being that made sure the natives would remain in their "nonplace," Jews in theirs, and so on. It is no wonder that today the one issue that electrifies Israel as a society is the problem of the Palestinians, whose negation is the most consistent thread running through Zionism. And it is this perhaps unfortunate aspect of Zionism that ties it ineluctably to imperialism — at least so far as the Palestinian is concerned Rodinson again:

> The element that made it possible to connect these aspirations of Jewish shopkeepers, peddlers, craftsmen, and intellectuals in Russia and elsewhere to the conceptual orbit of imperialism was one small detail that seemed to be of no importance: Palestine was inhabited by another people.[17]

Zionist Population, Palestinian Depopulation

I have been discussing the extraordinary unevenness in Zionism between care for the Jews and an almost total disregard for the non-Jews or native Arab population in conceptual terms. Zionism and European imperialism are epistemologically, hence historically and politically, coterminous in their view of resident natives, but it is how this irreducibly imperialist view worked in the world of politics and in the lives of people for whom epistemology was irrelevant that justifies one's looking at epistemology at all. In that world and in those lives, among them several million Palestinians, the results can be detailed, not as mere theoretical visions, but as an immensely traumatic Zionist effectiveness. One general Arab Palestinian reaction toward Zionism is perfectly caught, I think, in the following sentence written by the Arab delegations's reply in 1922 to Winston Churchill's White Paper: "The intention to create the Jewish National Home is to cause the disappearance or subordination of the Arabic population, culture and language."[18] What generations of Palestinian Arabs watched therefore was an unfolding design, whose deeper roots in Jewish history and the terrible Jewish experience was necessarily obscured by what was taking place before their eyes as well as to those in Palestine. There the Arabs were able to see embodied

> a ruthless doctrine, calling for monastic self-discipline and cold detachment from environment. The Jews who gloried in the name of socialist worker interpreted brotherhood on a strictly nationalist, or racial basis, for they meant brotherhood with Jew, not with Arab. As they insisted on working the soil with their own hands, since exploitation of others was anathema to them, they excluded the Arabs from their regime. . . . They believed in equality, but for themselves. They lived on Jewish bread, raised on Jewish soil that was protected by a Jewish rifle.[19]

The "inventory" of Palestinian experience that I am trying to take here is based on the simple truth that the exultant or (later) the terrorized Jews who arrived in Palestine were seen essentially as foreigners whose proclaimed destiny was to create a state for Jews. What of the Arabs who were there? was the question we must feel ourselves asking now. What we will discover is that everything positive from the Zionist standpoint looked absolutely negative from the perspective of the native Arab Palestinians.

For they could never be fit into the grand vision. Not that "vision" was merely a theoretical matter; it was that and, as it was later to determine the character and even the details of Israeli government policy toward the native Arab Palestinians, "vision" was also the way Zionist leaders looked at the Arabs in order later (and certainly at that moment) to deal with them. Thus, as I said earlier, I have in mind the whole dialectic between theory and actual day-to-day effectiveness. My premise is that Israel developed as a social polity out of the Zionist thesis that Palestine's colonization was to be accomplished simultaneously for and by Jews *and* by the displacement of the Palestinians; moreover, that in its conscious and declared ideas about Palestine, Zionism attempted first to minimize, then to eliminate, and then, all else failing, finally to subjugate the natives as a way of guaranteeing that Israel would not be simply the state of its citizens (which included Arabs, of course) but the state of "the whole Jewish people," having a kind of sovereignty over land and peoples that no other state possessed or possesses. It is this anomaly that the Arab Palestinians have since been trying both to resist and provide an alternative for.

One can learn a great deal from pronouncements made by strategically important Zionist leaders whose job it is, after Herzl, to translate the design into action. Chaim Weizmann comes to mind at once, as much for his extraordinary personality as for his brilliant successes in bringing Zionism up from an idea to a conquering political institution. His thesis about the land of Palestine is revealing in the extent to which it repeats Herzl:

> It seems as if God has covered the soil of Palestine with rocks and marshes and sand, so that its beauty can only be brought out by those who love it and will devote their lives to healing its wounds.[20]

The context of this remark, however, is a sale made to the Zionists by a wealthy absentee landlord (the Lebanese Sursuk family) of unpromising marshland. Weizmann admits that this particular sale was of *some*, by no means a great deal, of Palestine, yet the impression he gives is of a *whole* territory essentially unused, unappreciated, misunderstood (if one can use such a word in this connection). Despite the people who lived on it, Palestine was therefore *to be made* useful, appreciated, understandable. The native inhabitants were believed curiously to be out of touch with history and, it seemed to follow, they were not really present. In the following passage, written by Weizmann to describe Palestine when he first visited there in 1907, notice how the contrast between past neglect and forlornness and present "tone and progressive spirit" (he was writing in 1941) is intended to justify the introduction of foreign colonies and settlements.

> A dolorous country it was on the whole, one of the most neglected corners of the miserably neglected Turkish Empire. [Here, Weizmann uses "neglect" to describe Palestine's native inhabitants, the fact of whose residence there is not a sufficient reason to characterize Palestine as anything but an essentially empty and patient territory, awaiting people who show a proper care for it.] Its total population was something above six hundred thousand, of which about eighty thousand were Jews. The latter lived mostly in the cities. . . . But neither the colonies nor the city settlements in any way resembled, as far as vigor, tone and progressive spirit are concerned, the colonies and settlements of our day.[21]

One short-term gain was that Zionism "raised the value of the . . . land," and the Arabs could reap profits even if politically the land was being cut out from underneath them.

As against native neglect and decrepitude, Weizmann preached the necessity of Jewish energy, will, and organization for reclaiming, "redeeming" the land. His language was shot through with the rhetoric of voluntarism, with an ideology of will and new blood that appropriated for Zionism a great deal of the language (and later the policies) of European colonialists attempting to deal with native backwardness. "New blood had to be brought into the country; a new spirit of enterprise had to be introduced." The Jews were to be the importers of colonies and colonists whose role was not simply to take over a territory but also to be schools for a Jewish national self-revival. Thus if in Palestine "there were great possibilities," the question became how to do something about the fact that "the will was lacking. How was that to be awakened? How was a cumulative process to be set in motion?" According to Weizmann, the Zionists were saved from ultimate discouragement only because of "our feeling that a great source of energy was waiting to be tapped — the national impulse of a people held in temporary check by a mis-guided interpretation of historic method."[22] The "method" referred to was the Zionist tendency hitherto to rely on great foreign benefactors like the Rothschilds and "neglect" the development of self-sustaining colonial insti-tutions on the land itself.

To do this, it was necessary to visualize and then to implement a scheme for creating a network of realities — a language, a grid of colonies, a series of organizations — for converting Palestine from its present state of "neglect" into a Jewish state. This network would not so much attack the existing "realities" as ignore them, grow alongside them, and then finally blot them out, as a forest of large trees blots out a small patch of weeds. A main ideolog-ical necessity for such a program was acquiring legitimacy for it, giving it an archaeology and a teleology that completely surrounded and, in a sense, outdated the native culture that was still firmly planted in Palestine. One of the reasons Weizmann modified the conception of the Balfour Declaration from its favoring the establishment of a Jewish National Home to favoring a "reestablishment" was precisely to enclose the territory with the oldest and furthest reaching of possible "realities." The colonization of Palestine proceeded always as a fact of repetition: the Jews were not supplanting, des-troying, breaking up a native society. That society was itself the oddity that had broken the pattern of a sixty-year Jewish sovereignty over Palestine which had lapsed for two millennia. In Jewish hearts, however, Israel had al-ways been there, an actuality difficult for the natives to perceive. Zionism therefore reclaimed, redeemed, repeated, replanted, realized Palestine, and Jewish hegemony over it. Israel was a return to a previous state of affairs, even if the new facts bore a far greater resemblance to the methods and suc-cesses of nineteenth-century European colonialism than to some mysterious first-century forebears.

Here it is necessary to make someting very clear. In each of the projects for "reestablishing" Jewish sovereignty over Palestine there were always two fundamental components. One was a careful determination to implement

Jewish self-betterment. About this, of course, the world heard a great deal. Great steps were taken in providing Jews with a new sense of identity, in defending and giving them rights as citizens, in reviving a national "home" language (through the labors of Eliezer Ben Yehudah), in giving the whole Jewish world a vital sense of growth and historical destiny. Thus "there was an instrument [in Zionism] for them to turn to, an instrument which could absorb them into the new life."[23] For Jews, Zionism was a school—and its pedagogical philosophy was always clear, dramatic, intelligent. Yet the other, dialectically opposite component in Zionism, existing at its interior where it was never *seen* (even though directly experienced by Palestinians) was an equally firm and intelligent boundary between benefits for Jews and none (later, punishment) for non-Jews in Palestine.

The consequences of the bifurcation in the Zionist program for Palestine have been immense, especially for Arabs who have tried seriously to deal with Israel. So effective have Zionist ideas about Palestine been for Jews—in the sense of caring for Jews and ignoring non-Jews—that what these ideas expressed to Arabs was *only* a rejection of Arabs. Thus Israel itself has tended to appear as an entirely negative entity, something constructed for us for no other reason than either to keep Arabs out or to subjugate them. The internal solidity and cohesion of Israel, of Israelis as a people and as a society, have for the most part, therefore, eluded the understanding of Arabs generally. Thus to the walls constructed by Zionism have been added walls constructed by a dogmatic, almost theological brand of Arabism. Israel has seemed essentially to be a rhetorical tool provided by the West to harass the Arabs. What this perception entailed in the Arab states has been a policy of repression and a kind of thought control. For years it was forbidden ever to refer to Israel in print; this sort of censorship led quite naturally to the consolidation of police states, the absence of freedom of expression, and a whole set of human rights abuses, all supposedly justified in the name of "fighting Zionist aggression," which meant that any form of oppression at home was acceptable because it served the "sacred cause" of "national security."

For Israel and Zionists everywhere, the results of Zionist apartheid have been equally disastrous. The Arabs were seen as synonymous with everything degraded, fearsome, irrational, and brutal. Institutions whose humanistic and social (even socialist) inspiration were manifest for Jews—the kibbutz, the Law of Return, various facilities for the acculturation of immigrants—were precisely, determinedly inhuman for the Arabs. In their body and being, and in the putative emotions and psychology assigned to them, the Arabs expressed whatever by definition stood *outside, beyond* Zionism.

The denial of Israel by the Arabs was, I think, a far less sophisticated and complex thing than the denial, and later the minimization, of the Arabs by Israel. Zionism was not only a reproduction of nineteenth-century European colonialism, for all the community of ideas it shared with that colonialism. Zionism aimed to create a society that could never be anything but "native" (with minimal ties to a metropolitan center) at the same time that it determined not to come to terms with the very natives it was replacing with new (but essentially European) "natives." Such a substitution was to be absolutely economic; no slippage from Arab Palestinian to Israeli societies would occur, and the Arabs would remain, if they did not flee, only as docile, subservient objects. And everything that did stay to challenge Israel was viewed not as something *there*, but as a sign of something *outside* Israel and Zionism bent on its destruction—from the outside. Here Zionism literally took over the typology employed by European culture of a fearsome Orient confronting the Occident, except that Zionism, as an avant-garde, redemptive Occidental movement, confronted the Orient *in* the Orient. To look at what "fulfilled" Zionism had to say about the Arabs generally, and Palestinians in particular, is to see something like the following, extracted from an article printed in *Ma'ariv*, October 7, 1955. Its author was a Dr. A. Carlebach, who was a distinguished citizen and not a crude demagogue. His argument is that *Islam* opposes Zionism, although he does find room in his argument for the Palestinians.

> These Arab Islamic countries do not suffer from poverty, or disease, or illiteracy, or exploitation; they only suffer from the worst of all plagues: Islam. Wherever Islamic psychology rules, there is the inevitable rule of despotism and criminal aggression. The danger lies in Islamic psychology, which cannot integrate itself into the world of efficiency and progress, that lives in a world of illusion, perturbed by attacks of inferiority complexes and megalomania, lost in dreams of the holy sword. The danger stems from the totalitarian conception of the world, the passion for murder deeply rooted in their blood, from the lack of logic, the easily inflamed brains, the boasting, and above all: the blasphemous disregard for all that is sacred to the civilized world . . . their reactions—to anything—have nothing to do with good sense. They are all emotional, unbalanced, instantaneous, senseless. It is always the lunatic that speaks from their throat. You can talk "business" with everyone, and even with the devil. But not with Allah. . . . This is what every grain in this country shouts. There were many great cultures here, and invaders of all kinds. All of them—even the Crusaders—left signs of culture and blossoming. But on the path of Islam, even the trees have died. [This dovetails perfectly with Weizmann's observations about "neglect" in Palestine; one assumes that had Weizmann been writing later he would have said similar things to Carlebach.]
> We pile sin upon crime when we distort the picture and reduce the discussion to a conflict of border between Israel and her neighbors. First of all, it is not the truth. The heart of the conflict is not the question of the borders; it is the question of Muslim psychology. . . . Moreover, to present the problem as a conflict between two similar parts is to provide the

Arabs with the weapon of a claim that is not theirs. If the discussion with them is truly a political one, then it can be seen from both sides. Then we appear as those who came to a country that was entirely Arab, and we conquered and implanted ourselves as an alien body among them, and we loaded them with refugees and constitute a military danger for them, etc. etc. . . . one can justify this or that side—and such a presentation, sophisticated and political, of the problem is understandable for European minds—at our expense. The Arabs raise claims that make sense to the Western understanding of simple legal dispute. But in reality, who knows better than us that such is not the source of their hostile stand? All those political and social concepts are never theirs. Occupation by force of arms, in their own eyes, in the eyes of Islam, is not all associated with injustice. To the contrary, it constitutes a certificate and demonstration of authentic ownership. The sorrow for the refugees, for the expropriated brothers, has no room in their thinking. Allah expelled, Allah will care. Never has a Muslim politician been moved by such things (unless, indeed, the catastrophe endangered his personal status). If there were no refugees and no conquest, they would oppose us just the same. By discussing with them on the basis of Western concepts, we dress savages in a European robe of justice.

Israeli studies of "Arab attitudes"—such as the canonical one by General Harkabi[24]—take no notice of such analyses as this one, which is more magical and racist than anything one is likely to encounter by a Palestinian. But the dehumanization of the Arab, which began with the view that Palestinians were either not there or savages or both, saturates everything in Israeli society. It was not thought too unusual during the 1973 war for the army to issue a booklet (with a preface by General Yona Efrati of the central command) written by the central command's rabbi, Abraham Avidan, containing the following key passage:

> When our forces encounter civilians during the war or in the course of a pursuit or a raid, the encountered civilians may, and by Halachic standards even must be killed, whenever it cannot be ascertained that they are incapable of hitting us back. Under no circumstances should an Arab be trusted, even if he gives the impression of being civilized.[25]

Children's literature is made up of valiant Jews who always end up by killing low, treacherous Arabs, with names like Mastoul (crazy), Bandura (tomato), or Bukra (tomorrow). As a writer for *Ha'aretz* said (September 20, 1974), children's books "deal with our topic: the Arab who murders Jews out of pleasure, and the pure Jewish boy who defeats 'the coward swine!' " Nor are such enthusiastic ideas limited to individual authors who produce books for mass consumption; as I shall show later, these ideas derive more or less logically from the state's institutions themselves, to whose other, benevolent side falls the task of regulating Jewish life humanistically.

There are perfect illustrations of this duality in Weizmann, for whom such matters immediately found their way into policy, action, detailed results. He admires Samuel Pevsner as "a man of great ability, energetic, practical, resourceful and, like his wife, highly educated." One can have no problem with this. Then immediately comes the following, without so much as a transition: "For such people, going to Palestine was in effect going into a social wilderness—which is something to be remembered by those who, turning to Palestine today, find in it intellectual, cultural and social resources not inferior to those of the Western world."[26] Zionism was all foregrounding; everything else was background, and it had to be subdued, suppressed, lowered in order that the foreground of cultural achievement could appear as "civilizing pioneer work."[27] Above all, the native Arab had to be seen as an irremediable opposite, something like a combination of savage and superhuman, at any rate a being with whom it is impossible (and useless) to come to terms.

> The Arab is a very subtle debator and controversialist—much more so than the average educated European—and until one has acquired the technique one is at a great disadvantage. In particular, the Arab has an immense talent for expressing views diametrically opposed to yours with such exquisite and roundabout politeness that you believe him to be in complete agreement with you, and ready to join hands with you at once. Conversation and negotiations with Arabs are not unlike chasing a mirage in the desert: full of promise and good to look at, but likely to lead to death by thirst.
>
> A direct question is dangerous: it provokes in the Arab a skillful withdrawal and a complete change of subject. The problem must be approached by winding lanes, and it takes an interminable time to reach the kernel of the subject.[28]

On another occasion, he recounts an experience which in effect was the germ of Tel Aviv, whose importance as a Jewish center derives in great measure from its having neutralized the adjacent (and much older) Arab town of Jaffa. In what Weizmann tells the reader, however, there is only the slightest allusion to the fact of Arab life already existing there, on what was to be the adjacent future site of Tel Aviv. What matters is the production of a Jewish presence, whose value appears to be more or less self-evident.

> I was staying in Jaffa when Ruppin called on me, and took me out for a walk over the dunes to the north of the town. When we had got well out into the sands—I remember that it came over our ankles—he stopped, and said, very solemnly: "Here we shall create a Jewish city!" I looked at him with some dismay. Why should people come to live out in this wilderness where nothing would grow? I began to ply him with technical questions, and he answered me carefully and exactly. Technically, he said, everything is possible. Though in the first years communications with the new settle-

ment would be difficult, the inhabitants would soon become self-supporting and self-sufficient. The Jews of Jaffa would move into the new, modern city, and the Jewish colonies of the neighborhood would have a concentrated market for their products. The Gymnasium would stand at the center, and would attract a great many students from other parts of Palestine and from Jews abroad, who would want their children to be educated in a Jewish high school in a Jewish city.

Thus it was Ruppin who had the first vision of Tel Aviv, which was destined to outstrip, in size and in economic importance, the ancient town of Jaffa, and to become one of the metropolitan centers of the eastern Mediterranean.[29]

In time, of course, the preeminence of Tel Aviv was to be buttressed by the military capture of Jaffa. The visionary project later turned into the first step of a military conquest, the idea of a colony being later fleshed out in the actual appearance of a colony, of colonizers, and of the colonized.

Weizmann and Ruppin, it is true, spoke and acted with the passionate idealism of pioneers; they also were speaking and acting with the authority of Westerners surveying fundamentally retarded non-Western territory and natives, planning the future *for them.* Weizmann himself did not just think that as a European he was better equipped to decide for the natives what their best interests were (e.g., that Jaffa *ought to be* outstripped by a modern Jewish city), he also believed he "understood" the Arab *as he really was.* In saying that the Arab's "immense talent" was "in fact" for never telling the truth, he said what other Europeans had observed about non-European natives elsewhere, for whom, like the Zionists, the problem was controlling a large native majority with a comparative handful of intrepid pioneers:

> It may well be asked how it is that we are able to control, with absurdly inadequate forces, races so virile and capable, with such mental and physical endowments. The reply is, I think, that there are two flaws to be found: —the mental and moral equipment of the average African. . . . I say that inherent lack of honesty is the first great flaw. . . . Comparatively rarely can one African depend upon another keeping his word. . . . Except in very rare instances it is a regrettable fact that this defect is enlarged rather than diminished by contact with European civilization. The second is lack of mental initiative. . . . Unless impelled from the outside the native seldom branches out from a recognized groove and this mental lethargy is characteristic of his mind.[30]

This is C. L. Temple's *Native Races and Their Rulers* (1918); its author was an assistant to Frederick Lugard in governing Nigeria and, like Weizmann, he was less a proto-Nazi racist than a liberal Fabian in his outlook.

For Temple as for Weizmann, the realities were that natives belonged to a stationary, stagnant culture. Incapable therefore of appreciating the land they lived on, they had to be prodded, perhaps even dislocated by the initiatives of an advanced European culture. Now certainly Weizmann had the additional rationalizations behind him of reconstituting a Jewish state, saving Jews from anti-Semitism, and so on. But so far as the natives were concerned, it could not have mattered initially whether the Europeans they faced in the colony were Englishmen or European Jews. Then too, as far as the Zionist in Palestine or the Britisher in Africa was concerned, he was realistic, he saw facts and dealt with them, he knew the value of truth. Notwithstanding the "fact" of long residence on a native territory, the non-European was always in retreat from truth. European vision meant the capacity for seeing not only what was there, but what *could* be there: hence the Weizmann-Ruppin exchange about Jaffa and Tel Aviv. The specific temptation before the Zionist in Palestine was to believe — and plan for — the possibility that the Arab natives would not *really* be there, which was doubtless a proven eventuality (a) when the natives would not acknowledge Jewish sovereignty over Palestine and (b) when after 1948 they became legal outsiders on their land.

But the success of Zionism did not derive exclusively from its bold outlining of a future state, or from its ability to see the natives for the negligible quantities they were or might become. Rather, I think, Zionism's effectiveness in making its way against Arab Palestinian resistance lay *in its being a policy of detail*, not simply a general colonial vision. Thus Palestine was not only the Promised Land, a concept as elusive and as abstract as any that one could encounter. It was a specific territory with specific characteristics, that was surveyed down to the last millimeter, settled on, planned for, built on, and so forth, *in detail*. From the beginning of the Zionist colonization this was something the Arabs had no answer to, no equally detailed counterproposal. They assumed, perhaps rightly, that since they lived on the land and legally owned it, it was therefore theirs. They did not understand that what they were encountering was a discipline of detail — indeed a very culture of discipline by detail — by which a hitherto imaginary realm could be constructed on Palestine, inch by inch and step by step, "another acre, another goat," so Weizmann once said. The Palestinian Arabs always opposed a *general* policy on general principles: Zionism, they said, was foreign colonialism (which strictly speaking it was, as the early Zionists admitted), it was unfair to the natives (as some early Zionists, like Ahad Ha'am, also admitted), and it was doomed to die of its various theoretical weaknesses. Even to this day the Palestinian political position generally clusters around these negatives, and still does not sufficiently try to meet the detail of Zionist enterprise; today there are, for example, seventy-seven "illegal" Zionist colonies on the West Bank and Israel has confiscated about 27 percent of the West Bank's Arab-owned land, yet the Palestinians seem virtually powerless physically to stop the growth or "thickening" of this new Israeli colonization.

The Palestinians have not understood that Zionism has been much more than an unfair colonialist master against whom one could appeal to all sorts of higher courts, without any avail. They have not understood the Zionist challenge as a policy of detail, of institutions, or organization, by which people (to this day) enter territory illegally, build houses on it, settle there, and call the land their own—with the whole world condemning them. The force of that drive to settle, in a sense *to produce*, a Jewish land can be glimpsed in a document that Weizmann says "seemed to have anticipated the shape of things to come" as indeed it did. This was an "Outline of Program for the Jewish Resettlement of Palestine in Accordance with the Aspirations of the Zionist Movement"; it appeared in early 1917, and it is worth quoting from:

> The Suzerain Government [that is, any government, Allied or otherwise, in command of the territory] shall sanction a formation of a Jewish company for the colonization of Palestine by Jews. The said Company shall be under the direct protection of the Suzerain Government [that is, whatever went on in Palestine, should be legitimized not by the natives but by some outside force]. The objects of the Company shall be: a) to support and foster the existing Jewish settlement in Palestine in every possible way; b) to aid, support and encourage Jews from other countries who are desirous of and suitable for settling in Palestine by organizing immigration, by providing information, and by every other form of material and moral assistance. The powers of the Company shall be such as will enable it to develop the country in every way, agricultural, cultural, commercial and industrial, and shall include full powers of land purchase and development, and especially facilities for the acquisition of the Crown lands, building rights for roads, railway harbors, power to establish shipping companies for the transport of goods and passengers to and from Palestine, and for every other power found necessary for the opening of the country.[31]

Underlying this extraordinary passage is a vision of a matrix of organizations whose functioning duplicates that of an army. For it is an army that "opens" a country to settlement, that organizes settlements in foreign territory, that aids and develops "in every possible way" such matters as immigration, shipping, and supply, that above all turns mere citizens into "suitable" disciplined agents whose job it is to be on the land and to invest it with their structures, organization, and institutions.[32] Just as an army assimilates ordinary citizens to its purposes—by dressing them in uniforms, by exercising them in tactics and maneuvers, by disciplining everyone to its purposes—so too did Zionism dress the Jewish colonists in the system of Jewish labor and Jewish land, whose uniform required that only Jews were acceptable. The power of the Zionist army did not reside in its leaders, nor in the arms it collected for its conquests and defense, but rather in the functioning of a whole system, a series of positions taken and held, as Weizmann says, in agriculture, culture, commerce, and industry. In short, Zionism's "company" was the translation of a theory and a vision into a set of instruments for holding and developing a Jewish colonial territory right in the middle of an indifferently surveyed and developed Arab territory.

The fascinating history of the Zionist colonial apparatus, its "company," cannot long detain us here, but at least some things about its workings need to be noted. The Second Zionist Congress meeting in Basel, Switzerland (August 1898), created the Jewish Colonial Trust Limited, a subsidiary of which was founded in Jaffa in 1903 and called the Anglo-Palestine Company. Thus began an agency whose role in the transformation of Palestine was extraordinarily crucial. Out of the Colonial Trust in 1901 came the Jewish National Fund (JNF), empowered to buy land and hold it in trust for "the Jewish people"; the wording of the original proposal was that the JNF would be "a trust for the Jewish people, which . . . can be used exclusively for the purchase of land in Palestine and Syria." The JNF was always under the control of the World Zionist Organization, and in 1905 the first land purchases were made.

From its inception as a functioning body the JNF existed either to develop, buy, or lease land—only for Jews. As Walter Lehn convincingly shows (in a major piece of research on the JNF, on which I have relied for the details I mention here)[33] the Zionist goal was to acquire land in order to put settlers on it; thus in 1920, after the Palestinian Land Development Company had been founded as an agency of the JNF, a Palestine Foundation Fund was created to organize immigration and colonization. At the same time, emphasis was placed institutionally on acquiring and holding lands for "the Jewish people." This designation made it certain that a Zionist state would be unlike any other in that it was not to be the state of its citizens, but rather the state of a whole people most of which was in Diaspora. Aside from making the non-Jewish people of the state into second-class citizens, it made the Zionist organizations, and later the state, retain a large extraterritorial power in addition to the vital territorial possessions over which the state was to have sovereignty. Even the land acquired by the JNF was—as John Hope Simpson said in 1930—"extraterritorialized. It ceases to be land from which the Arab can gain any advantage either now or at any time in the future." There was no corresponding Arab effort to institutionalize Arab landholding in Palestine, no thought that it might be necessary to create an organization for holding lands "in perpetuity" for the "Arab people," above all, no informational, money-raising, lobbying work done—as the Zionists did in Europe and the United States—to expand "Jewish" territory and, paradoxically, give it a Jewish presence and an international, almost metaphysical status as well. The Arabs mistakenly thought that owning the land and being on it were enough.

Even with all this sophisticated and farsighted effort, the JNF acquired only 936,000 dunams of land (a dunam being roughly a quarter of an acre) in the almost half-century of its existence before Israel appeared as a state; the total land area of mandate Palestine was 26,323,000 dunams. Together with the small amount of land held by private Jewish owners, Zionist land-holding in Palestine at the end of 1947 was 1,734,000 dunams, that is, 6.59 percent of the total area. After 1940, when the mandatory authority restricted Jewish land ownership to specific zones inside Palestine, there continued to be illegal buying (and selling) within the 65 percent of the total area restricted to Arabs. Thus when the partition plan was announced in 1947 it included land held illegally by Jews, which was incorporated as a *fait accompli* inside the borders of the Jewish states. And after Israel announced its statehood, an impressive series of laws legally assimilated huge tracts of Arab land (whose proprietors had become refugees, and were pronounced "absentee landlords" in order to expropriate their lands and prevent their return under any circumstances) to the JNF. The process of land alienation (from the Arab standpoint) had been completed.

The ideological, profoundly political meaning of the "company's" territorial achievements illuminates the post-1967 controversy over the fate of Arab land occupied by Israel. A large segment of the Israeli population seems to believe that Arab land can be converted into Jewish land (a) because the land had once been Jewish two millennia ago (a part of Eretz Israel) and (b) because there exists in the JNF a method for legally metamorphosing "neglected" land into the property of the Jewish people.[34] Once Jewish settlements are built and peopled, and once they are hooked into the state network, they become properly extraterritorial, emphatically Jewish, and non-Arab. To this new land is added as well a strategic rationale, that it is necessary for Israeli security. But were these things simply a matter of internal Israeli concern, and were they sophistic arguments intended only to appeal to an Israeli constituency, they might be analyzed dispassionately as being no more than curious. The fact is, however, that they impinge—as they always have—on the Arab residents of the territories, and then they have a distinct cutting edge to them. Both in theory and in practice their effectiveness lies in how they Judaize territory coterminously with de-Arabizing it.

There is privileged evidence of this fact, I think, in what Joseph Weitz had to say. From 1932 on, Weitz was the director of the Jewish National Land Fund; in 1965 his diaries and papers, *My Diary, and Letters to the Children*, were published in Israel. On December 19, 1940, he wrote:

> . . . after the [Second World] war the question of the land of Israel and the question of the Jews would be raised beyond the framework of "development"; amongst ourselves. *It must be clear that there is no room for both peoples in this country.* No "development" will bring us closer to our aim, to be an independent people in this small country. If the Arabs leave the country, it will be broad and wide-open for us. And if the Arabs stay, the country will remain narrow and miserable. When the War is over and the English have won, and when the judges sit on the throne of Law, our people must bring their petitions and their claim before them; and the only

solution is Eretz Israel, or at least Western Eretz Israel, *without Arabs. There is no room for compromise on this point!* The Zionist enterprise so far, in terms of preparing the ground and paving the way for the creation of the Hebrew State in the land of Israel, has been fine and good in its own time, and could do with "land-buying"—but this will not bring about the State of Israel; that must come all at once, in the manner of a Salvation (this is the secret of the Messianic idea); and there is no way besides transferring the Arabs from here to the neighboring countries, *to transfer them all*; except maybe for Bethlehem, Nazareth and Old Jerusalem, *we must not leave a single village, not a single tribe.* And the transfer must be directed to Iraq, to Syria, and even to Transjordan. For that purpose we'll find money, and a lot of money. And only with such a transfer will the country be able to absorb millions of our brothers, and the Jewish question shall be solved, once and for all. There is no other way out. [Emphases added.][35]

These are not only prophetic remarks about what was going to happen; they are also policy statements, in which Weitz spoke with the voice of the Zionist consensus. There were literally hundreds of such statements made by Zionists, beginning with Herzl, and when "salvation" came it was with those ideas in mind that the conquest of Palestine, and the eviction of its Arabs, was carried out. A great deal has been written about the turmoil in Palestine from the end of World War II until the end of 1948. Despite the complexities of what may or may not have taken place, Weitz's thoughts furnish a beam of light shining through those events, pointing to a Jewish state with most of the original Arab inhabitants turned into refugees. It is true that such major events as the birth of a new state, which came about as the result of an almost unimaginably complex, many-sided struggle and a full-scale war, cannot be easily reduced to simple formulation. I have no wish to do this, but neither do I wish to evade the outcome of struggle, or the determining elements that went into the struggle, or even the policies produced in Israel ever since. The fact that matters for the Palestinian—and for the Zionist—is that a territory once full of Arabs emerged from a war (a) essentially emptied of its original residents and (b) made impossible for Palestinians to return to. Both the ideological and organizational preparations for the Zionist effort to win Palestine, as well as the military strategy adopted, envisioned taking over territory, and filling it with new inhabitants. Thus the Dalet Plan, as it has been described by the Zionist historians Jon and David Kimche, was "to capture strategic heights dominating the most likely lines of advance of the invading Arab armies, and to fill in the vacuum left by the departing British forces in such a way as to create a contiguous Jewish-held area extending from the north to the south."[36] In places like Galilee, the coastal area from Jaffa to Acre, parts of Jerusalem, the towns of Lydda and Ramla, to say nothing of the Arab parts of Haifa, the Zionists were not only taking over British positions; they were

also filling in space lived in by Arab residents who were, in Weitz' word, being "transferred."

Against the frequently mentioned propositions—that Palestinians left because they were ordered to by their leaders, that the invading Arab armies
were an unwarranted response to Israel's declaration of independence in May
1948—I must say categorically that *no one has produced any evidence of such orders
sufficient to produce so vast and final an exodus.*[37] In other words, if we wish to
understand why 780,000 Palestinians left in 1948, we must shift our sights
to take in more than the immediate events of 1948; rather, we must see the
exodus as being produced by a relative lack of Palestinian political, organizational response to Zionist effectiveness and, along with that, a psychological
mood of failure and terror. Certainly atrocities, such as the Deir Yassin massacre of 250 Arab civilians by Menachem Begin and his Irgun terrorists in
April 1948, had their effect. But for all its horror, even Deir Yassin was one
of many such massacres which began in the immediate post-World War I
period and which produced conscious Zionist equivalents of American
Indian-killers.[38] What probably counted more has been the machinery for
keeping the unarmed civilian Palestinians away, once they had moved (in
most cases) to avoid the brutalities of war. Before as well as after they left
there were specific Zionist instrumentalities for, in effect, obliterating their
presence. I have already cited Weitz in 1940. Here he is on May 18, 1948,
narrating a conversation with Moshe Shertok (later Sharett) of the Foreign
Ministry:

> Transfer—*post factum*; should we do something so as to transform the exo-
> dus of the Arabs from the country into a fact, so that they return no
> more? . . . His [Shertok's] answer: he blesses any initiative in this matter.
> His opinion is also that we must act in such a way as to transform the exo-
> dus of the Arabs into an established fact.[39]

Later that year, Wetiz visited an evacuated Arab village. He reflected as
follows:

> I went to visit the village of Mu'ar. Three tractors are completing its de-
> struction. I was surprised; nothing in me moved at the sign of the destruc-
> tion. No regret and no hate, as though this was the way the world goes. So
> we want to feel good in this world, and not in some world to come. We
> simply want to live, and the inhabitants of those mud-houses did not want
> us to exist here. They not only aspire to dominate us, they also wanted to
> exterminate us. And what is interesting—this is the opinion of all our boys,
> from one end to the other.[40]

He describes something that took place everywhere in Palestine but he seems
totally unable to take in the fact that the human lives—very modest and
humble ones, it is true—actually lived in that wretched village meant some-

thing to the people whose lives they were. Weitz does not attempt to deny the villagers' reality; he simply admits that their destruction means only that "we" can now live there. He is completely untroubled by the thought that to the native Palestinians he, Weitz, is only a foreigner come to displace them, or that it is no more than natural to oppose such a prospect. Instead, Weitz and "the boys" take the position that the Palestinians wanted to "exterminate" them—and this therefore licenses the destruction of houses and villages. After several decades of treating the Arabs as if they were not there at all, Zionism came fully into its own by actively destroying as many Arab traces as it could. From a nonentity in theory to a nonentity in legal fact, the Palestinian Arab lived through the terrible modulation from one sorry condition to the other, fully able to witness, but not effectively to communicate, his or her own civil extinction in Palestine.

First they were inconsequential natives; then they became absent ones; then inside Israel after 1948 they acquired the juridical status of less real persons than any individual person belonging to the "Jewish people," whether that person was present in Israel or not. The ones who left the country in terror became "refugees," an abstraction faithfully taken account of in annual United Nations resolutions calling upon Israel—as Israel had promised—to take them back, or compensate them for their losses. The list of human indignities and, by any impartial standard, the record of immoral subjugation practiced by Israel against the Palestinian Arab remnant is blood-curdling, particularly if counterpointed with that record one hears the chorus of praise to Israeli democracy. As if to pay that wretched 120,000 (now about 650,000) for its temerity in staying where it did not belong, Israel took over the Emergency Defense Regulations, used by the British to handle Jews and Arabs during the mandate period from 1922 to 1948. The regulations had been a justifiably favorite target of Zionist political agitation, but after 1948 they were used, *unchanged*, by Israel against the Arabs.

For example, in those parts of Israel that still retain an Arab majority, an anachronistic but no less effective and detailed policy of "Judaization" goes on apace. Thus just as Ruppin and Weizmann in the early days foresaw a Tel Aviv to "outstrip" Arab Jaffa, the Israeli government of today creates a new Jewish Nazareth to outstrip the old Arab town. Here is the project described by an Israeli in 1975:

> Upper Nazareth, which was created some fifteen years ago, "in order to create a counterweight to the Arab Nazareth," constitutes a cornerstone of the "Judaization of the Galilee" policy. Upper Nazareth was erected upon the hills surrounding Nazareth as a security belt surrounding it almost on all sides. It was built upon thousands of acres of lands which were expropriated high-handedly, purely and simply by force, from the Arab settlements, particularly Nazareth and Rana. The very choice of the name "upper" Nazareth, while the stress is upon *upper*, is an indicator of the attitude

of the authorities, which give the new town special privileges according to their policy of discrimination and lack of attention regarding the city of Nazareth, which is, in their eyes, at the very bottom of the ladder. The visitor to Nazareth can acknowledge with his own eyes the neglect and lack of development of the city, and if from there he goes "up" to upper Nazareth, he will see over there the new buildings, the wide streets, the public lights, the steps, the many-storied buildings, the industrial and artisan enterprises, and he will be able to perceive the contrast: development up there and lack of care down there; constant government building up there, and no construction whatever down there. Since 1966 the [Israeli] Ministry of Housing has not built a single unit of habitation in old Nazareth. [Yoseph Elgazi in *Zo Hadareh*, July 30, 1975.]

The drama of a ruling minority is vividly enacted in Nazareth. With all its advantages, upper — that is, Jewish — Nazareth contains 16,000 residents; below it, the Arab city has a population of 45,000. Clearly the Jewish city benefits from the network of resources for Jews. Non-Jews are surgically excluded. The rift between them and the Jews is intended by Zionism to signify a state of absolute difference between the two groups, not merely one of degree. If every Jew in Israel represents "the whole Jewish people" — which is a population made up not only of the Jews in Israel, but also of generations of Jews who existed in the past (of whom the present Israelis are the remnant) and those who exist in the future, as well as those who live elsewhere — non-Jews in Israel represent a permanent banishment from their as well as all *other* past, present, and future benefits in Palestine. The non-Jew lives a meager existence in villages without libraries, youth centers, theaters, cultural centers; most Arab villages, according to the Arab mayor of Nazareth, who speaks with the unique authority of a non-Jew in Israel, lack electricity, telephone communications, health centers; none has any sewage systems, except Nazareth itself, which is only partly serviced by one; none has paved roads or streets. For whereas the Jew is entitled to the maximum, the non-Jew is given a bare minimum. Out of a total work force of 80,000 Arab workers, 60,000 work in Jewish enterprises. "These workers regard their town and villages as nothing but places of residence. Their only prosperous 'industry' is the creation and supply of manpower."[41] Manpower without political significance, without a territorial base, without cultural continuity; for non-Jews in Israel, if they dared to remain after the Jewish state appeared in 1948, there was only the meager subsistence of being *there*, almost powerless except to reproduce themselves and their misery more or less endlessly.

Since occupying the West Bank and Gaza in 1967, Israel has acquired approximately a million more Arab subjects. Its record has been no better, but this has not been surprising. Indeed, the best introduction to what has been taking place in the Occupied Territories is the testimony of Israeli Arabs who suffered through Israeli legal brutality before 1967. See, for instance, Sabri

Jiryis's *The Arabs in Israel* or Fouzi al-Asmar's *To Be an Arab in Israel* or Elia T. Zwrayk's *The Palestinians in Israel: A Study in Internal Colonialism*. Israel's political goal has been to keep the Arabs pacified, never capable of preventing their continued domination by Israel. Whenever a nationalist leader gains a little stature, he is either deported, imprisoned (without trial), or he disappears; Arab houses (approximately 17,000) are blown up by the army to make examples of nationalist offenders; censorship *on everything written by or about Arabs* prevails; every Arab is directly subject to military regulations. In order to disguise repression and to keep it from disturbing the tranquility of Israeli consciousness, a corps of Arab experts — Israeli Jews who understand the Arab "mentality" — has grown up. One of them, Amnon Lin, wrote in 1968 that "the people trusted us and gave us a freedom of action that has not been enjoyed by any other group in the country, in any field." Consequently,

> Over time we have attained a unique position in the state as experts, and no one dares to challenge our opinions or our actions. We are represented in every department of government, in the Histadrut and in the political parties; every department and office has its "Arabists" who alone act for their minister among the Arabs.[42]

This quasi government interprets, and rules the Arabs behind a facade of privileged expertise. When, as I have noted elsewhere, visiting liberals wish to find out about "the Arabs," they are given a suitably cosmetic picture.[43] Meanwhile, of course, Israeli settlements on occupied territories multiply (over ninety of them since 1967); the logic of colonization after 1967 follows the same pattern, resulting in the same displacements of Arabs as before 1948.[44]

There are Zionism and Israel for Jews, and Zionism and Israel for non-Jews. Zionism has drawn a sharp line between Jew and non-Jew; Israel built a whole system for keeping them apart, including the much admired (but completely apartheid) kibbutzim, to which no Arab has ever belonged. In effect, the Arabs are ruled by a separate government premised on the impossibility of isonomic rule for both Jews and non-Jews. Out of this radical notion it became natural for the Arab Gulag Archipelago to develop its own life, to create its own precision, its own detail. Uri Avneri put it this way to the Knesset:

> A complete government . . . was created in the Arab sector, a secret government, unsanctioned by law . . . whose members and methods are not known . . . to anyone. Its agents are scattered among the ministries of government, from the Israel Lands Administration to the ministry of education and the ministry of religions. It makes fateful decisions affecting [Arab] lives in unknown places without documents and communicates them in secret conversations or over the telephone. This is the way decisions are made about who goes to the teachers' seminar, or who will obtain

a tractor, or who will be appointed to a government post, or who will receive financial subsidies, or who will be elected to the Knesset, or who will
be elected to the local council—if there is one—and so on for a thousand
and one reasons.[45]

But from time to time there have been inadvertent insights into government for Arabs in Israel given to watchful observers. The most unguarded
example was a secret report by Israel Koenig, northern district (Galilee) com-
missioner of the ministry, written for the then Prime Minister Yitzhak Rabin
on "handling the Arabs in Israel." (The full text was subsequently leaked to
Al-Hamishmar on September 7, 1976.) Its contents make chilling reading, but
they fulfill the assumptions of Zionism toward its victims, the non-Jews.
Koenig frankly admits that Arabs present a demographic problem since unlike Jews, whose natural increase is 1.5 percent annually, the Arabs increase
at a yearly rate of 5.9 percent. Moreover, he assumes that it is national policy
for the Arabs to be kept inferior, although they may be naturally susceptible
to nationalist restlessness. The main thing, however, is how to make sure that
in areas like Galilee the density of the Arab population, and consequently its
potential for trouble, be reduced, contained, weakened. Therefore, he suggested that it is necessary to

> expand and deepen Jewish settlement in areas where the contiguity of the
> Arab population is prominent, and where they number considerably more
> than the Jewish population; examine the possibility of diluting existing
> Arab population concentrations. Special attention must be paid to border
> areas in the country's northwest and to the Nazareth region. The approach
> and exigency of performance have to deviate from the routine that has been
> adopted so far. Concurrently, the state law has to be enforced so as to limit
> "breaking of new ground" by Arab settlements in various areas of the
> country.

The quasi-military strategy of these suggestions is very near the surface.
What we must also remark is Koenig's unquestioning view of the Zionist imperatives he is trying to implement. Nothing in his report intimates any
qualms about the plainly racial end his suggestions promote; nor does he
doubt that what he says is thoroughly consistent with the history of Zionist
policy toward those non-Jews who have had the bad luck to be on Jewish
territory, albeit in disquietingly large numbers. He goes on to argue—
logically—that any Arab leaders who appear to cause trouble should be
replaced, that the government should set about to "create" (the word has an
almost theological tone very much in keeping with Jewish policy toward
Arabs) "new [Arab] figures of high intellectual standard, figures who are
equitable and charismatic," and completely acceptable to the Israeli rulers.
Moreover, in "dissipating" the restless nationalist leaders, whose main sin
seems to be that they encourage other natives to chafe at their enforced inferi-

ority, the government should form "a special team . . . to examine the personal habits of . . . leaders and other negative people and this information should be made available to the electorate."

Not content then with "diluting" and manipulating the Arab citizens of Israel, Koenig goes on to suggest ways for economically "neutralizing" and "encumbering" them. Very little of this can be effective, however, unless there were some method of somehow checkmating the "large population of frustrated intelligentsia forced by a mental need to seek relief. Expressions of this are directed against the Israeli establishment of the state." Koenig appeared to think it natural enough for Arabs to be kept frustrated, for in reading his suggestions there is little to remind one that Arabs are people, or that his report was written not about Jews by a Nazi during World War II, but in 1976 by a Jew about his Arab co-citizens. The master stroke of Koenig's plan comes when he discusses the social engineering required to use the Arab's backward "Levantine character" against itself. Since Arabs in Israel are a disadvantaged community, this reality must be enhanced as follows:

a) The reception criteria for Arab university students should be the same as for Jewish students and this must also apply to the granting of scholarships.

A meticulous implementation of these rules will produce a natural selection [the Darwinian terminology speaks eloquently for itself] and will considerably reduce the number of Arab students. Accordingly, the number of low-standard graduates will also decrease, a fact that will facilitate their absorption in work after studies [the plan here is to make certain that young Arabs would easily be assimilated into menial jobs, thus ensuring their intellectual emasculation].

b) Encourage the channeling of students into technical professions, the physical and natural sciences. These studies leave less time for dabbling in nationalism and the dropout rate is higher. [Koenig's ideas about the incompatibility between science and human values go C. P. Snow one better. Surely this is a sinister instance of the use of science as political punishment; it is new even to the history of colonialism.]

c) Make trips abroad for studies easier, while making the return and employment more difficult—this policy is apt to encourage their emigration.

d) Adopt tough measures at all levels against various agitators among college and university students.

e) Prepare absorption possibilities in advance for the better part of the graduates, according to their qualifications. This policy can be implemented thanks to the time available (a number of years) in which the authorities may plan their steps.

Were such ideas to have been formulated by Stalinists or Orwellian socialists or even Arab nationalists, the liberal outcry would be deafening. Koenig's suggestions, however, seem universally justified by the logic of events pitting a small, valiant Western population of Jews against a vast and amorphous, metastasizing and ruinously mindless Arab population. Nothing in Koenig's report conflicts with the basic dichotomy in Zionism, that is, benevolence toward Jews and an essential but paternalistic hostility toward Arabs. Moreover, Koenig himself writes from the standpoint of an ideologist or theorist as well as from a position of authority and power within Israeli society. As a ruler of Arabs in Israel, Koenig expresses both an official atten- tion to the well-being of Jews, whose interests he maintains and protects, and a paternalistic, managerial dominance over inferior natives. His position is therefore consecrated by the institutions of the Jewish state; licensed by them, he thinks in terms of a maximum future for Jews and a minimal one for non-Jews. All of these notions are perfectly delivered in the following paragraph from his report:

> Law enforcement in a country with a developing society like that of Israel is a problem to be solved with flexibility, care and much wisdom. At the same time, however, the administrative and executive authority in the Arab sector must be aware of the existence of the law and its enforcement so as to avoid erosion.[46]

Between Weizmann and Koenig there exists an intervening period of several decades. What was visionary projection for the former became for the latter a context of actual law. From Weizmann's epoch to Koenig's, Zionism for the native Arabs in Palestine had been converted from an advancing en- croachment upon their lives to a settled reality — a nation-state — enclosing them within it. For Jews after 1948, Israel not only realized their political and spiritual hopes, it continued to be a beacon of opportunity guiding those of them still living in Diaspora, and keeping those who lived in former Palestine on the frontier of Jewish development and self-realization. For the Arab Palestinians, Israel meant one essentially hostile fact and several unpleasant corollaries. After 1948 every Palestinian disappeared nationally and legally. Some Palestinians reappeared juridically as "non-Jews" in Israel; those who left become "refugees" and later some of those acquired new Arab, European, or American identities. No Palestinian, however, lost his "old" Palestinian identity. Out of such legal fictions as the nonexistent Palestinian in Israel and elsewhere, however, the Palestinian has finally emerged — and with a con- siderable amount of international attention prepared at last to take critical no- tice of Zionist theory and praxis.

The outcry in the West after the 1975 "Zionism is racism" resolution was passed in the United Nations was doubtless a genuine one. Israel's Jewish achievements — or rather its achievements on behalf of European Jews, less so for the Sephardic (Oriental) Jewish majority — stand before the Western world; by most standards they are considerable achievements, and it is right that they not sloppily be tarnished with the sweeping rhetorical denunciation associated with "racism." For the Palestinian Arab who has lived through and who has now studied the procedures of Zionism toward him and his land, the predicament is complicated, but not finally unclear. He knows that the Law of Return allowing a Jew immediate entry into Israel just as exactly prevents him from returning to his home; he also knows that Israeli raids killed thousands of civilians, all on the acceptable pretext of fighting terrorism,[47] but in reality because Palestinians as a race have become synonymous with unregenerate, essentially unmotivated terrorism; he understands, without perhaps being able to master, the intellectual process by which his violated humanity has been transmuted, unheard and unseen, into praise for the ideology that has all but destroyed him. *Racism* is too vague a term: Zionism is Zionism. For the Arab Palestinian, this tautology has a sense that is perfectly congruent with, but exactly the opposite of, what it says to Jews.

Western and Israeli intellectuals have continued to celebrate Israel and Zionism unblinkingly for thirty years. They have perfectly played the role of Gramsci's "experts in legitimation," dishonest and irrational despite their protestations on behalf of wisdom and humanity. Check the disgraceful record and you will find only a small handful — among them Noam Chomsky, Israel Shahak, I. F. Stone, Elmer Berger, Judah Magnes — who have tried to see what Zionism did to the Palestinians not just once in 1948, but over the years. It is one of the most frightening cultural episodes of the century, this almost total silence about Zionism's doctrines for and treatment of the native Palestinians. Any self-respecting intellectual is willing today to say something about human rights abuses in Argentina, Chile, or South Africa, yet when irrefutable evidence of Israeli preventive detention, torture, population transfer, and deportation of Palestinian Arabs is presented, literally nothing is said. The merest assurances that democracy is being respected in Israel are enough to impress a Daniel Moynihan or a Saul Bellow, for instance, that all is well on the moral front. But perhaps the true extent of this stateworship can only be appreciated when one reads of a meeting held in 1962 between Martin Buber and Avraham Aderet, published in the December 1974 issue of *Petahim*, an Israeli religious quarterly. Aderet is extolling the army as a character-building experience for young men, and uses as an instance an episode during the 1956 war with Egypt when an officer ordered a group of soldiers simply to kill "any Egyptian prisoners of war . . . who were in our hands." A number of volunteers then step forward and the prisoners are duly shot, although one of the volunteers avers that "he closed his eyes when he shot." At this point Aderet says: "There is no doubt that this test can bring a confusion to every man of conscience and of experience of life, and even more so to young boys who stand at the beginning of their lives. The bad thing which happened is not the confusions in which those young men were during the time of the deed, but in the internal undermining which took place in them afterwards. " To this edifying interpretation, Buber — moral philosopher, humane thinker, former bionationalist — can say only: "This is a great and true story, you should write it down." Not one word about the story's horror, or of the situation making it possible. But just as no Jew in the last hundred years has been untouched by Zionism, so too no Palestinian has been unmarked by it. Yet it must not be forgotten that Palestinians were not simply a function of Zionism. Their life, culture, and politics have their own dynamic and ultimately their own authenticity.

NOTES

1. I. F. Stone, "Confessions of a Jewish Dissident," in *Underground to Palestine, and Reflections Thirty Years Later* (New York: Pantheon Books, 1978).

2. See Sabri Jiryis, *The Arabs in Israel* (New York: Monthly Review Press, 1976); a powerful case is made also by *The Non-Jew in the Jewish State: A Collection of Documents*, ed. Israel Shahak (privately printed by Shahak, 2 Bartenura Street, Jerusalem), 1975.

3. See *Imperialism: The Documentary History of Western Civilization*, ed. Philip D. Curtin (New York: Walker, 1971), which contains a good selection from the imperialist literature of the last 200 years. I survey the intellectual and cultural backgrounds of the period in *Orientalism*, chapters 2 and 3.

4. Desmond Stewart, *Theodor Herzl* (Garden City, N.Y.: Doubleday, 1974), p. 192.

5. Antonio Gramsci, *The Prison Notebooks: Selections*, ed. and trans. Quintin Hoare and Geoffrey Nowell Smith (New York: International, 1971) p. 324. The full text is to be found in Antonio Gramsci, *Quaderni del Carcere*, ed. Valentino Gerratana (Turin: Einaudi Editore, 1975), vol. 2, p. 1363.

6. See Hannah Arendt, *The Origins of Totalitarianism* (New York: Harcourt Brace Jovanovich, 1973), p. 129.

7. Harry Bracken, "Essence, Accident and Race," *Hermathena*, 116 (Winter 1973), pp. 81–96.

8. See Curtin, *Imperialism*, pp. 93–105, which contains an important extract from Knox's book.

9. George Nathaniel Curzon, *Subjects of the Day: Being a Selection of Speeches and Writings* (London: Allen & Unwin, 1915), pp. 155–56.

10. Joseph Conrad, *Heart of Darkness* in *Youth and Two Other Stories* (Garden City, N.Y.: Doubleday, Page, 1925), p. 52.

11. Ibid., pp. 50–51.

12. Agnes Murphy, *The Ideology of French Imperialism, 1817–1881* (Washington: Catholic University of America Press, 1948), pp. 110, 136, 189.

13. Amos Oz, a leading Israeli novelist (also considered a "dove"), puts it nicely: "For as long as I live, I shall be thrilled by all those who came to the Promised Land to turn it either into a pastoral paradise or egalitarian Tolstoyan communes, or into a well-educated, middle-class Central European enclave, a replica of Austria and Bavaria. Or those who wanted to raise a Marxist paradise, who built kibbutzim on biblical sites and secretly yearned for Stalin to come one day to admit that 'Bloody Jews, you have done it better than we did.' " *Time*, May 15, 1978, p. 61.

14. See Neville J. Mandel, *The Arabs and Zionism before World War I* (Berkeley: University of California Press, 1976), and Yehoshua Porath, *The Emergence of the Palestinian-Arab National Movement*, Vol. I, *1918–1929* (London: Frank Cass, 1974).

15. See the forthright historical account in Amos Elon, *The Israelis: Founders and Sons* (1971; reprinted New York: Bantam Books, 1972), pp. 218–24.

16. Maxime Rodinson, *Israel: A Colonial-Settler State?* trans. David Thorstad (New York: Monad Press of the Anchor Foundation, 1973), p. 39.

17. Ibid., p. 38.

18. Quoted in David Waines, "The Failure of the Nationalist Resistance," in *The Transformation of Palestine*, ed. Ibrahim Abu-Lughod (Evanston, Ill.: Northwestern University Press, 1971), p. 220.

19. Ibid., p. 213.

20. Chaim Weizmann, *Trial and Error: The Autobiography of Chaim Weizmann* (New York: Harper & Row, 1959), p. 371.

21. Ibid., p. 125.

22. Ibid., pp. 128–29, 253.

23. Ibid., p. 128.

24. Yehoshafat Harkabi, *Arab Attitudes to Israel* (Jerusalem: Keter Press, 1972). Harkabi was chief of military intelligence until he was dismissed in 1959 by Ben-Gurion. He later became a professor at the Hebrew University and an expert Arabist, indeed the principal propagandist in Israel against everything Arab and/or especially Palestinian. See, for example, his virulently anti-Palestinian book (distributed gratis in this country by the Israeli embassy) *Palestinians and Israel* (Jerusalem: Keter Press, 1974). Surprisingly, General Harkabi has recently become a "dove" and a supporter of the Peace Now movement.

25. Reproduced in *Haolam Hazeh*, May 15, 1974. *Haolam Hazeh*'s editor, Uri Avnery, has written an interesting, somewhat demagogic book, worth looking at for the light it sheds on Israeli politics: *Israel without Zionism: A Plea for Peace in the Middle East* (New York: Macmillan, 1968). It contains vitriolic attacks on people like Moshe Dayan, whom Avnery describes essentially as "an Arab-fighter" (cf. Indian-fighters in the American West).

26. Weizmann, *Trial and Error*, p. 130.

27. Ibid., p. 188.

28. Ibid., pp. 215–16.

29. Ibid., p. 130.

30. C. L. Temple, *The Native Races and Their Rulers* (1918; reprinted London: Frank Cass, 1968), p. 41.

31. *Trial and Error*, pp. 156–57.

32. On the army as a matrix for organizing society, see Michel Foucault, "*Questions à Michel Foucault sur la géographie*," *Hérodote*, 1, 1 (first trimester 1976), p. 85. See also Yves Lacoste, *La Géographie, ça sert, d'abord, à faire le guerre* (Paris: Maspero, 1976).

33. Details taken from Walter Lehn, "The Jewish National Fund," *Journal of Palestine Studies*, 4 (Summer 1974), pp. 74–96.

34. As an example, consider the fate of Umm al-Fahm, a large Arab village given to Israel by King Abdallah of Jordan in 1949 according to the Rhodes agreement. Before 1948 the village owned 140,000 dunams, with a population of 5,000. In 1978 there were about 20,000 Arab inhabitants of Umm al-Fahm, but the village's land had been reduced to 15,000 dunams, almost all of it rocky and poor for cultivation. All the best land was confiscated by various "legal" decrees, including the 1953 Law of Land, Insurance and Compensation. The greatest irony perhaps is that two socialist kibbutzim—Megiddo and Givat Oz—were built on the confiscated Arab land. What was left was turned over to a moshav, or cooperative agricultural settlement.

35. Joseph Weitz, *My Diary and Letters to the Children* (Tel Aviv: Massada, 1965), vol. 2, pp. 181–82.

36. Jon and David Kimche, *A Clash of Destinies: The Arab-Jewish War and the Founding of the State of Israel* (New York: Praeger, 1960), p. 92. See also the two important articles by Walid Khalidi, "The Fall of Haifa," *Middle East Forum*, 35, 10 (December 1959), pp. 22–32; and "Plan Dalet: The Zionist Blueprint for the Conquest of Palestine," *Middle East Forum*, 37, 9 (November 1961), pp. 22–28.

37. The most thorough study ever made of the Palestinian exodus, after a combing of every Arab newspaper and broadcast of the period, revealed absolutely no evidence of "orders to leave," or of anything except urgings to Palestinians to remain in their country. Unfortunately, the terror was too great for a mostly unarmed population. See Erskine Childers, "The Wordless Wish: From Citizens to Refugees," in *The Transformation of Palestine*, ed. Ibrahim Abu-Lughod (Evanston, Ill.: Northwestern University Press, 1971), pp. 165–202. Childers, an Irishman, was a free-lance journalist when he conducted his research; his findings are devastating to the Zionist case.

38. See Avnery, *Israel without Zionism*.

39. Weitz, *My Diary*, vol 3, p. 293.

40. Ibid., p. 302.

41. Tawfiq Zayyad, "Fate of the Arabs in Israel," *Journal of Palestine Studies*, 6 (Autumn 1976), pp. 98–99.

42. Quoted in Jiryis, *The Arabs in Israel*, p. 70.

43. See Saul Bellow, *To Jerusalem and Back* (New York: Viking, 1976), pp. 152–61 and passim.

44. John Cooley, "Settlement Drive Lies Behind Latest Israeli 'No,' " *Christian Science Monitor*, July 25, 1978, makes it clear that Israel plans officially to populate the West Bank with a Jewish majority (1.25 million) by the year 2000, and that Yamit (in the Rafah salient—occupied Sinai) is being planned as a major Israeli city, under construction now. According to Arye Duzin, Chairman of the Jewish Agency, Yamit "must always remain under Jewish sovereignty" as forecast by the Zionist Executive in 1903. Many of the settlements are to be filled with South African Jews (hence Israel's close military—indeed nuclear—cooperation with South Africa, and its particularly cordial relations with Prime Minister John Vorster, a convicted Nazi), Americans, and of course Russians.

45. Jiryis, *Arabs in Israel*, p. 70.

46. The full text of the Koenig Report was printed in an English translation in *SWASIA*, 3, 41 (October 15, 1976).

47. Take as an example the raid on Maalot by Palestinians in May 1974. This event has now become synonymous with Palestinian terrorism, yet no U.S. newspaper took note of the fact that for two consecutive weeks before the incident, Israeli artillery and air power were used to bombard southern Lebanon mercilessly. Well over 200 civilians were killed by napalm and at least 10,000 were made homeless. Still, only Maalot is recalled.

CHAPTER 15

Racism and the Innocence of Law

Peter Fitzpatrick

> *. . . with us there is nothing more consistent than a racist humanism since the European has only been able to become a man through creating slaves and monsters.*[1]

Introduction

In liberal views of the world, law is manifestly incompatible with racism. Where racist practice infects law that can only be something aberrant and remediable. Exploring the British situation as a case, I will argue that on the contrary racism is compatible with and even intregral to law. I try to show that the very foundational principles of law as liberal legality import racism into law, those principles of equality and universality that stand in their terms opposed to racism. The aim is not to dismiss law, nor to expose liberal legality as a sham. But nor is it to retrieve law and add to the list of obviously desirable variants on how to combat racism through law, such as recent "left strategies."[2] The point is, rather, to make such "acts, gestures, discourses which . . . had seemed to go without saying become problematic, difficult, dangerous."[3] A note on the term "racism": I will use it in an extended way to cover both belief and practice.

Thanks to Fiona Kinsman, Lydia Pepple, Guy Smith, and Industrial Tribunals for a lot of help with the cases. Thanks to Dave Reason for much else.

Liberal Capitalism and the Specificity of Racism

Initially, I will set the argument in contrary Marxist views of racism. One, usually attributed to Marx, sees a fundamental incompatibility between racism and capitalism of a developed, liberal variety. With its integral assertions of equality and universalist morality, such a capitalism stands opposed to racist divisions and this for good economic reasons.[4] Far from seeing such capitalism and racism as opposed, the alternative Marxist tradition finds them compatible, even symbiotic. In economic terms racism operates to provide cheap labor and to constitute a sector of "the reserve army of labor." Politically, racism divides the working class and counters the transformative potential of that class. There are numerous dimensions to this. In the annals of war and imperialism, race has often served to unite a "white" working class and bourgeoisie. Racial division has been a powerful strategic tool of employers both in undermining white workers and in gaining their support.

These abrupt accounts may seem overly functionalist. But they do have large historical warrants. So much is that so that in the dispute between them one cannot be accepted as right and the other dismissed as wrong. What they support, rather, is a picture of conflicting forces within capitalism. And what this disagreement indicates is the inability of Marxism to provide a surpassing theoretical elaboration that encompasses racism. This need not provoke a rejection of Marxism, nor should it occasion surprise if we see Marxism as confronting a specific history of liberal capitalism. That confrontation does have things to say about racism. But it could also be the case that engaging with a specific history of racism can say things about liberal capitalism. In those rare moments when critical social theory has considered racism, it has tended to be taken on as an extra, as a discrete actor in a scenario devised without it in mind. Or that has been so until recently. There are now emergent academic visions not just of the historical specificity of race but also of its current centrality and significance.[5] It is, however, difficult to establish the significance of racism in a society whose self-presentation denies that significance. Monuments to liberalism can hardly acknowledge foundations of racism. It follows that racism in its legitimate forms will not be explicit. It will be found in forms of, for example, crime and social degeneration, community and culture, nation and society. That is, the form both substitutes for explicit racism and provides a means of asserting that what is involved is not racism but something different.

The liberal denial of racism prompts certain strategies in establishing its significance. One could be seen as a root-and-branch strategy, a strategy that seeks constitutive compatibilities between liberalism and racism. This large challenge has begun to be taken up in philosophical and historical work.[6] As I interpret it, this work points to the origins of racism in the liberal Enlightenment project, which, with its claims to universality, comprehensiveness, and consistency, sets a fateful dimension. It can only relate to those excluded from the project through slavery or semislavery by saying that they are qualitatively different. This imperative, this terrifying consistency puts the enslaved and the colonized beyond the liberal equation of universal freedom and equality by rendering them in racist terms as qualitatively different. This identity in essential difference, particularly in the figure of the feckless African, becomes a counter in the making of the disciplined, "liberal" individual in the West. Racism was, in short, basic to the creation of liberalism and the identity of the European.

Another strategy for extracting racism's significance entails a short-cut through liberalism. This could be called a strategy of telling instances. By this I mean instances, often seemingly insignificant or evanescent, that convincingly anticipate or provoke demotic responses. Jokes and politicians provide an abundance of these. Take the statement on January 30, 1978, of Thatcher as leader of the parliamentary opposition, a statement that immensely boosted both the popularity of the Conservative party and the salience of "immigration" as an electoral issue. She said that

> people are really rather afraid that this country might be swamped by people with a different culture. And, you know, the British character has done so much for democracy, for law, and done so much throughout the world, that if there is a fear that it might be swamped, people are going to react and be rather hostile to those coming in.[7]

As Martin Barker has so skillfully shown, all the elements of racism are contained in this and numerous other recent political evocations of culture, community, and the miasma of unexpired imperial dreams.[8] To take one other instance, Crossman's diaries as a cabinet minister provide a candid account of anticipating a demotic response. The Labour government in the 1960s changed its policy and practice on immigration to an "illiberal" one so as to "out-trump the Tories," otherwise "we would have been faced with certain electoral defeat in the West Midlands and the South East."[9]

So far, there are two broad lines to the argument. One focuses on liberal capitalism and traces a basic conflict within it in that liberal capitalism opposes yet is maintained by racism. The other line of argument focuses on racism. It asserts the specificity and the significance of racism. That dimension intersects with the history of liberal capitalism indicating integral connections between racism and liberalism. I will now add law to the mixture.

Law as Racism

Liberal cosmology provides a particular protection of law's innocence. Law is radically separate from "material life" and can also act on and order that life: with liberal society "[p]articular self-interest must be constrained by universalistic legal and motivational structures; in this sense, the formal rationality of civil society must dominate the substantive rationality of material life."[10] In line with assertions of the centrality and significance of racism, we may ask what point is to be given to the experience of those for whom law is not separate from, much less able to order or correct that part of material life called racism. Lord Scarman could provide a celebrated confirmation that " '[i]nstitutional racism' does not exist in Britain" in a report that was an instance of it.[11] In this he was implicitly confronting and dismissing a phrase that black people used to encapsulate their experience of law and of state action.[12] That experience is not simply a contained "different voice" that stands along with, if opposed to, liberal self-presentation. It can also be given point in founding a critical engagement with that self-presentation. An immediate problem is the powerful closure erected around liberal legality. Being radically separate from and ordering of material life, law cannot be brought into definitively complicitous comparisons with that life. Sympathetic connections between law and racism can be presented as exceptional and remediable, with the exceptional serving to contrast and confirm the great virtue of the norm.[13] Indeed, the very terms of that separation — terms of universalistic ordering, terms operatively realized in liberal legality — are ostentatiously opposed to racism. Against accusations of racism, then, law's innocence is unassailable.

If we "respect" the terms of separation, that is, if we are not simply to reduce them to something else such as economic relations or treat them merely as a mask for something else, then the only way of integrally linking law with racism is to attack the foundation and show that those very terms of separation are racist. Law could then be seen as contradictory, as integrally opposed to and supportive of racism. I will argue that, metaphorically speaking, law positively acquires identity by taking elements of racism into itself and shaping them in its own terms. Yet law also takes identity from its opposition to and separation from racism. But this very opposition is not innocent, for it operates by containing and constraining law. Law, as a result, and contrary to the principle of universality, is unable assuredly to counter racism. That is not just to say, along with assertions of critical legal scholars about the family and workplace, that by not entering areas where racism or sexism is prevalent law implicitly confers powers on those who are dominant within them.[14] Such a line of argument leaves law competent to intervene and counter that power and, of course, liberal legality is only a claim about competence, about being able to cover things, not about actual coverage. The point here is that racism marks constitutive boundaries of law, persistent limits on its competence and scope. Being so limited, law proves to be compatible with racism. I will argue, further, that it is the combination of this compatibility with law's claims to universalist competence that creates and heightens racism.

I will try to support that ambitious agenda in a way that may seem disappointingly and inaptly modest. That is, I will explore particular aspects of the operation of the Race Relations Act 1976. Although there may be a provocative persuasiveness in establishing racism in legislation aimed at countering it, there does remain the small problem of how the general assertions about law and racism that I have just indicated can be established in such a particular way. But to borrow from Foucault's "rule of double conditioning," a localized exercise of power with its "precise and tenuous relations" is effective only as a distinct but related part of a "general strategy" of power. The general strategy is, in turn, distinct but dependent for its effectiveness on the localized exercise of power.[15] The study of the localized is, in this light, necessary. It will also implicate the general. Specifically, an exploration of certain "precise and tenuous relations" involved in the Race Relations Act reveals persistent limits beyond which law will not proceed, limits erected in an overlapping of confining categories and discretions, and in the constitution of a domain of the normal. When we seek to move beyond these limits, we find on their borders "general strategies" drawing on racism, strategies that involve the power of capital and nation. This general dimension makes intelligible what would otherwise be mysterious in the limiting of localized instances. The approach from a localized instance cannot, of course, present some comprehensive, much less structured picture of the general. But I am arguing that effective general elements are invoked by it.

The Bounds of Law in the Race Relations Act

The British Race Relations Act 1976 enabled people to take civil action in respect of discrimination in certain areas of life on "racial grounds."[16] Persons discriminate if on racial grounds they treat someone less favorably than they treat or would treat others. There is also indirect discrimination, which is the imposition of requirements or conditions having a discriminatory effect in that they disproportionately disadvantage racial groups, are to the detriment of the person alleging discrimination, and cannot be otherwise justified. For example, educational requirements for a job that are in excess of what can be justified for the work to be done could indirectly discriminate against racial groups who are educationally "disadvantaged."

Almost all cases brought under the legislation concern employment. Employment cases are taken to an administrative court called an industrial tribunal. Awards that may be made in employment cases comprise damages for material loss and for injury to feelings, a declaration of the rights of the complainant and a recommendation that the employer take remedial action.

Damages cannot be awarded in cases of indirect discrimination while there is no intent to discriminate. The Act also constitutes and empowers a governmental Commission for Racial Equality, which is "to work towards the elimination of discrimination." Greatest emphasis is given to its broad power to investigate discriminatory practices, to issue nondiscrimination notices and take court proceedings to have these enforced.

I will explore employment cases under the legislation, focusing on aspects of universalistic legal ordering. These are the form of universal individual right and the mode of adjudication, adjudication being the subjection of competing claims to universally applicable, impartially applied standards. I do not make the common, but infinitely contestable, assertion found in critical legal studies that with legislation like this the form of right constitutes racial (or gender) oppression in terms of the action of individuals and thereby denies its wider "social" or "structural" determinants.[17] But this branch of critical legal studies is a source of assertions suggesting boundaries imported by the form of right, boundaries we can seek in the legislation and in the legal processes it generates. This will involve the mundane and the obvious — quotidian rules of evidence and questions about the burden of proof, for example. But, as I try to show, a multitude of oppressions are effected by the mundane and the obvious.

Right is attached to the individual legal actor who has to assert this right against the person allegedly in breach of a correlative duty. That breach is a matter of individual wrongdoing. It is something aberrant, a particular episode that disturbs the normal course. It calls for the occasional and discontinuous intervention of legal remedies. These remedies, in turn, need only reassert the normal course, need only focus on the act of the wrongdoer and correct or compensate for it. The form of right deals with deviation, and racism in liberal societies has to be a deviation. This correspondence provides a temptation to which the Race Relations Act succumbs in the basic remedy against "discrimination." In legal and liberal terms discrimination is a matter of intentional wrongdoing inflicted by one individual on another. The only significant remedy provided in the legislation is damages seen as redress, as affirming the norm. The complainant, the person wronged, has the onus of establishing that the norm has been disturbed. This "burden of proof" is in practice a heavy one. As I will show later, industrial tribunals reflect the ethos of law and liberalism and take racial discrimination to be exceptional indeed.[18] There is also the banal paradox that making discrimination legally culpable has rendered it more elusive and intractable to remedial action. Unless the person supposedly discriminating is unaware or intemperate enough to provide it, it is difficult to get direct evidence of discrimination. The evidence, that is, will usually be circumstantial. Such evidence is never conclusive. It is clear from the cases that circumstantial evidence is accepted as proving discrimination, as discharging the burden of proof, only very exceptionally. Such constant rejections of complainants are facilitated by narrowing the type of knowledge that can be used in support of a claim. This narrowing is in terms of the individualistic nature of the relation and dispute between the parties. There is a concretizing here of the form of right in the adversarial process. The adversaries, for example, are to be left on their own. The tribunal will only rarely help a litigant, and it often explicitly refuses to do so. Evidence going beyond these individualistic dimensions will be rejected or given little weight. Instances of such evidence include social survey evidence of racial disadvantage in employment generally or statistical information about the "racial" composition of the employer's work force. In the same vein, the remedy of recommending that the employer take remedial action cannot extend beyond what is necessary to redress the adverse effect on the complainant. But the most potent dimension of individuality in the legal process here is that of intention. The unsurpassed aptness of a rejected applicant is not evidence of racial discrimination because she or he may have been rejected on other grounds. And such grounds, as tribunals repeatedly recognize, can include the most vague and the most irrational. Constantly, tribunals uphold employers' purported rejection of applicants in such terms as demeanor, personality, ability to fit in, and even in terms of favoritism on the part of the employer. Obviously racially based decisions can be thus justified or obscured with ease. Tribunals also engage here in a revealing slippage, one that purports to follow on from intentionality but goes beyond legal justification in such terms. For what they assert is that such decisions are the prerogative of the employer, that they have to accept the employer's assessment and even the terms in which it is made. As a matter of course the impermeability of the employer's power is affirmed.

It is convenient now to be fair and credit the legislation with attempts to transcend the limits imported by the form of right and the related idea of discrimination. But these attempts, I now argue, end up confirming and reinforcing the original limits. The Commission for Racial Equality is given ostensibly broad powers to investigate discrimination and to issue a nondiscrimination notice. Any threat that this power may be effective is avoided by its reduction in the lineaments of the form of right. Thus, a nondiscrimination notice can only relate to particular acts. The Commission's power to issue a subpoena for information is restricted to investigations where the Commission suspects a named person of discriminatory acts, and there has already to be material supporting "a reasonable suspicion."[19] That position is reached with the aid of judicial interpretation, an interpretation that reflects a splenetic attitude to conferring judicial-type power on an administrative body thereby denying, in the view of the judges, adequate protection for the individual: "You might think that we are back in the days of the Inquisition. . . . You might think that we were back in the days of the General Warrants," thought Lord Denning. He appropriated control of this power for the judges, where it has remained. The court was "free to balance the public interests involved," those between the "immense powers" given to the Commission "to compel the disclosure of confidential information" and "the importance to the public services and industrial concerns" of preserving that confidentiality.[20] Less spectacularly, the Act in s.38(3)(a) confers a similar discretion by obliquely applying rules of evidence relating to discovery. A similar study can be told about discovery in its more general application in cases before tribunals. Discovery does have a particular significance in such cases, for it is "designed to offset the probative disadvantage which the complainant would otherwise suffer" because evidence of discrimination will usually be in the hands of the employer.[21] Discovery tends to be successful when the information is narrowly focused on the applicant or the alleged act of discrimination. But "confidentiality" almost invariably excludes discovery of more extensive information held by the employer such as details of the competitors for a job or for promotion. Inevitably, it is for the tribunal to exercise a discretion here in terms of what is "necessary for dispensing fairly of the proceedings."[22] In short, where the Act provides modes compensating for the limits entailed in the form of right, the limits are extended to confine these modes. Should this not suffice to protect the portals of capital, then adjudicators are to exercise their discretion, in both senses of the word.

The most revealing instance of this strategy is provided by indirect discrimination. Such discrimination is, in part, constituted in categories of the form of right. Action is brought by the individual who must have sustained harm. But there is no purposive wrongdoing involved. The causal element springs from the disproportionate effect the employer's "requirement or condition" has on a racial group. Tenaciously, the form of right shapes the outcome because damages cannot be awarded while the employer did not intend to discriminate. But the core of indirect discrimination, the salience of the effect on a racial group, goes beyond the realm of individual right. Here, legal inquiry and legal ordering cannot be confined to some episodic wrongdoing. They must now penetrate the realm of the employer, examining and assessing potentially any "requirement or condition" relating to employment. But the potency of indirect discrimination was soon countered in judicial applications of the exemption from indirect discrimination of a requirement or condition shown to be justifiable. This was rendered in terms of, variously, what was reasonable or commonsensical, or what was acceptable to right-thinking people and such, or it was simply a question of fact unique to each case. Judicial creativity enters again with an expedient balancing, the desirability of eliminating discrimination being balanced against the demands of the employer's enterprise. In this, judges and tribunals again explicitly recognize that employers are to be left with their autonomy; they ought to be able to decide what is best for business.

In looking at the two types of universalistic ordering, I have so far concentrated on the form of right and have considered the mode of adjudication only from that perspective. Adjudication sustained the form of right as a confining category and restrained extensions beyond it by the apt use of discretion and the recognition of the employer's autonomy. I will now focus more exclusively on the process of adjudication. We can start with the banality that law cannot be mechanically applied. Adjudication requires a productive impetus, a positive going-out to recognize and shape claims. We can continue with another banality: that, as it is usually put, the values of adjudicators influence their decisions. I will try to establish this not in the sense of values intruding on otherwise pristine standards and processes of adjudication, but in the sense of values constituting these standards and processes. Such standards and processes, in turn, form a particular but comprehensive perspective that quite simply includes the interests of some and excludes the interests of others. This is not a matter of remediable bias or some such. It is a matter of a whole sensibility. Adjudicators cannot be responsive to interests they cannot comprehend. Nor can they respond through standards and processes that obscure and deny these interests rather than reveal them. The productive impetus needed to recognize claims in adjudication does not operate to recognize claims founded in such interests. Where the claims are insistent and potentially disruptive, they are explained away as something else, something understood within the particular perspective, understood in the domain of the normal. I will now expand and illustrate that argument.

Adjudicative standards and processes are not pure creations. They are responsive to and draw on wider rationalities operating beyond adjudication and law. With industrial tribunals, there is an explicit mode of incorporating such wider rationalities, since, in addition to a legally qualified chairperson, tribunals are composed of two "wing" members drawn respectively from employers' and trade union organizations. Such people are likely to be more responsive to "good industrial relations" than to adopt a radical view toward the notorious racism of employers and trade unions.[23] They are not likely to transcend the traditional hostility of employers and unions to anti-discrimination legislation.[24] The failure, for example, of "industry machinery" to discern discrimination under the previous Race Relations Act was almost complete.[25] The point can be made dramatically by looking at cases where a wing member has some specialist background in "race relations." Commenting on "the experience of adjudication in the first eighteen months of the Act," Lustgarten notes that "in *every* case in which there was a split tribunal decision against the complainant, the non-specialist wingmen joined the chairman to make the majority."[26] That experience, with but few exceptions, has continued since. We are, it would seem, dealing here with two worlds. The inability of industrial tribunals to respond to one of them was starkly evident even before the Race Relations Act of 1976 in cases of unfair

dismissal brought under employment protection legislation. Despite numerous such cases involving a racial element, "[i]n not one case . . . [had] there
been an express finding that dismissal was for racial reasons."[27] Nor does the
legally qualified chairperson inhibit the abject responsiveness of wing members to prevailing rationalities. The chairperson is more likely than these
members to find against the complainant. But disagreement among tribunal
members is quite exceptional. Uniformity is promoted in the chairperson's
tending to be a dominating influence. This dominance is fostered in the technical nature of the process. Despite original aspirations to informality and accessibility, industrial tribunals have become increasingly legalistic. Hence,
although they are never great, the chances of success are very slim without
expert assistance.[28] Often tribunals assert that they are not bound by technical rules of evidence, such as the rule against admitting hearsay evidence, but
almost as often this is merely a prelude to applying such rules. More generally, the crudities of such rules, of the adversarial process, of the standard
tricks of advocacy designed to block the truth, all serve to exclude evidence
of an often subtle and intractable racial oppression.[29] This, in sum, is a circumscribed ritual of reassertion of a world in which such oppression is
nonexistent or rare.

What if evidence of racial discrimination survives these exclusions? Exceptionally a complainant will succeed as a result. Much more usually, the
evidence is made to conform to the domain of the normal in two ways. In
one, apparent evidence of the employer's discrimination is understood by the
tribunal as something else. So, a particular hostility to the applicant is understood as a communications problem, as bad management practice, or as the
result of pressure or health problems. Alternatively, the domain of the normal reduces evidence of the employer's discrimination to a less challenging
dimension. So, the complainant is, in terms of the common *canard*, paranoid
or oversensitive or the acts complained of are "trivial."[30] But this is the
"triviality of the sand," to borrow Auden's phrase. What is happening is that
the massive reality of oppression is being rejected or reduced to the insignificant, whereas the employer's reality is being accepted and elevated to the
determinant. It is not so much a matter that the employer's account is believed whereas the complainant's is not. The grinding normality is that the
employer's account serves to call forth and to confirm what is already there,
what is already known.

Of course, industrial tribunals are not the sole occupants of the field of adjudication. But they do have something close to sole occupancy of a crucial
part of it. Factual questions and questions of the weight of evidence will, as
a matter of law, rarely be disturbed on appeal. Appellate courts will have a
decisive influence on tribunals in determining questions of law and thereby
providing precedents which tribunals have to follow. There is also the
vaguer question of appellate "values" influencing tribunals. On both these

counts the constant refrain has been one of restriction, reinforcing the perspective generated within tribunals. In its interpretation, race relations legislation has not been construed expansively under, say, the "mischief rule" as befits the remedying of an acknowledged social evil. Rather, appeal courts see the Race Relations Act as having to be interpreted strictly, especially as they restrict "the liberty which the citizen has previously enjoyed at common law" to discriminate.[31] Such judicial invocation of positive legal liberties also characterizes, as we have seen, the balancing of confidentiality and the employer's autonomy against the desirability of eliminating discrimination. This line of argument may accord well with the demonstration by critical legal scholars (and others) that "the legal process at large and its discrete doctrinal components . . . are fundamentally indeterminant and manipulable," and that adjudication draws on no ultimate and principled resolution but is, rather, a "political" process.[32] The argument here is different, however. We have seen that in the process of adjudication some elements when weighed in the balance have more or less persistently been found wanting. What happens is that these seeming choices are not simply made, but themselves make the community of law. With this community, apparently disjoint or indeterminant elements do configure in heirarchies that, if not invariant, are at least usual. Judges relate to the overall ordering ethos of community in such ultimate and revealing terms as what is "sensible" and "reasonable," what conforms to "the fitness of things," and to "common sense."[33] These are not masks for an unbounded, "political" discretion. They are, rather, borders beyond which the recognition of constraint cannot proceed in terms of the community's particular traditions and particular rationalities.

Law, Race, and the Liberal World

This community of law, like any community, is not generated purely internally. Through industrial tribunals, as we have seen, the community of law incorporates and integrally relies on a particular yet operatively comprehensive perspective. This perspective joins with the confining categories and obscuring discretions of the form of right and of the legal process to set law's bounds. These bounds restrict law but in so doing they maintain its integrity in its relation to the power of employers.[34] Law is, however, constituted not just in opposition to other types of power but also in the positive assimilation of wider, sustaining identities. There are identities predisposed toward racism with which law is intimately involved. One is the modern figure of society as a contained unit with a "typical" membership.[35] The other is the distinct but not greatly dissimilar figure of the nation: liberal "legality . . . celebrates and elevates the law to an exalted status as the expression of unity in the nation."[36] Neither these identities nor law take on a racist dimension without its specific historical addition. Such an addition is, of course, frequent and Britain is conspicuously not an exception. In line with my earlier argument, the addition of racism effects the unity of society and nation and serves to constitute the identity of its members.

I will now explore law's connections with the particularity of society and nation and relate these connections to law's universalistic pretensions. The argument will develop through instances. One is the very genius of the common law with its combination of universalistic "reason" with a "strange and . . . incoherent" (English) particularism.[37] In Dicey's seminal account of constitutional law, the combination becomes a prerogative of the "English." The resulting "rule of law" is not English in the sense that it should be confined to England. It is just that in less happy climes, such as Belgium, its existence is much more attenuated.[38] Adjusting Dicey's paean to our concern with a more mundane reality of legal procedure, Lord Denning recently could find a betrayal of "England" and Empire in a small challenge posed by the European Communities (Amendment) Bill to the "English adversary system."[39] To put the argument before instances descend any further, such ethnocentric elevations of law are an inevitable reconciliation of law's palpable national connections with its transcendent universalist claims.[40] In the result, law is captured as an expression of national superiority. When that superiority incorporates racism, law is likewise captured as an expression of it.

It is hardly surprising, then, that the resort to law as a symbol of race and nation should be so facile, so common, and so effective.[41] Thus, to return to the strategem of the telling instance and to Thatcher's contribution, she precisely echoes the imperialist claim to law as a gift we gave them, gave those "people with a different culture," people who did not have law, who did not give it to the world and who in remaining essentially alien have failed to assimilate the gift adequately. Almost in passing, the not-so-distinctive contributions of the higher judiciary to this "new racism" have also at times assumed telling dimensions.[42] But for law the most telling has probably been the immense popular response to Powell's speech in 1968, in which racial division in Britain prompted some characteristic visions: "[L]ike the Roman, I seem to see 'the River Tiber foaming with much flood.' " His prop and target were provided by the then Race Relations Bill, an antidiscrimination measure even more limited and more anemic than the current legislation. Yet Powell presented it with great effect as "a one-way privilege," as "legal weapons" that "the stranger" can now use "to overawe and dominate the rest."[43] Gilroy has acutely located a potency of Powell's appeal here in the "debasement" and "perversion" of what was pure law and English law. This "ultimate symbol of national culture" is traduced through "blacks being afforded limited legal protection."[44]

Indeed, both the critics and the supporters of race relations legislation agree that its purpose is to bring black people "discriminated" against into society.[45] But, as the aptly named Whitelaw as Home Secretary put it: for equal rights, responsibilities, and opportunities to be extended to such people, they should "demonstrate their commitment to our society" and abandon cultural and linguistic isolation.[46] The Race Relations Acts are seen not just as a powerful means for black people to achieve this, but also as a privilege given to them and as an advantage over white people. This is not just Powell's perception but a popular one.[47] It is also, incidentally, one that is wrong in that the legislation protects people of any race and cases brought by white people are not infrequent. But the error is much more extensive than that. The race relations legislation has had little reforming effect.[48] The failure of the oppressed successfully to use such powerful, privileging legal means thus confirms their essential inadequacy. Reform, in the guise of a succession of Race Relations Acts, like so much reform becomes part of the problematic, creating and sustaining that which it purports to counter.

Law, in short, is tied to a particular community that excludes those whom law would include through race relations legislation. In the liberal worldview, as we saw, law erects a universal inclusiveness, transcending and ordering material life. It is true that law as legal rules only directs what should happen and so cannot be held specifically accountable. But the liberal worldview does entail a general and a strong claim for law's competence. If the powerful and persistent ministrations of law do not bring certain racial identities into society that must be because the identities are essentially different and naturally incapable. This is but a continuation of that legacy of the Enlightenment in which those constantly beyond the liberal equation have to be qualitatively different from those within it.

Conclusion

I started questioning the manifest opposition between liberal legality and racism by drawing on a conflict in Marxist accounts of racism. This conflict indicated that racism was incompatible yet symbiotic with liberal capitalism in Britain. This same conflict pointed toward the specificity and the enormous significance of racism. But no matter what the significance of racism, law seemed to escape any complicitous connections with it. This was because, in the liberal worldview, law was a form of universalistic ordering that transcended material life. Yet if the universalistic terms of that transcendence could, paradoxically, be held racist, then law could still be rendered accountable. To begin establishing that, I took a seemingly perverse course of looking at instances of universalistic legal ordering that were not only minutely localized but also explicitly opposed to "racial discrimination." These instances were the operation of the form of right and of the mode of adjudication in employment cases under the Race Relations Act of 1976.

A detailed study of such instances showed that there were certain persistent limits, certain bounds beyond which law did not proceed in countering racism. What, in an immediate sense, stood on the other side of those bounds and checked law's advance was the power and autonomy of employers. Law thus marked out areas in which the racism of employers could operate. But the relation of law to racism was seen to be more intimate. Between law and the employer, mediating and constituting the necessary distance separating them, was a comprehensive yet particular perspective generated in adjudication that "naturally" and racially set law's limits and, in the same moment, denied effect to the contrary experience of black people. This perspective inhabited the community of law, which, in turn, evoked and integrally relied on a wider, racially conceived society and nation. For these entities, law was an operative figure of great social impact. In this, law was seen to be readily involved in extensive racist strategies. Its contributions to racism were also more distinctive, however. Law's claims to universalistic ordering contrasted with its confinement in terms of specific national community. The disjunction, as we saw, is resolved by making that community and its law the incarnation of a rational universal ordering. Those of a "different culture" are not, however, merely excluded from superior reason. When, as in the Race Relations Act, its beneficent and potent modes are extended to them in terms of universalistic ordering but then withdrawn in implicit terms of community, a gap opens that is filled by the attribution to them of an insuperable inadequacy.

NOTES

1. J. P. Sartre, "Preface," to F. Fanon, *The Wretched of the Earth* (New York: Grove Press, 1967), p. 22.

2. See G. Ben-Tovim et al., "Race, Left Strategies and the State," *Politics and Power*, 3 (1981), p. 153.

3. M. Foucault, "Questions of Method: An Interview with Michel Foucault" *I. & C.*, 8 (1981), p. 3, p. 12.

4. See A. Szymanski, "Race, Sex and the U.S. Working Class," *Social Problems*, 21 (1973–74), p. 706, for an account and strange application of these Marxist views on race.

5. See, for example, Centre for Contemporary Cultural Studies, *The Empire Strikes Back: Race and Racism in 70s Britain* (London: Hutchinson, 1982).

6. See, for example, P. Fryer, *Staying Power: This History of Black People in Britain* (London: Pluto, 1984), chapter 7.

7. As quoted in M. Barker, "Racism—The New Inheritors," *Radical Philosophy* 21 (1984), p. 2, p. 4.

8. Ibid.

9. As quoted in J. Rex and S. Tomlinson, *Colonial Immigrants in a British City: A Class Analysis* (London: Routledge & Kegan Paul, 1979), p. 61.

10. Poole, "Reason, Self-Interest and 'Commerical Society': The Social Content of Kantian Morality," *Critical Philosophy* (1984), p. 24, p. 42.

11. *The Brixton Disorders 10–12 April 1981: Report of an Inquiry by the Right Honourable the Lord*

Scarman, O.B.E. (1982; Penguin ed.), p. 209; Barker and Beezer, "The Language of Racism," *Internal Socialism* (1983), p. 108.

12. A Sivanandan, "Race, Class and the State: The Black Experience in Britain," *Race and Class*, 17 (1976), p. 347.

13. For example, Scarman, *Brixton Disorders*, p. 119.

14. Cf. some targets N. Rose, "Beyond the Public/Private Division: Law, Power, and the Family," in P. Fitzpatrick and A. Hunt (eds.), *Critical Legal Studies* (Oxford: Blackwell, 1987), p. 61.

15. M. Foucault, *The History of Sexuality, Volume I: An Introduction* (Harmondsworth: Penguin, 1981), pp. 99–100.

16. The summaries in the text are supported in ss. 1, 2, 6, 17, 20, 43, 48–51, and 54–58 of the Act.

17. For example, Freeman, "Legitimizing Racial Discrimination through Antidiscrimination Law: A Critical Review of Supreme Court Doctrine," *Minnesota Law Review*, 62 (1978), p. 1049.

18. Statements about legal process draw on a survey of judgments in cases before industrial tribunals and employment appeals tribunals. The records of most are kept in the Central Office of the Industrial Tribunals. I will happily supply people interested with record numbers of cases supporting or instancing the various statements. I will refer here to cases from which quotations are taken. The name of a case followed only by a number refers to its record in the Central Office.

19. *R.V. Commission for Racial Equality, Exparte Hillingdon Borough Council* (1982) 1 Q.B. 276.

20. *Science Research Council v Nassé* (1979) 1 Q.B. 144 at pp. 172–73.

21. *British Library v. Palyza and Another* (1984) I.C.R. 504 at p. 508.

22. Ibid., p. 507.

23. *Francis v. Newey and Eyre Limited* 20743/80.

24. See, for example, A. Lester and G. Bindman, *Race and Law* (Harmondsworth: Penguin, 1972), pp. 126–130.

25. Select Committee on Race Relations and Immigration, *Minutes of Evidence (Race Relations Board)*, *Session 1973–74* (January 24, 1974), p. 28.

26. L. Lustgarten, *Legal Control of Racial Discrimination* (London: Macmillan, 1980), p. 196 (emphasis in original).

27. I. A. Macdonald, *Race Relations: The New Law* (London: Butterworths, 1977), p. 122.

28. V. Kumar, *Industrial Tribunal Applicants under the Race Relations Act 1976: A Research Report* (London: Commission for Racial Equality, 1986).

29. On tricks of advocacy see Paynter, "Presenting Your Case: A Guide to Effective Advocacy before the Industrial Tribunal: Part Two," *The Lawyer* (1984), p. 14. Other points were dealt with earlier.

30. *Shah v. Richards Longstaff Ltd.* 26623/84. On the *canard* see D. J. Smith, *Unemployment and Racial Minorities* (London: Policy Studies Institute, 1981), p. 158.

31. Per Lord Diplock in *Dockers' Labour Club and Institute, Ltd. v. Race Relations Board* [1974] 3 All E.R. 592 at p. 598.

32. Hutchinson and Monahan, "Law, Politics and the Critical Legal Scholars: The Unfolding Drama of American Legal Thought," *Stanford Law Review*, 36 (1984), p. 199 at pp. 211–12.

33. P. Goodrich, *Reading Law: A Critical Introduction to Legal Method and Techniques* (Oxford: Blackwell, 1986), p. 152.

34. The point is developed more generally in Fitzpatrick, "Law and Societies" (1984) 22 *Osgoode Hall Law Journal*, 22 (1984), p. 115.

35. P. Hirst and P. Woolley, *Social Relations and Human Attributes* (London: Tavistock, 1982), chapters 2 and 3.

36. C. Sumner, *Reading Ideologies: An Investigation into the Marxist Theory of Ideology and Law* (London: Academic Press, 1979), p. 293.

37. D. Little, *Religion, Order and Law: A Study in Pre-Revolutionary England* (Oxford: Blackwell, 1968), p. 172.

38. A. V. Dicey, *Introduction to the Study of the Law of the Constitution* (1885; rpt. London: Macmillan, 1959), chapter 4.

39. 480 *H. L. Debs.*, cols. 249–51, 265 (October 8, 1986).

40. Law's inter- and subnational existences do not detract from its powerful national configuration.

41. For an enthralling account and analysis of instances see P. Gilroy, *"There Ain't No Black in the Union Jack": The Cultural Politics of Race and Nation* (London: Hutchinson, 1987), chapter 3.

42. Barker and Beezer, "Language of Racism," and Lester and Bindman, *Race and Law*, pp. 90–91.

43. E. Powell, *Freedom and Reality* (Kingswood: Paperfront, 1969), pp. 286, 289.

44. Ibid., chapter 3.

45. For example, Sivanandan, "Race, Class and the State," and Home Office, *Racial Discrimination* (1975; Cmnd. 6234), p. 6.

46. "Whitelaw Seeks to Reassure Immigrants on Equal Rights," *Guardian*, July 12, 1980.

47. See, for example, A. Phizacklea and R. Miles, "Working-class Racist Beliefs in the Inner City," in R. Miles and A. Phizacklea (eds.), *Racism and Political Action in Britain* (London: Routledge & Kegan Paul, 1979), p. 113.

48. C. Brown and P. Gay, *Racial Discrimination: 17 Years After the Act* (London: Policy Studies Institute, 1985).

CHAPTER 16

One Nation under a Groove: The Cultural Politics of "Race" and Racism in Britain

Paul Gilroy

> *How much is here embraced by the term* culture. *It includes all the characteristic activities and interests of a people; Derby Day, Henley Regatta, Cowes, the twelfth of August, a cup final, the dog races, the pin table, the dart board, Wensleydale cheese, boiled cabbage cut into sections, beetroot in vinegar, nineteenth century Gothic churches and the music of Elgar.*
>
> T. S. Eliot

> *While there is some community of interest called Britain and common institutions and historical experiences called British, and indeed a nationality on a passport called British, it is not an identity which is self contained. . . . Britain is a state rather than a nation. The British state imposed upon the English, Scottish, Welsh and part of the Irish peoples and then imposed world wide, is an inherently imperial and colonial concept at home and abroad. The British state cannot and should not be an object of affection, save for those who want to live in a form of authoritarian dependency.*
>
> Dafydd Elis Thomas

Studying the politics of "race"[1] necessitates tracing at least two separate yet intertwined threads of history. The first involves mapping the changing contours of racist ideologies, the semantic fields in which they operate, their special rhetoric, and their internal fractures, as well as their continuities. The second centers on the history of social groups, both dominant and subordinate, that recognize themselves in terms of "race" and act accordingly. Neither of these histories is reducible to the other, and they reciprocate in a complex

---

I would like to thank Vron Ware and Mandy Rose for their help with this essay (which was completed in December 1987).

·r over time bringing together the myths of descent with the manage-
of conquest and the negotiation of consent. The groups we learn to
ν as "races" are not, of course, formed simply and exclusively by the
power of racial discourses. The intimate association between ideas about race
and the employment of unfree labor in plantation slavery, "debt peonage,"
apartheid, or the coercive use of migrant labor should be a constant warning
against conceptualizing racial ideologies as if they are wholly autonomous.
Race may provide literary critics with "the ultimate trope of difference," but
the brain-teasing perplexities of theorizing about race cannot be allowed to
obscure the fact that the play of difference in which racial taxonomy appears
has extradiscursive referents. At different times, economic, political, and cultural factors all play a determining role in shaping the character of "races."
The power of race politics can be used as a general argument for realist conceptions of ideology that emphasize referential conceptions of meaning and
defend a problematic of relative or partial autonomy.[2]

Races are not, then, simple expressions of either biological or cultural
sameness. They are imagined — socially and politically constructed — and the
contingent processes from which they emerge may be tied to equally uneven
patterns of class formation to which they, in turn, contribute. Thus ideas
about race may articulate political and economic relations in a particular society that go beyond the distinct experiences or interests of racial groups to
symbolize wider identities and conflicts. Discussion of racial domination
cannot therefore be falsely separated from wider considerations of social sovereignty such as the conflict between men and women, the antagonism between capital and labor, or the manner in which modes of production develop and combine. Nor can the complexities of racial politics be reduced to
the effect of these other relations. Dealing with these issues in their specificity
and in their articulation with other relations and practices constitutes a profound and urgent theoretical and political challenge. It requires a theory of
racisms that does not depend on an essentialist theory of races themselves.

These methodological observations help to negotiate a critical distance
from positivist and productivist Marxian and neo-Marxian approaches that
risk the reduction of race to a mystical conception of class as well as those
that have buried the specific qualities of racism in the difficulties surrounding
the analysis of ideology in general. Pursuing a radical analysis of race and racism within the broad framework supplied by historical materialism requires
a frank and open acknowledgment of its limitations. Yet Marxism understood in Richard Wright's phrase as a "transitory makeshift pending a more
accurate diagnosis"[3] can provide some valuable points of departure. If the capacity of race and racism to slide between the realm of "phenomenal forms"
and the world of "real relations" means that they have baffled and perplexed
Marxian orthodoxy,[4] there is much to learn from the radically historical approach that has emerged from some of the more sophisticated applications

of Marx's insights. Working from an explicitly Marxian perspective. Stuart Hall puts it like this:

> Racism is always historically specific. Though it may draw on the cultural traces deposited by previous historical phases, it always takes on specific forms. It arises out of present — not past — conditions. Its effects are specific to the present organisation of society, to the present unfolding of its dynamic political and cultural processes — not simply to its repressed past.[5]

This important observation points squarely at the plurality of forms in which racism has developed, not simply between societies but within them also. It underlines the idea that there is no racism in general and consequently there can be no general theory of race relations or race and politics. More important, a perspective that emphasizes the need to deal with racisms rather than a single ahistorical racism also implicitly attacks the fashionable overidentification of race and ethnicity with tradition, allowing instead the opportunity to develop a view of contemporary racisms as responses to the flux of modernity itself.[6]

This perspective places severe limitations on analysis of particular local racisms. It demands that the development of racist discourses must be periodized very carefully and that the fluidity and inherent instability of racial categories is constantly appreciated. With these qualifications in mind, I want to examine some aspects of recent race politics in Britain, by looking, first, at the particular contemporary forms of racist discourse and, second, at the distinctive political outlook articulated by the expressive cultures of England's black settlers.

The starting point for this inquiry must be an acknowledgment of Britain's postcolonial decline and crisis. Although this crisis originates in the economic sphere,[7] it has a variety of features — economic, political, ideological, and cultural. They are not wholly discrete and although they are definitely discontinuous, they are experienced as a complex unity of many unsynchronized determinations. How then is this unity constructed? I want to suggest that ideas about race that are produced by a new and historically specific form of racism play a primary role in securing it. This crisis is thus *lived* through a sense of race. A volatile populist racism has become an obvious political feature of this crisis. But racism is more than simply an increasingly important component of a morbid political culture. It has also become part of how the different elements of this protracted "organic" crisis have become articulated together.[8]

The centrality of racism to this crisis does not, however, mean that the word "race" is on everybody's lips. It bears repetition that racism changes and varies historically. It is essential to remember that we are not talking about racism in general but British crisis racism in particular. One of the ways in which this form or variety of racism is specific is that it frequently operates without any overt reference to either race itself or the biological notions of difference that still give the term its commonsense meaning. Before the rise of modern scientific racism in the nineteenth century the term "race" did duty for the term "culture."[9] No surprise, then, that in its postwar retreat from racism the term has once again acquired an explicitly cultural rather than a biological inflection.

The stress and turbulence of crisis have induced Britons to clarify their national identity by asking themselves a question first posed by Enoch Powell: "What kind of people are we?" Their self-scrutiny has prompted a fascination with primary, ascribed identities that is manifested in an increasingly decadent peoccupation with the metaphysics of national belonging. Examining contemporary British ideas about race and their relationship to notions of nationhood and national belonging in particular can therefore tell us something about the crisis as a whole.

It would appear that the uncertainty the crisis has created requires that lines of inclusion and exclusion that mark out the national community be redrawn. Britons are invited to put on their tin hats and climb back down into their World War II air raid shelters. There, they can be comforted by the rustic glow of the homogeneous national culture that has been steadily diluted by black settlement in the postwar years. That unsullied culture can be mystically reconstituted, particularly amidst national adversity when distinctively British qualities supposedly emerge with the greatest force and clarity. The analogy of war is extensively employed, not just in attempts to represent black immigration and settlement as the encroachment of aliens but around the politics of crime and domestic political dissent. Industrial militants and black settlers have come to share the designation "The Enemy Within." In 1982, real war off the coast of Argentina provided, in the words of one New Right ideologue, an opportunity for the nation to discover "what truly turns it on." From this perspective, which has provided a cornerstone for popular, commonsense racism, blacks, trapped by the biology of their skin shade into a form of symbolic treason, are excluded from the national community because their cultures have obstructed the acquisition of that special hallmark of a true patriotism: the willingness to lay down one's life for one's country.

The culturalism of the new racism has gone hand in hand with a definition of race as a matter of difference rather than a question of hierarchy. In another context Fanon refers to a similar shift as a progression from vulgar to cultural racism.[10] The same process is clearly seen in the cultural focus that marked the inauguration of the apartheid system in 1948.

Culture is conceived along ethnically absolute lines, not as something intrinsically fluid, changing, unstable, and dynamic, but as a fixed property of social groups rather than a relational field in which they encounter one another and live out social, historical relationships. When culture is brought into contact with race it is transformed into a pseudobiological property of communal life.

Thus England's black settlers are forever locked in the bastard culture of their enslaved ancestors, unable to break out into the "mainstream" alternative. Their presence in the ancient territory of the "Island Race" becomes a problem precisely because of their difference and distance from the standards of civilized behavior that are second nature to authentic (white) Britons. The most vocal ideologists of the English New Right[11] — Powell himself, John Casey, and Ray Honeyford — stress not only that they are not racists but that they have no sense whatever of the innate superiority of whites or the congenital inferiority of blacks. They profess allegiance to the nation rather than the race and identify the problems of contemporary black settlement in terms of cultural conflict between the same groups that were once misrecognized as biologically distinct races. This cultural sense of race has posed key problems for antiracist strategy and tactics.

As the distance from crude biologism has increased, the question of law has become more important as a marker for the cultural processes involved. English law is presented as the summit of the national civilization, the pinnacle of Britain's historic achievements. An unwritten constitution distills the finest qualities of the national community and enshrines them in a historic compact to which blacks are unable to adhere. Black violations of the law supply the final proof of their incompatibility with Britain. Their "illegal immigration" and a propensity to street crime confirm their alien status. These specific forms of lawbreaking, as I have shown elsewhere, are gradually defined as a cultural attribute of the black population as a whole.

One significant continuity with the colonial setting can be identified in the way that the most potent symbols of the national culture are not merely racialized but gendered too. Once-proud Britannia has, like her declining nation, fallen on hard times. A resurgent nativist politics has recast her as an aged white woman. Initially violated by Powell's demons, the "wide-grinning picaninnies" who chase her through the streets chanting "racialist," she is, with the onset of their adolescence, terrorized by them again when they turn to more financially remunerative forms of harassment like mugging. The predatory figure of the black rapist also makes an appearance here, demonstrating the failure of the civilizing process and the resistance of black culture to its evangelical imperatives.[12]

For a long while, the question of black criminality provided the principal means to underscore the *cultural* concerns of this new racism. Its dominance helped to locate precisely where the new racism began — in the bloody nightmare of the old woman pursued through the streets by black children. However, crime has been displaced recently at the center of race politics by another issue that points equally effectively to the supposed incompatibility of different cultures sealed off from one another forever along ethnic lines. This too uses images of the black child to make its point. It seems that the cultural sins of the immigrant parents will be visited on their British-born children. Where once it was the mean streets of the decaying inner city that hosted the most fearsome encounter between white Britons and their most improbable and initimidating other—black youth—now it is the classrooms and staffrooms of the nation's inner-city schools that frame the same conflict and provide the most potent terms with which to make sense of racial difference.

The recent publication of *Anti-racism: An Assault on Education and Value*[13] confirmed that the school has become the principal element in the ideology with which the English New Right has sought to attack antiracism. It is essential to understand *why* its burgeoning anti-antiracism has shifted the emphasis from crime to education. Although it poses a range of different strategic difficulties, the change may be less significant than it may first appear. Schools are defined by the Right as repositories of the authentic national culture that they transmit between generations. They mediate the relation of the national community to its youthful future citizens. Decaying school buildings provide a ready image for the nation in microcosm. The hard-fought changes that antiracists and multiculturalists have wrought on the curriculum come to exemplify the debasement of all genuine British culture. Antiracist initiatives that supposedly denigrate educational standards are identified as an assault on the "traditional virtues" of British education. This cultural conflict is a means through which the dynamics of power are transposed and whites become a voiceless ethnic minority oppressed by the antiracist policies of totalitarian Labour local authorities. In the same ideological movement, the racists are redefined as the blacks and their allies, and Mr. Honeyford becomes a tenacious defender of freedom who is invited into the inner sanctums of government as a consultant.

If the importance of culture rather than biology is the first quality that marks this form of racism as something different and new, the special ties it discovers between race, culture, and nation provide further evidence of its novelty. The expansive ideology of the Commonwealth and the Imperial family of nations bonded in common citizenship has given way to a more parochial and embittered perspective that sees culture in neat and tidy national formations. The family remains a key motif, but the multiracial family of nations has been displaced by the racially homogeneous nation of families. The nation is composed of even, symmetrical family units that, like Mr. Honeyford's beleaguered inner-city school, transmit folk traditions between generations. The emphasis on culture allows nation and race to fuse. Nationalism and racism become so closely identified that to speak of the nation is to speak automatically in racially exclusive terms. Blackness and Englishness are constructed as incompatible, mutually exclusive identities. To speak of the British or English people is to speak of the *white* people.

Brief consideration of the British general election of summer 1987 allows

us to see these themes and conflicts played out with a special clarity. The
theme of patriotism was well to the fore and a tussle over the national flag
was a major feature of the campaign. The Labour party pleaded for Britain
to heal its deep internal divisions and become "one nation again," whereas the
Conservatives underlined their success in "putting the Great back into Britain" by urging the electorate not to let the Socialists take this crucial adjective
out again. Significantly, this language made no overt reference to race, but
it acquired racial referents. Everyone knows what is at stake when patriotism
and deference to the law are being spoken about. The seamless manner in
which the themes of race, culture, and nation came together was conveyed
by a racist leaflet issued in the north London constituency of Bernie Grant,
a black Labour candidate who had achieved national prominence in the after-
math of the 1985 riots as an apologist for the rioters. It was illustrated by a
picture of his head grafted on to the hairy body of a gorilla. It read:

> Swing along with Bernie, it's the very natural thing
> he's been doing it for centuries and now he thinks he's king
> He's got a little empire and he doesn't give a jot
> But then the British are a bloody tolerant lot
> They'll let him swing and holler hetero — Homo — Gay
> And then just up and shoot him in the good old British way.

These lines signify a powerful appropriation of the rights and liberties of
the freeborn Briton once so beloved of the New Left. The rhyme's historical
references demonstrate how completely blackness and Britishness have been
made into mutually exclusive categories, incompatible identities. It would
appear that the problems Bernie represents are most clearly visible against the
patterned backdrop of the Union Jack. The picture of him as a gorilla is
necessary on the leaflet because its words make no overt mention of his inferior biology. The crime for which he may be justifiably lynched is a form
of treason, not the transgression involved in mere racial inferiority. The
poem knits together images invoking empire, sovereignty, and sexuality (an
allusion to the local council's progressive policy on lesbian and gay rights),
with its exhortation to violence. There is nothing about this combination of
themes that marks it out as the exclusive preserve of the Right. The leaflet
provides a striking example of how the racism that ties national cultures to
ethnic essences, which sees custom, law and constitution, schools and courts
of justice beset by corrosive alien forces has moved beyond the grasp of the
old Left/Right distinction. The populist character of the new racism is crucial.
It works across the lines of formal politics as well as within them. It can link
together disparate and antagonistic groups leading them to discover the morbid pleasures of seeing themselves as "one nation," inviting them to draw

comfort from a mythic sense of the past[14] as it is reconstructed as historical memory in the present.

As a political issue, concern with the erosion of the national culture is perhaps spontaneously identified with the self-consciously conservative postures of the Right. The emphasis on crime and the law that identified the early stages of the new cultural racism also emerged from that quarter. However, many of the same ideas about what race, nation, and culture mean and how they fit together are held more broadly. Sections of the Left have recently stressed the issues of crime and patriotism without regard for any of their racial connotations. More significantly and ironically, some vocal factions inside the black communities have also sought to emphasize the cultural incompatibility of Afro-Caribbean and Asian settlers with Britain and Britishness. Ultra-Right, New Left, and black nationalists can accept variations of the idea that Britain may be a multiracial society but is not yet and may never be a multiracial nation.

The convergence between the Left and Right over what race means in contemporary Britain can be illustrated by looking at Raymond Williams's brief discussion of race in *Towards 2000*.[15] In this passage, Williams not only proved himself unable to address the issue of racism, he unwittingly echoed Powell in arguing that there was far more to authentic "lived and formed" national identity than the rights conferred by the "alienated superficialities" of formal citizenship. For blacks denied access to meaningful citizenship by the operation of a "grandfather clause" these legal rights are rather more than superficial. Indeed, they have constituted the substance of a protracted political conflict with which Williams is clearly unfamiliar. I am not suggesting that Conservative and Socialist positions are the same but rather that a significant measure of overlap now exists between them. An absolutist definition of culture tied to a resolute defense of the idea of the national community appears uncompromisingly in both.

Themes and concepts that parallel the outpourings of the new racists have appeared in the political pronouncements of many of Britain's black cultural nationalists. Often, the theories and preoccupations of the white racists have simply been inverted to form a thoroughly pastoral account of black culture. This has been combined with an extreme version of cultural relativism that relies for its effect on a *volkish* ethnic absolutism. Here too the family is the key unit out of which nationality is built and the central means of cultural reproduction.

Where the racists have measured black households against the idealized nuclear family form and found them wanting,[16] this black politics has viewed black children as the primary resource of the race with predictable consequences particularly in terms of the continued subordination of women. Where this tendency is strongest, particularly in local government agencies where black professionals have been able to consolidate their power, a special concern with black fostering and adoption policy has emerged as the primary vehicle for black cultural nationalism. This issue has precipitated a debate over the capacity of white families to provide an environment in which black culture and identity can be nurtured. It has achieved a symbolic currency far beyond its immediate institutional context. An absolutist conception of cultural or ethnic difference appears here to underpin the fear that new forms of slavery are being created in the placement of black children in white families for adoption or fostering and the consequent belief that racial identity necessarily overrides all other considerations. The class character of the political formation organized around this ideology cannot be elaborated here. It would appear, however, that these potent symbols of a racial community and its beleaguered boundaries play an important role in securing the unity of an emergent black petite bourgeoisie and in mystifying their intrinsically problematic relationship to those they are supposed to serve, particularly in a social work setting. Belief in the transcendental racial essence capable of uniting the black professionals with their dispossessed black clients conjures away awkward economic and historical complexities and occludes the conspicuous divergence of interests between the never employed and the cadre of black bureaucrats employed by the local state to salve their misery.

This divergence within the black communities is significant because the logic of Britain's crisis is itself a logic of cultural and political fragmentation. The recent history of race politics can be identified by the decomposition of open, inclusive definitions of "blackness" that facilitated political alliances by accommodating the discontinuous histories of Afro-Caribbean and Asian-descended people. The more restrictive definitions that emerged to take their place and restrict the term "black" to those of Afro-Caribbean ancestry betoken a general retreat into the dubious comfort of ethnic particularity. However, this fracturing process is far more extensive than its intraethnic dimensions suggest. The economic effects of the crisis are, for example, unevenly developed in the most radical manner; they are unevenly distributed even within the same city. It has become commonplace to speak of Britain as two nations—an exploited and immiserated north bearing the brunt of deindustralization and a more affluent south. These definitions of the nation are more than competing metaphors. They correspond to important changes in the mode of production itself and the geography of class formation and political representation. The Labour party presides over the north and the inner cities almost without challenge. The Conservatives enjoy a similar monopoly of power in the more prosperous and suburban areas. Amidst these divisions, to answer the pleas for aid from the ailing north, where notions of region and locality have provided an important axis of political organization, with the language of nationalism and patriotism, is fundamentally misguided. The racial connotations that emerge with this rhetoric work actively to distance black citizens from the system of formal politics as a whole. The counterposition of local and national identities makes nonsense of the idea of a homogeneous national culture. The intensity with which it has emerged as a political problem suggests a deeper crisis of the nation-state.

Elsewhere in *Towards 2000* Williams has suggestively described the nation-state as being simultaneously both too large and too small a unit for the necessary forms of political interaction required by the advancement of radical democracy during the years ahead. Seeing the nation as a totality of different societies constructed for different purposes allows us to ask how these may learn to coexist; and in particular, what role the cultural politics of Britain's black settlers and their British-born children may play in creating the pluralistic ambience in which people are able to discover positive pleasure in their inescapable diversity.

An understanding of the limitations of the nation-state as a form is central to the sense of the African diaspora as a cultural and political unit that anchors black English political culture. The majority of Britain's blacks are postwar settlers, but their refined diaspora awareness is more than a reflection of the proximity of migration. It corresponds directly to the subordinate position Britain's small and diverse black population has occupied within the vast network of cultural and political exchange that links blacks in Africa, the Caribbean, the United States, and Europe. Until very recently, this country's identifiably black culture has been created from the raw materials supplied by blacks elsewhere, particularly in America and the Caribbean.

In one sense, the political network that made this cultural relationship possible was a direct product of the commercial traffic in slaves. The activities of eighteenth- and nineteenth-century abolitionists, the transnational and international organization of antislavery activities and Pan-African initiatives[17] prepared the way for the great gains of the Garvey movement. Each of these phases of black self-organization consolidated independent means of communication between the different locations within the diaspora. What principally concerns us here is the cultural character of these developments: the special premium they have placed on expressive culture — music, song, and dance. Artistic forms have produced and sustained an interpretive community outside the orbit of formal politics in a long sequence of struggles that has been irreducibly and simultaneously both cultural and political. The internationalization of the leisure industries and the growth of important markets for cultural commodities outside the overdeveloped world have provided new opportunities for the consolidation of diaspora awareness. The popular Pan-Africanist and Ethiopianist visions inherent in reggae were, for example, carried to all the corners of the world as an unforeseen consequence of selling the music of Jamaica beyond the area in which it was created. The ideologies and sign systems of Afro-American Black Power, in part, traveled by a similar route. The narrow nationalism we saw in the politics of the emergent black petite bourgeoisie contrasts sharply with the voice of the social movement that has been articulated through the language, styles, and symbols of the diaspora. Britain's black population is comparatively small and heterogeneous. Britain has no ghettos along the American model or any residential communities comparable to the Bantustans and squatter camps of South Africa. The blackest areas of the inner city are, for example, between 30 and 50 percent white. Here, the idea of the black community necessarily expresses something more than just the physical concentration of black people. The term has a special moral valency and refers above all to a community of interpretation whose cultural cohesion has sometimes enabled it to act politically. This is a community bounded by language and by cultural forms that play an ethical and educative role. Although the collapse of certainties once provided by class identity, class politics, and class theory has been a pronounced feature of the recent period in Britain, it is also a community that has been articulated, at a number of points, with the contemporary structures of class relations. In the encounter between black settlers and their white inner-city neighbors, black culture has become a class culture. There is more to this transformation and adaptation than the fact that blacks are among the most economically exploited and politically marginal sections of the society, overrepresented in the surplus population, the prison population, and among the poor. From the dawn of postwar settlement, diaspora culture has been an ambiguous presence in the autonomous institutions of the working class. Two generations of whites have appropriated it, discovering in its seductive forms meanings of their own. It is now impossible to speak coherently of black culture in Britain in isolation from the culture of Britain as a whole. This is particularly true as far as leisure is concerned. Black expressive culture has decisively shaped youth culture, pop culture, and the culture of city life in Britain's metropolitan centers. The white working class has danced for forty years to its syncopated rhythms. There is, of course, no contradiction between using black culture and loathing real live black people, yet the informal, long-term processes through which different groups have negotiated each other have intermittently created a "two-tone" sensibility that celebrates its hybrid origins and has provided a significant opposition to "commonsense" racialism.

It is often argued that the spontaneity of black musical forms, their performance aesthetic, and commitment to improvisation have made them into something of a magnet for other social groups. Certainly the centrality that issues of sexuality, eroticism, and gender conflict enjoy within black folk cultures has given them a wide constituency. Their Rabelaisian power to carnivalize and disperse the dominant order through an intimate yet public discourse on sexuality and the body has drawn many outsiders into a dense and complex network of black cultural symbols. These aspects of black forms mark out a distinct field of political antagonisms that I do not intend to examine here. Instead, I want to explore the equally distinctive *political* character of these forms and the urban social movement they have helped to create and extend.

The politics of this movement are manifested in the confluence of three critical, anticapitalist themes that have a historic resonance in diaspora culture and can be traced directly and indirectly back to the formative experience of slavery. Together they form a whole but nonprogrammatic politics that has sustained Britain's black settler populations and their white inner-city associates. The first theme deals with the experience of work, the labor process, and the division of labor under capitalism. It amounts to a critique of productivism—the ideology that sees the expansion of productive forces as an indispensable precondition of the attainment of freedom. In opposition to this view of production, an argument is made that sees waged work as itself a form of servitude. At best, it is viewed as a necessary evil and is sharply counterposed to the more authentic freedoms that can only be enjoyed in nonwork time. The black body is here celebrated as an instrument of pleasure rather than an instrument of labor. The nighttime becomes the right time, and the space allocated for recovery and recuperation is assertively and provocatively occupied by the pursuit of leisure and pleasure.

The second theme focuses on the state. It addresses the role of law in particular and, in challenging capitalist legality to live up to the expansive promises of its democratic rhetoric, articulates a plea for the dissociation of law from the processes of domination. The legal institutions on which Babylon's order of public authority rest do not provide equal rights for all. The version of justice they peddle is partial and inseparable from the system of economic interests that capitalist legality simply guarantees. The coercive brutality of the state is seen as an intrinsic property of these institutions. The exterminism and militarism that characterize them are denounced, not only where they reach into people's lives as the police or army but for the way that they symbolize the illegitimate nature of the capitalist state in general. This mystified form of rule is unfavorably compared to two quite different standards of justice: first, a divine version that will ultimately redress the miscarriages of earthly "man-made" law and, second, an alternative secular moral standard—truth and right—that derives its legitimate power from popular sovereignty. It is significant that capitalist legality is understood to have denied blacks the status of legal subjects during the slave period.

The third theme concentrates on the importance of history understood as a discontinuous process of struggle. An affirmation of history and the place of blacks within it are advanced as an antidote to the suppression of temporal perception under capitalism. This theme also answers the way in which racism works to suppress the historical dimensions of black life offering a mode of existence locked permanently into a recurrent present where social existence is confined to the roles of being either a problem or a victim.

The contemporary musical forms of the African diaspora work within an aesthetic and political framework that demands that they ceaselessly reconstruct their own histories, folding back on themselves time and again to celebrate and validate the simple, unassailable fact of their survival. This is particularly evident in jazz, where quotes from earlier styles and performers make the past actually audible in the present. This process of recovery should not be misunderstood. It does not amount to either straightforward parody or pastiche. The stylistic voices of the past are valued for the distinct register of address each offers. The same playful process is evident in the less abstract performances that define Washington's "Go-Go" dance funk. This style consists of a continuous segue from one tune to the next. The popular black musics of different eras and continents are wedded together by a heavy percussive rhythm and an apparently instinctive antiphony. A recent concert in London by Chuck Brown, the kingpin of the Go-Go saw him stitch together tunes by Louis Jordan, Sly Stone, Lionel Hampton, Melle Mel, and T-Bone Walker into a single epic statement. Reggae's endless repetition of "versions" and the tradition of answer records in rhythm and blues betray a similar historical impulse.

The core themes I have identified overlap and interact to generate a cohesive but essentially defensive politics and a corresponding aesthetic of redemption from racial subordination. The critique of productivism is reinforced and extended by the structural location of black labor power in Britain and the other overdeveloped countries. It is also tied to the movement among young blacks that actively rejects the menial and highly exploitative forms in which work is made available. The concern with history demands that the experience of slavery is also recovered and rendered vivid and immediate. It becomes a powerful metaphor for the injustice and exploitation of contemporary waged work in general.

The anticapitalist politics that animate the social movement against racial subordination is not confined to the lyrical content of these musical cultures. The poetics involved recurrently deals with these themes, but the critique of capitalism is simultaneously revealed in the forms this expressive culture takes and in the performance aesthetic that governs them. There is here an immanent challenge to the commodity form to which black expressive culture is reduced in order to be sold. It is a challenge that is practiced rather than simply talked or sung about. The artifacts of a pop industry premised on the individual act of purchase and consumption are hijacked and taken over into the heart of collective rituals of protest and affirmation, which in turn define the boundaries of the interpretive community. Music is heard socially and its deepest meanings revealed only in the heat of this collective, affirmative consumption. Struggles over the commodification of black music are reflected in a dialectical conflict between the technology of reproduction and the subcultural needs of its primary consumers in the "race market." Here, the pioneering use of live recordings occupying the whole side of a long-playing disk, issuing the same song in two parts on different sides of a forty-five, and putting out various mixes of a song on one twelve-inch disk to facilitate scratch mixing are all part of the story. Musicians and producers for whom the "race market" is the primary constituency are reluctant to compromise with the commercial formats on which the music business relies. Where they are able to exercise control over the form in which their music is issued, black artists anticipate this specific mode of consumption and privilege it. Records are issued in an open, participative form that invites further artistic input. The Toaster or MC (rapper) adds rhymes and comments to the wordless version of a tune that is routinely issued on the reverse of the vocal version. Several different versions of the same piece are issued on a single record. Twelve-inch disks that allow for extended playing time are favored. Thus the original artifact negotiates the supplementary input of other artists unseen and unknown yet anticipated by the original creator of the music.

The clubs, parties, and dances where these creative negotiations between original and supplementary performances take place are governed by a dramaturgy that prizes the local, immediate, and seemingly spontaneous input above all. Leaving behind the passive role of spectator to which they would be assigned by Western convention, these audiences become instead active participants. In this metaphysics of intimacy, race mediates the social relation between internal pain and its externalization in cathartic performance. The audience's association with the performer dissolves Eurocentric notions of the disjunction between art and life, inside and outside, in the interplay of personal and public histories for which the traditions of the black church serve as a model and an inspiration.[18] The complex, dialogic rituals involved become sources of profound pleasure in their own right, particularly where singers and musicians encounter a crowd directly. The musical countercultures of black Britain are primarily based on records rather than live performances, but the same aesthetic of performance applies. Music recorded on disks loses its preordained authority as it is transformed and adapted. In reggae, soul, and hip-hop subcultures the disk that appears in the dominant culture as a fixed and final product is extended and reconstructed as it becomes the raw material in a new creative process born in the dialogue between the DJ, the rapper or MC, and the dancing crowd. A range of de- and reconstructive procedures—scratch mixing, dubbing, toasting, rapping, and beatboxing—contribute to new layers of local meaning. The original performance trapped in plastic is supplemented by new contributions at every stage. Performer and audience alike strive to create pleasures that can evade capture and sale as cultural commodities. A hostility to commercial trafficking in black music has grown so steadily that the majority of black clubs and leisure spaces are actively disinterested in the latest new records, forsaking them in favor of old and hard-to-obtain disks in an antiaesthetic cult known as the "Rare Groove" scene. Popularized by the illegal pirate radio stations that deal exclusively in the various styles of black music, this fashion has placed a special premium on politically articulate American dance-funk recordings from the Black Power period. Because it cannot be bought, the pleasures in hearing a particular tune are severed from the commercial relations of pop. Dislocated from the time and place in which they were created, disks like Hank Ballard's 1968 "How You Gonna Get Respect? You Haven't Cut Your Process Yet"[19] become abstract metaphysical statements on the nature of blackness. The same process applies to music imported into Britain's black communities from the Caribbean. Again, for both reggae and soul-based traditions, the polysemic qualities of black speech add to the subversive potency of the DJ's and MC's language games.

These issues can be examined further by considering the impact of "I Know You Got Soul," an American hip-hop record that was the most popular item in London's black clubs for several months at the beginning of 1987. The record was a new version of Bobby Byrd's sixteen-year-old Black Power anthem. Snatches of his original version were still clearly audible, but it had been transformed by the addition of a drum machine and an unusually clever and poetic rap. Eric B. and Rakim, the creators of the new version, declared themselves emphatically committed to a ghetto constituency, people who, as Rakim put it when I spoke to him, "turn to music because they got nothin' else." The record affirms this commitment by celebrating the concept of soul that is thought to be fundamental to black experience. "You listen to it . . . the concept might break you." Its dense, dizzy sound privileges and anticipates a public hearing: "Sit by the radio hand on the dial, soon as you hear it pump up the volume." But the public sphere to which it is addressed is defined against the dominant alternative to which blacks enjoy only restricted access. This is an altogether different forum bounded by the strictures of race and community and marked out by the naming process that gave these young men their identity as performers. The Soul Power the record manifests is also the force that binds their listeners together into a moral, even a political community. For black Britain constructing its own distinct culture from material supplied by the United States and the Caribbean, "I Know You Got Soul" brilliantly tied a sense of exclusive contemporary style to an older, positive message of self-respect and political autonomy that derives its power from the American black movement of the 1960s. The disk, an adaptation and transformation of an earlier piece that retained the original within its own fractured form, was scratched, dubbed, and made over time and time again in the dancehalls, parties, and other leisure spaces of Britain's black community. Its consumption by Afro-Caribbean and Asian-descended Britons and their white friends, lovers, and associates defines the boundaries of a utopian social movement. This movement aims to defend and extend spaces for social autonomy and meets the oppressive power of racial capitalism with the radical aspiration that one day work will no longer be servitude and law no longer equated with domination. Thus the territoriality of identity is counterposed to the territoriality of control. An immediate, nonnegotiable politics is infused with a powerful sense of locality and a rootedness in tradition. "It ain't where you're from," intones Rakim, "its where you're at."

It is interesting to note that at the very moment when celebrated Euro-American cultural theorists have pronounced the collapse of "grand narratives" the expressive culture of Britain's black poor is dominated by the need to construct them as narratives of redemption and emancipation. This expressive culture, like others elsewhere in the African diaspora, produces a potent historical memory and an authoritative analytic and historical account of racial capitalism and its overcoming. There are of course many problems in trying to hold the term "postmodernism" together. It refers simultaneously and contradictorily to modernization, to a cognitive theory, to a change in the cultural climate in the overdeveloped countries, and to an aspect of the logic of late capitalism. The concept may have some value as a purely heuristic device, but it seems often simply to serve to validate another equally Eurocentric master narrative from which the history and experiences of blacks remain emphatically absent. Fredric Jameson, for example, views postmodernism as "the cultural dominant."[20] However, all the constitutive features of the postmodern that he identifies — the new depthlessness, the weakening of historicity, the waning of affect — are not merely absent from black expressive cultures but are explicitly contradicted by their repertoire of complete "hermeneutic gestures." These cultural forms use the new technological means at their disposal, not to flee from depth but to revel in it, not to abjure public history but to proclaim it! They have created their own thoroughly subversive means to inhabit what Jameson calls "the bewildering new world space of late multi-national capital."

There is, in the history of these forms, a suggestion that the grand narrative of reason is not being brought to an end but itself transformed, democratized, and extended. This transformation that sees the center of ethical gravity shift away from "the West" is mistakenly identified as the end of reason. Forms of rationality are being created endlessly. The postmodernists' claim that the present moment is *the* moment of rupture contains echoes of earlier European obsessions with the precise timing of the new dawn. Rather than seek to substitute an aesthetic radicalism for a moral one as the spokespersons for postmodernism have implicitly and explicitly suggested, the expressive culture shows how these two dimensions can be aligned in a complex sensibility sometimes utopian, sometimes fiercely pragmatic.

The movement it articulates has coalesced somewhere between what Jean Cohen has called the "identity-oriented" and "resource-mobilisation" paradigms for comprehending social action.[21] It is neither a class nor, of course, a racially homogeneous grouping. Its identity is a product of immediate local circumstances but is apprehended through a syncretic culture for which the history of the African diaspora supplies the decisive symbolic core. Partly because religious language conveys an intensity of aspiration for which there is no secular alternative, this culture has a spiritual component. As we have already seen, it views the body as itself an important locus of resistance and desire. The body is therefore reclaimed from its subordination to the labor process, recognized as part of the natural world, and enjoyed on that basis. Third, and most important, this movement can be identified by its antipathy to the institutions of formal politics and the fact that it is not principally oriented toward instrumental objectives. Rather than aim at the conquest of political power or apparatuses, its objective centers on the control of a field of autonomy or independence from the system.

The distinctive political perspective that emerges from this movement can lead us to a more scrupulous and detailed periodization of modernity itself. The modernizing processes in which commodification and industrialization come together with the political institutions of formal democracy have had *regional* as well as temporal characteristics. It is therefore useful to reconceptualize the struggles of African diaspora populations not simply as anti-capitalist but as a product of one of modernity's most significant and enduring countercultures. Capitalism, industrialization, and their political counterparts are differentiated and then analyzed in their articulation. The social movement that is the contemporary heir to a non-European radical tradition[22] has a more total critique of them than that currently spoken in furtherance of the struggle to emancipate labor from capital.

Identifying this radical tradition unburdened by the dream of progress and a positivistic faith in the easy certainties of Marxian science returns us to the question of whose master narratives are collapsing and whose growing stronger? This inquiry in turn provides a further cue to shift the center of debate away from Europe, and to explore other encounters with modernity that a dogmatic postmodern perspective ignores or dismisses as peripheral. As C. L. R. James argued long ago, the history of communism ought to reckon with political communities for whom the "enthusiasm of 1789" relates to Port-au-Prince before it relates to Paris.[23] Why is it so difficult to think through the relationship between them? To put it another way, it is not, as J.-F. Lyotard puts it in *Le Différend*, only the "annihilation named Auschwitz" that now requires a formal transformation of what counts as history and as reality, of our understanding of reference and the function of the proper name.[24] These problems have been the substance of diaspora culture through slavery and since. The people whom June Jordan has eloquently called "the stubborn majority of this world"[25] have had a variety of complex and problematic relationships to "modernity." This has been true from the moment when Africans, detached from an identifiable location in space and time, became Negroes — in the West but not organically of it — and acquired the "double vision" that a subordinate position entails. As slaves, their exclusion from universal human categories demanded the acquisition and validation of an authentic humanity. It is also relevant that their experiences as unfree working populations engaged in industrial capitalist production have been accorded secondary status behind those of the industrial proletariat by four generations of Marxist theoreticians.

Questions of political economy aside, studying the distinct "intertextual" traditions of the African diaspora alone demands extensive adjustments to the conceptualization of modernization, modernity, and aesthetic modernism. The idea of a "Populist" modernism is a useful preliminary means to comprehend the cultural and political strategies that have evolved not only where European philosophy and letters have been bent to other purposes by Nella Larsen, Richard Wright, James Baldwin, David Bradley, Alice Walker, or most self-consciously in Amiri Baraka's black Baudelaire, but also to make sense of the secular and spiritual *popular* forms — music and dance — that have handled the anxieties and dilemmas involved in a response to the flux of modern life.

The cultural politics of race can be more accurately described as the cultural politics of racism's overcoming. It challenges theories that assert the primacy of structural contradictions, economic classes, and crises in determining political consciousness and collective action. Traditions of radical politics arising from groups whose enduring jeopardy dictates that the premises of their social existence are threatened may, in our postindustrial era, be more radical than more obviously class-based modes of political action. The high level of support for the striking miners and their families inside Britain's black communities during the recent coal dispute seems to indicate that these different varieties of radicalism can be brought together. During that industrial dispute, highly dissimilar groups were able to connect their fates across the divisions of "race," ethnicity, region, and language. For a brief period, inner-city populations and the supposed vanguard of the orthodox industrial proletariat shrank the world to the size of their immediate communities and began, in concert, to act politically on that basis. In doing so, they supplied a preliminary but nonetheless concrete answer to the decisive political questions of our age: how do we act locally and yet think globally? How do we connect the local and the immediate across the earthworks erected by the division of labor?

NOTES

1. The themes and problems discussed in this essay have been elaborated in my book *There Ain't No Black in the Union Jack: The Cultural Politics of Race and Nation* (London: Hutchinson, 1987).

2. One version of this problematic appears in the work of Stuart Hall, particularly his 1980

paper "Race, Articulation and Societies Structured in Dominance," published in the UNESCO reader, *Sociological Theories: Race and Colonialism*. See also his "Signification, Representation, Ideology: Althusser and the Post-Structuralist Debates," in *Critical Studies in Mass Communication*, 2 (June 1985). A similar position is sketched on somewhat different ground by Alex Callinicos in his "Postmodernism, Post-Structuralism and Post-Marxism?" *Theory Culture and Society*, 2 (1985). Both pieces draw heavily on the work of Volosinov and Bakhtin.

3. "The Voiceless Ones," *Saturday Review*, 16 (1960).

4. I am thinking here of Robert Miles's *Racism and Migrant Labour* (London: Routledge & Kegan Paul, 1982); and John Gabriel and Gideon Ben Tovim's essay "Marxism and The Concept of Racism," *Economy and Society*, 7 (May 1978).

5. Hall, "Racism and Moral Panics in Post-war Britain," in Commission for Racial Equality (ed.), *Five Views of Multi-racial Britain* (London: 1978).

6. *Shamanism, Colonialism and The Wild Man: A Study in Terror and Healing* (Chicago: University of Chicago Press, 1987). Michael Taussig's absolutely brilliant study of race and colonial terror is an excellent example of what can be achieved. Less inspiring but worth investigating nonetheless are Orlando Patterson's *Ethnic Chauvinism: The Reactionary Impulse* (New York: Stein & Day, 1977), and Anthony D. Smith's *Ethnic Revival in The Modern World* (Cambridge: Cambridge University Press, 1981).

7. Andrew Gamble, *Britain in Decline* (London: Macmillan, 1981).

8. Apart from *There Ain't No Black*, see Centre for Contemporary Cultural Studies (eds.), *The Empire Strikes Back* (London: Hutchinson, 1982); and S. Hall et al, *Policing the Crisis* (London: Macmillan, 1979).

9. Nancy Stepan, *The Idea of Race in Science: Great Britain 1800–1960* (London: Macmillan, 1982).

10. Frantz Fanon, *Toward the African Revolution* (Harmondsworth: Pelican, 1967).

11. A useful account of the development of the English New Right is provided in R. Levitas (ed.), *The Ideology of the New Right* (London: Polity, 1985). See also *The New Right Enlightenment: Young Writers on the Spectre Haunting the Left* (Sevenoaks: Economic and Literary Books, 1985). The men referred to here are part of an influential grouping around the journal *Salisbury Review*. Ray Honeyford in particular became something of a celebrity when he opposed the introduction of "antiracist and multicultural" teaching methods into the inner-city school where he was headmaster.

12. See Vron Ware and Mandy Rose, *The White Woman's Burden: In Search of a Feminist Antiracism* (London: Verso, forthcoming).

13. Frank Palmer (ed.), *Anti-racism: An Assault on Education and Value* (London: Sherwood Press, 1986).

14. See Patrick Wright's *On Living in an Old Country* (London: Verso, 1985).

15. Raymond Williams, *Towards 2000* (London: Chatto, 1983).

16. A concern with the supposedly pathological forms in which black family life develops is shared by Lord Scarman's report into the 1981 riots in London and Daniel Moynihan's report *The Negro Family and the Case for National Action*. This convergence and the image of family breakdown in racist ideology is discussed by Errol Lawrence in the CCCS volume, *The Empire Strikes Back*.

17. I am thinking here of the settlement of Sierra Leone and of the travels of black abolitionists in Britain and Europe. On the latter see C. Peter Ripley (ed.), *The Black Abolitionist Papers*, Vol. 1 (Chapel Hill: University of North Carolina Press, 1985), and Clare Taylor (ed.), *British and American Abolitionists* (Edinburgh: Edinburgh University Press, 1974). For Sierra Leone see Immanuel Geiss, *The Pan-African Movement* (London: Methuen, 1974).

18. Gerald L. Davis, *I Got the World in Me and I Can Sing It, You Know: A Study of the Performed African-American Sermon* (Philadelphia: University of Pennsylvania Press, 1985).

19. Hank Ballard and the Dapps, "How You Gonna Get Respect?" (King Records, K6196).

The cut is also included on the 1969 album "You Can't Keep a Good Man Down" (King, K1052).

20. Frederic Jameson, "Postmodernism or the Cultural Logic of Late Capitalism," *New Left Review*, 146 (July–August 1984).

21. Jean Cohen, "Strategy or Identity: New Theoretical Paradigms and Contemporary Social Movements," *Social Research*, 52 (Winter 1985).

22. Cedric J. Robinson, *Black Marxism: The Making of the Black Radical Tradition* (London: Zed Press, 1982).

23. C. L. R. James, *The Black Jacobins* (London: Allison & Busby, 1985).

24. J.-F. Lyotard, *Le Différend* (Paris: Minuit, 1983). See also Meaghan Morris, "Postmodernity and Lyotard's Sublime," *Art and Text*, 16 (Summer 1984).

25. June Jordan, *Civil Wars* (Boston: Beacon Press, 1981).

CHAPTER 17

Paradoxes of Universality

Etienne Balibar
Translated by Michael Edwards

That theories of nationalism, and even the strategies and affects of national-ism, are always caught in the "contradiction" between simultaneous tenden-cies toward universality and particularism is a received idea that lends itself to infinite developments and illustrations. Indeed, nationalism aspires to uniformity and rationality; it is expansive. And yet it cultivates the symbols, the fetishes of an autochthonous national character, which must be preserved against dissipation. What interests me here is not the generality of this con-tradiction, but the way in which it is exhibited by racism itself and the role racism plays in its development.

In fact, we see that racism figures on both sides, the universal and the par-ticular. The excess that racism represents with respect to nationalism, and therefore what it adds to nationalism, tends at one and the same time to universalize it, correcting in sum its lack of universality, and to particularize it, correcting its lack of specificity. In othe words, racism simply adds to the ambiguity of nationalism, not only on the theoretical plane—in many respects, racism has supplied nationalism with the only theories it has[1]—but also on the practical plane, which means that through racism, nationalism en-gages in a "blind pursuit," a metamorphosis of its ideal contradictions into material ones.

In adding to the side of the particular, racism becomes a *supernationalism.* Ordinary nationalism is perceived to be weak, a compromise position in a universe of inexpiable competition or war. Racism wishes to be a "compre-hensive" nationalism.[2] But comprehensive nationalism has no meaning (or

Extracted from "Racisme et nationalisme," in Etienne Balibar and Immanuel Wallerstein, *Race, Nation, Classe* (Paris: Editions La Découverte, 1988).

chance) unless it is founded on the integrity of the nation, within and without. This is the double function of the notion of *frontier*, to which I shall return. What theoretical racism calls "race" or "culture" (or both) is therefore a birthright of the nation, a historical backbone, a concentration of qualities that belong "exclusively" to the nationals: it is in the race of "its children" that the nation can contemplate its true identity at its purest. Consequently, it is to the race that the nation must cleave. Ultimately the nation must identify itself, spiritually as well as physically or carnally, with the race, the "patrimony" to be protected from all degradation (and as for the race, so for the culture as substitute for, or interiority of, the race). This means, of course, that racism is the permanent breeding ground of the demand that "lost," expatriate individuals and populations (e.g., Germans of the Sudetenland, Tyrol, etc.) be annexed ("returned") to the national "body," a demand that, we know, is closely associated with the *pan-ic* developments of nationalism — Pan Slavism, Pan Germanism, Pan Arabism. But this means above all that racism leads ineluctably to an excess of "purism" regarding the nation: for the nation to be *itself* — for it to be strong, dominant, for it to save itself and resist its enemies — it must be racially and/or culturally pure. It must therefore isolate the "exogenous," "interbred," "cosmopolitan" elements within, then eliminate and expel them. This is an obsessive imperative, capable of purely and simply *creating* its own objects (racism is thus an essential aspect of the generalized "projective field" of political alienation) and in all cases directly responsible for the "racialization" of populations and social groups whose collective features will be designated stigmata of exteriority and impurity. Anti-Semitism (today racism toward the Arab immigrant) epitomizes this schema. And when the Jew and the Arab do not exist, they are invented.

Of course this process of constructing race as supernationality entails its own practical contradictions, its own blind pursuit. In principle there would have to be a way to recognize, through some sure criterion based on origin or behavior, the "true nationals" or the "essential nationals": the "French French," the "English English" of whom Ben Anderson speaks in connection with the cast hierarchy and categorization of civil servants in the British Empire, the "German Germans" — see the distinction made by Nazism between *Volkszugehörigkeit* and *Staatsangehörigkeit* — the authentic Americanness of the WASP, without overlooking obviously the whiteness of the Afrikaner "citizen." But in practice they have to be constructed by means of ambiguous juridical conventions or cultural particularities. As a result, the quest for nationality through race is necessarily doomed, since racial or cultural "purity" is merely the name of this quest, this obsession. Moreover, it always turns out that in actual practice the criteria invested with a "racial" (and a fortiori cultural) meaning are largely criteria of social class; or else they wind up symbolically "selecting" an elite that already happens to be selected by the inequalities of economic and political classes; or else it turns out that the "cultural identity" are the most *doubtful*. These effects run directly counter to the nationalist objective, which is not to re-create an elitism, but to found a populism: not to expose the historical and social heterogeneity of the "people," but to exhibit their essential unity. This is why racism always tends to function *in reverse*, following the mechanism that has already been mentioned in connection with the role of anti-Semitism in European nationalisms: the racial-cultural identity of the "true nationals" remains invisible, but it is inferred from (and assured by) its opposite, the alleged, quasi-hallucinatory visibility of the "false nationals": Jews, "wops," immigrants, *indios, natives*, blacks. One might as well say that it remains forever uncertain and in danger: that the "false" are *too* visible will never guarantee that the "true" are visible *enough*.

These reflections reveal the underlying ambivalence of the signifier "race" (and its substitutes) from the standpoint of national unity and identity. In seeking to identify and circumscribe the shared essence of the nationals, racism inevitably embarks on the obsessive quest for a "core" of unobtainable authenticity, shrinks the boundaries of nationality, and destabilizes the historical nation. Whence this casuistry: if it must be admitted that French nationality includes innumerable successive generations of migrants, their spiritual incorporation will be justified by their capacity to assimilate, understood as a predisposition to Frenchness, but the question can always be raised (as in the past about the *conversos* under the Inquisition) whether this assimilation is not superficial, mere appearance. From there, to the extreme, a stupefying reversal of the racial phantasm: since there is no way to *find* racial-national purity or to guarantee its source in the origins of the people, it must be *fabricated* after the idea of a (super)national Superman. Such is the meaning of Nazi eugenics, but it must be said that the same orientation inhabits all the sociotechniques of human selection, even a certain tradition of "typically British" education, and that it reemerges today in the "pedagogic" applications of differential psychology (whose ultimate weapon is IQ). This also explains the rapidity with which one passes from racism as supernationalism to racism as *supranationalism*.

⌊We must take seriously the fact that the racial theories of the nineteenth and twentieth centuries (from "Indo-European" origin to the "Aryan myth," and from there to "Western specificity") define communities of language, of descent, of tradition that fail to coincide, as a general rule, with actual nations, the historical states, although these theories always refer to one or another of them.⌋ This means that in theoretical racism *the dimension of universality* is always present. If it is true, however, that there does not exist *one* unique racist theory, but *several* theories, which are tied to particular nationalisms, we may suppose that each racism is a "specific universalization" of nationalism. It is this dimension and its extreme consequences that I would now like to examine.

We need not dwell on the fact, in itself important (I will return to it later), that the classic racial myths, in particular Aryanism, refer initially not to the nation but to the class, in an aristocratic perspective, except to point out that, under these conditions, the "superior" race (or the superior races, i.e., Gobineau's "pure" races) can by definition never coincide with, and especially never restrict itself to, the totality of the national population.[3] Consequently, the "visible" (because institutional) national collectivity must adjust its aspirations and, if possible, its transformations according to another, "invisible," collectivity, which transcends frontiers and is by definition transnational. But what was true of the aristocracy and might appear to be the transitory consequence of the modes of thought of an era when nationalism is only beginning to establish itself remains true of *all* later racist theories, whether their imaginary referents are of a biological (in fact: somatic) or cultural historical order. Skin color, shape of the head, intellectual predispositions, wit are *beyond* positive nationality: it is only the other side of the obsession with purity that we have encountered. There follows from this a paradox, which many analysts have run up against: there well and truly exists an "internationalism," a racist "supranationalism," that tends to idealize certain timeless, or pseudotemporal, communities such as "the Indo-Europeans," "the West," "civilized man" (thus communities both open and closed, without frontiers, or whose only frontiers are, as Fichte said, "interior," inseparable from the individuals).

Here the excess of racism over nationalism works in the opposite direction, distending it, inflating it to the dimensions of an infinite totality. Whence the more or less grotesque similarities to and borrowings from theology, "gnosis." Whence also the risks of sliding toward racism that universalist theologies run when they are rigidly subjugated to modern nationalism (the "Arab-Islamic nation").

But this dimension of universality plays an essential role in the constitution of nationalism itself. Thus anti-Semitism has functioned on a *European* scale. Each nationalism has seen in the Jews—themselves contradictorily thought of as irreducibly inassimilable to others and as cosmopolitical, as people rooted in history and yet uprooted—*its* special enemy and the representative of *all* its other "hereditary enemies" (in France the Jew is a "German," in Germany a "Slav"). But all the nationalisms have thus had the same foil, the same "stateless person," who has been a latent component of the very idea of Europe, as land of "modern" national states.[4] At the same time the European, or Euro-American, nations fiercely competing for the world's colonial spoils recognized an identity and an "equality" in this very competition, which they baptized "white." Here again a racial signifier transcends national differences and organizes transnational solidarities, so as, in return, to assure the effectiveness of nationalism.

Let us go a step further: when certain historians claim to identify a *universalist* design in nationalism—meaning by that a pretension and a program of cultural imperialism (imposing on all humanity an "English," "German," "French," "American," or "Soviet" conception of man and universal culture)—all the while sidestepping the question of racism, their argument is at best incomplete. For it is only *qua* racism—or *qua* "ethnocentrism," if one prefers; but I fail to see any difference, once it is a matter of the absolute, innate, "natural" superiority of the white race, Western values, and so on—that imperialism has been able to transform itself from a simple enterprise of conquest into a project of universal domination, the founding of a "civilization": that is to say, insofar as the imperialist nation has been pictured and presented as the particular instrument of a more essential mission or destiny, one that other peoples cannot fail to acknowledge.

It is not surprising to find, in these circumstances, that contemporary racist movements, beginning with Nazism have given rise to the formation of international "Axes," what Wilhelm Reich provocatively called "nationalist internationalism"[5]—provocatively but justly, because he was seeking to understand the mimetic effects of this paradoxical internationalism and of another internationalism, which tended more and more to become an "internationalist nationalism," as Communist parties, following the example of the "homeland of socialism" (and around and below it), turned themselves into "national parties," sometimes exploiting anti-Semitism. Even more decisive was the symmetry that, since the middle of the nineteenth century, contrasted the representation of history as "class struggle" and as "race struggle," both thought of as "international civil wars" in which the destiny of humankind plays itself out. Both of them are in this sense supranational: with the one significant difference that class struggle is supposed to dissolve nationalities and nationalisms, whereas race struggle is supposed to establish the immortality and hierarchy of nations, and so permits nationalism to fuse the specifically national element and the socially conservative element (militant antisocialism and anticommunism).

This leads us to the conclusion that is perhaps hardest to admit, yet is undeniable when contemplated seriously: racism is unquestionably *a philosophy of history*, and, above all, *this philosophy is itself a humanism*. Let me clarify, in order to remove the foreseeable ambiguities: I mean a theoretical humanism. Racism is a philosophy of history, or better yet a historiosophy, by which I mean a philosophy that *merges* with an interpretation of history, but makes history the consequence of a "secret" hidden and revealed to men about their own nature and birth; a philosophy that *reveals the invisible cause* of the destiny of societies and peoples, ignorance of which accounts for degeneration or for the historical power of evil. Of course there are aspects of historiosophy in providentialist theologies of history, in philosophies of progress, evolutionist philosophies in general, but also in dialectic philosophies. Marxism is not exempt, which contributes significantly to feeding the effects of symmetry between "class struggle" and "race struggle," between the motor of progress and the enigma of evolution, hence to the possibilities of transition and transfer from one ideological universe into another. This symmetry nevertheless has very clear *limits*. I am not thinking so much of the antithesis of rationalism and irrationalism, the definition of which runs the risk of circularity, nor of the antithesis of historical optimism and pessimism, although it is true (and practically conclusive) that most racist philosophies present themselves as inversions of the theme of progress, in terms of decadence, degeneration, degradation of race, culture, identity, and national integrity.[6] Rather I have in mind the fact that a historical dialectic — unlike a historiosophy of race or class struggle, or of the antagonism between "the elite" and "the masses," or of the competition between adapted and nonadapted types of humanity — can never present itself as the simple elaboration of a Manichaean theme. It has to explain not only the "struggle" or "conflict" but also *the historical constitution* of the forces and forms in conflict; in other words, it has to ask some critical questions regarding its own representation of the course of history. The historiosophies of race and culture are, from this point of view, radically acritical.[7]

Definitely there does not exist a *single* racist philosophy of history or historiosophy, all the more so since the latter does not always take the form of a system. In taking up elsewhere the question of contemporary neoracism,[8] we have already encountered some of its historical and national variations: the myth of "race struggle," evolutionary anthropology, "differentialist" culturalism, sociobiology, and so forth. Around this constellation there revolve sociopolitical discourses and techniques such as demography, criminology, and eugenics. It would be advisable also to retrace the various genealogies of racist theories that, via Gobineau or Chamberlain, but also the psychology of nations and sociological evolutionism, sink their roots into the anthropology and natural history of the Enlightenment.[9] In short, what I wish to underline is the persistence, in these theories, of the humanist problematic.

In fact, theoretical racism has been unable to establish itself except as humanism. What masks it from us, and makes us hesitate to admit it and draw its consequences, is in the first place the chronic confusion between *theoretical* and *practical* humanism:[10] if we identify the latter with a politics and an ethics of the defense of human rights, without limitations or exclusions, we can easily see that racism and humanism are incompatible, and we understand without difficulty why effective antiracism has had to set itself up as a "consistent" humanism. From this it does not follow, however, that practical humanism is necessarily based on a theoretical humanism (i.e., on a doctrine that makes of human beings, *qua* individuals or *qua* species, the origin and the end of rights, both declared and instituted). It can also be based on a theology, or a secular wisdom that subordinates the idea of human beings to that of nature, or else, what is clearly different, on an analysis of social conflict and liberation movements that substitutes specific social relations for the generality of human beings and the human species. Conversely, the necessary link of antiracism with practical humanism—which I propose to read the other way round, that is, to invert:[11] *today practical humanism can exist as such only if it is, in the first place, an effective antiracism*—in no way prevents theoretical racism from also being a theoretical humanism. This means quite simply that the conflict here unfolds in the space of humanism, or by means of theoretical instruments that humanism supplies.

It could be shown distributively, by analyzing a large number of variants of racist discourse, or genealogically, by following the trajectory of racist themes from the eighteenth-century speculations on the origin of the diversity of human races to the current anthropological doctrine of the transhistoric universality of cultural differences.[12] The tricky part is obviously the examination of "biological" racisms, which are at the origin of the widespread idea that racism is theoretically an *antihumanism*, since it values "life" to the detriment of properly human values: knowledge, personal dignity. There is confusion and error here. Confusion, because the "biologism" of racial theories (from anthropometry to sociobiology) does not value life as such, even less an application of biology; rather it is a *vitalist metaphor*, more or less subtle, for certain social values—energy, initiative, and generally all representations of mastery and domination; or on the contrary, passivity, sensuality; or even solidarity, *esprit de corps*, and generally all representations of societal "consensus" and "organic" unity. This vitalist metaphor is associated with a hermeneutics or a "clinical analysis" [*clinique*] that turns *somatic* features into the stigmata and symptoms of psychological and cultural "units." There is also error, because biological racism itself has never been a way of *dissolving* human specificity in the vaster totality of life, evolution or nature, but on the contrary a way of using pseudo-biological notions to *constitute* the human species and improve it or preserve it from decline (it is here that the Nietzschean dialectic of the "Superman" and the "higher man" can enlighten us). As Colette Guillaumin has put it so well: "These marked categories of biological difference are placed, and considered to be, at the very heart of the human species. This remark is of paramount importance. Indeed the human species is the key notion in relation to which racism has constituted itself and continues daily to constitute itself."[13] It would not be so difficult to organize intellectually the fight against racism if the "crime against humanity" had not been perpetrated in the name and by means of a humanist discourse. It is this fact, perhaps first and foremost, that brings us face to face with what, in another context, Marx called the "underside" of history, from which nevertheless it in fact derives its reality.

From this standpoint, it is possible to list some of the intellectual operations that are at work in theoretical racism (and are linked to the "desire to know" of everyday racism). There is first *the fundamental operation of classification*, that is to say, the reflection within the human species of the difference that constitutes it, the search for the criteria according to which men are men: What makes them so? To what extent are they men? What kind of men are they? This classification is presupposed by any hierarchical organization and can lead to it, because the more or less coherent construction of a hierarchical table of the groups that make up the human species is a privileged representation of its unity *in* and *through* inequality. But it can be self-sufficient, as pure "differentialism." (At least it can appear to be so because, as I have explained elsewhere in response to several recent analyses of contemporary racist discourse,[14] the criteria of differentiation cannot be "neutral" in practice: they incorporate sociopolitical values that are often challenged and that have to be imposed via the detour of ethnicity or culture. Differentialism *shifts* the discrimination of classified groups toward the criteria of classification themselves—it is a "secondary" racism—just as it shifts the naturality of "races" toward the naturality of "racist attitudes.") Classification and hierarchy are above all else operations of naturalization, or more accurately, the projection of historical and social differences onto an imaginary nature. But here again we must not let ourselves be taken in by the obviousness of the result. "Human nature," in conjunction with a system of "natural differences" at the heart of the human species, is no immediate category. In particular, it necessarily incorporates sexual schemata, on the side of "effects" or symptoms (racial "characteristics," whether psychological or somatic, are always sexualized) and on the side of "causes" (interbreeding, heredity): whence the central importance of the theme of *genealogy*. But genealogy is anything but a category of "pure" nature; it is a symbolic category permeated with juridical connotations (legitimacy of descent). Thus contradiction is latent in the naturalism of race, which not only falls within the province of the imaginary, but must reach beyond itself toward a "supernature." The nature of racism is not one of proportional causes and effects, immanent regulations: it is a nature that is "inherent," "immemorial," always already valorized.[15]

This first aspect immediately introduces a second: any theoretical racism necessarily refers to *anthropological universals*. It is even, in a sense, the way in which theoretical racism chooses and combines them that specifies it, and it is the succession of anthropological universals, backed up by the history of science, of law, of world economy, that constitutes its doctrinal evolution. Among these universals are to be found of course the notions of "the genetic heritage of humanity" or "the cultural tradition," but also more specific concepts such as human *aggression* or, conversely, "preferential" *altruism*,[16] which lead to different (unequally valued) variations of the ideas of "xenophobia," "ethnocentrism," and "tribalism." (We find here the opportunity for double-dealing that permits "neoracism" to mount a rear attack on the antiracist critique: sometimes directly dividing humanity and organizing it into a hierarchy, sometimes turning itself into an explanation of the "natural necessity" of racism itself.) And these ideas in turn are based on other universals, either sociological and structural (for example, the idea that endogamy is a more or less codified condition and norm of every human group, and hence that exogamy is an object of universal anguish and prohibition) or psychological (for example, imitation, suggestion, and "hypnotic contagion" — the old standbys in the psychology of crowds).

In all these universals we find the *same question* repeated: *the difference between humanity and animality.* This difference should in no way be dismissed, but retaining it causes a problem. Its problematic character is reemployed in interpreting the "conflicts" of human society and human history. In classic social Darwinism, we thus find the paradoxical figure of an evolution that must *extract* humanity properly so called (i.e., culture and technological mastery of nature, including that of human nature: eugenics) from animality, but *by means* that typify animality (survival of the "fittest"), in other words by an animal competition *between* degrees of humanity ("nearest" to and "furthest" from animal origins). In contemporary sociobiology and ethology, "socio-affective" behaviors of individuals and groups (aggression and altruism) are represented as the indelible mark of animality in evolved humanity. One could get the impression that this theme is totally absent from differentialist culturalism. I believe that it is nonetheless to be found there, in an oblique form, in the frequent coupling of the discourse of cultural difference with that of ecology (as if the isolation of cultures were the precondition for the preservation of the "natural habitat" of the human species), and particularly in the unallayed metaphorical representation of cultural categories in terms of individuality, reproduction, interbreeding. Let us not forget that we are at present discussing not conventionally defined scientific concepts but words, that is to say, signifiers and their imaginary effects. The animality of man, in man and against man (whence the systematic "bestialization" of racialized individuals and human groups) is the particular method that theoretical racism adopts in thinking about human historicity. It is a historicity that is paradoxically immobile, if not regressive, even when it provides a stage for the affirmation of the "will" of the higher men.[17]

Just as racist movements represent the paradoxical and, in certain circumstances, all the more effective synthesis of the contradictory ideologies of revolution and reaction, so too theoretical racism represents the ideal unity of transformation and fixity, or repetition and destiny. The "secret" whose exposure it continually replays is that of a humanity forever emerging from animality, and of a humanity eternally menaced by the grip of animality. That is why, when it substitutes the signifier "culture" for the signifier "race," it must always attach that culture to a "heritage," a "lineage," a set of "roots," all signifiers of the imaginary face-off between man and his origins.

It would, however, be a mistake to think that theoretical racism is incompatible with transcendence, as certain well-intentioned critics of culturalism have it. These critics, moreover, commit the same error with respect to nationalism, of which they see only the romantic, vitalist, particularist forms.[18] Racist theories necessarily involve an aspect of sublimation, an *aesthetic* idealization of the species: this is why the sublimation must be achieved by the description and valorization of a certain *type of man*, who exhibits the human ideal, in both body and mind—from yesterday's "German" and "Celt" to the "gifted" of today's "developed" nations (so much the better if they pump iron and run the marathon). This ideal connects at one and the same time with the man of the origins (nondegenerate) and with the man of the future (the Superman). It is a critical point, as much for understanding the way in which racism and sexism are articulated (the importance of the phallic signifier in racism) as for connecting racism to the process of exploitation of labor and political alienation. (An analysis of the aesthetic interpretation of social relations, as the contribution of racism to the constitution of the "projective field" of politics, needs to be developed elsewhere.) Even the idealization of the pragmatic and technocratic values of decisiveness, efficiency, entrepreneurial spirit, presupposes an aesthetic sublimation (it is not by chance that the modern executive, whose enterprises must dominate the planet, is both an athlete and a seducer). And the symbolic reversal that, in the socialist tradition, has prized the figure of the *worker* as the fully realized type of future humanity and the "bridge" between extreme alienation and extreme power, is accompanied, we know, by a great emphasis on the aesthetic and the sexual that has permitted its "co-opting" by fascism, and obliges us also to ask ourselves which elements of racism have historically reverted to "socialist humanism."[19]

In the excess of meaning and activism that marks the transition from nationalism to racism *within* the field of nationalism itself (and crystallizes its distinctive violence), the side that wins paradoxically is not therefore particularism but universalism: a deranged but indisputable variant of humanism.[20] Racism can function as supernationalism, which is in fact its dominant practical function, only when it can introduce into its representation of history and politics a universal theme both supra- and extranational.

NOTES

1. It has often been suggested that nationalism, unlike the other leading political ideologies of the nineteenth and twentieth centuries, *lacks theory* and theoreticians; cf. Benedict Anderson, *Imagined Communities: Reflections on the Origin and Spread of Nationalism* (London: Verso, 1983);

Isaiah Berlin, "Nationalism: Past Neglect and Present Power," in *Against the Current: Essays in the History of Ideas* (New York: Viking, 1980). I shall take up this question later in connection with the philosophy of history.

2. *Nationalisme intégral* is the key notion in the doctrine of Charles Maurras (1868–1952), leading theoretician of French nationalism and founder of *Action Française*. Cf. Eugen Weber, *The Nationalist Revival in France, 1905–1914* (Berkeley: University of California Press, 1959).

3. On Gobineau, cf. in particular Colette Guillaumin's essay, "Aspects latents du racisme chez Gobineau," in *Cahiers Internationaux de Sociologie*, 42 (1967).

4. It is notably through the common exclusion of Jews—later Arabs—by all the nations, even though born from the dissolution of the former politico-theological unity of the Middle Ages, that the signifier "Christendom" has come to mean "Europe" or European civilization. Naturally some intellectuals have also forged the idea according to which Europe as such does not exist *without the Jews* and the Jewish tradition: thus the Jews, who have no territory of their own in Europe, no national *status*, would be the catalyst of the community of European peoples and of the "consciousness" of their destiny. Thus we are presented with a myth mirroring the myth of Christendom. And the game of mirrors can go on: when the "Judeo-Christian dialogue" is begun, the essence of Europe is at stake, etc.

5. Cf. Wilhelm Reich, *Les Hommes dans l'Etat* (Paris: Payot, 1978); French trans. of *Menschen im Staat: Die emotionale Pest der Menschheit* (Frankfurt: Nexus, 1972).

6. The introduction of the "pessimistic" theme of degeneration in racist social Darwinism, when it obviously has no function in the Darwinian theory of natural selection, is an essential stage in the ideological exploitation of the theory of evolution (playing on the ambiguity of the notion of *heredity*). But all racism is not *categorically* "pessimistic," although it is *hypothetically* pessimistic: the superior race (culture) is lost (and human civilization with it) *if* it winds up "drowned" in the ocean of inferiors. Differentialist variant: *all* the races (cultures) are lost (and therefore the one and only human civilization) if they drown each other in the ocean of their diversity, if the "order" that they together make up degenerates into the entropy of homogenized "mass culture." Historical pessimism leads to a voluntarist or decisionist conception of politics: only a radical decision, expressing the antithesis of pure will and the natural course of events—thus the antithesis of men of will and passive men—can thwart, indeed reverse, the decline. Whence the dangerous proximity that is established when Marxism (and more generally socialism) drives its representation of historical determinism all the way to *catastrophism*, which in turn calls for a "decisionist" response (a decisionist conception of revolution).

7. Nietzsche's ambiguity derives from his development, with respect to racist historiosophy, of a second-order reflection that follows two inextricably tangled orientations. On the one hand, starting with the unrelenting critique of anti-Semitic demagogy, there emerges an excessive Manichaeism, privileging the aesthetic intelligence of the elite over the "resentment" of the masses: a superracism, as it were. On the other hand, a critical genealogy of the very concepts that make all historiosophy possible: pessimism, will, power, good and evil, and in the last analysis the concepts of humanism as they reside also in evolutionism and historical determinism.

8. Etienne Balibar, "Y amt-il un néo-racisme?", in Balibar and Wallerstein, *Race, Nation, Classe*.

9. Cf. in particular the works of Michèle Duchet, *Anthropologie et histoire au Siècle des Lumières* (Paris: Maspéro, 1971); "Racisme et sexualité au XVIIIᵉ siècle," in Léon Poliakov (ed.), *Ni juif ni grec: Entretiens sur le racisme*, vol. 2 (Paris-The Hague: Mouton, 1978); "Du noir au blanc, ou la cinquième génération," in Léon Poliakov (ed.), *Le Couple interdit: Entretiens sur le racisme*, vol. 3 (Paris-The Hague: Mouton, 1980). The recent book by Louis Sala-Molins, *Le Code Noir, ou le calvaire de Canaan* (Paris: PUF, 1987), supplies the politico-juridical counterpoint: slavery as legal concept.

10. I borrow the distinction between theoretical and practical humanism (or antihumanism) from Louis Althusser.

11. [The author's reference is to Marx's Postface to the second edition of *Capital*, vol. 1, trans. Ben Fowkes (New York: Vintage Books, 1977), p. 103 – Trans.]

12. The anthropological writings of Roger Bastide and Michel Leiris epitomize antiracist theorizing because, unlike Lévi-Strauss, they adopt a position counter to this postulate.

13. *L'Idéologie raciste: Genèse et langage actuel* (Paris-The Hague: Mouton, 1972), p. 6.

14. "Y amt-il un néo-racisme?"

15. On Nature as "phantasmic Mother" in racist and sexist ideologies, cf. C. Guillaumin, "Nature et histoire: A propos d'un 'matérialisme,' " in *Le Racisme: Mythes et sciences*, ed. Maurice Olender (Brussels: Complexe, 1981). On symbolism and the imaginary in genealogy, cf. Pierre Legendre, *L'Inestimable Objet de la transmission* (Paris: Fayard, 1985).

16. See the way in which sociobiology organizes "altruistic sentiments" into a hierarchy: first the immediate family, then the extended family – kin altruism – then the ethnic community. Cf. Martin Barker, *The New Racism: Conservatives and the Ideology of the Tribe* (London: Junction Books, 1981; Frederick, Md.: Aletheia Books, 1982). [See Barker's essay in this volume. – Ed.]

17. It will be said that there is nothing new or specific about this configuration, which is as eternal as the unconscious (cf. Poliakov et al., *Homes et bêtes: Entretiens sur le racisme*, vol. 1 [Paris-The Hague: Mouton, 1975]), as old as the metaphorical correspondence between the classification of animal species and the perception of sociological differences (cf. the works of Lévi-Strauss on the "savage mind" and his critical discussion of the notion of "totemism"). I will reply first that the idea of archaism that lurks in these objections is itself ambiguous: it suggests that racism *would be the manifestation of the unconscious*, or the vestige of an "ethnic mind," now lost, nostalgia for which racism would embody. Second, what matters is the distortion to which contemporary ideologies submit the categories of animality and humanity: they form part, no longer of a cosmology, but of a history, whose motor, differential of movement, they exhibit. There follows not, as Georges Bataille postulates (*La Souveraineté*, in *Oeuvres complètes*, vol. 8 [Paris: Gallimard, 1976], p. 371), the "sacred character of the difference between man and animal," but the *use* of this difference as signifier of the "sacred," name of the origins and ends of man, in a racist theory of history. There would be moreover a good deal of work to be done (I do not know if it has been undertaken) in the images and practices of *zoophilia* associated with racism (dogs, but also horses and monkeys). Cf. some brief remarks in Max Horkheimer and Theodor W. Adorno, *Dialectic of Enlightenment*, "Man and Animal," trans. John Cumming (New York: Herder & Herder, 1972), pp. 252–55.

18. Cf. Alain Finkielkraut, *La Défaite de la pensée* (Paris: Gallimard, 1987).

19. On Nazism's aesthetic interpretation of social relations, there exists a vast literature: cf. Philippe Lacoué-Labarthe, *La Fiction du politique* (Paris: Bourgois, 1988). In *The Nazi Question: An Essay on the Interpretations of National Socialism (1922–1975)*, trans. Robert Hurley (New York: Pantheon Books, 1981), p. 12, Pierre Ayçoberry notes that Nazi aesthetics "has the function of obliterating the traces of class struggle by situating each category in its proper niche in the folkish community: the uprooted peasant, the athlete and prodution worker, the woman at home." Cf. also A. G. Rabinbach, "L'Esthétique de la production sous le III⁹ Reich," in *Le Soldat du travail: Guerre, fascisme et taylorisme*, ed. Lion Murard and Patrick Zylberman, *Recherches*, no. 32/33 (September 1978).

20. Hannah Arendt, speaking of "supersense" in the concluding remarks to *The Origins of Totalitarianism*, 1st ed. (New York: Harcourt, Brace, 1951), pp. 432ff. (cf. also 2nd ed., 1958, chapter 13), does not relate it to a process of idealization, but to the terrorist constraint that would be inherent in the mania for "ideological consistency"; even less to a variety of humanism, rather to the absorption of human will into the anonymous movement of History or Nature, which the totalitarian movements propose to "accelerate." (For Arendt herself, humanism is synonymous with transcendence.)

CHAPTER 18

The Social Formation of Racist Discourse

David Theo Goldberg

⌊The history of racism is given definition by changes in the conception of "race." The concept of race crept into European languages in the fifteenth century, and its scientific and popular usage peaked in the eighteenth and nineteenth centuries. Its unfortunate traces continue to mark social and political thought and experience. The link between racism and race is obvious: racism is generally considered to be discrimination against others in virtue of their putatively different racial membership. The social abuse we have come this century to call "racism" mirrors in some respects the linguistic and conceptual abuse perpetrated under the banner of race. The various redefinitions of race, and transformations in the technologies of racial classification and recognition partially reflect and are reflected in the differing forms assumed by racism since the Enlightenment.⌋

⌊There is considerable historical variation both in the conception of races and in the kinds of social expression we characterize as racist.⌋⌈The challenge consists in establishing a general theory in virtue of which the disparate phenomena commonly considered racist can be conceived—and opposed.⌈ ⌊For ultimately the efficacy of a theory *about* racism is to be assessed in terms of the ways in which it encourages and makes possible resistance to racism.⌋

⌊I will argue that racism is to be conceptualized at a deep structural level in terms of a group of central constitutive elements. These elements furnish

I discussed drafts of this essay with the Greater Philadelphia Philosophy Consortium Workshop, and with the Law and Society Workshop at New York University. I am grateful to the participants in both groups for their helpful comments. I would like especially to thank Peter Fitzpatrick for his careful critical reading and comments. This paper was completed with the assistance of a grant from the Office of Special Projects, Drexel University.

the key to a unified account of racism. The history of racism will be read in terms of reinterpretations and transformations of these elements (or of additions to them) in light of new problematics, changed circumstances, or trenchant criticisms. Further complicating the temporal ruptures and conceptual discontinuities of racist history is the relatively recent proliferation of explanatory accounts of racism's rise, functions, logics, and practices. In some instances, the misrepresentations thus encouraged have fueled rather than dowsed racism. Part of the challenge, then, would be to show how these accounts fit into the general theory of racism to be developed here. However, this task lies largely beyond my present scope.

[Racism will be characterized here in terms of a model for picking out racists on the basis of the kinds of beliefs they hold. Racists are those who explicitly or implicitly ascribe racial characteristics of others that they take to differ from their own and those they take to be like them. These characteristics may be biological or social. The ascriptions do not merely propose racial differences; they assign racial preferences, and they express desired, intended, or actual inclusions or exclusions, entitlements or restrictions. Racist acts based on such beliefs fall under the general principle of *discriminatory behavior against others in virtue of their being deemed members of different racial groups*. However, in some cases behavior may be deemed racist on the basis only of its outcome. The mark of racism here will be whether the discriminatory behavior reflects a persistent pattern *or* could reasonably have been avoided. Thus, I intend to include as racist, for example, the behavior of nonprejudiced prosecutors who use their peremptory challenges to exclude blacks from juries in the trials of black defendants solely for the sake of securing a conviction. Racist institutions are those whose formative principles incorporate and whose social functions serve to institute and perpetuate the beliefs and acts in question.[1]

The cluster of properties suggested here are offered as general guidelines that, given specific circumstances, will help to determine whether a belief, intention, act, consequence, principle, rule, or institution is racist. Instead of specifying necessary and sufficient conditions, we cannot say more than that all things racist bear to each other family resemblances. There is "a complicated network of similarities overlapping and criss-crossing: sometimes overall similarities, sometimes similarities of detail."[2]

The challenge here is to develop a theoretical framework sufficiently wide in scope to include these detailed similarities and differences. The hypothesis I will explore is that racism is to be considered in terms of a *field of discourse*.[3] As a theoretical construct, the discursive field of racism is sufficiently broad to incorporate the various entities constitutive of racism. Taken independently, these constitutive entities fall under the category of *expressions*. Racist expressions include beliefs and verbal outbursts (epithets, slurs, etc.); acts and their consequences; and the principles on which racist institutions are based.

Yet the "field of racist discourse" is a designation intended also to include the set of texts that undertake to analyze and explain racism's historical formations and logics.

On this view, beliefs and descriptions are theoretically basic. Beliefs and descriptions are directly accessible to analysis and interrogation. Acts and their consequences, or institutions and their principles, must be described, translated first into texts, to furnish a form appropriate for analysis. Beliefs and expressions may be conveyed either directly (spoken, enacted) or indirectly (reported, in writing). The former are transcribable likewise into the latter, and so they are open to analysis on the same basis.

At the most general level of description, the domain of racist discourse is populated by two sets of texts: the expressive and the analytic. Racism has been variously analyzed as rationalizations for psychosexual fear, economic or social disparities; for cultural exclusions; or for political entitlements. I have argued elsewhere that racism is not inherently irrational, that some racist responses to given circumstances and available evidence may be rational, although they are never moral.[4] Yet racist texts are constituted by beliefs in the narrower sense. They are expressions of racist principles, supposed justifications of differences, advantages, claims to superiority (whether considered "natural" or "developed"), and of racist practices and institutions. These expressions have assumed widely divergent forms: scientific, linguistic, economic, bureaucratic, legal, philosophical, religious, and so forth.

Interpreting racism as a field of discourse can be used accordingly to organize the family resemblances among the data of racism. But the concept will be used in this discussion also as an explanatory device. The primary puzzles here are how and why the forms of racist expression have changed over time. Mapping the field of racist discourse will enable us to address them.

A well-defined field of discourse arises out of a *discursive formation*. This consists of a totality of ordered relations and correlations — of subjects to each other and to objects; of economic production and reproduction, cultural symbolism and signification; of laws and moral rules; of social, political, economic, or legal inclusion and exclusion. The sociodiscursive formation consists of a range of rules: "is's" and "oughts," "do's" and "don'ts," "cans" and "cannots," "thou shalts" and "thou shalt nots." Conditions of existence, production and reproduction, preservation, transformation and dissolution at a given historical conjuncture define an *object* that can be spoken of. They determine also the *mode* in terms of which the object can be analyzed, its elements named and classified, its functions explained. Rules constitutive of a discursive field are promoted in this elaboration of object and mode.[5]

Racism exists as the effect of — that which is given rise to by — established relations between subjects and institutions, economic and social practices; by patterns and principles of conduct and ethics, classificatory systems and technologies of power. Racism is not simply present in these relations, nor is it reducible to them or to any one of their constitutive elements. Hence the failure of any attempted explanation of racism solely in terms of economic determinism, sociological or biological reductionism.[6]

Specifying racism's "genealogy" and "ontology" in this way highlights a point often overlooked. [The ethnocentrisms of socioepistemic conjunctures prior to the seventeenth century, although forerunners of racism, were not themselves forms of racist expression. "Slavery" and "barbarianism" are discursive objects that were differently constituted and structured than racism.] They make no legitimating appeal to any concept having its originary place in scientific discourse the way race has. There is a wide schism between these earlier forms of subjection, exclusion or subjugation, and racism. This rupture is reflected in the discourses defining these disparate phenomena.

Three general factors make up the methodological terrain of sociodiscursive fields: sociohistorical conjuncture; formal components and relations constitutive of the discourse; and the subjective expression or internalization and use of the discourse — here, racism — by subjects. My concern to account for the "success" of racism in pervading cultures leads me to focus on the formal structure of racist discourse, and on its assumption and expression by individual (racist) subjects.[7]

The Structures of Racist Discourse

In a field of discourse like racism what is generally circulated and exchanged is not simply truth but truth claims or representations. These representations draw their efficacy from traditions, conventions, institutions, and tacit modes of mutual comprehension.[8] Analysis of the representations must reveal the objects to which they refer, and the styles of reference found in the figures of speech and metaphors as well as in the categories and expressions of the discursive field. But the analysis must uncover more than this. In the relations between the expressions lies a *grammar*; and underlying the categories representing the objects is a *preconceptual plane* or set of *primitive terms*. Analysis of the structures of racist discourse must seek to explain both the grammar and preconceptual primitives.

The Grammar of Racist Discourse

The question here is whether a unified grammar of racist discourse can be identified. For if it cannot, much more than simply the grammar's existence is thrown in doubt. Skeptics may gather strength in claiming that the public expression of racism has been much less pronounced than its critics charge.

The implications for public policy and for moral judgments of individual behavior are thus considerable.

It has been shown that the unity of an individual work is partially determined by lexical distribution and the connectivity of vocabulary in it.[9] The discursive unity of racism—what marks it off as a discourse separate from others—is not so strictly determinable. The field of racist discourse cuts across different languages, works, acts, and institutions. Although the assumptions, principles, and purposes of racist discourse might loosely circumscribe its content, the discursive unity is not so well defined as it is for a given work. It fails to furnish a foundation sufficiently firm for textual determination by lexical distribution and vocabulary periodicity. Clearly the unity of racist discourse cannot be established on narrow grammatical grounds.

Cornel West has suggested that the unity of racist discourse is a product of the "structure of modern discourse . . . the controlling metaphors, notions, categories and norms that shape the predominant conceptions of truth and knowledge in the modern West." This "complex configuration of metaphors, notions, categories, and norms produces . . . [a] . . . normative gaze" that in turn "produces and promotes such an object [white supremacy] of modern discourse." The unity of racist discourse accordingly is "a product of" and is "promoted by" these controlling metaphors, notions, categories, and norms, that "produce and prohibit, develop and delimit forms of rationality, scientificity and objectivity which set parameters and draw boundaries for the intelligibility, availability and legitimacy of certain ideas."[10]

One can object to each of the claims West seems to be making here. Discursive unity is not a product of figures of speech (including metaphors). Discourse is only expressed by such means, and partially so. The metaphors of racist discourse are not reducible to a single form: "Nigger dogs" and "Blacks (or Red Indians) are savages"[11] differ in form, substance, and probably in the specificity of their purposes from "the Jewish conspiracy" or Chamberlain's "Aryan race-soul," but also from "Sambo, the typical plantation slave [as] docile but irresponsible, loyal but lazy, humble but . . . lying and stealing."[12] It is not simply that color racism and anti-Semitism differ in virtue of the fact that blacks are referred to as animals and Jews only in the context of some abstruse mythology. For Jews are often described in terms of animal imagery;[13] and a color racism relying on character-trait stereotyping need have no recourse to animal metaphors.[14]

It might be suggested—at least this is one way of reading West—that discursive unity is a function either of a prevailing corpus of norms or of a prevailing style. These norms would be established in terms of a series of descriptive statements about others that delimit the way we perceive them.

Style, in turn, is the dominant mode of discursive expression. Neither is adequate to the task of unifying racist discourse.

The discourse of racism does not consist simply in descriptive representations of others. It includes a set of hypothetical premises about human kinds (e.g., the "great chain of being," classificatory hierarchies, etc.), and about the differences between them (both mental and physical). It involves a class of ethical choices (e.g., domination and subjugation, entitlement and restriction, disrespect and abuse). And it incorporates a set of institutional regulations, directions, and pedagogic models (e.g., apartheid, separate development, educational institutions, choice of educational and bureaucratic language).[15] Norms or prescriptions for behavior are contextually circumscribed by specific hypotheses, ethical choices, regulations, and models. Yet no unidirectional norms are basic to racist discourse: a decision that one race is intellectually inferior to another may be taken as the basis of a norm of exclusion from educational institutions, or of the concentration of special resources.

Similarly, the mode of racist expression—its style—may be interpreted variously as aversive, academic or scientific, legalistic, bureaucratic, economic, cultural, linguistic, religious, mythical, ideological, and so on. Racist descriptions, hypotheses, choices, modes, and rules of discourse have altered over time. This precludes the possibility of establishing a singular transhistorical stylistic or normative pattern.

A complementary criticism can be launched against attempts to establish discursive unity on the basis of common objects referred to, or common themes developed and spoken about, in the discourse of and concerning racism. Anti-Semitic statements pick out objects different from those racist statements that objectify blacks. The theme of an anti-Semitic slur (e.g., "Communist conspirators!" as grounds for excluding Jews from trade unions or political office)[16] largely differs from that of antiblack ones ("Dumb nigger!" as the ground for restricting blacks to manual labor or slavery). Various objects are named, described, analyzed, and judged—in a word, they *emerge—in* the discourse, just as themes are chosen, delineated, and developed *in* speaking. Determined by the discursive field, these objects and themes cannot be all that differentiates the discourse of racism from other discourses.

Themes and objects emerge only in discourse, delineated by the set of norms, principles, hypotheses, and choices, and articulated in figures of speech and styles. The grammar of racist discourse assumes coherence and uniqueness only when compared from the vantage point of the discourse as a whole with another discursive field. If discursive unity is to be achieved, it can only be a product of those underlying factors that directly generate the discursive field. Foucault calls this set of factors the *preconceptual* level.[17] I have already suggested that they be likened to "primitive terms" in an artificial language. Grammatical changes in descriptions, hypotheses, rules, models, norms, and styles are reflected in transformations in the preconceptual grounds of racist discourse. The structural unity of racist discourse must be sought in a transformational schema of its preconceptual set, and "in the interplay between their location, arrangement and displacement."[18]

The Preconceptual Grounds of Racist Discourse

The preconceptual set consists of those factors of power, including dominant values, that directly enable the expression of racist discourse. These conceptual primitives are not abstract a priori essences; they do not constitute an ideal foundation of the racist discursive formation. On the other hand, the set of primitives are not to be confused with the actual concepts and terms by which racist discourse is usually expressed. These primitives are manifestations of relations of power vested in and between historically located agents, and they are effects of a determinate social history. Factors of power vested in and between historically located agents effect rules that determine the transformations, inferences, and references for the field of discourse. They generate the concepts and categories in terms of which racism is expressed and comprehended. Thus, these preconceptual factors define in a general way the expression of those agents, and only those, who speak and act in terms of racist discourse.

It follows that the unity of racist discourse is not given in any purportedly ahistorical durability of racism. The discourse of racism transforms—arises, alters, and perhaps will eventually disintegrate—both with actual social conditions and with conceptual reformulations. The coherence of the racist project, then, is a function of the preconceptual elements that have structured racist dispositions. These include classification and order, value and hierarchy; differentiation and identity, discrimination and identification; exclusion and domination, subjection and subjugation; entitlement and restriction, and in a general way, violence and violation. Historical derivation of these preconceptual elements or primitives of racial discourse requires illustration.

Classification is basically the scientific extension of the epistemological drive to place phenomena under categories. The impulse to classify data goes back at least to Aristotle. Yet classification is established as a fundament of scientific methodology only as function of the "*esprits simplistes*" of the seventeenth century and the Enlightenment.[19] With its catalogues, indices, and inventories, classification establishes an ordering of data; it thereby furnishes systematicity to observation.[20] Yet it claims also to reflect the natural order of things. As such, this ordering of representations always presupposes value: Nature ought to be as it is; it cannot be otherwise.[21] The seemingly naked body of pure facts is veiled in value.

The data that lent themselves most readily in the eighteenth century to systematic seeing, to representations by rules, were clearly those of biology and natural history. Extended to human affairs, the pervasive spirit of simplicity sought to reproduce for social relations the sort of simple order thought to inhere in nature.[22] Hence the application of categories of speciation (racial classification, etc.) to human groupings on the basis of natural characteristics. Perhaps the major assumption underlying anthropological classification at the same time was that identification of races in terms of their differentia is adequate to establish the laws of behavior for their members.

So, classification is central to scientific methodology; and scientific method, in turn, was taken to furnish the ideal model of rationality. The capacity for rationality, however, was considered the mark of humanity. It seemed, obvious, then, that the anthropological ordering into a system of races in terms of rational capacity would establish a *hierarchy* of humankind. The race represented by the classifiers was considered to stand at the hierarchical apex. Racial ordering accordingly implied a racial hierarchy, and a behavioral expectation. The rational hierarchy was thought to be revealed through its physical—natural—correlates: skin color, head shape, body size, smell, hair texture, and so on. This engendered a metaphysical pathos, an aesthetic empathy or aversion. Because it was putatively natural, this pathos was considered rational.[23]

Thus racial classification—the ordering of human groups on the basis of putatively natural (inherited or environmental) differences—implied a racial hierarchy of races. The derivation of hierarchy from classification rested on the long-standing assumption that the universe is perfectly intelligible to reason, and on the *principle of gradation* inherent in this. Formulated initially as Aristotle's "hierarchy of being," this principle was adopted later as a fundament of Christian thought. It evolved systematically "from a less to a greater degree of fulness and excellence."[24] The neutrality and distantiation of the rational scientist created the theoretical space for a view to develop of subjectless bodies. Once objectified, these bodies could be analyzed, categorized, classified, and ordered with the cold gaze of scientific distance.

So, the principle of gradation was employed to ground racial classification. Classification, then, could claim to provide an objective ordering. The subjectivity of aesthetic taste and judgment, of empathy and aversion, was applied to this objectification of human subjects. The full weight of eighteenth-century science and rationality, philosophy, aesthetics, and religion thus merged to circumscribe European representations of others.[25] This reduction of human subjects to abstract bodies had the objectifying effect of enabling their subjection to the cold scientific stare of Europeans and their descendants.

The principle of gradation carries also a moral implication: higher beings are considered of greater worth than lower ones.[26] The chain of elements—classification, order, value, hierarchy—is supposed to delineate the realm of possibilities at each level of existence. If "ought implies can," the range of moral imperatives is thereby delineated and a ladder of command accordingly authorized. The ladder of command consists in a hierarchy of imperatives and injunctions that simultaneously reflects and cements the putative racial order. This hierarchy of command is promoted by a complex configuration of power relations and its representations. Yet the structure of commands serves also to perpetuate the given relations of power.[27] For example, various interpretations of the principle of gradation considered it justifiable to treat "lower racial orders" as animals, subjecting their members to forms of labor and living conditions otherwise reserved for animals. Polygenicists like Edward Long reasoned that because "Negroes" and whites are incapable of forming properly fertile hybrids ("mulattoes"), they must constitute different species. Long held that "Negroes" are not properly human and ought not to be treated as such. A century later, leading scientists and social theorists in Europe and the United States encouraged inferences in the same vein.[28] The principle of gradation, it could be said, is at once a principle of degradation.

Classification, order, and value are fundamental to the forms of rationality we have inherited. Socially, it is evident that we still labor under the constraints of this rationalized authority. We order our relations with others in its light. The principle of racial hierarchy is now widely considered obsolete. This has motivated various responses to racist thinking and discourse. The most widespread is that the concepts of *inferiority* and *superiority* implicit in "racial hierarchy" are part of a buried scientific paradigm. It would follow that the ladder of command they authorize has no scientific or rational legitimacy. At best, the theory of racism is thought accordingly to be like the phlogiston theory of gases in the Enlightenment: despite empirical discoveries and new scientific paradigms, the phlogiston theory persisted to the turn of the nineteenth century.[29] At worst, racism is dismissed as a crude rationalization for the domination and subjugation of others. A more sophistic response has been the denial that racist principles any longer exist: if the principle of natural hierarchy has been abandoned, there can be no concept of racist superiority commanding acts or authorizing differential distributions.[30]

In abandoning appeals to superiority connoted by hierarchical classification, racists are committed neither to irrationality and rationalization nor to extinction. History for the moment aside, although hierarchy may not be implicit in the concept of racial classification *difference* surely is. This is borne out by the synonym "racial differentiation." *Difference* and *identity* inhere in the concept of race, furnishing the grounds for racial classification. Domination of a particular race is established in respect of a series of differences from other individuals or groups, and by virtue of a series of identities between like beings. The choice of what is to count as a relevant difference or identity is not determined simply by the prevailing discursive primitives outlined earlier. The choice is overdetermined in that it is circumscribed by various assumptions effective in social or scientific discourse at the time.[31]

Racial differentiation—the discrimination *between* races and their purported members—is not in and of itself racist. Racial identity, even when externally ascribed, implies unity. When this identity is internalized it prompts identification, a sense of belonging together. Only then does racial differentiation begin to define otherness, and discrimination *against* the other becomes at once *exclusion* of the different.[32] Elaboration of racial differences and identities has sufficed since the seventeenth century as the leading mode of determining exclusions and inclusions. In contemporary terms, it allows racists to applaud the debunking of social hierarchies. Yet it serves, in the same breath, to establish unity for modern racist discourse.

Exclusion on the basis of difference furnishes common ground for the transformational schema generated by classification. *Differential exclusion* is the most basic primitive term of the deep structure definitive of racist discourse. As the basic propositional content of racist desires, dispositions, beliefs, hypotheses, and expressions (including acts, laws, and institutions), racial exclusion motivates the entire superstructure of racist discourse. Most notably, racial exclusion establishes the racial mark of entitlement and restriction, endowment and appropriation. So racial exclusion functions in at least two general ways. It serves as *presumption* in the service of which rules or rationalizations may then be formulated or offered. Or it may be concluded as the *outcome* of practical deliberation in some domain—in economics, say, or pedagogy, or legislation.

The institutional "success" of racial exclusion in its various forms presupposes a suitable authority. The authority is required to distinguish the beneficiaries of the entitlement (those who would enjoy the fruits of the endowment) from those to be restricted in their enjoyment or denied their rights, goods, and services. Now the sense of belonging together is too vague as such to furnish a mode of discriminate differentiation and exclusion. The sense of belonging must either manifest in or be predicated on establishment of an authority (institutional or personal) in the body or person(s) of whom group members partially recognize themselves. By internalizing this authority and subjecting themselves to the law thus authorized and enforced, group members incorporate themselves and establish cohesion. In this way, the group so constituted acquires also a privileged moral position.[33]

This identification of, with, and by means of an authoritative body thrusts the question of the mode of exclusion to a prior level. It may be evident that the sense of identity with others is encouraged or cemented by mutual recognition of an authority. Yet it is not clear what the primary motivating factors of a sense of mutual belonging could be. If this is established, it remains an open question whether the authority in fact appeals to these factors as the underlying modes of differentiation and exclusion, and as a foundation for moral privilege. Moreover, initiation and promotion of a group's self-recognition in the form of an authority may not be contractual at base. Promotion and manipulation of group self-consciousness may be a function — in a peculiar way — of some assumed theoretical (or ideological) corpus.

Social Power and the Body of Racist Discourse

Each *episteme* is characterized by a "regime of rationality." This consists not simply in a collection of objective truths to be discovered and affirmed, but in what Foucault calls a "general politics of truth." A set of discursive rules emerges from an economy of epistemological production in virtue of which "truth" may be differentiated from "falsity."[34] At issue in any such economy are competing interpretations of the language of truth, assertion, and representation — in a word, "knowledge."

Foucault suggests that "nothing is more material, physical, corporeal than the exercise of power," or (in my terms) than the exercise of authority. If this is so, then authority can be something ideal. The drive to exercise authorial power — whether out of the pure pleasure of the act or as a means to further ends — clothes itself in the theoretical fashions of rationality. Authority is established and exercised only by being vested with the force of discrimination, exclusion, and enforcement. If the canons of value and taste in which authority resides have the power to effect material ends, it must be that these canons themselves embody material force.[35]

Racist discourse has for the most part dominated the definition of otherness, and furnished the material power for the forceful exclusion of the different. To succeed so long in doing this, racist discourse has to be grounded in the relations of bodies to each other, and in ways of seeing (other) bodies. Voyages of discovery and imperialist drives may have prompted the presumption of general differences among conquering populations and conquered; yet the rise of racist discourse was rendered *theoretically* possible only by a change in paradigm from the seventeenth century onward of viewing human subjects. The new philosophical assumption that bodies are but machines naturally divorceable from minds promoted novel developments in technologies of physical power and bodily discipline. These technologies of discipline and power were superimposed on human subjects; they encouraged docility by reducing subjectivity to physical dimensions and correlates.[36]

So racist discourse may be seen to acquire unity in terms of bodily relations, that is, in certain forms of "the investment of the body, its valorization, and the distributive management of its forces."[37] This unity highlights the material force at racism's heart. The "distributive management of bodies" enabled by color racism, for example, extended the space in which capital accumulation, the growth of productive forces, and the massive generation and redeployment of surplus value could take place. It is in virtue of racist discourse and not merely rationalized by it that such forced manipulations of individual subjects and whole populations could have been affected.

I have suggested that racial exclusion finds whatever authority it has in a discourse of the body, and that this "body talk" (so to speak) forges an underlying though abstract unity for the discourse of racism. More must be said by way of establishing the body as an object of analysis.

From the standpoint of human subjects, nothing is more "natural" to think and speak about than the body. It is directly experienced; its deficiencies are immediately felt; and it is the receptacle of pleasures and pains, desires and needs. The bodies of others are unproblematically observable, confronted, and engaged. In other words, the body is central to ordinary experience. It offers a unique paradigm: it is a symbol of a "bounded system" whose parts and functions are related in a complex structure, and whose substance is confined by boundaries and limits that are fragile, vulnerable, and threatened. By extension, the body may be found to stand for the body politic, to symbolize society.[38]

As a mode of exclusion, racist discourse assumes authority and is vested with power, literally and symbolically, in bodily terms. They are human bodies that are classified, ordered, valorized, and devalued. They are human bodies that, because of their differences, are forced to work, alienated from their labor product, disenfranchised or restricted in their right of social entry and mobility. Corporeal properties furnish also the metaphorical medium for distinguishing the pure from the impure, the diseased from the clean and acceptable, the included from the excluded. Classification of differences determines order. Hierarchy is established on the basis of a value of purity — whether interpreted biologically (in terms of "blood" or "genes"), hygenically (in terms, for instance, of body odor), culturally (for example, language as signifying the evolution of thought patterns and rational capacity), or even environmentally (character, like nose shape and size, as determined by climate). Impurity, dirt, disease, and pollution are expressed as functions of the transgression of classificatory categories, as too are danger and the breakdown of order. Actively undertaking to transgress or pollute the given order necessitates reinventing order by way of confinement and artificially imposed separation.[39] So anti-Semitic representations have often been deployed to exclude "Jewish bodies" from European neighborhoods or active participation in European economies, and Palestinian presence on the West Bank has been curtailed in the name of purity and order.

Moreover, techniques of racial prohibition inherited the repressive apparatuses formerly imposed against leprosy and witchcraft. These were redefined in light of newly evolved technologies of insanity. Aided by the theoretical tools of modern science, they were tailored to contemporary social conditions.[40] This heritage of repressive exclusion is best exemplified by the case of Robben Island, off the South African shores of the Cape of Good

Hope. There lepers first, then the mentally insane, and now black political rebels have been incarcerated. Thus Robben Island has come to signify, in the symbolism of South African politics, the wider artificial incarceration of others, their general exclusion—only lately in terms of race—that it is the point of South Africa's "separate development" policy to police.

Instruments of exclusion—legal, cultural, political, or economic—are forged by subjects as they mold criteria for establishing racial otherness. Racism is promoted—perhaps entailed—by this discourse of the body, with its classificatory systems, order, and values, its ways of "seeing" particular bodies, and most fundamentally its modes of exclusion. Paradoxically, racist discourse has succeeded in drawing social subjects together. It has served to unify them as subjects of authority. Subjects have been able to recognize identity in terms of this discourse, as too they can be identified by it. The discourse of racism furnishes a cohesive foundation for the body politic, a continuity in time, across authorities. It is a discourse authors of the law might invoke as justification of entitlements or restrictions, endowments or lacks, incorporation or disenfranchisement.

Thus racist discourse enters the domains of morality and legality as a set of foundational claims. Its asserted title to establish differences is taken as an objective basis of inclusion and exclusion, whether natural or historical. This is offered, in turn, as a primary ground of entitlements, of rights of accessibility (to enfranchisement, opportunity, or treatment), and of endowments (goods and the means thereto); and conversely, of denial (disenfranchisement or restriction), of prohibition (to entry, participation, or services), and of alienation (of goods and the means to them). In general, the discourse of racism "justifies" the exclusion of others by denying or ignoring their respective claims. It encourages active interference in establishing what the excluded, the disenfranchised, and the restricted are entitled to and can properly expect.

This question of exclusion and entitlement is exemplified most vividly by immigration policy. Eugenicists addressed the political, legal, and moral issues of immigration from the standpoint of their "scientific" findings. Earlier this century prominent eugenicists in the United States and Britain argued that members of alien racial stocks should be excluded or severely restricted from entering these respective countries to prevent weakening or to improve the biological quality of the local stock. In Britain, East European Jews were especially singled out.[41] In the United States, the national quota on population entrance from any country in Europe was reduced to 2 percent of residents of that origin in the nation in 1890. "Orientals" were eventually excluded altogether, culminating in the complete ban on Japanese immigration in 1924. The European Bill had the intended effect of favoring among immigrant stocks the "desirable" English, Irish, Germans, and Scandinavians over the "inferior stocks" of new immigrants from Eastern and Southern Europe.[42] More recently, exclusion, disenfranchisement, restriction of entry and mobility, and denial of the means to fulfill needs and wants have been justified in South Africa, Thatcher's Britain, and Israel. Although not racially explicit in formulation, the new U.S. immigration restrictions, Germany's *Gastarbeit* policy and France's migrant labor system are racist in effect: they restrict entry of members of undesirable population (or racial) groups.[43]

I have argued that the formal apparatus of racist discourse has multiple overlapping determinations. They include the economy of power and its relations pertaining at a given historical conjuncture, a new way of looking at bodies, and new modes of speaking about others. This new mode of speaking is defined in terms of technologies of classification and the analysis of differences and identities; new forms of institutionalized prohibition—for instance, on bodily contact implied by the concept of heredity, or on land tenure implied by the appeal to historically granted land rights. As a discourse of exclusion, racism appeals either to inherent superiority or to differences. These putative differences and gradations may be strictly physical, intellectual, linguistic, or cultural. Each serves two functions: it purports to furnish the basis for justifying differential distributions or treatment, and it represents those very relations of power that prompted them.

The discursive unity of racism is promoted by transformational structures effected from the schema of preconceptual primitive terms laid out earlier. At specific sociohistorical conjunctures this schema generates the concepts peculiar to the enunciation of racism at that time and place, and thereby the categories, stereotypes, expressions, metaphors, styles, and themes expressed in the field of racist discourse. To establish racism specifically as a discourse, however, the preconceptual schema must give rise also to racist hypotheses and presumptions, indeed, to racist argumentation, reasoning, and rationalization.

If the widespread employment and influence of racist discourse is to be fully comprehended, it is the *persuasiveness* of argumentation that must be accounted for. This suggests a factor of the racist discursive formation that remains to be analyzed. To show how agents have so readily expressed racist discourse, it must be illustrated how agents subject themselves to modes of expression, making these modes of expression their own; whom subjects direct these expressions and reasoning at, and why; and what subjects might aim to gain from this way of expressing themselves.

The Racist Subject

Adoption of racist discourse has been widespread. It has been assumed across classes, nations, social and ethnic groups; in different places, at different times, and under widely varying conditions. This cannot be explained solely in socioeconomic, political, or historical terms. Such explanations are singular in ignoring a central feature: the persuasiveness of racist discourse, that is, its compelling character for agents. Similarly, the prevailing presumptions of racism's irrationality, and of the "false consciousness" of racists, stress the psychosis of the racist personality rather than his or her persuasion, conscious belief and conviction, or rational willingness.[44] To comprehend this widespread domestication of racist discourse, the question of human agency and the formation of subjectivity must be addressed.

I have suggested that a primary factor in the formation of social groups is the self-recognition of group members in the image of an authority (whether institutional or personal). This recognition may be realized in terms of various media. *Interpellation* is the process by which individuals are "hailed" or called to subjectivity by others, and so it presupposes mutual recognition by agents. The formation of subjectivity is thus inherently social. Emile Benveniste argues that individuals are interpellated as subjects in and by means of language.[45] This hypothesis raises the possibility of a novel framework in conceiving the constitution of the subject: as the point of convergence, the bodily intersection, of multiple discourses. Whatever properties and (Kantian) categories are thought to constitute humans *qua* human, individuals are defined as *subjects* by way of social discourses. Discourses are the intermediary between self and society; they mediate the self as social subject.[46]

Discourses like racism are the products of the economy of power, the interrelations of bodies, produced and refined in practice. However, social discourses do not just reflect the economy of power, with its characteristic relations of domination, subjugation, and exclusion. Once initiated, social discourses are placed in the arsenal of the "practico-inert,"[47] ready to be passed along, inherited, reproduced, and transformed to suit prevailing conditions. By converging with other discourses and interiorized by the individual, the discourse of racism comes to define not only subjectivity but also otherness. It molds the subject's relations with others. Subjects' actions are rendered meaningful to themselves and others in light of the values this discourse, as others, makes available or represents to the parties involved.[48] In this way, racist discourse—reproduced, redefined perhaps, and acted on—reconstitutes the relations of power that produced them.

Just as language furnishes a key for becoming conscious of oneself as distinct from the world, social discourse provides the means for social self-definition. Naming one's race, on the plane of racial identity, functions similarly to naming oneself at the level of self-consciousness and self-identity. The possibility of the former necessitates self-recognition by the individual in the image of the social fathers (e.g., white leaders, the nation's founding fathers, a Jewish Jehovah, the Aryan Superman, etc.), as self-consciousness presupposes self-recognition by youths in their own patriarchal (or matriarchal) heroes. Each level of subjection—to authoritative discourses or to racial authority—is established by way of sociolinguistic symbols. These symbols incorporate general rules and taboos that represent The Law: the "Law of Authority" in general, or the "Racial Law" in particular. Once internalized, these discursive bodies of law, and others like them, give social definition to the subject.

This analogy between the forms of law constitutive of the social subject is obviously assymetrical. The "Patriarchal Law of Authority" is central to the constitution of human subjectivity in a way in which "Racial Law" and racist discourse are not. The Law of Authority serves perhaps as a model, an ideal, for the definition of individual subjectivity by social discourses. This is partially reflected in the fact that it is for the most part less wrenching to abandon the likes of Racial Law, to give up racist discourse, than it is to transgress the Law of Authority, although of course there are times when these will be coincidental. This renunciation or shift to other discourses, like modifications internal to the discourse, might reflect more or less subtle changes in the economy of power. It is possible, however, that they are in some ways determined rather by features specific to the psychological and bodily formation of agents themselves.

The social subject, I have maintained, consists in the intersection of social discourses in the body. The dimensions brought by the body to the equation are the (bounded) capacities to desire and to think. It is discourses, though, that furnish the media for thought and for articulation of desires. Kant's famous dictum may be emulated to express the state of subjectivity: discourses without desires are empty, desires without discourses blind.[49] Because human subjects fail to act save on the impulsion of desires, discourses on their own would be unmotivated. Hence they would be empty, in the sense of producing no effect. Conversely, a desire not yet defined by a discourse could only be blind (indiscriminate). The intentions, motives, dispositions, expressions, and acts of the racist are obviously discourse specific. These determinations by discourse may be conscious and explicit, or inadvertent as with unconscious slips and misstatements that reveal repression and wish fulfillment.[50]

On the conscious level, discourses articulate and thereby give definition to intentions, dispositions, reasons, and goals. The general intention, disposition, desire, or goal of the racist may be expressed as (relative) *racial exclusion*. The extension of this expression may include both specific racist goals and reasons (whether cited as justification or rationalization). Racists may intend, desire, or be disposed to exclude racial others with the goal in mind of domination or subjugation; of maximizing profit by maintaining a cheap labor force, a reserve army of labor; of reserving jobs for members of what they take to be their own race; or of maintaining indigenous culture; and so on. As reasons for or as the general principles they take to inform their acts, racists may offer the goals themselves or various other categories of reason. These include, although they may not be limited to, scapegoating (e.g., a conspiracy theory), rationalizations (like inferiority), or rational stereotyping (e.g., a normative judgment appealing to factual evidence). These motivations a subject may have to act in a racist way are complemented by other factors. They include fear, whether brought on by the threat of physical force or psychologically induced; and conformism, that is, the behavioral disposition, imposed or merely encouraged, to conform to the needs of the community.[51] Such factors, in turn, may be a function of racist discourse in the process of reinforcing itself.

The field of racist discourse is a product of sociodiscursive praxis in determinate historical circumstances. The power of racist discourse conjoins with the power of other discourses — notably although not only those of class, gender and (lately) nation — to determine the subjectivity of agents at a given time and place. What begins to emerge from this racial subjectivizing is a subjection to violence. The violence of racism afflicts both the objects of racist acts and the racist subject. Violence is inherent in racist discourse. Subjects are defined in general by the discourses of difference. So subjects recognize themselves for the most part only in contrast to others. The recognition of the self in the other remains an alienated identity, an "identity-in-otherness." Self-determination is a precondition for self-recognition or self-conscious identity. This assertion of self-determination requires that the other — literally the other's otherness — be negated or canceled. Where this "identity-in-the-other" is racially predicated or defined by racial discourse, the drive to self-consciousness may become a negation of the racial other, the other's exclusion. Tabulating racial differences as an order of what Sartre calls "alterity," defining others so as to exclude them, is at once to constitute the other as enemy, to engage him or her in relations of violence.[52]

This establishment of the other *as* other is promoted by the initial drive to establish self-identity by identifying *with* the other. Negating others, denigrating them, becomes in part thus also self-negation and self-denigration.[53] The pleasure of violating another is not simply a product of self-assertion. It involves, although often self-deceptively, also the masochistic perversion of self-violation. By contrast, in responding to this violence the other may vacillate between the hardships of active resistance and the relative comforts of passive resignation. This hesitation signifies prior acquisition of the preconditions of the victim's own subjection and violation. The subjection at work here all too often presupposes acquiescence by the victims to the preconcepts of the discourse that motivated their exclusion: persecution approaching self-persecution (the "persecution complex") and then projected as the vicious persecution of others. Anti-Semitism illustrates the point: the modes of Jewish subjugation are reproduced in Israeli exclusion and violence against Palestinians.

Nevertheless, the self-assertive drive to determine one's conscious identity reveals an ambiguity in the determination of subjectivity by racial discourse. For, in negating another subject's *racially* defined otherness, the possibility of compatibility and solidarity beyond race may be entertained. The problem of dissolving racist discourse is thus dialectically posed.

Against Racist Discourse

I have argued that the issues concerning the discourse of racism may be addressed on three levels: sociodiscursive economies of power and value; formal or "grammatical" structures; and subjective expression. I have focused here primarily on the second, and more speculatively on the third. It is clear at every level that racist discourse consists of multiple determinations. These include sets of practices, expressions, disciplines, and institutions; relations of power, struggles, and repressions; violations and violence. I leave to another occasion a detailed demonstration of how the transformational schemata for racist primitive terms, categories, and concepts are actualized historically by subjects and expressed in determinate circumstances.

I must leave to another occasion also development of my contention that the prevailing mode of analyzing racism in the social sciences serves subtly to entrench rather than to dissolve the discourse of racism. I should say only that much of the standard studies of racism in the behavioral sciences like social psychology perpetuate presuppositions and concepts that have been fundamental to the history of racist expression. Thus, empirical research in these disciplines continues to presuppose the existence of races and racial differences, if not of "racial attitudes," whether conceived as natural or social. The research, then, forms part of disciplines that constitute social subjects as passive objects — of examination, classification, and calculation. In failing to examine their own presuppositions, these disciplines perpetuate racial categories and the constitution of subjects in racial terms. They contribute inadvertently therefore to the potential for racist discourse to persist.[54]

Further, there is a need to distinguish here, as in respect of other forms of socially unacceptable practices, between *cruelty* and *coercion*. Coercion is often ignored in favor of cruelty. Analysts presume, on the basis of evidence that institutional cruelty of a racist kind has been outlawed, that the repugnant forms of racist expression no longer exist. If temptations to racist expression are to be fully resisted, there is a need to confront racially motivated and effected coercion. Such coercion may assume the form of perpetuated impoverishment, social exclusion, maintenance of artificial differences, artificial institutional exclusivity, and so forth. Acquiescence to and participation in coerced practices is no mark of their social acceptability or moral justifiability. It is of the nature of coercion that the coerced have few if any viable alternatives to the practices with which they are confronted. Resistance to racist discourse requires actively opposing practices coercive as much as cruel.[55]

Discursive resistance includes but is not limited to political resistance. The latter involves organized collective activity aiming to alter the distribution of power. Resistant activities may range from unbridled violence at the extreme to highly organized and rationally planned opposition.[56] Discursive formations of a social sort, like racism, are more diffuse than political institutions. They are accordingly more difficult to confront directly. To succeed in dissolving racist discourse, then, opposition must assume suitably diverse forms.

In general, the line of analysis adopted here suggests that the factors fundamental in opposing racist discourse and practice are three in kind: first, the radical alteration of its socioeconomic determinants, and not just internal modification of some of its constitutive elements; second, transformation and extinction of the formal components, its grammar and language. Serious efforts to this effect in literary theory and in disciplines like anthropology have already begun.[57] Yet resistant practices need to be directed against more than the intellectual culture in which racist discourse enshrouds itself. They must be encouraged at the center of populist political practices. An obvious example concerns opposition to the projected hegemony of English as the only official language of administration in the United States; another, the discriminatory effects of capital punishment or voter apportionment. Widespread dissolution of racist discourse, however, is likely to occur only once the grammatical or linguistic features are rendered irrelevant to or inconsistent with the material determinants of the first level. This suggests the third possible approach. The particular forms of subjective racist expression must be ended by altering subjective practice. This amounts to abandoning racist discourse on a conscious psychological plane. Abandonment might be prompted by a realization that the discourse no longer serves the subject's individual or group-related purposes. More to the point, though, abandonment must be encouraged by attacking racist reasoning or expression at every occurrence. The primary undertaking here is to promote competing social discourses in light of which subjects' desires, motives, dispositions, and goals will be defined.

This latter strategy necessitates developing appropriate counterdiscourses to racism across every domain: social, political, legal, economic, historical, cultural, biological, and perhaps most fundamentally, moral. These discourses must inform the formation of social subjectivity. Active opposition and resistance must be encouraged in light, say, of egalitarian theories, a commitment to discourses of extensive equalities in rights, claims, and powers. There is a need to proceed with caution here. The discourse promoting resistance to racism must not prompt identification with and in terms of categories fundamental to the discourse of oppression.[58] Resistance must break not only with *practices* of oppression, although its first task is to do that. Resistance must oppose also the *language* of oppression, including the categories in terms of which the oppressor (or racist) represents the forms in which resistance is expressed.

Here, and finally, it may prove useful to distinguish between a discourse of authoritative orders and injunctions coercively imposed on subjects, and a discourse constructively assumed because it authorizes and articulates acceptable acts and thereby empowers the oppressed. It is to the task of formulating the latter that any comprehensive stance against racism now beckons us.

NOTES

1. David Theo Goldberg, "Racism and Rationality," unpublished ms.

2. Ludwig Wittgenstein, *Philosophical Investigations*, trans. G. E. M. Anscombe (Oxford: Basil Blackwell, 1968), #68.

3. The view that racism consists in a field of discourse is explicitly suggested by Cornel West, and less directly by Edward Said in his stimulating analysis of Orientalism. West simply summarizes in brief the bare threads of Foucault's original specification of the concept of "discursive field," applies it to a limited "genealogy of racism," and suggests how it might be incorporated into a more sophisticated Marxist historiography. By contrast, Said's more detailed investigation streamlines the concept's applicability to the specific confines of Orientalism. This is more institutionalized than the object of my concern. Cf. Cornel West, *Prophesy Deliverance! An Afro-American Revolutionary Christianity* (Philadelphia: Westminster Press, 1982), pp. 47–68; Edward Said, *Orientalism* (New York: Pantheon Books, 1978), pp. 1–4. See also Said's "Zionism from the Standpoint of Its Victims," in this volume.

4. Goldberg, "Racism and Rationality."

5. Cf. Michel Foucault, *The Archaeology of Knowledge*, trans. A. Sheridan-Smith (London: Tavistock, 1972), pp. 38, 45, 179.

6. For a fuller argument supporting this claim, see David Goldberg, "Raking the Field of the Discourse of Racism," *Journal of Black Studies*, 17 (Fall 1987), pp. 58–71.

7. Although various sociohistorical conjunctures of racism have been widely discussed, omissions, misrepresentations, and misunderstandings persist. I discuss some of these in "Raking the Field of the Discourse of Racism." Paul Gilroy's recent critique is exemplary. Paul Gilroy, *There Ain't No Black in the Union Jack* (London: Hutchinson, 1987). See also Gilroy's "One Nation under the Groove," in this volume.

8. Said, *Orientalism*, pp. 21–22.

9. "Once the system of content has been settled in outline not only the main items of the vocabulary needed for the expression, but also their relative frequencies are, by and large, determined, the system of content determining how often a particular word will appear in combination with other words." Gustav Herdan, *Type-Token Mathematics*, quoted in Peter Caws, "On the Determination of the Text," in *About French Poetry from Dada to "Tel Quel*," ed. Mary Ann Caws (Detroit, Mich.: Wayne State University, 1974), pp. 278–79.

10. West, *Prophesy Deliverance!* pp. 50, 49, 53. Two general features should be noted about West's analysis. First, he substitutes the concepts of "production" and "promotion" for "determination." His aim is thereby to evade difficulties internal to Marxist analysis. But it is difficult to discern in his analysis any real difference in the *use* of the substitutes. Second, West considers modern racism (which he equates with "white supremacy") to be a *product* of modern discourse,

one of its *objects*. However, he has taken the view — at least in conversation — that racism is itself a discourse.

11. The former is taken from Joseph Baldwin, *The Flush Times of Alabama and Mississippi* (New York: Appleton, 1853), p. 300. For the latter representation in antebellum Southern literature, see Alan Rose, *Demonic Vision* (Connecticut: Archon Books, 1976), pp. 46ff.

12. See Houston Stewart Chamberlain, *The Foundations of the Nineteenth Century*, ed. George Mosse (New York: Howard Fertig, 1968), pp. 542ff. Alfred Rosenberg, Hitler's court philosopher, made much of this notion in *Race and Race History*, ed. R. Pois (New York: Harper & Row, 1970), pp. 35ff. For the depiction of Sambo in historical sources, see Joseph Boskin, *Sambo* (Oxford: Oxford University Press, 1986).

13. "[Jewish elders] have the tenacity of a snake, the cunning of a fox, the look of a falcon, the memory of a dog, the diligence of an ant and the sociability of a beaver." Hermann Goedsche (under the pen name of Sir John Radcliffe) in his novel *Biarritz*, (1868). Quoted in George Mosse, *Towards the Final Solution: The History of European Racism* (New York: Howard Fertig, 1978), p. 117.

14. For a comprehensive collection of analyses, see Henry Louis Gates, Jr. (ed.), *"Race," Writing, and Difference* (Chicago: University of Chicago Press, 1986); Sander Gilman, *Pathology and Difference* (Ithaca, N.Y.: Cornell University Press, 1984); Tzvetan Todorov, *The Conquest of America* (New York: Harper & Row, 1984). See also Nancy Stepan, "Race and Gender: The Role of Analogy in Science," in this volume.

15. Cf. Foucault, *Archaeology of Knowledge*, p. 33.

16. An entry in Himmler's diary associates Jews with reds. Examples abound in which Jews are identified as "red." Mosse, *Towards the Final Solution*, p. 178.

17. Cf. Foucault, *Archaeology of Knowledge*, pp. 32–36.

18. Ibid., p. 60.

19. Arthur Lovejoy, *The Great Chain of Being* (New York: Harper Torchbooks, 1960), pp. 7ff. If introduction of words into the language is any guide, "classification" appears only in the eighteenth century. L. Febvre, "The Problem of Unbelief in the Sixteenth Century," in *Historians at Work*, ed. Peter Gay and George Cavanaugh (New York: Harper & Row, 1975), p. 111.

20. "Every note should be a product of number, of form, of proportion, of situation." Carolus Linnaeus, *Philosophie Botanique*, #299. Quoted in Michel Foucault, *The Order of Things* (New York: Random House, 1970), p. 134. Foucault calls this ordered observation "seeing systematically."

21. Peter Caws, "Order and Value in the Sciences," in *The Concept of Order*, ed. P. Kuntz (Seattle: University of Washington Press, 1968), p. 106.

22. Lovejoy, *Great Chain of Being*, p. 8.

23. The assumptions and reasoning are uniform, whether those of Kant's hardheaded rationalism or Buffon's and Lamarck's environmentalism. Although author of the principle that "all men are (created) equal," Jefferson believed that nature condemned the "Negro" to inferiority on the scale of being: "Blacks, whether originally a distinct race or made distinct by time and circumstance, are inferior to the whites in the endowment both of body and mind." Thomas Jefferson, *Notes on the State of Virginia* (Chapel Hill: University of North Carolina Press, 1954), p. 143. These premises run clear through Darwinism, eugenicism, and the IQ movement. Cf. Stephen Jay Gould, *The Mismeasure of Man* (New York: Norton, 1981).

24. Lovejoy, *Great Chain of Being*, p. 317.

25. The Protestant Episcopal Bishop of Kentucky in 1883: "Instinct and reason, history and philosophy, science and revolution alike cry out against the degradation of the race by the free commingling of the tribe which is the highest (whites) with that which is the lowest (blacks) in the scale of development." Quoted in Charles Herbert Stember, *Sexual Racism* (New York: Harper Colophon, 1976), p. 38.

26. Lovejoy, *Great Chain of Being*, p. 320.

316   David Theo Goldberg

27. Cf. Louis Dumont, *Homo Hierarchus* (Chicago: University of Chicago Press, 1970), pp. 66–67.

28. "The planters do not want to be told that their Negroes are human creatures . . . they . . . [are] no better than dogs or horses." Edward Long, *History of Jamaica* (New York: Arno Press, 1972), vol. 2, pp. 270–71. Long appealed to his contemporary, David Hume, in justification of his racist views: "Mr. Hume presumes, from his observations of native Africans, to conclude, that these are inferior to the rest of the species, and utterly incapable of all the higher attainments of the human mind." Long, p. 376. Cf. David Hume, "Of National Character," in *Philosophical Works*, ed. T. H. Green and T. H. Grose (Aalen: Scientia Verlag, n.d.), vol. 3, esp. p. 252n.1.

29. Cf. D. Eckberg, *Intelligence and Race* (New York: Praeger, 1979), foreword by J. Garcia, pp. vii–viii.

30. This reasoning is quite widespread in popular thinking. It is implicit, philosophically, in Michael Levin's claim that the use of the term "racist," like "sexist," is scientifically and morally illegitimate. Michael Levin, "Sexism Is Meaningless," *St. John's Review* (Autumn 1981), p. 40, n.12. Cf. Gilroy, *There Ain't No Black in the Union Jack*, pp. 60ff., and this volume.

31. Foucault, *The Order of Things*, pp. 138ff. Cf. Terry Eagleton, "Wittgenstein's Friends," *New Left Review*, 135 (1982), pp. 66–67.

32. "Belonging together" is Heidegger's term. Martin Heidegger, *Identity and Difference*, trans. Joan Stambaugh (New York: Harper Torchbooks, 1969), pp. 25–26. Identification may be motivated by a variety of factors: economic, political, legal, cultural, linguistic, historical, psychological, or psychoanalytic. It may be more or less rational.

33. Cf. Wilhelm Reich, *The Mass Psychology of Fascism* (New York: Simon & Schuster, 1970), pp. 46–47. Cf. E. Erikson, "The Concept of Identity in Race Relations," in *The Negro American*, ed. T. Parsons and K. Clark (Boston, Mass.: Riverside Press, 1965), pp. 227–53; Louis Althusser, "Ideology and Ideological State Apparatuses," in *Lenin and Philosophy*, trans. Ben Brewster (London: New Left Books, 1971), pp. 170–71. The institutional authority may be as abstract as *the nation*. See Gilroy, "One Nation under the Groove," and Etienne Balibar, "Paradoxes of Universality," both in this volume.

34. Michel Foucault, "Truth/Power," in *Power/Knowledge*, ed. Colin Gordon (New York: Pantheon Books, 1980), p. 131.

35. Foucault, "Body/Power," in *Power/Knowledge*, pp. 57–58. Cf. Edward Said, "The Problem of Textuality: Two Exemplary Positions," in *Aesthetics Today*, ed. M. Philipson and P. Gudel (New York: Meridian Books, 1980), p. 120; and Said, *Orientalism*, pp. 19–20.

36. Michel Foucault, *Discipline and Punish*, trans. A. Sheridan-Smith (New York: Pantheon Books, 1977), pp. 135–69. The coherence drawn by racism from the general discourse of the body may be gleaned from the fact that racist metaphors often turn on corporate references. This may function directly or indirectly. For the former, consider Hume's likening of "negroes" to parrots, or former U.S. Secretary of the Interior James Watt's equations, in a speech on September 27, 1983, of Jews and blacks with "cripples." For the latter, consider the common attribution of the symbolism of dirt to blacks and Arabs. Cf. Julia Kristeva, "Ours to Jew or Die . . . ," this volume.

37. Foucault, *Discipline and Punish*, p. 138.

38. Cf. Mary Douglas, *Purity and Danger* (London: Routledge & Kegan Paul, 1966), p. 115.

39. Ibid., pp. 125; 2–4; 103–4; 162. Cf. Dumont, *Homo Hierarchies*, pp. 47–48; 60. Some eugenicists bemoan the biological vices of racial miscegenation and hybridization between "inharmonious stocks." See Nancy Stepan, *The Idea of Race in Science* (New York: Archon Books, 1982), p. 130.

40. See Bryan Easlea, *Witchhunting, Magic and the New Philosophy* (Hassocks, Sussex: Harvester Press, 1980), p. 33.

41. Karl Pearson, a leading eugenicist in Britain, suggested that only those immigrants be

admitted who displayed physical and mental abilities 25 percent higher than the native British mean. K. Pearson, "The Problem of Alien Immigration in Britain Illustrated by an Examination of Russian and Polish Jewish Children," *Annals of Eugenics*, 1 (1925–26), pp. 1–127. Cf. P. Mudge, "The Menace to the English Race and Its Tradition of Present Day Immigration and Emigration," *Eugenics Review*, 2 (1920), pp. 202–12. See Stepan, *Idea of Race in Science*, p. 130.

42. This bill was advocated by Albert Johnson, Republican Chair of the House Committee on Immigration. In 1923, Johnson was elected president of the Eugenics Research Association. Eugenic presuppositions had wide influence. In 1922, U.S. Vice-President Coolidge claimed in a popular essay that biological laws reveal the deterioration of Nordics when mixed with other races. Thomas Gossett, *Race: The History of an Idea in America* (New York: Schocken Books, 1966), p. 466.

43. For a discussion of recent immigration policy of both Tory and Labor parties in Britain, see Martin Barker, *The New Racism* (London: Junction Books, 1981), pp. 12–29. Cf. Gilroy, *There Ain't No Black in the Union Jack*.

44. These presumptions militate against insistence on moral responsibility of racists. See Goldberg, "Racism and Rationality."

45. Emile Benveniste, *Problems of General Linguistics* (Miami: University of Miami Press, 1971); cf. Althusser, "Ideology and Ideological State Apparatuses," pp. 179ff.

46. I do not mean to imply that the individual, theoretically or historically prior to this discursive intersection, is just a blank tablet, an empty receptacle. One may have an immediate intuition of one's individuality that nevertheless may be actualized and expressed only in and by means of language. Nor need this commit us to untenable forms of relativism. Some physical states and psychological dispositions (e.g., emotions) may be innate although incapable of recognizable expression in a discursive vacuum. Expressions (including acts) are mediated largely by the discourses definitive of the agent's subjectivity. Cf. G. W. F. Hegel, *The Phenomenology of Mind*, trans. J. B. Baillie (New York: Harper Torchbooks, 1967), pp. 529ff; A. Lemaire, *Jacques Lacan*, trans. D. Macey (London: Routledge & Kegan Paul, 1977), p. 53.

47. The "practico-inert" is the "material product of past *praxis*," Jean-Paul Sartre, *Critique of Dialectical Reason*, trans. A. Sheridan-Smith (London: New Left Books, 1976), pp. 318–20.

48. Cf. Jacques Lacan, *Ecrits*, trans. A. Sheridan-Smith (New York: Norton, 1977), pp. 1–7; Althusser, "Ideology and Ideological State Apparatuses," p. 181; Paul Hirst, *On Law and Ideology* (London: Macmillan, 1979), pp. 64ff; M. Shapiro, *Language and Political Understanding* (New Haven, Conn.: Yale University Press, 1981), p. 130.

49. Kant's deep insight: "Without sensibility no object would be given to us, without understanding no object would be thought. Thoughts without content are empty, intuitions without content are blind." Immanuel Kant, *Critique of Pure Reason*, trans. Norman Kemp-Smith (New York: St. Martin's Press, 1965), p. 93.

50. For the distinction between conscious and unconscious factors in the determination of the text, see Caws, "On the Determination of the Text," pp. 274ff.

51. For remarks on fear, see Goran Therborn, *The Ideology of Power and the Power of Ideology* (London: Verso Books, 1980), pp. 94ff. For an account of *conformism* in Heidegger's work, see John Haugland, "Heidegger on Being a Person," *Noûs* (1982), pp. 15–25.

52. Sartre, *Critique of Dialectical Reason*, p. 720.

53. Cf. Hegel, *Phenomenology of Mind*, pp. 229–40.

54. Cf. Goldberg, "Is Racism Inherently Irrational"; Gilroy, *There Ain't No Black in the Union Jack*, p. 105.

55. For an analysis of the distinction between cruelty and coercion with respect to slavery, see G. Frederickson and C. Lasch, "Resistance to Slavery," in *American Slavery: The Question of Resistance*, ed. J. Bracey, A. Meier, and E. Rudwick (Belmont, Calif.: Wadsworth, 1970), p. 179.

56. Ibid., pp. 180–82.

57. See, for example, Gates, *"Race," Writing, and Difference*; the "minority discourse" issues

of *Cultural Critique*, Spring and Fall 1987; J. Fabian, *Time and the Other: How Anthropology Makes Its Object* (New York: Columbia University Press, 1983); Michael Taussig, *Shamanism, Colonialism and the Wild Man* (Chicago: University of Chicago Press, 1987); Francis Barker et. al. (eds.), *Europe and Its Others* (Colchester: University of Essex Press, 1985); Gilroy, *There Ain't No Black in the Union Jack*; Said, *Orientalism*.

58. Examples of the failure so to distinguish abound: The black separatist movement is a case in point. Another concerns tactics of resistance used by plantation slaves: slow work and malingering undermined the plantation economy but reinforced the stereotype of laziness; slave destruction of property fueled the stereotype of incompetence; self-mutilation increased labor costs but steeled the stereotype of barbarianism. On resistance to the slave economy, see R. A. Bauer and A. H. Bauer, "Day to Day Resistance to Slavery," in Bracey, Meier, and Rudwick, *American Slavery*, p. 38. I do not mean thus to devalue the significance of slave resistance. For a problematizing of this and related issues, see the exchange between Todorov and Gates in Gates (ed.), *"Race," Writing, and Difference*.

CHAPTER 19

Critical Remarks

Henry Louis Gates, Jr.

I

> *And this is the highest pitch of humane reason: to follow all the links of this Chain, till all their secrets are open to our minds; and their works advanc'd or imitated by our hands. This is truly to command the world; to rank all the varieties and degrees of things so orderly upon one another; that standing on the top of them, we may perfectly behold all that are below, and make them all serviceable to the quiet peace and plenty of Man's life.*
>
> Thomas Sprat, *The History of the Royal Society* (1667)[1]

Thomas Sprat's words speak eloquently of a period in which the ancient conception of the *scala naturae* could sponsor — with its metaphysics of continuity and hierarchy — a burgeoning science of natural history. Effortlessly identifying imperial and scientific conquest, they speak of the will to classify and its reward: a harmonious social order continuous with a perfectly comprehended natural order. In the middle of the next century, the *Encyclopédie* expressed the same cosmology with only slightly diminished confidence:

> Beings are connected with one another by a chain of which we perceive some parts as continuous, though in the greater number of points the continuity escapes us . . . [therefore] the art of the philosopher consists in adding new links to the separated parts, in order to reduce the distance between them as much as possible. But we must not flatter ourselves that gaps will not still remain in many places.[2]

It is clear, however, that the Enlightenment need to address biologically the nature of the physical differences among people reflects a profound shift in the terms of debate. Graphic accounts of the worlds discovered by courageous navigators, along with, for example, the progressively more exact cartographical approximation of the African continent, introduced a mass of information that demanded some logical framework through which natural philosophers could digest the world as readily as scriptural sanction had allowed. And the European discovery of Africa provided a feature — color — distinctive enough to become a convenient sign to measure various differences among human beings.[3]

The simplest classificatory schemes fasten upon one characteristic that a given group shares but which another group does not, then arranges all specimens into types accordingly. Dr. Thomas Towns, for instance, in a letter dated Barbadoes, March 26, 1675, and published in the Royal Society's *Philosophical Transactions*, argued that the Africans' blood was black, a premise expanded to include variously their brain, skull, and semen.[4] This inclination to classify by color, however exaggerated on occasion, became basic to the classification of the human species in the work of François Bernier in 1684. Bernier does discuss possible alternative bases for classification — including differences of hair, stature, shape of nose and lips — but he settles on color in dividing the human species into four subdivisions. The historic interest of his scheme is that it provides a means of classification that would avoid the implications of continuity and gradation.[5] In this respect, Bernier's approach reached its fullest and most prescriptive form in the work of Linnaeus in the 1730s. Linnaeus — like Johann Friedrich Blumenbach later — explicitly avoided the notion that variety in the human species implies hierarchy, as the *scala naturae* suggested. Pursuing this logic, Christianus Emmanuel Hoppius, Linnaeus's student, could thus suggest that what separated the cultivated European from Hottentots and wild boys was a lack of education.[6]

Even with its metaphysics of continuity and hierarchy, however, a logical tension quickly made itself felt in the context of the Anti-Slave Trade debates. How fine were the links in the chain of being and where did they segment — where were the limits of speciation, of any grouping larger than the individual? Here was a site for critique internal to the generative discourses of eighteenth-century anthropology, and it caused no end of trouble. A mid-eighteenth-century disquisition of Soame Jenyns is typical, in that the instability of categories is evident and unremarked:

> From this lowest degree in the brutal Hottentot, reason, with the assistance of learning and science, advances, through these various stages of human understanding, which rise above each other, till in a Bacon or a Newton it attains the summit.[7]

Moving from a type to a token, the passage represents the hierarchy within a type (a type of Englishman in this case) as identical *in kind* to the divisions between varieties and species.[8] (Where ranks the Newton of the Hottentots?) And the same uncertainty could be employed strategically by the antislavery advocate:

If Negroes are to be Slaves on account of colour, the next step will be to enslave every mulatto in the kingdom, then all the Portuguese, next the French, then the brown complexioned English, and so on till there be only one free man left, which will be the man of the palest complexion in the three kingdoms.[9]

Notice that this classic *reductio* is predicated on the principle of continuity, a principle that was consistent with — indeed, typically allied with — the belief in an order fixed eternally by divine will that is also an order defined by hierarchical gradations.

And this form of *reductio* could eventuate in a more radical rejection of the realist metaphysics of classification, such as we find in the sort of nominalism that was receiving renewed intellectual support in the work of John Locke. A medieval topos with Platonic antecedents, the realist-nominalist dispute recrudesced with a different inflection in the context of the Enlightenment sciences of man, and was quickly enlisted in the Anti-Slave Trade debates. Further, the achieved stature of Locke's *Essay Concerning Human Understanding* itself contributed to the rejection of "the whole business of *genus* and *species*" by some of the greatest naturalists in the latter third of the eighteenth century; indeed, its argument would serve more generally as grounds for the reinterpretation of gradation, plenitude, continuity, and fixity, all buttresses to a "science of man" that was reexamining its notional foundations.

In the Sixth Chapter of Book III of the *Essay*, Locke distinguished between real and nominal essences: "Nor indeed *can we* rank and *sort things*, and consequently (which is the end of sorting) denominate them *by their real essences*, because we know them not." In short,

Our distinguishing substances into species by names is not at all founded on their real essences; nor can we pretend to range and determine them exactly into species, according to essential internal differences.

For "*the boundaries of the species, whereby men sort them, are made by men.*"

The *reductio* from continuity can be distinguished from the more general nominalist skepticism about kinds, but the two worked well in tandem. Here is Buffon (adopting a position he later relinquished): "In general, the more one increases the number of one's divisions, in the case of the products of nature, the nearer one comes to the truth; since in reality individuals alone exist in nature."[10] Bonnet amplifies on the point:

If there are no cleavages in nature, it is evident that our classifications are not hers. Those which we form are purely nominal, and we should regard them as means relative to our needs and to the limitations of our knowledge. Intelligences higher than ours perhaps recognize between two individuals which we place in the same species more varieties that we discover between two individuals of widely separate genera. Thus these

intelligences see in the scale of our world as many steps as there are individuals.[11]

As a reasoned response to the presuppositions of racialist essentialism, this
passage summarizes not just the wisdom of his time, but of ours. Juxtapose
to Bonnet's statement some observations in a recent volume of American Left
political theory, almost two and a half centuries later:

> The differences between two randomly selected white people are likely to
> be greater than the differences between the average genetic
> characteristics—if they are discernible at all—for blacks and whites, Native
> Americans and Asians, and so on.
>   The division of the human species into races is biologically—though not
> socially—arbitrary. We could differentiate humans along countless axes,
> such as height, weight and other physical features. If we assigned racial cat-
> egories to groups of humans with different heights—for example, for every
> foot of height from four feet up determines a new race—we would be more
> biologically precise than the usual racial designation by skin color. For no
> fixed biological boundary exists between Asian and Caucasian, black and
> Indian, whereas a fixed boundary does exist between those who are shorter
> than five feet and those who are between five and six feet.[12]

We can easily see the same skepticism about the categorization (the insistence
that differences within the groups are no less than those without) as well as
the principle of continuity ("no fixed biological boundary"). And although
Bonnet's science did not have space for the currently privileged biological
principle of genetics (at least in its modern forms), there is no reason to think
he would have disagreed with any of the propositions expressed in here. Indeed, my survey of an eighteenth-century field of discourse has not been
motivated by a genealogical interest in an "earlier" stage than our own: what
is enlightening about the Enlightenment debate is that the terms of debate set
out so clearly remain *our* terms.

To be sure, the story I have been telling so far reduces (in the venerable fashion of thin intellectual history) an array of complexly conflictual discourses
on human classification to a tidy *récit*. Against a realist metaphysics of classification is ranged a nominalist skepticism, as discourse to counterdiscourse.
But staging this debate in the era preceding the emergence of nineteenth-
century race science allows me to bring out a few points, that would later
be obscured. The dispute is not, in principle, empirical: more information
about the variety of human countenance and behavior could not decisively
settle the issue one way or the other. Even though the ascendancy of those
two intellectual strains—the principle of continuity, and nominalism about
kinds—led to the decline, by mid-eighteenth century, of the habit of thinking
of the natural order in terms of fixed divisions, it did not lead to the decline

of the research program of classification. For Bonnet, to return to our example, the imperative was to subtilize, make ever finer distinctions, to find kinds within kinds without succumbing to atomism. (He quoted with approval Leibniz's axiom "Nature makes no leaps," as he pursued the comparative studies of *visage*.) Plainly, the difference between Bonnet and the authors of *Liberating Theory* is not how much they know. For all the lurid fascination it holds for us, nineteenth-century race science is, on the whole, bad science, even by internal standards; argument with the Enlightenment's natural historians, on the other hand, immediately raises questions that are more foundational—and foundational even to our own antiracist discourses.

In sum, what we have inherited from the Enlightenment—I hope my brief excursus makes this claim plausible—is a conceptual grammar of antiracism. The reverse discourses of the Enlightenment have become our own reverse discourse and frame our own posture of rejection. Inasmuch as we ritually decry essentialism, we remain conceptually sutured to it. Inasmuch as we ritually decry techniques of "naturalization," we remain wedded to a certain ideology of the natural as a contrastive. Locke's sweeping skepticism about kinds has been localized and transmuted to the narrower confines of the social, its cohesions and divisions: a legacy I will call cultural nominalism.[13] So we must ask whether the Enlightenment stance of antiessentialism, which continues to frame the issues for us in the theoretical register, remains adequate for us. How—if I may recur to Bonnet—has it served us as "means relative to our needs and to the limitations of our knowledge"?

II

Theory excels at a variety of tasks. In its normative mode, which is to denaturalize, it has served us well as a sort of consumer advocate, issuing warnings about those ideological products for everyday use. But it is not much good at exploring the relations between social identity and political agency. For that is, in an important sense, not a merely theoretical problem.

"This is the risk," Derrida warns, explicitly opposing an Enlightenment model of universalism: "The effect of Law is to build a structure of the subject, and as soon as you say, 'well, the woman is a subject and this subject deserves equal right,' and so on—then you are caught in the logic of phallogocentrism and you have rebuilt the empire of Law." These are thoughtful words by a critic whose stands on sexism and racism have been exemplary. But since the empire of law has never been unbuilt, the admonition not to rebuild it does give one pause. The constitution of the Western male subject, after all, has enjoyed quite a different history from that of its racial or sexual others. Consider the irony: precisely when those "others" gain the complex wherewithal to define a countervailing subjectivity in the republic of Western culture, our theoretic colleagues declare the subject to be mere mystification. It is hard not to see this as the critical version of the grandfather clause, the double privileging of categories that happen to be, as it were, preconstituted, a position that seems to leave *us* nowhere, invisible and voiceless. The universalism that undergirds poststructural antiuniversalism is finally seen in its inability to comprehend the *ethnos* as anything other than mystification, magic, or mirage—or what once would have been called false consciousness.

And while the so-called death of the subject may be a theoretical triviality, its rhetorical deployment is more problematic. Starting with the recognition that the "reflexive actor" is not simply a given, a subjectivity existing prior to and independently from language, we too quickly decided that its factitious pedigree made it an effect of linguistic determination. But that did not quite follow. As Anthony Giddens observes, once we see the subject as imbricated in the broader matrix of social practices, the flux of social life, we find that the subject is not only an effect of language but a participant in an articulated realm of social practices that, far from constraining its agency, are its very conditions of possibility.[14] The subject is dead, long live the subject. The familiar Wittgensteinian point is that you cannot simply opt out of a form of life, and you cannot *mean* outside one, either.

So far I have been discussing social identity and political agency as if they were logically connected, and so they are. If one is not (as de Beauvoir wrote) born a woman, one is not, as Donna Haraway has pointed out, even born an organism, in that even this most basic category is ideologically inflected and socially constructed. (In the context of nineteenth-century race science, Nancy Stepan has expertly revealed the operation of tendentious analogies and metaphors collusive in sexual and racial debasement; at the same time, she reminds us that metaphors are—to advert to the title of a book she cites—things we live by.) And since self-identification proves a condition for agency, the imperatives of social change require us to construct ourselves, just as *all* the furniture in the social universe was. The utopian aspect of the theory project is the implicit hope that we can now divest ourselves of our social identities, when there is not another one to take its place. As a social theory, this may be the dream of content without (social) form. But we cannot become one of those bodiless vapor trails of sentience portrayed on that *Star Trek* episode (although often it seems like the universalists of theory want us to be just that). We cannot opt out of history; and while it may be a nightmare, as Joyce suggested, it is perhaps time to stop pinching ourselves.

So I want us to remark the treacherous non sequitur that moves us from "socially constructed" to essentially unreal. We typically go from "constructed" to "unstable," which is one non sequitur, or to "changeable by will" (which is a bigger problem still, given that "will" is yet another construction).

I suppose there is a lurking positivism in the sentiment, in which social facts are unreal compared to putatively biological ones. And post-Enlightenment theory is complicit with it because of the real ascendancy of what we might call a paradigm of dismantlement. Reversals do not work, we are told; dismantle the scheme of difference altogether. I do not deny the importance, on the level of theory, of the project; it is important to remember that "race" is *only* a sociopolitical category, nothing more: but it is also important to question the force of that "only." In its performative aspect, the proclamation of nonexistence of the Negro usually sounds like the old darky joke about the nigger in the chicken coop, denying his existence on the poultry's behalf. Spivak poses the question: can the subaltern speak? Possibly she can—but a chicken, never.

We are, of course, accustomed to other tensions and disjunctions between theory and praxis. What a leading deconstructive theorist describes as "the sense of loss of historical agency that accompanies the fragmentation of the self characteristic of social abstraction"[15] has bred its own resistance, manifest in the claims of—indeed, in the authority of—experience. Thus Barbara Christian forcefully defends the specificity of the black woman's cultural work as a preserve both discursive and experiential; and she is equally firm in warning against the tendency to homogenize the cultural achievement of black women, even through the ideology of tradition. Considering the construction of identity more generally, Appiah has observed that the "demands of agency may entail a misrecognition of its genesis";[16] and a sense of this is poignantly dramatized in Fanon's dialogue with Sartre. Reading Sartre's account of Négritude (as an antithesis preparatory to a "society without races," hence "a transition and not a conclusion"), Fanon reports: "I felt I had been robbed of my last chance":

> A consciousness committed to experience is ignorant, has to be ignorant, of the essences and the determinations of its being. . . . Sartre, in this work, has destroyed black zeal. . . . In any case, I *needed* not to know.

Has there ever been so eloquent a rage against the Medusan face of theory? Bhabha, at once joining forces with and recoiling from poststructuralism, asks "how we are to re-think 'ourselves' once we have undermined the immediacy and autonomy of self-consciousness" (which is to say, once we have placed "ourselves" between scare quotes), and this he says must be left as an open question.

The lesson holds equally about the historicity of our sexual categories. Foucault argues (and for the moment, let's take him at his word) that the "homosexual" as life form was invented sometime in the mid-nineteenth century. Now, if there is no such thing as a homosexual, then homophobia, at least as directed toward people rather than acts, loses its rationale. But you cannot respond to discrimination against gays by saying, "I'm sorry, I don't exist; you've got the wrong guy." The simple historical fact may have been that Stonewall was necessary—that the orchestration of community, and thus concerted action, proves necessary to take action against the very structures that, as it were, called the homosexual into being, subjecting certain people to this imaginary identity. To reverse Audre Lord, *only* the master's tools will ever dismantle the master's house.

In this regard, Said's exposition is illustrative of the predicament of the oppositional intellectual, not so much in its analysis of Zionism as in its representation of the Palestinian people. While Said has, as he says, no interest in a successful nationalism, his analysis cannot but inhabit a counternationalism: "The Palestinian was not simply a function of Zionism. His life, culture, and politics have their own dynamic and ultimately their own authenticity." As Said knows, the territorial conception of the nation—centered on the self-determining homeland of that (gendered) indigene—is historically no more "nature" to the colonized than to the European colonizer. The rhetoric of authenticity and of nationalism is no political embarrassment but is always an academic one; and Said is an academic, even if his humanism and political engagement lead him more in the direction of Friedrich List than Karl Marx.

And indeed, we can take it as axiomatic that modern racialism always inhabits—even while it may be inhabited by—the discourse of nationalism, as Balibar shows in his extremely clarifying exposition. Certainly the paradoxes of universality within particularism inhere in the institution of law in liberal capitalist societies, as Fitzpatrick demonstrates: law subsists on strong universalist claims even as "racism marks constitutive boundaries of law, persistent limits on its competence and scope."

What such considerations of nationality and race suggest is a lesson that many of the contributors to this volume have insisted on: that it is not necessarily progressive to say race is culture, insofar as culture is then simply allowed the function as race. Along these lines, Martin Barker has analyzed the rather Humean strategy that substitutes for the naturalness of race, the naturalness of racism. The culturalist counterpart of this—something Christian Delacampagne is wary of—would twin racism with some constitutive aspect of our culture, such as reason *in se*. A sociobiological pessimism (racism is in our nature, little can be done about it) finds here its antihumanist correlative (racism is, *mutatis mutandis*, a constitutive aspect of our very rationality; nothing—for us, at least—to do about it). In any case, the ease of translation should put us on our guard. As Paul Gilroy observes, "Before the rise of modern scientific racism in the nineteenth century, the term 'race' did duty for the term culture. No suprise, then, that in its postwar retreat from Fascism the term has once again acquired an explicitly cultural rather than a biological inflection." And indeed, the trojan horse of culture has today become a favored means of transport for the ideologies of race.

With Delacampagne, I think it is a mistake to hold that to eradicate racism, we must eliminate its most fundamental conditions of possibility. (In this respect, it is possible that Lucius Outlaw's account—with which I'm generally sympathetic—is both too pessimistic and too optimistic: too pessimistic in thinking we need radically to change the social order in order to change racial discourse; too optimistic, conversely, in thinking that we can radically change the existing order by changing racial discourse.) As any archaeologist will vouch, there is an art to superficiality, to knowing when *not* to dig deeper. Gun control is not about iron smelting, and antiracism should probably not turn on foundational issues in the philosophy of logic. The risk is always that of radically dehistoricizing, and so derealizing, the object of inquiry. But even here a delicate balance must be sought.

For our cultural nominalism cuts deepest in (what might be seen as its legitimate purview) the theorizing of race and of racism. In denying us recourse to universals, it calls into question the project of conducting a genealogy of racism, or of theorizing racism in any general way (but then what is more universalizing than theory?). And David Goldberg has rightly focused our attention on the problem. Thus Kristeva's *sémanalyse* of Céline's anti-Semitism brilliantly explores a rhetorical logic she sees as sustained by the "two common features" she identifies, but at the cost of derealizing its historical occasion. Of course, it is no accident that his animus is directed also against Negroes and Near Easterners, and that his opprobrium is often expressed through the imagery of homophobia; we can expect a more contextual survey would banalize its metaphorics. Pace Kristeva, anti-Semitism is never mere anti-semanticism, a quixotic stance against all symbolics.

But the imperative to historicize will, at the limit, be equally incapacitating. We are accustomed to seeing race (and racialism) as a construction, something essentially constituted an intelligible only within a given social formation. But this sort of cultural nominalism can lead to a skeptical extreme, in which (in John Guillory's words) we roll up history behind us like a carpet. If a term exhaustively derives its meaning from the social totality at any historical moment, then for the purposes of analysis—as a familiar *reductio* should suggest—yesterday is too long ago. But few intellectual projects are as important as an archaeology of racialism, and a successful one requires a sense of the extent to which cultural practices are (in the anatomical sense) articulated. Arriving at a serviceable "nominal essence" of our own grasp of the concept is the necessary propaedeutic to any *Ideologiekritik*, genealogy, or conceptual philosophical analysis—which is the unglamorous but indispensable service of Appiah's essay. That much forethought suggests a hypocrisy in holding history to a criterion of invariance to which we do not hold ourselves: as the medieval historian John Boswell notes about the historiography of sexual categories, "If these disparate patterns . . . can be

grouped together under a single heading in the present, why make such a fuss about a diachronic grouping?"[17]
Cultural nominalism tyrannizes through tautology. Once we have acknowledged that everything—including our conception of the social—is (in the relevant sense) socially constructed, the doctrine comes down to the hoary humanist maxim that man makes his own meaning. As to the hard political questions of human identity, of ethos and *ethnos*, of who we are and how we got that way, theory as such may live little to tell us, save through its silences.

NOTES

1. Thomas Sprat, *The History of the Royal Society* (London: Printed by T. R. for J. Martyn and J. Allestry, 1667), p. 110.

2. *Encyclopédie*, art. "Cosmologie." See Arthur O. Lovejoy's magisterial *The Great Chain of Being: A Study of the History of An Idea* (Cambridge, Mass.: Harvard University Press, 1936), esp. chapters 2, 6, and 8 which remains the standard treatment of the subject, and to which I am indebted; and its reconstruction in William F. Bynum, "The Great Chain of Being after Forty Years: An Appraisal," *History of Science*, 13 (March 1975), pp. 1–28.

3. The contrast in color between the Europeans and the Africans had long perplexed both; but it was in the eighteenth century that science first addressed the quandary. Richard Bradley's "five sorts of men" identified in 1721 turns largely on distinctions of color; Dr. John Mitchell, a physician "*from* Urbana *in* Virginia," published the results of his "Experiments and Observations" in an "Essay on that Strange *Phaenomenon* in Nature, the Cause of the Color of the Negroes," in the Royal Society's *Philosophical Transactions* in 1744. (Mitchell's work was meant to dispel the idea that the African's hue appeared to be black because of the presence of "that black juice" beneath his skin.) Pierre Maupertius's investigations of the patterns of heredity, which would prove to be so fundamental to genetic theory, were stimulated initially by a "white negro" who was brought to Paris, and pronounced by Voltaire to be one of a new race of men. Cornelius de Pauw in 1770 wrote an entire chapter ostensibly on the color of Indians, but devoted over half of it to the color of the African. Buffon and Peter Kalm, a pupil of Linnaeus's, both wrote of the matter at length. And Conway Zirkle has shown that many pioneering investigations into the hereditary transmission of acquired characteristic, from Marcello Malpighi on, concerned the human complexion (Conway Zirkle, "Early History of Inheritance," American Philosophical Society, *Transactions*, New Series, 35 [1946], part 2, pp. 91–151.

4. Dr. Thomas Towns, Letter submitted by a Mr. Lister to the Royal Society, Royal Society, *Philosophical Transactions* 10 (1675), p. 400. Buffon (*Natural History*, trans. [Smellie] vol. 3, pp. 202–2), seemed to believe this; but [Leslie], *New History of Jamaica*, p. 312, argued assuredly that African blood was "equally fair with" the European's. See also Romans, *Florida*, p. 55 DeP[auw], *Recherches Philosophiques sur les Americans*, 3 vols. (Berlin: G. J. Decker, 1770), vol. 2, pp. 27, 45–46.

5. See Winthrop Jordan, *White over Black* (Chapel Hill: University of North Carolina Press, 1968), pp. 217–18.

6. Christianus Emmanuel Hoppius, "Anthropomorpha" (Upsaliae, 1760), reprinted in *Caroli Linnaei, Amoenitates Academicae*, vol. 5, pp. 63–76; Thomas Bendyshe (trans.), "History of Anthropology," *Anthropological Society of London, Memoirs*, 1 (1863–64), p. 355.

7. Soame Jenyns, "Disquisitions on Several Subjects; Disquisition I: On the Chain of Universal Being," *The Works of Soame Jenyns* . . . , 2 vols. (London: T. Cadell, 1790), vol. 2, p. 133; and see Winthrop Jordan, *White over Black*, p. 224.

8. Not that the challenge must go unanswered. William Petty, one of the founders of the Royal Society in the mid-seventeenth century, seems to take up this point in insisting that "[though there existed] those differences between Man and [individual] man, there bee others more considerable, that is, between the Guiny negroes and the middle Europeans; and of negroes between those who live about the Cape of Good Hope [the Hottentots], which last are the most beastlike of all the souls [?Sorts?] of men with whom are Travellers are well acquainted"; Henry W. Landsdowne (ed.), *The Petty Papers: Some Unpublished Writings of Sir William Petty*, 2 vols. (London: Constable, 1927), vol. 2, p. 31. There are obvious difficulties in discussing "race" before that term had quite acquired its modern sense. Most natural historians of the eighteenth century regarded "racial" divisions among people as distinguishing what they called "varieties," rather than "species," the latter being stable across time and generations; the "separate origins" theory of racial difference was a distinctly minority view.

9. Purdie and Dixon's Williamsburg *Virginia Gazette*, August 20, 1772.

10. Cited in Lovejoy, *Great Chain of Being*, pp. 229–30.

11. C[harles] Bonnet, *The Contemplation of Nature*, 2 vols. (London: T. Longman, T. Becket, 1766; 2nd ed., 1769), vol. 1, p. 28.

12. Michael Albert, Leslie Cagan, Noam Chomsky et al., *Liberating Theory* (Boston: South End Press, 1986), p. 26.

13. The empiricist epistemology of the Enlightenment was predicated upon a conceptual separation of realms, the factual from the artifactual, the cultural from the natural; as Alasdair McIntyre writes, " 'Fact' becomes value-free, 'is' becomes a stranger to 'ought,' and explanation, as well as evaluation, changes its character as a result of this divorce between 'is' and 'ought' " (*After Virtue: A Study in Moral Theory* [Notre Dame: University of Notre Dame Press, 1981], p. 81). And while the thoroughgoing nominalism about universals we find in Hobbes and Locke has pretty much fallen by the wayside as regards the physical world, it has continued to rule in the (newly distinguished) realm of social (hence artifactual) signification. (The Enlightenment notions of objectivity have recently been questioned from various directions, for example, in the work of David Wiggins and John McDowell.)

14. Anthony Giddens, "Structuralism and the Theory of the Subject," *Central Problems in Social Theory* (Berkeley: University of California Press, 1979), pp. 29–95.

15. Wlad Godzich, "The Further Possibility of Knowledge," foreword to Michel de Certeau, *Heterologies* (Minneapolis: University of Minnesota Press, 1986), p. xx.

16. K. A. Appiah, "Social Forces, Natural Kinds," Science, Gender and Race panel of the Radical Philosopher's Association, American Philosophical Association Eastern Division Meeting, New York, December 1987.

17. John Boswell, "Towards the Long View: Revolutions, Universals, and Sexual Categories," *Salmagundi*, no. 58/59 (Fall 1982–Winter 1983), p. 95.

Notes on Contributors

Notes on Contributors

Kwame Anthony Appiah is a member of the Sage School of Philosophy at Cornell University. He is the author of *Assertions and Conditionals; For Truth in Semantics; Necessary Questions;* and *In My Father's House* (forthcoming).

Etienne Balibar is professor of philosophy at the University of Paris I (Panthéon-Sorbonne). He is the author of *Spinoza,* coauthor (with Louis Althusser) of *Reading Capital* and (with Immanuel Wallerstein) of *Race, Nation, Classe.*

Martin Barker teaches philosophy at Bristol Polytechnic. He is the author of *The New Racism.*

Roland Barthes was born in 1915. He was a professor at the College de France until his death in 1980. His books include *Mythologies, The Eiffel Tower, S/Z, The Pleasure of the Text,* and *Camera Lucida.*

Homi Bhabha is lecturer in English at Sussex University. He is the author of *Power and Spectacle: Colonial Discourse and the English Novel,* and of numerous articles on race and colonialism.

Barbara Christian is professor of Afro-American studies at the University of California, Berkeley. She is the author of *Black Women Novelists: The Development of a Tradition; Black Feminist Criticism;* and *Perspectives on Black Women Writers.*

Christian Delacampagne formerly lectured in philosophy and is at present director of the French Cultural Center in Cairo, Egypt. He reviews philosophical books for *Le Monde* and is the author of *L'Invention du Racisme.*

Frantz Fanon was born in Martinique in 1925. He studied psychiatry in France and practiced in Algeria, where he became a noted spokesman for the revolution. He died of cancer in 1961. He is the author of *The Wretched of the Earth; Black Skin, White Masks*; and *A Dying Colonialism*.

Peter Fitzpatrick is professor of law and social theory at the University of Kent. He is the author of *Law and State in Papua New Guinea* and coeditor of *European Critical Legal Studies*.

Henry Louis Gates, Jr., is professor of English, comparative literature, and African studies at Cornell University. He is the author of *Figures in Black: Words, Signs, and the Racial Self*, and editor of *"Race," Writing, and Difference* and *Black Literature and Literary Theory*.

Sander Gilman is Goldwin Smith Professor of Humane Studies at Cornell University and professor of psychiatry (history) at Cornell Medical School. His books include *Jewish Self-Hatred: Anti-Semitism and the Hidden Language of the Jews; Difference and Pathology: Stereotypes of Sexuality, Race, and Madness; Seeing the Insane*; and *On Blackness without Blacks*.

Paul Gilroy teaches sociology at the University of Essex. He is the author of *There Ain't No Black in the Union Jack* and coauthor of *The Empire Strikes Back*.

John L. Hodge is formerly an assistant professor of philosophy at California State University, Hayward. He is at present an attorney with the Legal Division of the Massachusetts Department of Public Welfare. He is the primary author of *The Cultural Bases of Racism and Group Oppression*.

Julia Kristeva is a psychoanalyst and teaches at the University of Paris VII. She is the author of *Tales of Love; Powers of Horror; Desire in Language; Revolution in Poetic Language*; and *About Chinese Women*.

Lucius Outlaw is professor of philosophy at Haverford College. He is the author of "On Race and Class. Or, on the Prospects of 'Rainbow Socialism' "; "Race and Class in the Theory and Practice of 'Emancipatory' Social Transformation"; and "The Deafening Silence of 'The Guiding Light': American Philosophy and the Problem of the Color Line."

Edward W. Said is Parr Professor of English and Comparative Literature at Columbia University. He is the author of *The Question of Palestine; The World, the Text, and the Critic; Orientalism; After the Last Sky*; and coeditor of *Blaming the Victims*.

Nancy Leys Stepan is professor of history at Columbia University. She is the author of *The Idea of Race in Science: Great Britain, 1800–1950* and *Beginnings of Brazilian Science*.

Selected Bibliography

Selected Bibliography

Adorno, T., E. Frenkel-Brunswick, D. Levinson, and R. N. Sanford, *The Authoritarian Personality*. New York: Harper & Row, 1950.

Baker, H. A. *Blues, Ideology, and Afro-American Literature: A Vernacular Perspective*. Chicago: University of Chicago Press, 1984.

Balibar, E. and I. Wallerstein. *Race, Nation, Classe*. Paris: Editions la Découverte, 1988.

Banton, M. *Racial and Ethnic Competition*. Cambridge: Cambridge University Press, 1983.

Banton, M. "Analytical and Folk Concepts of Race and Ethnicity." *Ethnic and Racial Studies*, 2 (1979), pp. 127–38.

——. "United States Racial Ideology as Collective Representation." *Ethnic and Racial Studies*, 10 (October 1987), pp. 466–68.

Barker, F., et al. *Europe and Its Other*. Colchester: University of Essex, 1985.

Barker, M. *The New Racism*. London: Junction Books, 1981.

Bell, D. *And We Are Not Saved: The Elusive Quest for Racial Reform*. New York: Basic Books, 1987.

——. *Race, Racism, and American Law*. 2nd ed. Boston: Little, Brown, 1980.

Ben-Tovim, G., et al. "Race, Left Strategies and the State." *Politics and Power*, 3 (1981).

——. *The Local Politics of Race*. London: Macmillan, 1986.

Bhabha, H. "Of Mimicry and Man: The Ambivalence of Colonial Discourse." *October*, 28 (1984), pp. 125–33.

Blaut, J. M. *The National Question and Colonialism*. London: Zed Books, 1987.

Boon, J. *Other Tribes, Other Scribes*. Cambridge: Cambridge University Press, 1985.

Bourne, J. "Cheerleaders and Ombudsmen: The Sociology of Race Relations." *Race and Class*, 21 (1980), pp. 331–52.

Carmichael, S., and C. Hamilton. *Black Power: The Politics of Black Liberation in America*. New York: Vintage, 1967.

Cashmore, E. *The Logic of Racism*. London: Allen & Unwin, 1987.

——. *Dictionary of Race and Ethnic Relations*. London: Routledge, 1988.

Cashmore, E., and B. Troyna, eds. *Black Youth in Crisis*. London: Allen & Unwin, 1982.

CCCS, eds. *The Empire Strikes Back*. London: Hutchinson, 1982.

Christian, B. *Black Feminist Criticism*. New York: Pergamon, 1985.

Cox, O. C. *Caste, Class and Race*. New York: Doubleday, 1948.

Cross, M., ed. *Restructuring Race: Ethnic Minorities and Industrial Change*. Cambridge: Cambridge University Press, 1988.

337

Cross, M., and M. Johnson. *Race and the Urban System.* Cambridge: Cambridge University Press, 1989.

Delacampagne, D. *L'Invention du Racisme.* Paris: Fayard, 1983.

Duffield, M. "New Racism . . . New Realism: Two Sides of the Same Coin." *Radical Philosophy,* 37 (Summer 1984).

Essed, P. J. M. *Everday Racism.* Claremont, Calif.: Hunter House, 1988.

Fabian, J. *Time and the Other: How Anthropology Makes Its Object.* New York: Columbia University Press, 1983.

Fanon, F. *A Dying Colonialism.* Harmondsworth: Pelican Books, 1970.

——. *Black Skin, White Masks.* New York: Grove Press, 1967.

——. *The Wretched of the Earth.* New York: Grove Press, 1963.

Gabriel, J. and G. Ben-Tovim. "The Conceptualization of Race Relations in Sociological Theory." *Ethnic and Racial Studies,* 2 (1979).

Gates, H. L. *Figures in Black: Words, Signs, and the Racial Self.* Oxford: Oxford University Press, 1987.

——. *The Signifying Monkey: A Theory of African-American Literary Criticism.* New York: Oxford University Press, 1988.

Gates, H. L., ed. *"Race," Writing, and Difference.* Chicago: University of Chicago Press, 1986.

—— *Black Literature and Literary Theory.* London: Methuen, 1984.

Gates, H. L., Jr., and D. La Capra, eds. *The Bounds of Race.* Ithaca, N.Y.: Cornell University Press, 1989.

Gellner, E. *Nations and Nationalism.* Oxford: Basil Blackwell, 1983.

Gill, D., and L. Levidow, eds. *Anti-Racist Science Teaching.* London: Free Association Books, 1987.

Gilman, S. *Difference and Pathology: Stereotypes of Sexuality, Race and Madness.* Ithaca, N.Y.: Cornell University Press, 1985.

Gilroy, P. *There Ain't No Black in the Union Jack.* London: Hutchinson, 1987.

Goldberg, D. T. "Is Racism Inherently Irrational?" *Philosophy of the Social Sciences* (1990).

——. "Reading the Signs: The Force of Language." *Philosophical Forum,* 18 (Winter-Spring 1987), pp. 70–91.

——. "Raking the Field of the Discourse of Racism." *Journal of Black Studies,* 18 (September 1987), pp. 57–71.

——, ed. "Apartheid: Special Double Issue on Racism in South Africa." *Philosophical Forum,* 18 (Winter-Spring 1987).

Gregory, D., and J. Urry, eds. *Racial Relations and Spatial Structures.* New York: Macmillan, 1985.

Hall, S., C. Critcher, T. Jefferson, J. Clark, and B. Roberts, eds. *Policing the Crisis: Mugging, the State, and Law and Order.* London: Methuen, 1978.

Harris, L., ed. *Philosophy Born against Struggle: Anthology of Afro-American Philosophy from 1917.* Dubuque, Iowa: Kendall Hunt, 1983.

Hartman, P., and C. Husband. *Racism and the Mass Media.* Totowa, N.J.: Rowman & Littlefield, 1974.

Hebdige, D. *Subculture: The Meaning of Style.* London: Methuen, 1979.

Higginbotham, A. L. *In the Matter of Color: Race and the American Legal Process.* Oxford: Oxford University Press, 1978.

Hodge, J., D. Struckmann, and L. Trost. *Cultural Bases of Racism and Group Oppression.* Berkeley: Two Riders Press, 1975.

Husband, C., ed. *"Race" in Britain.* London: Hutchinson, 1982.

Jackson, P., ed. *Race and Racism: Essays in Social Geography.* London: Allen & Unwin, 1987.

James, C. L. R. *A History of Negro Revolt.* London: Race Today, 1985.

——. *The Black Jacobins.* New York: Allison, 1938.

JanMohamed, A., and D. Lloyd, eds. "The Nature and Context of Minority Discourse." *Cultural Critique*, 6 (Spring 1987), pp. 5–220 and 7 (Fall 1987), pp. 5–266.

Jenkins, R., and J. Solomos. *Racism and Equal Opportunity in the 1980s*. Cambridge: Cambridge University Press, 1987.

Kochman, T., ed. *Rappin' and Stylin' Out: Communication in Urban Black America*. Champaign: University of Illinois Press, 1972.

Kristeva, J. *Powers of Horror*. New York: Columbia University Press, 1982.

Kushner, Tony. *The Persistence of Prejudice: Anti-Semitism in British Society During the Second World War*. Manchester: Manchester University Press, 1989.

Layton-Henry, Z., and P. Rich, eds. *Race, Government and Politics in Britain*. London: Macmillan, 1986.

Lewis, B. *The Political Language of Islam*. Chicago: University of Chicago Press, 1988.

Mackenzie, J. M. *Imperialism and Popular Culture*. Manchester: Manchester University Press, 1986.

Marable, M. *Black American Politics*. New York: Verso Books, 1985.

——. *Race, Reform and Rebellion: The Second Reconstruction in Black America, 1945–1982*. Macmillan, 1984.

——. *Blackwater Historical Studies in Race, Class-Consciousness and Revolution*. Dayton, Ohio: Black Praxis Press, 1981.

Miles, R. "Marxism versus the Sociology of 'Race Relations.'" *Ethnic and Racial Studies*, 7 (1984), pp. 217–37.

——. *Racism and Migrant Labor*. London: Routledge & Kegan Paul, 1982.

Miles, R. *Racism*. London: Routledge, 1989.

Miles, R., and A. Phizacklea, eds. *Racism and Political Action in Britain*. London: Routledge & Kegan Paul, 1979.

Mullard, C. *Racism, Power and Resistance*. London: Routledge & Kegan Paul, 1985.

Nelson, C., and L. Grossberg, eds. *Marxism and the Interpretation of Culture*. Chicago: University of Illinois Press, 1988.

Omi, M., and H. Winant. *Racial Formation in the United States: From the 1960s to the 1980s*. London: Routledge & Kegan Paul, 1986.

Patterson, O. *Slavery and Social Death*. Cambridge, Mass.: Harvard University Press, 1980.

——. *Ethnic and Social Chauvinism: The Reactionary Impulse*. Briarcliff, N.Y.: Stein & Day, 1977.

Phizacklea, A., and R. Miles. *Labour and Racism*. London: Routledge & Kegan Paul, 1980.

Prager, J. "American Racial Ideology as Collective Representation." *Ethnic and Racial Studies*, (1987), pp. 99–119.

——. "American Political Culture and the Shifting Meaning of Race." *Ethnic and Racial Studies*. 10 (January 1987), pp. 62–81.

——. "The Meaning of Difference: A Response to Michael Banton." *Ethnic and Racial Studies*, 10 (October 1987), pp. 469–72.

Reeves, F. *British Racial Discourse*. Cambridge: Cambridge University Press, 1984.

Rich, P. *Race and Empire in British Politics*. Cambridge: Cambridge University Press, 1986.

——. *White Power and the Liberal Conscience*. Manchester: Manchester University Press, 1984.

Richmond, A. H. *Immigration and Ethnic Conflict*. New York: St. Martin's Press, 1988.

Robinson, C. *Black Marxism: The Making of a Radical Tradition*. London: Zed Books, 1980.

Ross, R., ed. *Racism and Colonialism*. Leiden: Martinus Nijhof, 1982.

Rose, S., R. Lewontin, and L. Kamin. *Not in Our Genes*. New York: Pantheon Books, 1984.

Said, E. *The World, the Text, and the Critic*. Cambridge, Mass.: Harvard University Press, 1983.

——. *The Question of Palestine*. New York: Columbia University Press, 1979.

——. *Orientalism*. New York: Pantheon Books, 1978.

Schuman, H., C. Steeh, and L. Bobo. *Racial Attitudes in America*. Cambridge, Mass.: Harvard University Press, 1985.

Sivanandan, A. *A Different Hunger*. London: Pluto Press, 1982.

Smitherman-Donaldson, G., and P. A. Van Dijk, eds. *Discourse and Discrmination*. Detroit, Mich.: Wayne State University Press, 1988.

Solomos, J. *Black Youth, Racism and the State*. Cambridge: Cambridge University Press, 1988.

Spelman, E. *Inessential Woman*. Boston: Beacon Press, 1988.

Spivak, N. *In Other Worlds: Essays in Cultural Politics*. London: Methuen, 1987.

Stepan, N. *The Idea of Race in Science: Great Britain, 1800–1950*. London: Macmillan, 1982.

Todorov, T. *The Conquest of America*. New York: Harper & Row, 1984.

Van Dijk, T. *Communicating Racism: Ethnic Prejudice in Thought and Talk*. Beverly Hills, Calif.: Sage, 1987.

Van Horne, W., ed. *Ethnicity and Language*. Ethnicity and Public Policy Series, vol. 5. Madison: University of Wisconsin System, 1986.

———. *Ethnicity and Women*. Ethnicity and Public Policy Series, vol. 6. Madison: University of Wisconsin System, 1988.

Wellman, D. T. *Portraits of White Racism*. Cambridge: Cambridge University Press, 1977.

West, C. *Prophesy Deliverance: An Afro-American Revolutionary Christianity*. Philadelphia: Westminster Press, 1982.

Wilson, W. J. *The Truly Disadvantaged: The Inner City, the Underclass, and Public Policy*. Chicago: University of Chicago Press, 1987.

———. *The Declining Significance of Race: Blacks and Changing American Institutions*. Chicago: University of Chicago Press, 1980.

Index

Index
Compiled by Eileen Quam and Theresa Wolner

David Theo Goldberg is now at the School of Justice Studies, Arizona State University. He also has taught at Drexel University, New York University, and Hunter College. Goldberg co-directed *The Island*, a film on political imprisonment and the language of oppression in South Africa. He received his Ph.D. in philosophy from the City University of New York and his M.A. and B.A. in philosophy from the University of Cape Town, South Africa. Goldberg is author of *Ethical Theory and Social Issues* and was special guest editor for the double issue of *The Philosophical Forum*'s issue on apartheid. He is currently working on a book on racist discourse.